By
DEKE SHARON,
BEN SPALDING,
and
BRODY McDONALD

A CAP

PELLA

Foreword by BEN FOLDS

Alfred

ISBN-10: 1-4706-1667-X
ISBN-13: 978-1-4706-1667-0

© 2015 Alfred Music
Printed in the U.S.A

alfred.com

Chapter 12 musical examples used with permission:

BIG YELLOW TAXI
Words and Music by JONI MITCHELL
© 1970 (Renewed) CRAZY CROW MUSIC
All Rights Administered by SONY/ATV MUSIC PUBLISHING, 8 Music Square West, Nashville, TN 37203
All Rights Reserved

DON'T STOP BELIEVIN'
Words and Music by JONATHAN CAIN, NEAL SCHON and STEVE PERRY
© 1981 WEEDHIGH-NIGHTMARE MUSIC and LACEY BOULEVARD MUSIC
All Rights for WEEDHIGH-NIGHTMARE MUSIC Administered by WIXEN MUSIC PUBLISHING INC.
All Rights Reserved

Chapters 25 and 43 reprinted with permission from:

A CAPPELLA POP
A Complete Guide to Contemporary A Cappella Singing
By Brody McDonald
© 2012 Alfred Music
All Rights Reserved

This book is dedicated to the tireless veterans of a cappella: The people that spend their time starting singing groups, directing rehearsals, recruiting and training new members, arranging, recording, putting on events, sharing their knowledge without any expectation of compensation, sharing their voices with all who will listen. The people that understand the power that singing can have in bringing people together and improving their lives. The people that choose to spread harmony through harmony.

In other words, this book is dedicated to you.

TABLE OF CONTENTS

Chapters without an author credit were written by Deke Sharon, Ben Spalding, and Brody McDonald.

INSIGHTS

COMPETITIONS

Pentatonix

FOREWORD

By Ben Folds

A CAPPELLA is changing the world!

In a world where evidence was compelling to policy makers, Oakland School For The Arts' (a public school) "Vocal Rush," our youngest group on Season Four of *The Sing-Off*, would be Exhibit A, illustrating that arts in education produces well-rounded, focused, intelligent, well-spoken and happy students. The kind of students who are productive, but more importantly, innovative members of society. The data has shown us that test scores improved profoundly when academic classes are peppered with music classes. Students, like the young people of "Vocal Rush," breathe life into those stats. These kids are bad asses. I hope my generation is paying attention to *The Sing-Off*, and not just to "Vocal Rush," but to all that season's groups and what this form of music means in this era.

Besides being captivating—vocal groups with no instrumental accompaniment pulling off a massive sound—a cappella is actually timely. It's been growing for the past few decades slowly but surely, and has now reached critical relevant mass. Certainly current popular entertainment says something about our collective psyche and what our needs are. Our little show is back on the air precisely because there is something that resonates about all vocal music. It's the sound of life and kinda what the doctor ordered. Why? Because people need to, and have always needed to sing together. It's part of being human, and it shows us that we can actually work together in greater numbers, in harmony. Novel idea.

Most entertainment of the last decade has been the spectacle of dissonance. What I think we're seeing now is a need for some balance. Don't get me wrong. I'm always a sucker for cops chasing someone through an alley, a surly judge ordering some idiot to pay damages to his neighbor for vandalizing his porch, couples in fisticuffs on morning talk shows, pants on the ground, Congress trying to pass a budget, stage moms dolling their daughters up for beauty contests . . . you get my point. And yes, that IS entertainment, but years of exposure to that is why people are now embracing what seemed too nerdy to handle in 2009 when *The Sing-Off* first aired. We want some fresh air. Harmony feels good, sounds good and is healthy. That's why fans wouldn't let NBC drop *The Sing-Off*, and why a goofy show like ours got the best ratings in our time slot this past Monday night.

Also, a cappella music is cheap, and in a world where fiscal responsibility actually drove policy, it would be noted that it costs absolutely nothing to sing. Schools are cutting their music programs in an attempt to save money. But wait. A crazy thing is happening. This next generation of students is filling the musical education void by just doing it themselves. Each year sees more and more high school and a cappella groups working outside the school systems, coming together and teaching themselves some kind of voice leading, and arranging skills enough to perform, and in many cases, perform outstandingly. A cappella is the burgeoning university "Greek" system of the 21st century. The university is where much of this movement was fostered, but now we are finding that, for no money down, we can open mouths and sing.

Kids these days—what's up with them? They don't all think they'll be millionaires with a big record deal? And what's up with the hundreds of *The Sing-Off* contestants who have graced our purple stage over our five seasons? Not to mention the myriad performers on the show around the world, as we've now had shows in Europe, Asia, and Africa. They don't throw fits? They practice. They don't stay out extremely late. The TV handlers who are accustomed to following idiot reality contestants around cleaning up after them never have to babysit our contestants. Our contestants are here to make music.

None of the groups on *The Sing-Off* have ever had a diva. Most members of these a cappella groups are not professional musicians, and yet they're performing to a standard that's higher than many popular recording artists of my era. An a cappella group has to work together, in concert—they seem to sometimes not even understand competition itself. If you had invested in "a cappella stock" (no, it doesn't exist) a hundred years ago, your shares would have never depreciated. It's not a fad, and the stocks are gonna split—that's what the guy on Mad A Cappella Money said anyway.

So, thank you hundreds of a cappella groups out there who have started something that simply HAS to be represented on TV. Thank you to the fans who wouldn't let us go away, and thank you to anyone who tunes in and embraces their inner nerd (or for some of us, our outer nerd).

If you made it all the way through this foreword, Nick Lachey will give you a cookie.

SETTING THE STAGE

Quinta and a Half

CHAPTER 1

HISTORY OF CLASSICAL A CAPPELLA

By Joshua Habermann

In the beginning was a cappella. Long before there was any written history, there was singing; and there is every reason to believe that it was unaccompanied. The voice is, after all, the original instrument, coming built-in at birth. Though it's impossible to look back at those very early times, we can imagine that singing played a central role in communication and expression in pre-literate communities.

As societies became more organized, music came be to "institutionalized." Both church and state understood and made full use of its power. Unaccompanied singing played a significant role in the singing of the psalms in Jewish worship, and in the various forms of chant that developed in the early Christian church. These devotional melodies were monodic: a single melody without accompaniment. Many of these chants have survived to this day, and are some of the most beautiful melodies we have.

As invariably happens, over time people began to experiment. In the Middle Ages chants of various kinds were set, first against a static drone, and later against another moving line, moving first parallel and then independently of the original. With each innovation the texture of the music grew more complex, until the cultural flowering of the renaissance increased the rate of change significantly. In the early renaissance there was a move towards greater complexity as sacred and secular melodies were woven together, sometimes even resulting in songs in which the voices were in different languages.

The focus of this music was not yet on harmony (chords), but on fitting melodies together in a complementary and skillful way. At this time, instruments were creeping into the sacred music, and there was a certain interchangeability in which one line of a composition might be taken by a singer, while another might be taken by an instrumentalist. Nonetheless the voice was still the model, especially in the sacred music of the time, and composers sought to write melodies that sat well for the voice.

As we turn into the middle and late renaissance the trend is toward more parts, and a concept of equality among them. This was the flowering of polyphony, in which rather than having one

Five Good Reasons

dominant voice with the others subservient to it, each voice had its part to play in the musical conversation. The motets of Palestrina and Victoria of the late 16th and early 17th century are an example of this trend, in which each voice had its own melody, interwoven skillfully with those of the other voices to create a flowing fabric of sound. While four to six part compositions were the norm, it was not unusual to have much bigger forces, all the way up to Thomas Tallis' famous 40-part motet "Spem in Alium."

With each voice having its own role and speaking in different rhythms simultaneously, the text became hard to follow, and eventually the church declared that it was time for a simplification so that the words could be more easily understood. This trend was also present in the secular music of the day; the madrigals and chansons whose texts ranged from the high-minded poetry of Italian literary giants like Petrarch to some overtly racy lyrics. Despite the fact that some of the most saucy bits were hidden by double-entendre, no one had to dig too deep to understand madrigals such as this:

> *Fair Phyllis I saw sitting all alone,*
> *Feeding her flock near to the mountainside*
> *The shepherds knew not whither she was gone*
> *But after her lover Amyntas hied**
> *Up and down he wandered whilst she was missing*
> *When he found her oh then they fell a-kissing*
> *Up and down he wandered . . .*

---

* hied = hurried

Or this translation of a famous madrigal by Arcadelt, which, when we understand that death was associated with sexual release, takes on a whole new meaning:

The white, sweet swan dies singing,
And I, weeping, reach the end of my life.
Strange and different fate that he should die disconsolate
And I should die a blessed death, which
In dying fills me with joy and desire.
If, in dying, I were to feel no other pain,
I would be content to die a thousand deaths a day.

Once we have the cultural context, it's not hard to see that the songs of today and of centuries ago are not so different after all.

Alongside these bawdy madrigals, sacred music continued to develop, largely under the patronage of the church. Both a cappella and accompanied singing were widespread at this time, but as we move out of the 16th century, the renaissance aesthetic in which counterpoint was the norm begins to lose ground. With the new form of opera becoming very popular, the model begins to change, and melody with accompaniment was again favored over equal voices. In this way a text could be understood much more easily, and thus the dramatic action (or in the case of sacred music, the devotional scripture) could be followed.

The composers were not interested in going back to the monodic melodies of the Middle Ages, however. They liked all the harmonies that polyphony had provided, so instruments were introduced more and more into both sacred and secular music. An interest in theatricality (opera) and in virtuoso agility (coloratura) led to a new, Baroque style in which for the first time the voice was not the primary actor, but was to be accompanied by instruments of all kinds. It's at this time that purely instrumental music (up to then a relatively small part of the music that was being written and performed) began to take off. By the beginning of the 18th century composers were interested in writing *sinfonias*, the precursor to the modern symphony, which was only a few decades away.

Kettering-Fairmont Chorale

This trend continued in Europe into the classical period in the second half of the 18th century—the time of Mozart and Haydn. Most pieces were conceived with an instrumental component, which is why there is little a cappella music from this era. There were, however, certain religious traditions that did not allow instruments in their music: Russian Orthodox, and most notably for our purposes, the Puritans (Calvinists) who maintained an a cappella tradition of singing and brought it with them to the New World.

In the United States the small population and tough living conditions in the colonies meant a slow start to musical development. However, a cappella singing was well suited to the conditions, as it made few demands for resources. Itinerant singing masters would go from town to town teaching music and singing, as there were few instruments to be found on the frontier. As singing began to take root in the new world and people sought out opportunities to sing together, singing societies began to sprout.

Meanwhile, back in Europe a series of revolutions and wars in the late 18th and 19th centuries set the continent on a path towards political change. The old imperial orders began to crumble. Once hostilities ended there was a rise in prosperity, creating a new middle class with time and disposable income to study and enjoy music.

At the same time, composers were somewhat freed from the requirements of patronage and could take their music directly to the people via publishers, rather than writing for the church or the state. Singing societies (men's, women's and mixed) sprang up (especially in Germany and England) where a renewed interest in a cappella music during the 19th century led to new sacred and secular compositions without accompaniment.

Centerville High School Symphonic Choir

Back in the USA, waves of early 20th century immigration brought new Americans. They brought with them musical traditions that are still alive today. Choirs sprang up in areas of Moravian, German and Scandinavian communities, where singing traditions were particularly strong. The communities where those immigrants first settled are still some of the hotbeds of choral activity in the United States today.

In addition to immigration from Europe, the practice of slavery brought Western and African music elements together. This resulted in the creation of the African-American spiritual, which (like jazz) was a unique American fusion of disparate elements brought together by people who settled in the United States.

Spirituals became a mainstay of American choral repertoire, and in the 19th century groups such as the Fisk Jubilee Singers toured the world performing them. This reversed the long trend of the United States as purely an importer of musical culture, and paved the way for the uniquely American a cappella art forms to follow: barbershop, doo-wop, and eventually the current a cappella movement of the last decades.

"When you sing with a group of people, you learn how to subsume yourself into a group consciousness because a cappella singing is all about the immersion of the self into the community. That's one of the great feelings to stop being me for a little while and to become us."

—Brian Eno

"My friend and I sang an a cappella rendition of Extreme's 'More Than Words' at one of our football pep rallies in a desperate attempt to look cool. For a while, I wore pink Converse All Stars because I thought it made me seem daring and irreverent."

—Ed Helms

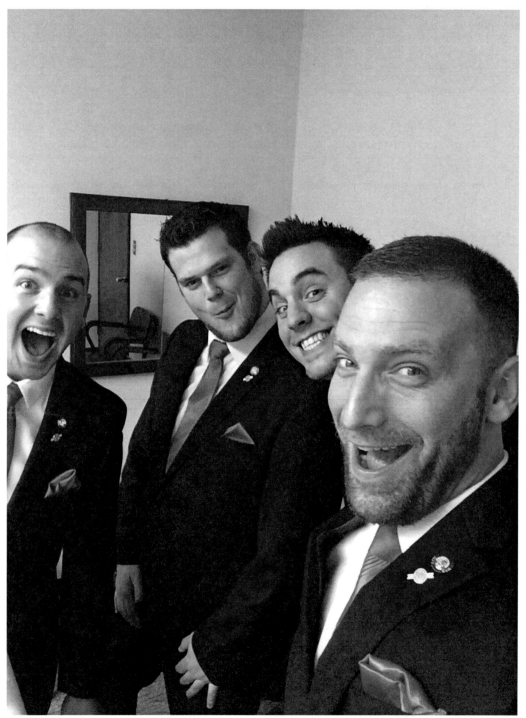

Boomtown

CHAPTER 2
HISTORY OF A CAPPELLA AS POPULAR MUSIC

By Joshua Duchan

By the early twenty-first century, a cappella groups who perform popular music have reached new heights of popularity and enthusiasm. However, they are merely the most recent entries in a long line of ensembles, stretching back centuries, who have sung the popular songs of their day. Whether college songs, barbershop, jazz, pop, R&B, or world music, a cappella has had a definite presence in the history of popular music and even had an impact on its course. What follows is a sketch of the history of a cappella and popular music. Of course, for each example of a group or song, there are many more that go unmentioned. But this section offers a brief survey to familiarize you with this history in a general sense.

The Eighteenth and Nineteenth Centuries: Singing at School

In America, people were singing a cappella before the United States was born, including both Native Americans and those who came from the Old World. Many colonists actually preferred to sing without accompaniment in religious services, which also happened to be an easier way of worshipping since it didn't require an expensive organ. In many cases, congregants didn't even need to know how to read a musical score; a religious official could simply sing a line and the congregation would then sing it back in a process known as "lining out." As church music took root, however, there were those who enjoyed it so much that they wanted to meet outside of church to sing at a more challenging level. This led to the establishment of "meeting house choirs." In order to satisfy the desire for more difficult repertory, many "singing schools" were founded to improve musical and vocal skills. Bostonian William Billings (1746–1800) was one of the most important singing school teachers. In addition to teaching, he also published books of instructional materials and compositions. There were many others who traveled the country too, teaching musical and vocal skills.

When young men attended college at this time—few women did, yet—they often brought their love of music and years of singing school experience with them to campus, where they sang religious music but also occasionally gathered to sing more secular songs, such as drinking tunes. These groups were particularly active at Harvard, Yale, and Dartmouth, and became more numerous around 1800. As time went on, the religious aspect faded and more emphasis was placed on fun. For example, early records of the Pierian Sodality, a Harvard group founded in 1808, make it clear that singing was only one third of the group's activities at each meeting; the others were enjoying wine and discussing women.

Until the middle of the nineteenth century, a cappella on campus was mostly an informal affair. That changed when Benjamin William Crowninshield established the Harvard Glee Club in 1858. Similar clubs soon followed at other schools, quickly branching out to the Midwest as the University of Michigan Men's Glee Club was founded the following year. At this point, they were strictly student-run groups; professors didn't begin directing them until around the turn of the twentieth century. Again, singing was only one of the ensemble's purposes, but it was an important one. Many clubs sang "serious" or classical music, but most also included "lighter fare," such as folk songs, school anthems, and drinking songs in their concerts. Glee clubs weren't yet huge choral societies, but they soon had enough members to field quartets and octets. These breakout groups often pursued a sort of harmony that would later be called "barbershop."

Indeed, barbershop emerged toward the end of the 1800s from both white and black American vocal traditions, combining their styles of singing and improvising in a cappella harmony. It was a great way to enjoy singing with friends, since it required each singer to pay close attention to the others in order to sound good. It could also satisfy those who wanted a challenge, since its harmonies were often complex, necessitating a good ear and plenty of practice.

GNU

It's no coincidence that barbershop emerged around the same time that the American popular music industry, called Tin Pan Alley, was taking off. The industry capitalized, on one hand, on the increased popularity of traveling musical shows that introduced new songs to audiences and, on the other, on increasingly affordable pianos that enabled everyday consumers to take their favorite songs home and play them over and over again. For the first time, the well-known songs were not only popular in one or two cities but across the country. And since the songs were usually fun tunes that expressed something about life at the time—such as the classic "In the Good Old Summer Time" written by Ren Shields and George Evans in 1902—they enjoyed wide appeal.

Forefront

It made sense, therefore, for singers to take these piano-vocal arrangements and set them for barbershop quartet instead, as doing so freed the performers from needing an instrument while providing them with familiar songs that would surely please their listeners. Some Tin Pan Alley songs were even published with four-part vocal arrangements for this purpose. The Whiffenpoofs, a collegiate a cappella group formed at Yale in 1909 from a subset of the Yale Glee Club, included many barbershop songs in their early repertory, which tells us something about how popular the tunes were on campus.

The Twentieth Century: A Cappella on Record

The beginning of the twentieth century saw the emergence of a new form of popular music in the United States: jazz. Not to be left out, many vocal groups enthusiastically took to the distinctive sound. One such group was the Mills Brothers, a quartet from Piqua, Ohio, who began singing together in the 1920s. They recorded a large number of jazz tunes and achieved particular popularity at the time. For example, they recorded the Original Dixieland Jazz Band's "Tiger Rag" several times in 1931 and 1932, including a version that was featured on the soundtrack to the 1932 film, *The Big Broadcast*.

One of the innovative things about jazz was the way it expanded the expressive possibilities of several instruments, including the trumpet and cornet, thanks largely to Louis Armstrong. The Mills Brothers were well aware of this and featured a cappella imitations of those instruments on their recordings. "Tiger Rag," for example, included not only a chorus-length scat section, but also an equally long—and remarkably convincing—vocalized horn solo. The fact that these voiced instrumental passages appear on all of their recordings of this song indicates how important they were to the group. And just so there was no confusion, some of their early records included a note that read, "no musical instruments or mechanical devices [were] used on this recording other than one guitar."

Where the Mills Brothers sang the popular music of their day a cappella, singers in the next generation continued the trend, setting their sights to rock 'n' roll. The result is the music that is known today as doo-wop, although that name wasn't used until a decade after the style emerged. Like glee clubs, barbershop, and many of the a cappella styles that would follow, doo-wop in the 1950s was mainly performed by amateur singers—often high school students—in big cities such as New York, Chicago, and Philadelphia. Unlike earlier a cappella styles, however, doo-wop tended to feature a soloist more prominently, while the remaining voices provided the accompanying background music; they even called it "backgrounding." The harmonies tended to be simpler than those of barbershop, but the arrangements more closely resembled the sound of later a cappella styles, especially in the way the background voices took on instrumental roles.

The 1950s was a time when the American recording industry included not only big labels like Columbia, RCA Victor, and Decca (known as "major labels"), but also an array of smaller outfits based in particular cities, such as King Records in Cincinnati, Sun Records in Memphis, and Chess Records in Chicago.

Street Corner Renaissance

These independent labels were often more willing to gamble on an unknown performer or band, including doo-wop groups. Thus, while some of doo-wop's biggest hits (such as "In the Still of the Night" recorded by the Five Satins in 1956) were heard on radio stations and sold in stores nationwide, the vast majority of doo-wop music tended to stay within its local market. Nonetheless, doo-wop was particularly popular in the 1950s and '60s, appealing across racial and ethnic lines with songs on universal themes of love and courtship, and was an important component of early rock 'n' roll.

A cappella remained a component of the popular music landscape as the twentieth century continued, albeit not always a particularly prominent one. Several successful records illustrate its staying power, however. One of them is Billy Joel's "The Longest Time" (1983), with its soaring falsetto, deep bass, and complex harmonies that seem to mix both doo-wop and barbershop with a pop sensibility. While this song remains the only a cappella track in Joel's catalog, just a few years later Bobby McFerrin would use an a cappella recording to propel himself into the mainstream spotlight. "Don't Worry, Be Happy" (1988), with its catchy hook, richly-layered vocal textures, and vocalized instrumental sounds, proved to audiences the potency of the human voice, aided by McFerrin's distinctive penchant for vocal acrobatics. It also won Grammy awards for Best Pop Vocal Performance, Song of the Year, and Record of the Year.

Where Billy Joel sang a cappella in a pop style and Bobby McFerrin did it with a reggae touch, Boyz II Men found success with R&B a cappella in their hit, "It's So Hard to Say Goodbye to Yesterday" (1991). Featuring long vocal runs and smooth harmonies, the quartet spent less time imitating instruments and more time providing a rich, silky support layer beneath each singer's passages of solo vocal display. The song also won Grammys for Best R&B Performance by a Duo or Group with Vocal while topping the R&B and Billboard Top 100 charts.

There were, of course, professional a cappella groups who may have sold fewer records but remained more closely focused on unaccompanied music, whether throughout their careers or for portions of it. Manhattan Transfer, a vocal jazz group, won Grammy awards in several categories for its a cappella album, *Mecca for Moderns*, in 1982. One of the record's tracks, "Boy From New York City," even became a Top 10 hit. Meanwhile, the Bobs, a quartet from San Francisco, garnered special notice in the *Contemporary A Cappella Newsletter*, published by the newly formed Contemporary A Cappella Society of America, in its April 1992 issue. By that time the group had already recorded five albums on several independent labels in the United States and abroad, consisting of both original songs and covers; their version of Lennon and McCartney's "Helter Skelter" earned a Grammy nomination in 1983. The Nylons, a Toronto-based group formed in 1978, also gathered a large a cappella fan base in the 1980s. The group enjoyed a Top 10 hit in 1987 with the song, "Kiss Him Goodbye."

This small pool of professional groups continued to grow as the turn of the century approached, as groups like Rockappella (founded in 1986), Five O'Clock Shadow (1991), and The House Jacks (1991) built an audience for popular style a cappella songs by singing a mix of covers and original fare. In some cases, they also achieved mainstream success: Rockappella, for example, is best known as the group who sang the theme song to the popular children's television show *Where in the World is Carmen Sandiego?*

Later professional a cappella groups, like the collegiate variety at the time, were more likely to incorporate vocal percussion into their performances. This method of making percussive and drum-like sounds using the voice, lips, and tongue (which has roots in early rap and hip-hop music) could provide additional rhythmic drive to a cappella songs.

Deke and The Filharmonic on the set of *Pitch Perfect 2*

The number of professional groups continued to increase after the turn of the century and can now be found in many major metropolitan areas, from Las Vegas (Mo5aic) to Orlando, Florida (Toxic Audio) to Washington, D.C. (The Capital Hearings). In many cases, members of professional groups are alumni of collegiate groups. In fact, the professional iteration of Straight No Chaser, which began singing in 2008, were all members of the collegiate group of the same name at Indiana University. Professional groups from outside the mainland United States also continue to gain prominence, including The Idea of North (from Australia), Nota (Puerto Rico), and Streetnix (Canada). The growth of a cappella festivals has contributed to this blossoming scene, including regular events such as the West Coast A Cappella Summit and its counterpart, the East Coast A Cappella Summit, as well as the more recent SoJam (in North Carolina) and ACappellaFest (Chicago).

A Cappella Comes Back to Campus

Within the span of just a few years toward the end of the twentieth century, young, aspiring singers could find plenty of commercially and musically successful models for a cappella music. In addition to decades of music education in public schools, the prominence of these recordings helped to inspire a new wave of a cappella on college campuses. Of course, with a legacy of glee clubs and earlier vocal ensembles, campuses had long been homes for a cappella music—after all, the famous Whiffenpoofs had been around for nearly a century. But the 1980s and 1990s saw a significant increase in the number of groups participating in the a cappella scene.

Historical data is incomplete, but an informal survey of the collegiate a cappella landscape conducted in the mid-2000s provides some evidence of the music's stunning growth. By 1980, approximately a hundred a cappella groups were active on American campuses, including the Whiffenpoofs and newer groups such as the Smiffenpoofs (formed at Smith College in 1936), the Kingsmen (Columbia University, 1949), the Friars (University of Michigan, 1955), the Beelzebubs (Tufts University, 1962), and the Clef Hangers (University of North Carolina, 1977). Most groups at this time were men's ensembles, although there were a significant number of women's groups as well. Few were mixed.

During the 1980s, the total number of groups more than doubled. The decade ended with nearly 250 groups, including almost equal numbers of men's and women's groups, while mixed groups made significant gains. Collegiate a cappella also expanded geographically, with groups formed at places like the University of Vermont, Washington University in St. Louis, York University in Toronto, the University of Georgia, the University of California, and Stanford University. The upward trend continued from 1990 to 2000, as over 300 new groups were established. By the mid-1990s, mixed groups overtook men's and women's as the most numerous.

By the mid-2000s, some estimated that there were 1200 active collegiate a cappella groups, mostly in the United States but also in Canada and parts of Europe and Asia. (By the next decade it has been suggested that the number is closer to 2000.) Moreover, the world of collegiate a cappella had grown to include not only groups singing mainstream, secular popular songs, but also those focused on various religious and ethnic identities (such as Christian, Jewish, Hindi, African-American, or purposely multicultural), particular subgenres (1950s rock 'n' roll, Broadway show tunes, sea chanteys), and even non-Western traditions (Stanford University's Talisman stands out in this regard).

Helping to propel this explosive growth was the formation of several organizations in support of a cappella music. Deke Sharon started the Contemporary A Cappella Society of America in 1991. In its early days, the Society began archiving a cappella arrangements in order to provide new groups with repertory. To this day, it continues to serve as an important mechanism for singers and groups, helping them connect and share ideas and music. In addition to hosting the Contemporary A Cappella Recording Awards and the A Cappella Community Awards,

Eleventh Hour

the Society also promotes a post-collegiate amateur a cappella "league" and a variety of other ventures aimed at supporting the music and its participants. The Recorded A Cappella Review Board website debuted in 1994, building on the success of the older Usenet internet discussion board, rec.music.a-cappella. It hosted detailed reviews of collegiate and professional albums as well as its own discussion forum, which was later folded into the Society's website. More recently, the A Cappella Education Association has joined the ranks of a cappella organizations. Its establishment by high school choral directors indicates its inclusion of high school a cappella within its purview, in addition to the collegiate level.

The annual *Best of College A Cappella* album series began in 1995 as a joint effort by Sharon and Adam Farb to promote collegiate a cappella music within and beyond the a cappella community. Since 1999, it has been administered by Varsity Vocals, the company—run almost entirely by collegiate a cappella alumni—that also oversees the International Championship of Collegiate A Cappella. That live competition was originally started in 1996 by Sharon and Farb as a national contest, but soon expanded internationally with the inclusion of Canadian groups. The competition extended to England in 2006, drawing entries from St. Andrews, Cambridge, and Oxford Universities, while the 2010 season included competitors from Pretoria, South Africa. A high school competition, the International Championship of High School A Cappella, was established in 2006.

To participate in the International Championship of Collegiate A Cappella, groups must first submit an application, including a recording from one of their performances. Accepted groups are then organized geographically; each section of the country (in the case of the United States) or the region as a whole (in the case of Europe and elsewhere) then hosts several first-round competitions, adjudicated by local experts. Competitors are evaluated according to a variety of criteria, including strictly musical qualities (tuning, blend, diction, etc.) as well as performance aspects (appropriateness of movement, transitions, professionalism, etc.). The highest scoring groups then advance to the local semifinal round, the winners of which move on to the final round, which is typically held in New York City.

Along with the rise of professional and collegiate a cappella, more advanced technology has made its way into both recording studios and, in some cases, live performances. As the turn of the twenty-first century approached, many groups began using the digital and computer-based tools of the studio to add effects to their voices, including guitar-like distortion and overdrive as well as echoes and pitch-shifting (especially dropping the bass singer's voice an octave or two lower in order to project a more powerful bass sound). A few took digital audio editing to an extreme, laying tens or hundreds of tracks of precisely trimmed and processed vocal sounds in order to better emulate the instruments used in a song's original recording, such as The Tufts Beelzebubs' recording of Styx's "Mr. Roboto," from *Code Red* (2003). As these kinds of effects became more common, some in the a cappella community began to debate the value of the changing sound of the music, asking whether digitally altered voices were a positive or negative development in the genre. Strong opinions emerged on both sides of the issue, which was often debated—in a somewhat ironic twist—in online discussion forums, a digital medium. In any case, the a cappella community witnessed a significant shift in the way many of its groups were making recordings, pushing them farther from the genre's choral roots and toward a more technologically informed pop sound.

In the Spotlight: A Cappella's Mainstream Moment

A cappella found itself in the media spotlight in the late 2000s and 2010s as a variety of efforts drew unprecedented levels of attention to the music. The trade book, *Pitch Perfect: The Quest for Collegiate A Cappella Glory* (2008), began the process, following three groups during the 2006–2007 academic year and offering their stories mixed with brief snapshots of other aspects of the a cappella world, from its history to its major personalities. The following year, Anoop Desai, a member of the University of North Carolina Clef Hangers, appeared on the eighth season of the hit television show, *American Idol*. That same year also saw the release of *Ben Folds Presents: University A Cappella!*, an album for which piano-rocker Ben Folds traveled the country recording collegiate groups singing covers of his compositions.

Street Corner Symphony

A cappella returned to TV with two important shows in the fall of 2009. The first was *Glee*, a musical comedy about a high school glee club. Although the show's music was largely accompanied, the second season introduced an a cappella group from a neighboring school, which provided opportunities for true a cappella songs (voiced by the Tufts University Beelzebubs) on the soundtrack. Then came *The Sing-Off*, a televised a cappella singing contest whose first season included several current or former collegiate groups; Ben Folds was one of the judges. The show was quickly renewed for additional seasons. As the president of the University of Virginia Hullabahoos said in a newspaper article covering the show, "[A] cappella was kind of dormant. Then, all of a sudden, it's something everyone knows about."

If anyone missed the memo, they certainly heard the message loud and clear when *Pitch Perfect*, a feature film based on the 2008 book, hit the theaters in 2012, featuring a fictional women's a cappella group as they compete in the national championship. Earning over $113 million worldwide, the film became the second-highest grossing music comedy, after *School of Rock* (2003). Its soundtrack included three songs that reached the Billboard Top 100 chart and ended up as the best-selling soundtrack in 2012 and 2013.

Naturally 7

Thus, it may seem like a cappella comes into its own in American pop culture only at the end of this story. And while it may be true that millions more know about a cappella thanks to the commercially successful books, albums, TV shows, and films of recent years, it is equally true that popular music has been sung, a cappella, for centuries. Indeed, as we look back at earlier forms of a cappella, we see the many things they have in common with today's version of the genre, including the emphasis on fun and camaraderie, the musical division between soloist and background singers, and the intricate and powerful harmonies. If the past is any indication of the future, then we should have centuries more of wonderful a cappella music to come.

"I make sure I sing a cappella to let people know I can sing."
—T-Pain

BARBERSHOP, DOO-WOP, AND POP

A brief comparison of Barbershop, Doo-Wop, and Contemporary Pop/Rock a cappella

BARBERSHOP	DOO WOP	CONTEMPORARY POP/ROCK
Late 19th century	Middle of 20th century	End of 20th century
Grew from current popular music	Grew from current popular music	Grew from current popular music
Spread in town community centers	Spread on urban street corners	Spread on radio, colleges, internet
Initially improvised from melody	Initially improvised from melody	Initially sheet music for harmony
Later codified and notated	Later codified and notated	Vocal percussion still not notated
Converges to homophonic: same words at the same time	Homophonic besides melody: background voices usually a unit	Polyphonic: melody, drums, bass, backs
Very little emphasis on sounding like instruments, if at all	Basic instrumental imitation: "bum" in bass, "doo" for chords	Complex, varied instrumental sounds: drums, bass, guitars, horns, etc.
Focus: harmony; ringing overtones	Focus: melody; soulful, loose, emotional	Focus: rhythm; constant driving groove
Complex harmonies (7th chords): frequently changing	Simple harmonies (triads): repeated harmonic patterns	Varied harmonies: simple-complex, frequent or infrequent changes
Formalized melody (pitch & rhythm)	Loose melody, improvisation	Loose melody, improvisation
Rhythm based on melody, constant or rubato	Constant, simple rhythm in backs, loose melodic rhythm in counterpoint	Complex driving rhythm in backs, loose melodic rhythm in counterpoint
Lyrics in all voices, usually	Lyrics in backs or "bum, doo"	Variety of sounds and syllables
Recordings done live	Recordings done live plus instruments	Recordings use lots of overdubbing
Amplified only if needed using a pair of microphones	Amplified sometimes lead vocal mic, then others	Amplified usually one mic per singer, two for VP

GETTING THE BAND TOGETHER

Broad Street Beat

CHAPTER 3
DECISIONS AND FINDING MEMBERS

Are you ready to start a group? There is a lot to learn, but there's no need to learn the hard way! This section will guide you from conceptualization to your first performance. You will learn the best way to find members, run auditions, structure your group, quickly build repertoire, and start performing.

Clear Vision

Before you start down the path of forming a group, you must have a clear vision of what the group will be. You must **begin with the end in mind.** How many singers will it have? Male, female, or mixed? What style of music will you sing? Will you be casual weekend warriors or full-time professionals? The following information will help guide you through some important considerations when forming a group.

Voice + Personality

As with most endeavors, the people you choose for your group are your greatest resource. During auditions, remember that voices make the music, but people make the group. Each member will not only bring their voice to the table, but also their personality, their musical goals, and their non-musical skills.

From a personality standpoint, you must all work well together. A barbershop singer once described his quartet as a "four-way marriage." Any group could be perceived as a musical marriage, and you must consider how the mix of personalities in your group can work together for the common good. "Birds of a feather flock together," and "opposites attract," are contradictory clichés. That's because both scenarios can work. There's no magic formula here. Simply being aware of human dynamics and observing how people work together will help you with your membership selection in the personality department.

Each singer has their own musical goals as well. When recruiting singers for your group, be as clear as you can about your musical goals: "Singers needed for professional cruise ship male doo-wop quartet" is bound to attract different singers than "singers desired for large, mixed, recreational a cappella group." By marketing your auditions properly, you will ensure you have generally like-minded people involved. The next step comes once those people have come through the door. You'll need to ask some follow-up questions and allow the auditionees to express what they want to get out of the group. For example: if you want to be the primary music arranger for the group and an auditionee says "I've been waiting for a group experience like this to showcase my arrangements," you'll want to discuss that potential conflict sooner rather than later.

Also, there are non-musical skills to consider. Do you need a treasurer for the group? How about a webmaster or someone who can create posters for each new gig? Discussing non-musical skills can be a great way to learn more about the auditionee as a whole, but can also help you break a musical "tie." Let's face it: if you have two great sopranos but one of them is an accountant willing to keep the books—you might have a tie-breaker. The higher your group sits on the "going pro" ladder, the more weight these non-musical abilities have. Getting off the ground requires a lot of sweat equity, so being able to divide that work among the membership is a blessing.

But before you start scrutinizing each individual's voice, business acumen and interpersonal style, you need to decide a few things:

Number of Voices

How many people do you want in your group? Four is a good minimum number. There have only been a handful of successful a cappella trios (usually folk music). With four members, you can have the traditional SATB, SSAA or TTBB composition, which will allow you to sing thousands of prearranged songs. If you're looking to have a classical, barbershop or doo-wop group, four is an excellent number.

A quintet will give you added musical versatility. Are you looking to perform more harmonically dense jazz arrangements or have one voice dedicated to vocal percussion? More and more nowadays, five is becoming the standard size for non-collegiate a cappella groups, as it allows for more complexity and can provide a more complete background when a voice steps forward to sing the lead.

Groups with six or seven members are sometimes a challenge; you have too few voices to double parts (having only one part doubled is generally a bad idea, especially if you're amplified) so you'll be forced to consistently sing fairly complex arrangements. Few fully-professional a cappella groups have sustained even a size of six. Those that have succeeded tend to tackle either difficult music with dense harmonies (many added chord factors like Take 6) or with vocal percussion and complex textures (like the House Jacks). Six or seven can be a good number for groups with a permanent vocal percussionist. After accounting for a lead singer, a bass, and a vocal percussionist, there are three or four people remaining to fill out the background parts.

If you're thinking about a group larger than seven, you're into small chorus territory. The members of your group will be perceived more as a unit than as individuals, and this alters how you approach the audience and your marketing angle. In very broad terms, if you'll forgive the analogy, you'll be moving more towards Chanticleer and away from N'SYNC or the Spice Girls. In other words: smaller groups are better for pop stylings, and large choral groups tend to be more of an "arts organization."

Seneca Junction Chorus

The one prominent exception to this is the scholastic a cappella scene. College, university and high school groups often have an average of 12–15 members. Such a large group singing pop music won't work on a professional basis (too many mouths to feed, and probably no help from arts and choral organizations since you're not "cultural," etc.), but for a scholastic group it's ideal. With ¼ to ⅓ of the group graduating each year, there will be enough of a core to move into the next year without losing much steam, and one or two members can be absent from a show without major repercussions. Also, because people may leave mid-semester due to bad grades or other pressures, a larger group size will minimize that damage.

Gender

What gender will comprise your group? You've got three choices: male, female, or mixed.

Male groups have been the most prominent lineup. Since the days of Gregorian chant, through barbershop and doo-wop, and even in today's vocal bands, men seem to enjoy singing together. The male voice typically has greater range than the female voice through the use of falsetto (think Frankie Valli high notes). Also, male voices start lower in the harmonic series, allowing more room for overtone production (an overtone is a high note that is produced when voices sing well together—it makes a group sound bigger and fuller than it is). Finally, there's a certain sex appeal a single-gender group seems to generate more often than mixed groups. Whatever the reason, the most popular lineup among small a cappella groups has been all-male.

However, mixed groups have grown tremendously in popularity over the years. Just a few years ago, it seemed the only mixed groups were choirs or jazz ensembles. This has been changing, as shown in the world of collegiate a cappella: ten years ago, fewer than fifteen percent of college a cappella groups were mixed. Today, mixed groups are the most common collegiate configuration, and their recordings and arrangements have proven to be the most trend-setting. The use of male and female voices together provides the greatest potential range of sounds. Also, if you're looking to stick to published and easy-to-get music, the number of SATB arrangements outnumbers all-male at around a 10:1 ratio. In the case of all-female arrangements, the ratio is closer to 30:1.

Female groups are currently the fewest in number. Don't look at this as a negative. This is a great opportunity! There is more room in the female category for groups to gain notoriety. If you have a great female group, you'll be in demand at a cappella festivals around the world. There is no specific reason there are so few all-female groups but the prevailing theory is that all-female groups cannot achieve the same range of sound a male or mixed group can. Without some abnormally low altos, female groups must stay in a very narrow vocal range, which then often leads to a lack of sonic variety. We have yet to see a mostly-female group that uses a male bass, but this is certainly a possibility, as is the possibility of an otherwise a cappella female group using an instrument (such as an upright bass or synthesizer) to fill out their bass range.

Style Of Music

A cappella groups are more stylistically versatile than most instrumental combos. Guitar bands and string quartets are limited in their sonic variety; an a cappella group can sing classical and pop songs back to back with equal prowess. The only limit to the range of the human voice is the ability of the singer. In other words, your choices are limitless. Nonetheless, there are some general categories that have arisen over time:

- Madrigal group
- Barbershop or Sweet Adeline Quartet
- Doo-wop quartet or quintet
- Close harmony/vocal jazz group
- Vocal band (including vocal percussion, etc.)

Many groups incorporate elements of at least one of these categories. What's even more exciting is that many groups blend a combination of styles to create their own unique sound. It's interesting to note that all of the above styles were developed through stylistic and sonic pioneering, and that before 1990, there weren't any vocal bands.

Having an idea of what kind of music you want to sing will make group auditions and repertoire selection much easier. Don't think you need to know everything right away if you intend to carve out a new sound. It's difficult to have a complete idea until you have voices in place. Nonetheless, a general concept is very useful.

Announce Auditions

If you are starting a new group from scratch, you'll have to hold open auditions. You will want to attract as many people as possible. A huge turnout at auditions would be considered a "pleasant problem." Yes, it takes a while to sort through a large pool of singers. However, your chances of finding great new members are increased.

To make sure your open auditions are well-attended, you should publicize them well. You'll want to announce them in multiple media and venues.

Ideas on how to announce your auditions:

- Local choruses
  Bring a flyer to a rehearsal and ask to make an announcement right before the break. Position your group as an opportunity for extra singing, not as a replacement for the chorus.

- Newspapers
  Classified ads are relatively inexpensive. If you have more than one paper in your area, advertise in all of them. Few people read the classifieds in more than one publication. Certainly in colleges, the campus newspaper is the place to advertise.

- Musician's publications
  In many cities, local musicians have a preferred publication or bulletin board. For example, many musicians post classifieds in Washington D.C.'s *City Paper*. Find out where your local musicians hang out and post there. Explore different genres. Often, the best modern a cappella group members have come from vocal rock bands, where they've learned to sing well, blend with other singers, and have practiced stage presence and style.

- CASA: The Contemporary A Cappella Society of America
  www.casa.org

- Social Media
  Use as many social media sites as you can, such as Twitter and Facebook.

- A Cappella Education Association (AEA)
  www.acappellaeducators.com

- Local Ambassadors
  CASA has a network of regional a cappella ambassadors that are, in many cases, the definitive source of a cappella information for their area. Let them know what you're up to, and ask if they have any suggestions or know of any potential members.

- A cappella events and concerts
  Bring a stack of flyers, wear a nametag, and network. Word of mouth is often the best way to find singers, and a cappella concerts bring together singers and generate new interest like nothing else.

Besides advertising, the best way for you to spread the word about your new group is to perform. Obviously you won't have all your members, but if you can put together a quartet of committed and talented people before starting auditions, you'll have a tremendous advantage. It is particularly easy for collegiate groups, where you can go sing in dining halls, before major functions, and during orientation week for the wide-eyed freshmen. Or just do some general "dormstorming," a term used to describe canvassing the dorms (often freshman dorms). If people can actually experience what you're doing instead of just reading about it, you'll easily generate much more interest.

As you're going through this process, be sure to keep a list of all people and contacts you meet. Even if they don't work out at present, you never know when you'll be looking for a new member. This information may prove invaluable to you some day in the future.

Attracting Good Members

Your existing personal reputation, as well as what you do before and during auditions, will greatly influence your ability to attract good singers. A singer will decide whether to audition based on what they know about your group. This means several things:

1. When recruiting, always consider the image you portray. You should make the group look enticing to the type of people you wish to attract. Make sure your print materials, audition posters, website, etc. are all in line with the image you are trying to project.

2. Be professional in your dealings with people. Be welcoming, return calls or emails promptly, and run the auditions in a professional manner. You can still be friendly and fun while being professional.

3. As you select your group, remember "quality over quantity." It is more important that the ability level of the group is where you want it rather than trying to hit an arbitrary target number. Make sure you have a musical threshold for your singers, and don't let anyone in who falls short. Also, make sure you are well-rehearsed before performing. The reputation that you eventually build through your performances will affect the level of singers that come out for subsequent auditions. This is particularly true for collegiate groups, where many of the auditionees tend to be people who have heard the group and liked it.

Your Perfect Member Profile

There are three major elements you're looking for in a potential member: talent, personality and commitment. Obviously each person is different, and no one is perfect. However, as you assess auditionees you can track them in each of these three important areas.

Talent

Talent is a difficult quality to assess. It's often used as an open-ended "catch-all" phrase. However, there are a number of helpful questions you might ask yourself to help focus your thoughts about the auditionee.

What kind of a singer is this person? Are they capable as a soloist? As a background singer? Are you be interested and "drawn in" watching this person on stage? How much experience do they have? What is their vocal range? What is the tone quality of their voice (light, bright, dark, strong, raspy, etc.)? How musical does this person seem? How well do they make adjustments when given direction?

Remember, you're not only looking at the person's talent as presented in the audition, but you're also interested in how that will translate to a stage, and how it will fit within your group.

Personality

A singer's personality isn't only important on stage. You also have to make sure an individual can get along with others, can conduct business, can handle other behind-the-scenes duties, and is generally responsible. Many groups have commented their success is greatly enhanced by being social outside of rehearsals and performances. During the audition process you'd be surprised how blinded people can get by an individual's raw talent. Sometimes a voice is so good it's hard to think of anything else. Make sure you take a sober step back and look at the whole person. In fact, when someone presents as "off the charts" talented, you have more time to explore those non-musical aspects of their personality. After all, they've proven very quickly that their vocal ability is not in question!

Commitment

Having a common level of commitment is crucial to a new group. If half of the members are looking for a Grammy® and the other half are only looking for a casual pastime, you're bound to hit conflict with almost every decision you make.

During the audition process, clearly spell out what the commitment will be. Put it in writing so there's no confusion. Spell out when rehearsals occur (what nights, how long), how many gigs you plan to sing per month, etc.

Example:

- Eleventh Hour

  ▷ Rehearsals: Monday and Wednesday evenings, 6–9 p.m.

  ▷ We average two gigs per month

  ▷ We will give members at least two weeks notice before accepting a gig

  ▷ Members are expected to respond to emails within 48 hours

A word of warning: just as a chain is only as strong as its weakest link, a group is only as effective as its least committed member/weakest singer/most difficult personality. Once your group is selected, make sure that the group expectations and calendar are always up-to-date and in print. If one person is consistently late for gigs or misses rehearsals, it must be addressed to avoid resentment or demoralization inside the group. Make sure you choose responsible, committed people. Then, together as a new group, you set goals and commit to each other.

UCF Voicebox

CHAPTER 4
A CAPPELLA GROUP CHECKLIST

Got a note from an ambassador wanting to take his region to the next level. He's got multiple a cappella festivals, a harmony sweepstakes, and ICCAs, but knows that a city's reputation starts and ends with its local groups.

So, this got us thinking: what elements are needed, and which things don't matter quite as much? (Note: this is not for all a cappella groups, but rather those that have a chance of blowing up in today's media.)

Needed: Soloist

Yes, everyone in your group must be able to sing well, but not all of them need to be amazing soloists. What do we mean by "amazing soloist?" A lead voice so compelling you would buy this person's solo album: Jeremy Lister, Scott Hoying, Margareta Bengtson/Jalkeus, Jerry Lawson. The group can share solos, but you need at least one person whose voice is world class.

Not Needed: Similar Voices

You'll have an easier time building a blend if you create a group around similar voices, but it's definitely not necessary. You can be Take 6 or you can be Straight No Chaser. Both are winning formulas.

Needed: Great Bass

After the soloist, the second loudest element in all popular music is the bass. That's how it should be in your group's mix as well, and that voice should be as low and as powerful as possible. The octave pedal can work, but if your group name isn't a palindrome (hello, Sonos/Arora!), we don't like your chances.

Not Needed: Great Vocal Percussionist

Not every contemporary group features vocal percussion. If you've got one, great. If that's not part of your sound, not a deal-breaker.

Needed: Original Music

Your ensemble will likely have more success with cover tunes than original tunes early on, but eventually having music that you're known for will become essential to keep you from simply being a cover band in the eyes of the public. Note that this isn't always an original song, but it can be: Straight No Chaser has found success with both "The Christmas Can Can" (old music, new lyrics, new concept), and "Who Stole The Egg Nog" (entirely new). An original arrangement can serve this purpose, but it has to be as arresting and memorable as, say, the remake of "Mad World."

Not Needed: Original Concept

Yes, it's excellent if your group has a new sound or approach, but we have to admit, there are plenty of bios boasting a sound and style unheard ever before in a cappella, and most fall short. Don't tell the world you're different. Show them. Don't focus on being amazingly different. Just be amazing. Not convinced? Nothing about Pentatonix on paper looks much different from many other groups. There's no huge fundamental concept behind it all, but the way they do what they do has indeed become revolutionary, and inspired millions.

Needed: Time Together

Lots of time. Ideally everyone lives in the same city and sings together every day for a year. Especially in the beginning. Build rapport, build a sound, build a character. You can make great recordings from a distance, but you're probably not going to have a great live sound until you're just a little bit sick of each other.

Not Needed: Veterans

Almost all of the biggest names in professional a cappella currently had nothing more than some high school and/or college a cappella experience when they started.

Needed: Momentum

It might be a viral video, an appearance on a television show, going on tour with a big artist, a six-month cruise ship gig, theme park gig, college tour— something to keep the group together and move you forward. It's partially about common experience, partially about time together, partially about building success.

Not Needed: All The Answers

You might not exactly know what style your group should adopt or what songs you should focus primarily on. Don't worry about having all of the answers early on. Instead, focus on answering the questions you can, and using the successes you have to help you answer the open questions as they become more clear.

The fact is, there is no one perfect formula, one easy path to success or excellence, especially in a market as diverse and as niche as a cappella. We're sure there are exceptions to the points above, and we could probably come up with some of our own with a few minutes—but the larger point We're trying to make is that you don't need everything to make a great group. You only need some things. And you probably already have some if not many of those things.

So what remains is the ability to focus and spend the time you have together building quality and momentum in ways that matter.

How are you supposed to know what matters? Oh, that's easy: get some outside perspective. Ask the experts. They're waiting by the phone, and Facebook, waiting for you to call!

A CAPPELLA AND THE GRAMMYS®

- The first big win for a cappella music at The Grammys came in 1988 when Bobby McFerrin's "Don't Worry Be Happy" won Record of the Year, Song of the Year, and Male Pop Performance.
- The American jazz group Manhattan Transfer won Grammys in 1980, 1981, 1982, 1983, 1985, 1988, and 1991, but none of their tracks were exclusively a cappella.
- The pop group Boyz II Men won their first Grammy in 1991 for *Cooleyhighharmony* in the category of Best R&B Performance By A Duo Or Group With Vocal, but not every track on the album was a cappella.
- Take 6 won Grammys in 1998 for Best Jazz Vocal Performance, Duo or Group for "Spread Love" and Best Soul Gospel Performance By A Duo, Group, Choir, or Chorus for "Take 6." In 1989 they won Best Gospel Vocal Performance By A Duo, Group, Choir or Chorus for "The Savior Is Waiting." Take 6 also won a Grammy in 1990 for Best Contemporary Soul Gospel Album for *So Much 2 Say*. They then won in 1991 for Best Jazz Vocal Performance for "He is Christmas." They won Best Contemporary Soul Gospel Album for *Join the Band* in 1994 and for *Brothers* in 1997. In 2002 they won a Grammy for Best R&B Performance by a Duo or Group With Vocal for their collaboration with Stevie Wonder "Love's In Need of Love Today."
- In 2008, the British a cappella vocal ensemble The King's Singers won a Grammy for Best Classical Crossover Album for *Simple Gifts*.
- In 2015 Pentatonix, along with their album producer/arranger Ben Bram, won a Grammy for Best Arrangement, Instrumental or A Cappella for "Daft Punk." It should be noted that this was the first time that this category existed (previously it was titled "Best Instrumental Arrangement") and the first time the term a cappella had been used in conjunction with the Grammys.

Twisted Moustache

CHAPTER 5
THE AUDITION

Introduction

Once you have advertised auditions and have a clear vision in your mind about what you want the group to be, you'll run the actual auditions. If you're starting out a group alone, you may find it difficult to audition members alone. A good solution is to find musicians whom you trust to participate in the first few auditions. These musicians can help you choose the group (if small) or some initial members (if large). In the case of a large group, you can work with those initial members to audition the rest of the group.

It is very important to take notes on the auditionees during each step of the process. Because you are analyzing each singer as they come through, it can be easy to have them start to blur together. A picture, audio recording, or video (just record part of each person's solo) will be very useful when remembering people and making decisions. There is no worse feeling than finishing several hours of auditions, only to not remember whom you liked the most.

Booking Auditions

Once interested persons have called, give them an audition date and time. Tell them anything they may need to prepare for the audition. You may even go as far as sending them some music in advance. You'll probably want them to come prepared to perform a solo for you, and you'll definitely want them to warm up prior to the audition. In any event, you'll want to let them know enough about what to expect that you see their best selves.

What to Include in the Audition

The audition itself should reflect the nature of the group you want to form and should include both elements of professionalism and enjoyable moments of camaraderie.

Before the audition itself, have the auditionee fill out a form including current contact information, relevant experience, and anything else you want to know. It also may help if the person brings a picture and/or resume. This is especially appropriate for professional groups.

There are many things you should make sure you cover during an audition:

Warm-ups

Although most singers will warm themselves up prior to an audition, warm-ups can be used as a way to learn about an auditionee's voice in a stress-free environment. Generally, if an auditionee is nervous, it will be at the beginning of the audition.

It's easy to use scales for the warm-up, which give you a chance to test their vocal range. Have them sing scale patterns up and down to test their vocal extremes and give you a sense of the quality of their voice in different registers. Be sure to have them take deep breaths and reassure them not to be nervous. Some light joking will help lighten the atmosphere.

Solo

Make sure each person has prepared a solo in advance of the audition. It should be something they know and preferably something that fits the style/potential repertoire of your group. In other words, no art songs for a doo-wop group audition. Have the person sing the song by themselves a cappella (no instrumental accompaniment CD and no other singer). Make sure the singer knows about this in advance, as this isn't easy for some. Hearing a person's naked voice is more telling than any other element of the audition. You'll hear vocal quality, interpretation, tuning, rhythm, dynamics and emotion—all in that single performance. Make sure to encourage the auditionee to truly perform the song for you, otherwise you may get all vocal precision and no spark. Occasionally you'll come across an excellent background singer who isn't a dynamic solo singer. This is okay as long as you have other great soloists in your lineup.

After the solo, you should "confer" with your fellow judges with a simple glance or pre-established signal (no need for a formal vote). If you're not at all interested in an individual at this stage, now is a good time to thank and dismiss the person. There is no need to go through the following steps with someone you know isn't right.

Vocal Ability, Tuning, and Precision

A cappella is demanding. You need to know your singers can sing complex passages in tune without being thrown off by other singers. Some good tests are:

- Play complex pitch patterns/intervals and have the auditionee sing them back to you—
  to check their pitch memory.

- Perform/play difficult rhythms and have the audition repeat them—
  to check their rhythmic sense.

- Sing and have the auditionee join you to match vowel sounds or vocal patterns—
  to check their ability to shape/mimic tone.

- Have the auditionee sing a musical phrase multiple times starting on different pitches—
  to check their ability to adjust quickly.

How Good is Their "Ear?"

Some singers can sing patterns or intervals back to you, but lack the ear to effectively harmonize. This is very important in a cappella singing and should be tested. Some good tests are:

- Play three notes consecutively on a keyboard and have the auditionee sing the middle note back to you. Start with simple chords and work your way to more complex combinations of notes.

- Hold three keys down indefinitely and have the auditionee sing the middle one to you.

You'll also get an idea for their ear as they learn songs with you. Be wary of singers who drift from their part to similar parts a third or fourth away.

Sight-Reading

It is important that you get a sense for how a singer learns music. Once your group is up and running, you'll set target dates for learning songs. Those who can't read music are forever dependent on external help: a recording, a friend playing the part, someone else singing the part. Those who can read music will have an easier time preparing on their own, and that's valuable.

Start by having the individual do a little sight-reading for you by simply looking at the music. If this is too hard, you can have them sight-read a simple passage while you and other members sing the other parts. (If you don't have enough members, you can play the parts on a keyboard.) If the right song is chosen, this type of group singing also satisfies the "blending" part of the audition, discussed later.

If this kind of "raw" sight-reading doesn't work, an alternative is to determine how quickly the person can learn by ear. Play or sing the part once, and then have the auditionee sing it back. The amount of time it takes for the person to get the part right will give you a rough indication of what you'll be dealing with in rehearsal. Often a person will not be a good sight-reader, but will still learn parts quickly with minimal teaching. This type of person inevitably becomes a better sight-reader as time goes on.

If your group is not planning or expecting any members to sight-read at all, but will be expecting people to learn music outside of rehearsal, you should give all auditionees music to learn on their own in advance of the audition. You can use either sheet music or a learning track.

Blending Test

In an a cappella group, it very important that the singers are able to match each other. Because a cappella groups make a wide variety of sounds (from harmonizing with the melody to making guitar or trumpet noises), singers must prove they are able to listen, analyze, adjust, and mimic.

- Listen—listen to other singers on the same part, listen to a given vocal model, listen to the rhythm section.

- Analyze—take what is heard and determine how that model sound is produced.

- Adjust—take steps to make their voice match the model.

- Mimic—produce sounds that match the model/other singers in the section.

One way to check a singer's ability to blend is to give them a "model" song in advance. Pick one song for each voice part (soprano, alto, tenor, bass). Have the auditionee come prepared to sing that song to you exactly as it was peformed on the recording, down to every slide, every breath, every nuance in the vocal line. A singer who can copy a vocal model is a singer who can blend.

Another way to test blend is to have auditionees learn a section of an a cappella song. Once the auditionee has learned their part, have them sing it with others. You may have to borrow some musical friends just for the audition. Listen for the singer's ability to blend in with the other voices, compensating pitch, timbre, and volume to match what they hear. Also make sure this person can hold their part and won't drift onto someone else's vocal lines. The point of this exercise is to see how an individual will do once a song is learned.

One important caveat with the blending test or any other time you're singing with the auditionee: make sure the existing group members (or your volunteer singers) know their parts and can sing the audition pieces well. It is important to have a constant, quality product against which you can measure the different auditionees. Also, you don't want to give the auditionee an escape hatch: "I was doing fine until that tenor came in early. That really messed me up!"

Depending on your group, the total depth and length of the audition may vary. For professional or semi-pro groups, long auditions or even multiple auditions are recommended to get a really good idea of the talent, ability, and personality of the singer. These pro auditions will usually be heavily weighted towards singing with the group and fitting into their lineup, filling the exact spot that is open. In the collegiate or high school scene, the opposite may be true: often there are so many interested singers that auditions must be run quickly. A fairly complete audition can be done in about 20 minutes. If you are blessed by exceptionally high turnout, you could consider doing a "first round" audition in which each singer is given a three-minute screening audition. Those who make the cut are then called back for a longer audition at a later date.

Austin Brown, Home Free

If you reach the end of your audition process and are still finding it difficult to choose between a few finalists, don't hesitate to schedule a callback. The callback should be formatted much like a full rehearsal. Also, be sure there's plenty of time to "hang out" with the singers as well as sing with them. Warm up together, learn music together, sing together. Focus on anything you feel is necessary to differentiate between the singers or find out more about a certain part of their vocal ability or personality. Remember, you'll be singing with this person for quite some time, so don't skimp during a callback. Take an hour or two to make sure all of your questions are answered completely. You can have more than one singer at a callback, but don't exceed four or five. If you have too many at once, you won't be able to pay attention to all of them.

Other Requirements

Some groups have specific requirements beyond singing. These could include movement, acting, or even playing instruments. If you have such requirements, you may need to customize your audition process. Make sure that the audition is structured to look for the all the qualities you require in a member. Don't hesitate to come up with some unique tests (choreography, acting, etc.), if your group is going to demand specific non-singing skills.

After the Audition

The next step after auditions is to make your decisions and cast the group. If you had help at the audition, meet as a panel. Otherwise, you're making the call solo. Consider all the auditionees, looking through the lens of your specific needs. Taking all the best individual singers won't guarantee you the best ensemble. Imagine you're looking to form a great basketball team. Picking the top five players in the NBA might not be the answer. What if four of the top five players are point guards, and you have one forward. Who's going to be your center? You need to balance the voice parts properly as well as have a good mix of soloists vs. background singers. A great group should be more than the sum of its parts.

As you work through the selection process, you might find yourself in a position where you don't have exactly what you need. Maybe you're missing a certain voice part or there are not enough singers with sight-reading skills. Before you go back into the audition process, see if you can make a good group out of the best singers that you do have. Maybe the format will be a little different than you expected, or maybe someone will be singing a voice part they didn't expect, but having a group comprised of good singers and people you like is more important than holding out for that perfect countertenor. There is definitely a tradeoff between taking the singers you can find and holding off for another round of auditions. Only you can can make that decision. Go with your gut.

Make sure you promptly contact each auditionee and let them know the outcome (either way). There's nothing worse than appearing for an audition and then never hearing back. Professionalism is paramount; contacting them by phone or letter is most polite. A good rule of thumb is to reach all the auditionees within two days of their audition. Try to talk to them personally, but leave a message after a few attempts have failed.

Another rule of thumb is to give the news quickly, without excuses or reasons. You can compare this to an apology. If you apologize for something and then follow up with a lengthy description of why you did what you did, you dilute the apology by trying to excuse your behavior. Similarly, telling a person exactly why you didn't take them is often worse than just saying "It's not a fit this time, but maybe something will work out in the future." If an auditionee asks why they weren't accepted, provide them with constructive feedback about their performance. Do not compare them to other auditionees; keep the call short and polite. Keep in mind that feedback is considered constructive if it would be helpful for their next audition.

WHAT'S IN A NAME?

Timeless. Your group will hopefully be going strong 30 years from now, perhaps long after you're not associated with it. Do you think the King's Singers planned to have their little college group become an international phenomenon?

Not "punny." Too many a cappella names play on a turn of phrase that's humorous to some but sends others running for the exits. If you want to have any coolness factor, stay away from puns.

Not everyone agrees, obviously. There seem to be more groups named "Nothing But Treble" than there are Canadian Provinces. Hardy har har.

Unique. Make sure no one else is using the name in the a cappella community or in your area. A couple of internet searches (acapedia, Google) and a look through the online yellow pages should do the trick. Don't forget that it might not be a vocal group that uses the name you are considering. "Michigan Mix" could be a concrete company!

Trips off the tongue.

Web address available. It's great to be able to say "check us out on rockapella.com" and not so great to have to say "find us on rockapella-band.net"

Spelling. People should know how to spell it when you say it. As much as they were a great group, +4Db could have been spelled "Plus Four Dee Bee" or a myriad of other ways. A difficult spelling makes it hard to find.

You like it. Probably goes without saying, right?

Other people like it. Make sure to bounce the name off a number of your peers/cohorts/family members before making the plunge. If they give it a thumbs-up, chances are you will, too.

Non-controversial. Stays away from controversial topics: race, religion, etc. You're going to have a hard time spreading harmony through harmony if your name rubs some people the wrong way or keeps them from being interested in your shows.

Style-neutral. Your name should avoid mentioning a style unless you're absolutely certain you want to focus primarily on that style. Forever. The Gospeltones are going to primarily draw from a specific fan base who will be expecting a certain type of music.

Regional. Something that mentions your area, if you're hoping to become ambassadors for your area and well known within it, but not tour the nation or the world (e.g. if you're creating a community chorus). "Deltacappella" for a group in Memphis TN is perfecto. Another option: Using your region before/within your group name, as in Marin Harmony or New York Voices.

First Meeting

Once your group is set, it's time to schedule a meeting to discuss your goals, expectations, and procedures. Set an agenda that allows the new members to contribute. You're a team now, and you'll have to all pull in the same direction. Answer any questions, and make sure everyone is on the same page before you move forward. You may want to sign a brief contract or letter of agreement to make things official.

Consider setting a two-month probation period to make sure all parties are pleased with the experience of singing together. This can be particularly important in professional groups. Audition processes can tell you a great deal, but only time together "in the trenches" will reveal a person's true behavioral patterns. Pay special attention to commitment. If an individual has a problem being on time or fulfilling responsibilities during the first couple of months, you should be very wary of continuing to work together.

Choosing a Name

Once you've chosen your members and decided what style of music you'll be performing, it's time to choose a name for the group.

Your group name is the single most important marketing decision you'll ever make. Names generate thoughts, particularly among those who have not heard your group perform. Look at the following group names and take note of your reactions. What do they bring to mind?

- Big Daddy and the Cool Cats
- The Revelations
- Jam 4 Reel
- Bushes and Briars
- The Swooners
- Golden Tradition

These groups are fictitious, but this exercise illustrates how your name immediately creates an impression. Your name is your calling card.

Style

It's not necessary for you to decide immediately what your group is going to sound like, but it is important for you to have some kind of general idea. Hopefully you've given this thought before auditions and have since come to an agreement as a group. Now that you're up and running, it's time to test the waters. Try different songs and arrangements. Experiment with vocal sounds. Switch parts. The process of solidifying your group's style will come with time, provided you're looking at least one step beyond covering other bands' material.

Fun

Never forget to have fun. No matter how hard you work, how much you achieve, or how far you feel you have to go, you have to have fun! In fact, some groups (high school, college, or semi-professional) exist primarily just to have a good time and share their love of music with others. These groups, although not as polished as their professional counterparts, often leave the audience with a comparably wonderful feeling and equally large smile on their faces.

Celebrate your achievements and successes. Enjoy each other's company. Share your music with those less fortunate than you. A cappella music has a strange, ineffable ability to strike a deep chord within people (those who sing as well as those who listen). Never forget the power of music to lift the human spirit.

Set Tone

CHAPTER 6
MANAGING REHEARSALS

Lets tackle the nitty-gritty issues that sometime make you crazy: teaching notes versus using learning tracks, how many songs per rehearsal, attendance management, sectionals versus group rehearsal, number of rehearsals before a gig, how much warm-up time, what kinds of warm-ups, when do you allow mistakes to happen and when do you stop and fix them, rehearsal discipline, and on and on. When you're done with this chapter, you'll be able to plan your rehearsals well to hopefully reduce some of the craziness!

Scheduling Rehearsals

When determining the frequency and length of rehearsals, it is important to consider your performance goals. If you meet once a week for two hours you'll likely take a long time before you have an hour's worth of music and a smooth show. If you can afford the time, rehearsing two or three times a week is exponentially better. The more often you rehearse, the less you forget between meetings. Once your show package is in place, you'll begin performing. Even if time is at a premium, make it a priority to regularly perform. A performance is worth 10 rehearsals when it comes to advancing the performance level of your group. Simply stated: you feel the heat. Therefore, as time progresses, it's ok to lose a rehearsal in lieu of a gig.

Typical college groups rehearse six to ten hours per week. Professional groups will require much more intense rehearsal as they're getting started and perhaps less rehearsal time as they transition into a more performance-heavy schedule. Semi-pro groups (where the members still have day jobs) often rehearse just once a week, even though more frequent rehearsals would definitely benefit them. It's a matter of priorities at that point.

Most groups have the tendency to socialize as well as sing during rehearsal time. Besides maximizing the **time** you can spend together, make sure you prioritize **music** as your first goal when spending that time together. By running well-structured rehearsals, you'll waste less time and ultimately have a better group. You can save time by doing business via email and phone. Share information and documents online. You'd be surprised how much time it can take to read through gig details, timetables, directions, etc. during a rehearsal. Anything that can be done apart, do it apart. Time together is rare and sacred.

Of course, some business will be necessary. Save those items for the end of each rehearsal. Discussions are like goldfish: they will grow to fit the space they are given. Save yourself some hassle and establish a habit of music first, then business. At times, you may even need to have separate music-only rehearsals and business-only meetings.

Elements of the Rehearsal

Rehearsal Order

Each rehearsal should begin with a warm-up. After that, you'll work on music for the bulk of rehearsal. This time should be structured based on how well each song is prepared. Sometimes you can add "special" activities mid-rehearsal to vary your routine or to target specific performance problems. Conclude the rehearsal with a brief business meeting covering any time-sensitive topics.

Warm-ups

Start exactly on time. If a member is late to rehearsal, cue them in silently.

Just as runners stretch before a run, singers should warm up their voices to ensure healthy vocal technique. However, warm-ups aren't just about getting the voice ready to sing. They help singers transition from the mental framework of their everyday life into the singular focus of rehearsal. Also, warm-ups help the group reconnect before the rehearsal begins.

In high-school, collegiate or non-professional groups, warm-up exercises often are focused towards the development of certain skills: blending ability, vowel matching, rhythmic abilities, tuning, etc. Often these types of exercises do more to effectively teach good singing technique than the actual song rehearsal. Towards that end, groups who are less experienced should plan more time each rehearsal for warm-ups as skill-builders. This type of longer warm-up session might take 15 minutes. Most warm-ups last between five to ten minutes. Once the singers are calibrated for rehearsal, it's time to dig into the music.

Music Rehearsal

Learning music is an important aspect of any rehearsal. Some groups can sight read well, others prefer to have the director play the parts on a keyboard one by one. Still others learn by ear, relying on having their parts sung to them or played on a learning track and memorized before rehearsal. Take the time initially to find out how each individual learns best, and come up with a system that will maximize your in-rehearsal productivity and minimize the amount of time your fastest learners have to wait for your slowest learners. This will reduce tension for all involved.

Four Stages of Song Preparation

When planning your rehearsals, it is helpful to understand that each song has four stages. If you make it clear to your singers where a song is in this spectrum, they will know what is expected of them at rehearsal.

Learning

From the first time seeing or hearing a song until the group can sing all of the notes through a song, they are learning the song. Ideally, much of this will be done outside of group rehearsal time, as it's the only stage that can be done individually.

Polishing

Polishing is the process of turning a chain of notes and markings into a song. This is the time to focus on the theme of a song and its emotional content.

Memorized

Once a song is memorized, not much time should need to be spent rehearsing it. It should be sufficient to pass through a song once or twice at the end of a rehearsal, making a few adjustments each time.

Performed

Once performed, no more rehearsal time should be needed on a song. Ideally, you'll have enough performances to keep these songs fresh and "rehearsed" while providing motivation to get songs through the memorization stage and into your repertoire.

Rehearse your music from newest to oldest (learning, polishing, memorized, performed)

If you have new music (**learning**), it is best to start while people are fresh and focused. Ideally, music has already been distributed in advance, perhaps with parts recordings. Try to minimize "note plunking," but don't be afraid to repeat difficult passages as needed. Make sure to teach dynamics and articulation from the beginning, so that they're "hardwired" into the brain. Move on to another song after 20–40 minutes, based on the attention span of your singers.

Next, work on songs or sections of songs that need specific attention (**polishing**). This could be a challenging key change, or a section with a tricky rhythm pattern you're trying to master. Maybe there's a chordal section that needs attention to refine the tuning. Such issues are handled in this portion of rehearsal. This is the most crucial level of song preparation. We like to call it *The Cycle*.

When we say *The Cycle* we're referring to a set pattern of how to rehearse one song. You'll polish a song very quickly when you follow this plan.

1. State the current musical goals for the song before beginning, so each singer is reminded of the plan.

2. Run-through of the entire song, noting trouble spots as you go (mark your music with a pencil if you're using music or jot quick notes on paper otherwise). Each person should mark areas where they need help. This gives singers a sense of ownership and helps build musical awareness.

3. Break down the song by sections (verse, chorus, etc.) and by part grouping (i.e. "let's hear whomever has the bell chord") to polish the trouble spots you uncovered in step 2.

4. Rebuild the song now that you have improved the target areas. Do this one section at a time, then gluing more sections together until you are running the song.

5. Perform the song for recording/capture (so you have a record of improvement against which to practice).

6. Set goals for the next rehearsal for this song.

Once songs reach a certain level of preparedness (**memorized**), it's time to sing them all the way through, saving your comments for the end. It's important to mentally reinforce the continuity of the song as well as to build physical stamina by singing it top to bottom without stopping. In this phase, you are also transitioning songs from **polishing** to **performed.** Oddly enough this is most difficult for perfectionists, who crinkle their nose at every tuning issue or wrong note. Full "performance situation" run-throughs will help them break this habit. This is especially important if you have members who "telegraph" errors to the audience through their facial expressions.

As the rehearsal winds towards the end, you might want to consider a quick run-through of one of your performance-ready pieces. Most groups stop rehearsing songs once they have been performed, but an occasional touch-up in rehearsal never hurt. Besides, if the song is so great it can't be improved, it's a great spirit-lifter just as you're likely getting fatigued.

Business

If you have business issues to address, use the last few minutes of rehearsal. Have an agenda and stick to it, as discussions can spiral out of control. Allow singers to remain after rehearsal to continue discussion. Form committees to handle logistics of projects. Handle issues "offline." Distribute information via paper and email, so there is no time lost writing down notes or updating calendars.

Special activities

Improvising

Some groups like to spend a portion of their singing time together improvising. Whether using a simple twelve-bar-blues form or just doing some free-form exploration, improv can be a rewarding experience. Note: if you do improvise and everyone is on board with it, consider taping each session. Sometimes a great song idea or arrangement texture arises, and it's great to have a reference recording.

Recording / Evaluation

Recording is an immensely beneficial tool for any performing group. While *The Cycle* contains time to record performances for future study, take the time to record a performance and then evaluate it immediately during rehearsal. When singers know they are being recorded for immediate evaluation, they perform differently. This is a very positive yet unspoken pressure to perform.

In addition, videotaping your group is an excellent way to see how you look when you sing. Disregard the video quality and look instead at facial expression, movement, and how the physicality of your group enhances the music.

Running the Set

As performance gets closer, sometimes you just need to run your whole set without stopping, complete with entrance to the stage, singing, talking, and exit. A great thing to do as you near performance is to videotape a set, watch the video, discuss it, then run it again.

Coaching

Consider bringing in an experienced coach or musical friend to work with the group. An outside opinion is always a good way to gain perspective, and sometimes a detached individual can address group issues without the distraction of internal dynamics. Let's face it: your group has to be together constantly. Sometimes relationship dynamics get in the way of direct performance critique. Let someone else point performance problems, then the whole group can pull together as a team to fix them.

Learning Tracks

Learning tracks allow people to work on music outside of rehearsal and come to rehearsal prepared. Learning tracks are most helpful if they are sung, but they are still acceptable if played on a piano/midi. Learning tracks are not available for most published sheet music. You can make your own learning tracks in software programs like Finale or Sibelius. If you hire custom arrangements, the arranger can often supply you with learning tracks as well.

Chesney Snow and Deke at Total Vocal in Carnegie Hall

Rehearsal Frequency

- Rehearse weekly at a minimum. Rehearse twice (or more) if possible.

- Plan to rehearse for a minimum of 90 minutes.

  ▷ If you rehearse longer, be sure to give the singers a break. They'll need it physically and for socializing with each other.

- Performances are more valuable than rehearsals. Schedule performances spread throughout the season with specific songs targeted for each one. Nothing inspires getting a song ready more than an upcoming gig!

Attendance

Require members to sign an attendance agreement or contract before they can join the group. The agreement should spell out the number of tardies or absences allowed and the consequences of exceeding those limits (usually dismissal from the group). If you can be flexible, specify which reasons are acceptable for being tardy.

Have an "official" clock in your rehearsal space and start rehearsals right on time, so that it is clear when someone is tardy. Keep written attendance notes so they can be referenced later. Address attendance issues in person, away from other singers, when a problem is clear.

Finally, dismiss singers on time from rehearsals, upholding your end of the agreement.

Discipline

Ideally, appoint someone other than the director to enforce quiet and focus. Section leaders can help both with small questions after a run through (be careful not to assume they're speaking out of turn) and with enforcing quiet. Allow some "loose" moments and be sure the group knows when they really need to focus and when they can relax a bit more and joke a bit. Be firm but not angry when quieting the group. Individuals who are disrupting too often should be dealt with outside of rehearsal.

Fun

For a director, rehearsal is your performance. Check your mood at the door and make the experience fun and productive. Plan some surprises for your group at non-critical rehearsals (e.g. just after a big concert) to avoid monotony. Move as quickly as you can through any part-teaching (unless it's a "dangerous passage"). People enjoy time well spent: "fast" is exciting and demands focus, and a focused rehearsal moves quickly.

It's a safe bet that everyone in the group likes to sing, so maximize singing and minimize your talking. Most directors like to talk too much! Find ways to make your feedback concise and also use non-verbal cues during the singing to streamline your rehearsal.

As you spend more time together, you'll fall into a comfortable rehearsal pattern that will best suit your group's talent, comfort, and needs.

A CAPPELLA ON TELEVISION

- Rockapella was the house band for the show *Where In The World Is Carmen Sandiego?* (1991–1996).

- On *The Simpsons* ("Homer's Barbershop Quartet" Sep. 30, 1993), Homer explains to his family that he, Skinner, Barney, and Apu were a famous barbershop quartet called the Be Sharps (voiced by The Dapper Dans) and they recorded an album in 1985. At the end of the episode the group reunites to perform a concert and they perform their hit number "Baby on Board."

- In an episode of *Mad About You* ("Surprise" Nov. 11, 1993), there is an a cappella group (Suave–Kevin Wommack, Bryant Woodert, Adam A, Labaud Jr.) performing in the subway station. Paul (Paul Reiser) pays them to sing to Jamie (Helen Hunt) for her birthday and they serenade her to "In the Still of the Night." At the end of that episode as the end credits are playing, Paul and Jamie listen to the same group singing the theme song as Paul keeps mentioning its familiarity and asking Jamie "How do I know this?" This is ironic because he co-wrote the theme song.

- Dr. Mark Sloan (Dick Van Dyke) frequently sang with the barbershop quartet Metropolis on the show *Diagnosis, Murder* (1993–2002).

- On *Friends* ("The One with All the Jealousy" Jan. 16, 1997), Monica (Courtney Cox) hooks up with the "poet" from work, who is a pompous foreigner. He calls her an empty vase in one of his poems. He later owned up that he was referring to all American women. Monica gets back at him by hiring a barbershop quartet (that performs a cappella) to humiliate him at the diner when he is making a pass at another woman.

- On *NewsRadio* ("Chock" Jan. 13, 1998), Dave (Dave Foley) gets visited on his birthday by three members of his college a cappella group that want him to quit his job and join their old group.

- On *Scrubs* (2001–2010), the character of Ted Buckland (Sam Lloyd) and his a cappella group The Worthless Peons (his real life group The Blanks) perform many times on the show

- On *American Idol* (2002–2016), contestants usually sing a cappella for the first rounds of judging.

- On the Da Ali G Show (2003-2004), the character of Ali G (Sacha Baron Cohen) is a wanna-be hip-hop artist and he engages in beatboxing from time to time, often improvising on the topic that is being discussed.

- On *How I Met Your Mother* ("The Slutty Pumpkin" Oct 24, 2005), Ted (Josh Radnor) goes to a Halloween party on the rooftop and there are former members of an a cappella group at Yale performing.

- On *The Office* (2005–2013) Andy Bernard (Ed Helms) is an alumnus of a fictitious a cappella group Cornell's Here Comes Treble and he doesn't hesitate to remind everyone of this. He regularly breaks into song, making recordings of himself covering multiple vocal parts on "Rockin' Robin" for his ring tone, and he serenades his girlfriend-to-be Angela (Angela Kinsey) with his a cappella buddies harmonizing over the speaker phone to ABBA's "Take a Chance On Me."

- On *Psych* ("High Top Fade Out" Sep. 25, 2009), one of the member's of Gus's (Dule' Hill) collegiate a cappella group is murdered. The remaining members seek out Shawn (James Roday) to help investigate since they are not on speaking terms with Gus. For that episode, the show even got Boyz II Men to perform the theme song a cappella.

- On *Glee* (2009–2015), the rival Dalton Academy Warblers that Blaine (Darren Criss) is a member of is an all-male a cappella group (played by the real-life Tufts University Beelzebubs).

- On *My Little Pony: Friendship is Magic* (2010), there is an a cappella group called The Ponytones.

- *Sing It On* (2015) is a reality television show, produced by John Legend, which follows five collegiate a cappella teams competing for first place at the International Championship of Collegiate A Cappella finals.

The Inversions

CHAPTER 7

GROUP ORGANIZATION

Leadership Roles

Every group is different, as the individuals in that group combine to make a unique dynamic. What every group has in common is that they need leadership and a division of responsibility. Who runs rehearsals? Who takes calls from interested gig opportunities? Who handles the finances? Whether your group will be run as a democracy (shared responsibility) or a benevolent dictatorship (one person doing all the work behind the scenes), make sure the responsibilities are clearly defined and understood by all.

The first step is to determine what roles need filled. Avoid the common pitfall of assuming you need common positions such as President, Vice President, Secretary, and Treasurer. While those might be common positions in clubs, a cappella groups have specific needs. In an a cappella group, some typical roles are:

- Musical Director (some call this "the pitch")
- Business Manager
- Tour/Performance Manager
- Treasurer
- President (usually same as Business Manager)
- Show Coordinator or Album Coordinator

You might not need ALL these offices. Even if you do, some roles could be combined. In some groups the musical director is also the business manager. If possible, it's better to have separate roles, as there's only so much one person can do. This is especially true when a group isn't working professionally. When the members have other priorities (day job, full load of classes, etc.), division of labor will make sure no one gets overloaded.

In any event, be sure to consider what roles your group NEEDS (and who is appropriate for those roles) before creating those positions. Build consensus within your group as to what roles should exist and who should fill them. In the case of scholastic groups, there is a need for plans to deal with office turnover as students graduate.

Another Round

The Musical Director

The role of director is the most important and influential role within a group. It combines elements of a musician, leader, organizer, consensus builder and conductor.

The most important tasks for a director are:

- Rehearsing
- Choosing the repertoire (original and cover songs)
- Choosing and modifying arrangements
- Determining soloists and who will sing which part
- Determining sets (song choice and order)
- Directing music on stage

It is essential that the director have the following skills:

- Musicality
- Impartiality and fairness
- Empathy
- Charisma
- Focus (ability to focus self and others while working)
- Perspective (knowing what's important and what isn't)
- Creativity

Below are some techniques and tips that will help the director maximize rehearsal time and minimize friction between singers.

- Be willing to sacrifice: put others' needs first

- Address problems directly

- Admit your errors

- Be willing: volunteer to do undesirable tasks

- Keep a good attitude

- Find opportunities for each member to shine on stage, whether with a solo or a smaller spotlight

- Take calculated creative risks, try new ideas or find a new sound

- Keep an open relationship with all members

- Separate business from music as much as possible

- Make most of rehearsal time by keeping on track

- Express your goals to everyone in advance

- Don't rely on the talents of any one member too much

- Work details of the music (like notes, dynamics) early because they are harder to fix later

- Be open to trying new ideas for both new and old songs

- Involve all singers in arrangement modification during rehearsals

- Involve others in creative decisions as much as they'd like

Crescendudes

- Make sure to choose songs with enough variety to address any situation
- Remain focused on stage, but don't forget that you're performing, too
- Ask group members for their opinions often, and let them speak without interruption
- Know your genre in a cappella, vocal music, and instrumental music
- Keep a copy of everything you do musically
- Listen to live or rehearsal tapes from time to time
- Make a professional recording
- Keep your eyes open and learn from all genres of the arts
- Relinquish power. Sometimes it's ok to let others make the decisions
- Make sure you and others enjoy the music you're making

Group Contract

In a college group, you should have an official charter or constitution. Talk to the university's student activities office or student government. They can give you examples so that you don't have to start from scratch. Such a charter may be a requirement of the school or a requirement in order for you to receive funding.

Professional groups have a different need. They are bound not by the laws of their school, but rather by the laws of the government. For this reason, it's a good idea to enter into a partnership agreement. The more professional the group, the more imperative this type of agreement is.

It is important to consider all aspects of group business before creating the partnership agreement. This can save time and headache down the road. Some issues to resolve include:

- Who owns the name? (The most valuable group asset)
- How are profits paid? (How often and in what format)
- Are departing members responsible for gigs and commitments agreed to before their departure was announced?
- Do you treat voluntarily-departing members differently from members who are expelled?
- Will everyone be paid equally, or do certain members get more money for executing certain duties?

Keeping Members

Losing and replacing members is the biggest threat to a group's success. Voices are not easily interchangeable. Each person has a different range, vocal quality, musical prowess, personality, etc. Although replacing a member could be a chance to get a more talented vocalist (to "trade up"), scrambling to fill a hole left when someone quits can be problematic.

How can you protect yourself? Have an agreement. Make everyone commit to the group for a certain length of time, perhaps a year or a school semester. This commitment will make all parties realize up front that they're signing on for a "run" (much like a musical theater production). Most groups hit some rough spots, especially early on. Having an agreement to participate fully until a certain date will create a feeling of stability. With good planning, you'll have enough payoff by the end of the "run" that people will be willing to stay on for another round.

Das Sound Machine rehearsing for *Pitch Perfect 2*

Kettering-Fairmont Fusion

CHAPTER 8
GROUP DYNAMICS

The loudmouth. The quiet one. The organizer. The flake. People are unique, like snowflakes. Your task—getting them to work together in perfect unison. In this chapter we'll draw on materials and techniques developed for the corporate world, and apply them to a cappella. You'll learn how groups interact, how your ensemble can understand each other, how to minimize friction, and how to work together *in harmony* to **create harmony**.

One of the most important parts of any successful a cappella group (or any group) is how well the members get along. This cannot be stressed enough. Take a moment and reflect on your family and friends. Our guess is that when you are working on a project, either **with** them or **for** them, you have a heightened desire to do a great job. You want things to go well because you care about the other people involved. It is also likely that if something goes wrong during the project, you are less likely to be upset because "you're in it together." Your relationship is more important than the movie, the yardwork, the lasagna, whatever the project is.

So it is with sports teams and musical ensembles. When the members are bonded, things always go better. Notice we didn't say "when the members are friends." It is unreasonable to think that every member of a given group will be friends. You might be friend-ly, or even just civil. That's different than bonded. People who have different personalities can be bonded together through music. The goal is to keep the creation of music front and center. That common goal is a social lubricant that helps the members interact whenever they are together. Over time, social relationships within any group will deepen, provided those musical seeds are sown. It's because people come together when they feel they are contributing to something bigger than themselves.

An a cappella group is a combination of three things: a creative ensemble, a business, and a family. Keep in mind that most people will stay happily involved if two of the three areas are satisfying for them. If the group is singing very rewarding musical material and the business side is providing a great paycheck, it likely doesn't matter if everyone feels like a family. On the other hand, if the music is great and you feel very much like a family, profit might be irrelevant. Maybe you sing with your best friends and land a gig making tons of money. Would you care if the music isn't awesome?

All that said, which of the three areas can you control? The area of greatest immediate control is the music. Make great music. The second area you can control is your internal dynamic. Do your best do strengthen relationships across the group. The last part is the business/money. So it follows: you make great music (first) and bond with your group, having lots of fun along the way (second). Because the product is good, people hire you (third), but even if they don't—*you're having a great time.* Get it?

General Conflict Resolution

Here are some simple pointers that can help in any group or one-on-one conflict situation:

Have Fun Together Regularly

A common mistake in any business or relationship is to focus primarily on things that are wrong or need to be changed. Eventually, no one will want to spend time together. Who wants to wallow in negativity?

"All work and no play makes Jack a dull boy." In other words, make sure you all have fun together, and celebrate your successes. This seed needs to be planted in advance and be watered regularly to grow. Don't expect a last minute trip to an amusement park to prevent an imminent group breakup. Just like in a marriage, you need to set aside time to enjoy each other.

Address Problems Right Away

Don't let little problems build up. It doesn't help to keep small annoyances bottled up. Eventually, small annoyances fester and grow until they erupt. It's much better to address them directly as they occur. For example, "It bothers me that we're starting rehearsal ten minutes late," or "I felt bad when you made that comment." Problems are much easier to deal with, understand, and move beyond when they are still small.

Identify The Problem

Remember that people are not problems. Actions (or inactions) are problems. Your singers have common goals: personal happiness and the success of the group. When you depersonalize problems, they become more easily managed. Example: "I really love singing with you, but it bothers me that you come with your music not learned. That gets in the way of us having fun together. Would you work on that for next time?"

Make An Appointment

If there's something you want to discuss, don't just launch into a diatribe. Ask if it's a good time to talk, and if not, make an appointment. Your group members will feel a lot more at ease in general if they know that rehearsal is not an environment for conflict.

Talk About Yourself

To keep from assigning blame to the other person when angry, start sentences with "I" and talk about your feelings, needs, or worries. When you focus discussions this way, you are communicating more clearly. Sentences that start with "I hate it when you . . ." don't count. Saying "I hate it when you never show up on time" will trigger defensiveness. Instead, try "I feel like I'm not respected when I have to sit here waiting."

You can also use the **feel, felt, found** formula. It goes something like this:

- I feel disrespected when I have to wait to start rehearsal

- I'm sure you have felt frustrated in the same way before

- What I have found is that a quick phone call helps those waiting to feel better

Mirror During Arguments

When having a heated discussion/argument, make sure to repeat what the other person says before launching into your own reply. This technique is called mirroring, and it helps convey to the other person that you are really hearing them.

You might say "I hear you saying that you want to add a new number to the show package. I agree with you. That would be great. My position is that we finish polishing our existing songs first so that we have a really great foundation on which to build."

Don't Make Demands

Know that you can't demand anything of anyone. All behavior changes need to be decided by the individual who's changing, and in a sense, that makes it a gift. No one wants to give a gift that's been demanded of them. Realize this, respect this, and approach your relationships accordingly.

Search For "Win-Win"

Business culture has co-opted what was once a hippie sentiment, but there is such a thing as a "win-win" solution, whether you wear Armani or tie-dye.

Solutions that resolve all members' problems are not always easy to find. They usually require all available pertinent information from each perspective, which means you all need to get past any defensiveness and bad feelings and open up completely. Only then can everyone lay out the facts that will allow a common solution to be found.

See Both Sides

Nothing is ever black or white. Nothing is ever right or wrong. See where you have made mistakes, and realize your own faults (especially when you're feeling holier-than-thou). You have faults. No one is perfect.

The key to resolving conflict is to understand the other person's position. Once you know this, you may have enough information to find a solution. Seek this information. Listen before talking.

Make Yourself Happy

Know what makes you happy, and spend time in your life actively pursuing these things. Everyone needs to be in charge of their own happiness. Some people expect others to make them happy, which is a very destructive thing in a relationship. Make sure you aren't expecting your groupmates to be anything they aren't, and don't depend on the a cappella group to make you happy.

The following quote is attributed to Abraham Lincoln: "Folks are usually about as happy as they make their minds up to be." Decide to be happy instead of letting your emotions ride completely on the next gig vote or repertoire discussion.

Don't Sweat It

Relax. Life is full of challenges and conflicts; you'll only make yourself and others around you less happy and able to deal with things if you heap lots of negative emotion on them. Laugh at yourself, and your situation, and realize that in the grand scheme of things, little you do right now will matter at all in a year from now—even to you. Being in a musical group is a rollercoaster ride, and you'll have a better time if you're able to appreciate the dips as well as swells.

Of course no person is perfect, and there are times that all of us collapse into destructive, unfocused anger. However, by making it a point to work on the interpersonal harmony of a group as well as your own happiness, you'll find that musical harmony is much easier to achieve.

Group Dynamics—A Cappella Style

In addition to using the above principals of effective communication and conflict resolution, there are some things that are specifically helpful to a group of musicians.

Focus On The Music

During rehearsal there can be times that are loose but you will avoid many issues by singing. Don't talk too much—just sing. The music director and/or leader shouldn't love to hear the sound of his own voice, nor try to talk through every little problem. Yes, direction is needed. Make it quick, then back to singing. Anything that is to be improved must be done and redone, not discussed to death.

Make Memories

Great things happen when you're actively performing. Sharing your music with an audience is just one way to make memories. Don't forget time spent backstage, at dinner, in the van on the way to the gig, in the hotel if you're on the road, etc. If you're out on the road performing you're going to create some amazing memories together. Go to festivals, get as many gigs as you can, tour, record, enjoy. Make memories to last a lifetime.

Work Hard/Play Hard

It should be clear by now that "it's about the music." BUT, it's also important that the group makes time for social activities. It's important that the group starts to enjoy each other's personalities outside of singing. Go to a movie together, go out to dinner, play miniature golf, etc. Being together for any reason is helpful.

Circle Up

This is a very simple exercise that you may quickly want to make a tradition before each major concert or performance. The group literally sits in a circle. As you go around the circle, each person has to say something that they enjoy about the person on their right. Each time you "circle up," each individual has to sit by a different person. This is a great way to generate great, positive feelings before hitting the stage.

And so we come back to the thoughts expressed at the beginning of this chapter: people will do a better job and go the extra mile for their friends and family. You have put together a group that will almost certainly become friends and likely will begin to feel like a family. Handle concerns as they come, remain open and honest, and celebrate your successes. You can't go wrong.

Camp A Cappella

Rockapella

CHAPTER 9

STEAL FROM THE BEST

By Deke Sharon

Perhaps you've just taken on a leadership role within your collegiate a cappella group, or you just founded one (congrats!). You want to be great, but you're not exactly sure what that means or how to do that. Stravinsky said, "great musicians steal," so why not steal the best practices from some of collegiate a cappella's best groups?

Best Tradition: Whiffenpoofs (Yale University)

The first, and still in some ways the best, with a group comprised entirely of the best male singers from all the other groups on campus who (almost) all take the year off and spend it touring the world.

No, you can't just set up a world tour, but you can see the value in tradition, and reinforce it as much as possible. Work closely with your admissions and alumni departments, performing both on campus and off. Create a network of contacts around the region, the nation, and eventually the world, which will create touring possibilities. Choose a school song that your group becomes known for and you can sing at events around the world.

Whiffenpoofs

Develop a look, a sound, a style, a tradition. It won't happen over night, but it will ensure your group has a long, prosperous future.

Best Alumni Organization: Beelzebubs (Tufts University)

The Bubs (my former group) just celebrated its 50th anniversary and over 80% of all Bubs, past and present, were there. How could there be such an amazing turnout?

Beelzebubs

Strong ties with the alumni have been at the core of the Bubs since it was first founded. Bub alums are invited to meet the new guys as soon as they're sung into the group (yes, at 4am), there is an annual event (Staag Nite) which is the BAA (Beelzebub Alumni Association) annual meeting, followed by a big dinner, concert by the current group and woodshedding til the wee hours. Alums are also invited to drop by rehearsals, given free tickets and great seats to all shows, contacted when the group will be performing in town, and generally revered by the current group.

Plus the BAA is a strong organization, keeping tabs on all former members, organizing events (like five year reunions, where alums get to see and sing with their old buddies), scholarships, music programs for teens, donations to the university, and so on. With a constant presence around the undergrads, the alums are able to help with music coaching, album production, arrangements, and advice, ensuring the undergraduate group maximizes their potential, and upon graduation, past members remain a Bub for life.

Best Transition to Professional Group: Straight No Chaser/Another Round (Indiana University)

It is now stuff of legend: Tape a concert, a decade later post some clips from your concert, have one clip go viral, get contacted by Atlantic Records, pull the old group back together, and become a national sensation. The original members of Straight No Chaser had no reason to expect their fate, but they did earn it by making the most of each opportunity and building on a strong musical and interpersonal foundation.

Plus SNC founder Dan Ponce recently created another professional group, called "Gentlemen's Rule", so now the group boasts two ten-member ensembles who record, tour, make videos, inspire others. The undergraduate group recently changed their name to "Another Round" to eliminate confusion with the professional group, and continue to make great music as undergrads.

If you're looking for a career in a cappella after college, you would do well to study this group's path and best practices.

Another Round

Best Trendsetters: Divisi (University of Oregon)

When Lisa Forkish and Evynne Hollens first started Divisi less than a decade ago, it would have been impossible for them to have anticipated the wild ride they were about to take, with a trip to the ICCA finals and a trophy that many feel should have been theirs, all documented in the first major book about collegiate a cappella, which was then optioned for a movie, which then became an international sensation.

How did such a young group at a college that was new to a cappella end up inspiring *Pitch Perfect*? First they had to inspire the collegiate a cappella world, which they did by creating a new sound, style and attitude within the female collegiate style, with lockstep precision, powerful and captivating performances that were strong and feminine but in no way "girly." Hair

Divisi

up, black collared shirts with red ties, lockstep choreography, and arrangements that demanded a deep rich vocal delivery may now seem almost cliché, but when they came on the scene it was both fresh and electrifying.

No, you can't copy them and expect to make major waves, but what you can do is develop a sound and style that sets your group apart.

And there are many other bests to be found in the annals of recent collegiate a cappella history. Best Spirit? Stanford Talisman in the mid-'90s, with an effortless delivery that captured a room immediately. Best Mixed Group Tradition? For almost fifteen years, U Penn Off The Beat was untouchable, with their own singing and recording style that landed them on BOCA more than any other. I could go on and on, as there has been something special about many collegiate groups over the past two decades.

And this perspective doesn't start and end with collegiate groups. Want your high school group to be great? Take a peek at what's been happening in Ohio with Eleventh Hour and Forte, or out West with Lisa Forkish's Vocal Rush. Same goes for professional groups, casual amateur groups, etc.

Learn your history, and steal from the best.

The House Jacks

CHAPTER 10

A VOICE, YOUR VOICE

By Deke Sharon

Ah, James Taylor. So simple, yet so good. He has a voice.

And when I say "a voice" I don't mean his vocal chords. Rather, I'm speaking of the combination of his characteristics and perspective that make him one of a kind. Plenty of singer-songwriters out there, only one James Taylor.

It's perhaps ironic then that we have so many voices in a cappella, but not nearly as many Voices. If you catch my meaning.

Would I like your group to develop its own voice, its own style? Very much. But before I start nudging you in that direction, I want to make sure you're ready.

Is your group good? Focused? Cohesive? Are you just singing for fun or are you hoping to do something new? The development of a voice can't be forced. It will happen when it's time, with a combination of experience and care.

In the case of one person, it's a very natural process, as no one told Elvis Costello or Tom Petty to sing in a particular way, write in a particular way, record in a particular way. Well, some people gave them advice, suggestions, perhaps even edicts (from their record label or manager), but in the end it was one man's journey, one man's sense of style.

In a cappella the process is different. It often starts with one person, usually a group's founder/director/arranger, but it's impossible for it to move forward without at least tacit approval or complicity. No one is dragged kicking and screaming into new territory. Moreover, since it involves multiple people, it's usually a more considered, discussed and perhaps cerebral process, requiring late night discussions, lengthy emails, disagreements, trial and error.

In hopes of making that process easier for your group, let me offer a few thoughts from my own and others' experiences:

- Start with what you know, what you like, what you want. This will likely be framed or described in terms of other groups. I've been told often that M-Pact was formed to be a hybrid of Take 6 and the House Jacks. Or it can be the result of a formula, just as Take 6 melds gospel songs, jazz harmonies and R & B vocal stylings. To be clear, this isn't a destination or even a pit stop along the way. It's more of a blueprint, an initial road map. Somewhere to start.

- Next, once you start on your path, do not turn back. In the case of the House Jacks, our plan was to be an original rock band, which meant original music. Cover songs were so much easier, and audiences could grab on to them right away, but we got advice from several other musicians who told us we'd turn a corner, and we'd begin to have fans who would like us for our music, not like us because we sang other people's music. Eventually this happened, and we were signed to a record label specifically because of our original music, but it took time and persistence. For years.

- Talk is cheap. Ideas are often easy. Execution is where the actual work happens, as the mechanics will often be very frustrating. We wanted conceptually to be a rock band, but what did that sound like? How could we make guitar sounds with our voices that would work in a live setting without effects? How could vocal percussion effortlessly weave into the sound of just a few voices on stage? Maybe this seems obvious now, but it was not obvious. Many things didn't work, and it took thought, and experimentation, and time to learn what would work.

- You might find the destination for your group is the journey itself. In the House Jacks, we're still trying different crazy things with each album which means we still run into walls, still come up with ideas and sounds that just don't work. By design we're constantly morphing, looking to reinvent ourselves and our sound, which will not necessarily be your group's goal. Some groups find a sound and stick to it, which is absolutely fine, and more common. No one is looking for Pentatonix or Straight No Chaser to change their sound; their fans want more of what they're doing, and there's no reason right now for a shift. If this concept isn't making much sense, consider pop music over the past 50 years: the Beatles and Madonna were/are shape-shifters; James Taylor and Willie Nelson are not. Up to you.

- It's not enough to just want to be different. As Ed Boyer wisely replied to a group asking him for advice as to how to be different, "what's different about you?" If you can't answer that question, you can't move to the next step. You have to know what you and your group does well in addition to knowing what other groups are doing, where the community and the sound has been, and where things will likely be going. If you're looking to build a city that will show up on the map, you need to know the map, and also where you currently are.

- Here's the tough one: You're not good at everything. I don't believe the tired adage that "anyone can do anything!" A 5'4" man cannot play in the NBA. Period. Stupid to try. Nor could Kobe be a jockey. The key to success is to find the nexus of your talents and your passions. I'm assuming if you're reading this, a cappella or at least vocal music is a passion, so you're well on your way. And you can sing, so again, there's going to be a sweet spot between desire and ability. But where is that desire? What's your personal style? Your life experience? How are you perceived by others? What's your personality? What do you have to say to others that's true, that's real, that's compelling? This is not the time to whine about being overweight or over 40. Exhibit A: Sweet Honey in the Rock. They will fill your spirit and make your soul soar, and they will in no way rely on many of the performing clichés you probably think are necessary to be successful in popular music.

A serious consideration of this last point is as far as I can get you on this journey. The self-honesty has to come from you, as do the searching, the testing, the discussing and disagreeing and wanting and failing and landing on your feet. I want to help you, and so do the people around you, if you'll ask for their help, and ask big, open, non-leading questions, and prepare yourself for the honest answers that might not be what you think you want to hear . . . but they're what you need to hear if you're going to find the Voice within your voices.

Why do I care? Because this, ultimately, is all that matters in music. Saying something meaningful to you in a way that's meaningful to others in a clear, direct, honest and unique voice. Communication. The a cappella community has a significant number of students, which is fantastic, and also many casual singers, which is also fantastic, and they can and should sing however they'd like without assuming the weight of pioneering genius in addition to the myriad technical and logistical hurdles they face.

But for those of you who are looking at a cappella professionally, or even semi-professionally, you're probably not only wanting to be great but wanting to be different and special . . . but you've got some college gigs and a cruise ship gig coming up and you need to learn "Gangnam Style." Art meets commerce, meets only so many hours in the day, meets different opinions . . .

Ensemble Nobiles

ARRANGING

BisCaydence

CHAPTER 11

CONTEMPORARY A CAPPELLA ARRANGING IN TEN STEPS

By Deke Sharon

Contemporary a cappella has been around for over a decade, resulting in a dynamic and rhythmic sound and style that differentiates it from barbershop, doo-wop, close harmony, and other a cappella styles. Learn how to create a great contemporary a cappella arrangement using this tried and true ten-step formula.

Step One: Choose a Song

Oddly, this is often the most difficult step. If you're a freelance arranger working on commission, the decision is made for you. If you are arranging for fun on your own, you have no restrictions. If you are a group's musical director, however, you have many considerations. Although it may be easy to come up with songs that would be fun to arrange, there is a question of what's <u>needed</u> in the repertoire. If diversity is important to you, consider barring songs that are by the same artist or composer or are stylistically the same.

Try to avoid songs that are often performed by other a cappella groups. Your group will make a name for itself much more quickly if you develop your <u>own</u> sound and your <u>own</u> repertoire. You should also be sure your group has a great first and last song and a great encore. Usually these songs will be most effective if they're up-tempo. Your group should also have at least one ballad at its disposal.

It should go without saying, but before you settle on a song, be sure you have someone in your group who can sing the solo if there is one. A great arrangement of a great song with a poor soloist will usually sound mediocre (or worse). The soloist is the most important vocalist in any song, and since, as the arranger, you're crafting everything around this central voice and melody, you'd better be sure that you have the right voice to get the job done.

EXERCISE: Which songs have made great a cappella arrangements? Which have made poor ones? Why?

For more in-depth information about arranging, please see the book *A Cappella Arranging* by Dylan Bell and Deke Sharon. Published by Hal Leonard #00333442.

Step Two: Listen To The Original Repeatedly

This learning principle is the same as in the study of a foreign language; listen to the song over and over again. While you're concentrating—and while you're not. You will begin to hear sounds, textures, rhythms, and chords that you never heard before, some of which are very subtle and mixed quietly in the background.

Many a cappella arrangements suffer from not integrating the subtle (often almost subliminal) musical elements that define a song. There are times when "doing the obvious thing" in an arrangement isn't the most effective thing to do. When you've listened to a song to the point that you can hear it in your head while it's not playing, you've fully integrated it. And you'll find that it helps later on when you don't need to listen back to the original recording as often.

> EXERCISE: Close your eyes and try to hear a recorded piece of music you know well in your head. Voices, instruments, and all, just as it is on the recording.

Step Three: Purchase The Sheet Music

Look at and listen to other arrangements of the song. "What? Isn't that cheating?" Let's put it this way: would you rather spend your time transcribing the melody and chords or focusing on the more creative elements of arranging? Stravinsky admitted to "stealing" musical ideas from others, and he wasn't the first great musician to do so. Whereas plagiarism occurs when someone copies a paragraph out of a book, there's no ownership of a musical texture or vocal lick or arranging trick. The artistry is in knowing when and where to use these various elements.

Caveat emptor: often there are mistakes or simplifications in the printed music (the melody and/ or the chords), but if you've more or less memorized the song, you'll catch these mistakes. All you need is a close approximation of the solo anyway, as the soloist should learn the solo directly from the recording. Also, there are sometime some interesting decisions made in vocal, piano or guitar arrangements that sometimes spark a new idea.

Most songs you'll want to arrange are in print and can be found at a music store or online. Other arrangements of a song can be heard on various a cappella albums and can be found in a number of places, such as CASA's site www.casa.org. Although you don't want to lift entire passages note for note (that's too blatant and not appreciated by the original arranger), you can see what decisions she made, appreciate what works well, and learn from the less effective sections.

Don't forget to consider the issues of securing arrangement permission and paying possible licensing fees to the song's publisher. Although you may consider it a headache or waste of time, you should always make sure this aspect is handled legally.

> EXERCISE: Name a great work of art that's based on another great work of art. How do they inform each other?

Step Four: Decide On A Form

Listening to and watching a cappella is a heightened experience. In a sense, everyone's a lead singer, and the audience has many more personalities to deal with than in a band, but not so many so that it's like watching a chorus. People concentrate and pay attention to a cappella more than most instrumental music, which is why less is often more. Say what needs to be said as efficiently as possible, and avoid unnecessary repetition.

If you think you don't understand this point, bring a stopwatch to an a cappella show and compare performed song lengths with the originals. A three-minute song on stage comes across as a full four-and-a-half-minute radio tune. Performing "Hey Jude" at its entire seven-minute length would be incredibly tiresome.

Since many songs are written for and recorded with instruments, there are often instrumental solos, long intros, and transitional passages that usually translate poorly to voices. If you've memorized your song completely (and you should have), try singing through it from start to finish and see where you lose interest. Chances are your audience will lose interest then, as well. Also, listen for what sounds stupid. Unless your group is well versed in vocal guitar solos, you'll want to skip them.

If you're having a hard time keeping everything straight because there are too many changes, consider making a sound file "splice/dub" with the sections in your new order. In the most rare of occasions, you'll find extreme measures are necessary. By weaving in another related song (possibly by the same artist) or by composing a short transition, you may find the answer. On the other hand, you may find that it's just not going to work, no matter what you do. Don't fret— come back to it later, and choose another song for now.

> EXERCISE: Can you recall a cappella arrangements where the form differed from that of the original? In what ways did that make the a cappella version more or less effective?

Step Five: Lay Out The Paper/Computer File/Sound File

It doesn't matter if you notate music on paper, use a music notation program, or arrange by ear into a digital recording program. Each method has benefits and hurdles, and all can result in superior artistry. It's a matter of personal choice. Whatever method you choose to record your arrangement, it's time to set your foundation.

You'll need to choose the number of staves and measures per page, which brings up the question of number of parts. If you have a small ensemble, your choice is made for you, as doubling only one or two parts will almost invariably cause an unwanted imbalance. If you're arranging for a small ensemble (like most collegiate groups), consider leaving at least two people per part unless you really know what you're doing. You'll get a much fuller sound and hedge your bet against singing out of tune.

Also, try to designate more basses (or second altos if you're arranging for a female group). Unless your group performs with microphones, the bass lines are often drowned out by screaming tenors. The bass voice is usually loudest on recordings, after the soloist, and a loud bass line casts overtones that help everyone tune better.

Be sure not to forget to factor in the soloist, and any extra parts, such as vocal percussion or duet lines, that need their own room on the paper. Once you have your final count, consider how many lines you need. The solo should be on the top line and may be joined by duet or trio parts. You should avoid having more than two parts per line, as the inner voice vocalists usually have difficulty following their chord factors in the middle of a cluster.

With two parts per line, the upper voice should have "stems up" throughout and the lower voice "stems down." Should you need to cross the voices, it will be clearly apparent to the singers. If your final count is three, four, or six lines, you'll want twelve-staff per page paper, and if you've arrived at five, ten-staff per page is also available. If you're arranging on computer, this isn't usually a concern—you can put each voice on its own line, and condense later. If you're recording to four-track, consider how many voices you want to use, and how many "bounces" you'll need to make it all fit.

Finally, "lay out" the song by counting the number of measures and making a note where each section (verse, chorus, bridge, etc.) begins. Next, fill in your clefs and key signatures. When you're done, you'll have a solid foundation that will allow you to work on sections in any order you'd like, without any confusion as to where you are or how it fits formally with the rest of the music.

Step Six: Write Out The Solo

Often you'll turn from section to section within your incomplete arrangement, and you'll need to know where you are at all times. Using your layout (the paper/computer file/sound file you just prepared), write or sing the solo line from the first measure through to the last, including all rests. Having the solo line written down will keep you from losing your place while you're arranging—it serves as a road map when you are turning from section to section.

Also, for small groups like quartets and quintets, the soloist's pitch and rhythm is important to consider at all times. Sometimes the soloist will be the only voice on a certain chord factor, and you'll need to know exactly where the solo will be. In these cases, it's worth the extra effort to make sure the solo line is exactly correct.

Remember that a soloist doesn't always sing exactly the same notes and rhythms as the written original, or as the last time she performed the song. For this reason, you should make a note on the music which sections of the melody need to be sung *as written* to make the arrangement work as you intend.

> EXERCISE: What shortcuts can you take when transcribing a solo, and what should you make sure is correct?

Step Seven: Write Out The Bass Line

Although you will likely change the bass line as you're writing in the upper background parts, you should at the very least put an outline of the bass on paper now. If the bass line in the original song is unique or memorable (a hook or clearly definable counter melody), it's desirable to duplicate it as closely as possible.

If it's not clearly definable, then you're free to weave a bass line of your own. Consider vocal range, roots of the chords, and the rhythmic feel of the original as primary factors. The bass line is the song's "second melody" and is usually the most recognizable line after the solo, so make it melodic, catchy, and fun.

Don't forget to take into consideration the little things like where your bass (or bass section) is going to breathe. Consider how fast your bass can articulate and how long he can hold a note. If you're not familiar with bass voices and their sounds and limitations, have your bass sing for you and listen to a few of the greats like Richard Greene (The Bobs), Alvin Chea (Take 6), Jimmy Hayes (The Persuasions), and Arnold Robinson (The Nylons). Each has a unique way of phrasing and articulating, and there's much to be learned from their recordings.

> EXERCISE: Without thinking about it in advance, sing the bass line to a couple current pop songs. In what way does translating the bass line into your voice change it from the original recording?

Step Eight: Write The "Uppers"

Apart from the solo, the other upper voices or "uppers" are usually treated as a unit in contemporary a cappella arranging. Examples of this include groups like Rockapella, Take 6 and The Nylons. But there are a myriad of things to consider when writing the uppers. So many things, in fact, that it's impossible to go into them all in any depth here. To give you a shove in the right direction, some of your considerations should be:

- Rhythmic variety (having these voices sing different rhythms from the solo and bass)
- Syllabic sounds (words? nonsense syllables?)
- Voice leading (avoiding unnecessary jumps; making the background lines melodic)
- Block chords vs. Counterpoint (all voices acting as a single unit vs. each line separate)
- Arpeggiation (voices working as a unit, but spelling out chords by singing one note at a time)
- Instrumental idioms (using the voices to imitate instrumental sounds or textures)
- Musical styles (taking ideas from classical, doo-wop, close harmony, pop, R&B, etc.)
- Quoting other songs (sometimes a fun, clever addition)

Of all of these ten steps, this one will prove the most time consuming, demanding, and ultimately most rewarding, as it's here that you get to be your most creative.

> EXERCISE: When is it most advantageous to have the "uppers" sing the same syllables and rhythms, and when is it best to have them differ?

Step Nine: The Final Touches

Now is the time to go back and "sing through" the entire arrangement in your head. It's best to turn your mental "editor" off when you're originally coming up with ideas, but you do need to turn it back on and look at your arrangement as a whole.

Some things to ask yourself as you do this:

- What does it need?

- Where is it too empty or too repetitious? Too busy?

- How do the sections fit together?

- Is there a build throughout the chart?

- Where are the weakest passages and how can you fix them?

    EXERCISE: In other creative processes, when do you know you're done? How does your "editor" help, and when does it get in the way?

Step Ten: Perform And Learn

If you thought you were finished when you copied and distributed your chart, you're wrong. A great arrangement is one that grows and changes with the group that sings it, and a great arranger is one who knows that no arrangement is finished until it is tailor-fit to a specific group. Don't let your ego get in the way of this crucial step in the arranging process; after you hear a proper sing-through and hear suggestions from the group, allowing yourself to make changes will only make the chart better. You will be respected and applauded for your flexibility.

When listening to the sing-through, your focus should be on your chart and the group's performance of it. How does the arrangement sound? Is it what you expected? What differs from your expectations, and do you like it or not? Be honest with yourself. Be open to trying a variety of ideas and suggestions. This is when you get to "mold your clay" and the most valuable learning experience you'll ever have as an arranger— use this time wisely.

In case you didn't realize it, many renowned composers and arrangers have had the luxury of writing for the best orchestras and choruses in the world, and they could write just about anything that they could imagine. You probably can't. Like it or not, you're arranging for your group, and it's your fault (not theirs) if the arrangement doesn't work. It's your job to make them sound their best. You can push their limits occasionally, but to push them you have to know them and work within their abilities.

And just as you'll push your group's limits, you should also push yours. There are plenty of standard arrangements in the world, and you're probably not interested in adding to the pile. To be a great arranger, you not only have to know how to write a standard arrangement, but also have the creativity and drive to do something new. Most instrumental arrangers approach a song with the initial question "What am I going to do differently?" On the other hand, many a cappella arrangers approach a song with the quandary "How can I make this sound the same, but with voices?" Consider putting yourself in a perspective that straddles and makes the most of both ways of thinking. The best arrangements manage to maintain the successful elements of an original version and also bring something new to the song.

Once you're finished, and your arrangement is safely in the repertoire, it's time to go back to step one!

Put it into practice

These ten steps hopefully sound simple and straightforward. Before you begin arranging the song that you've had in the back of your mind, however, it would be helpful to practice these ten steps. Choose a simple song that you know well, such as "America the Beautiful." Arrange it using the method described here. You may discover that you've been skipping valuable steps. Or, you may discover that there are some steps you prefer to do in a different order.

North Metro Bus

Boots 'n' Cats

CHAPTER 12

SINGING AND ARRANGING BY THE NUMBERS

By Deke Sharon

Although our current notational system was created for a cappella (by Guido D'Arezzo in the year 1,000 to standardize Gregorian chant notation), some of the greatest a cappella throughout time has been arranged and taught by ear.

This chapter aims to start you on the path of singing and arranging harmony without relying on sheet music or a detailed knowledge of chord factors and harmonic progressions. You've been listening to music since before you can remember, so the language of Western harmony is one you understand instinctively quite well. However, unless you've studied music theory, you likely don't realize how much you already know.

Melodic Numbers (1, 2, 3 . . .)

Let's start at the very beginning, as Maria Von Trapp famously sings in "The Sound of Music," and remember that our entire musical system is based on 8 note scales. In the language of solfege, that's Do Re Mi Fa Sol La Ti and back to Do an octave higher.

Assuming that most of you reading this have not studied solfege, it's easier for our purposes today to consider the notes by there number names: 1, 2, 3, 4, 5, 6, 7 and 8. To keep things simple, we're going to eliminate the number 8, knowing that for our purposes the octave will be clear enough. If you're singing the tonic note, the beginning of the scale as well as the end of the scale, consider that "1."

For example, let's look at what a few simple well known melodies look like when reduced to simple numbers:

- "Twinkle, Twinkle Little Star" 1-1-5-5-6-6-5

- "Silent Night" = 5-6-5-3 (note that a melody doesn't always start on "1")

- "Hallelujah Chorus" = 1-5-6-5 (note that the first note is above the others, which matters for melodic shape, but not for the purposes of harmony. In a chord, both the low and the high notes have the same function)

- "You Are My Sunshine" = 5-1-2-3-3 (the 5 in this case is below the 1, again not a concern harmonically)

- "Take Me Out To The Ball Game" 1-1-6-5-3-5-2 (note that the first and second notes are an octave apart, but for our harmonic purposes they're the same).

Why so many examples? We want to help you identify each note with its number, regardless of octave. This will become more clear as we start to harmonize by ear.

Those of you who are familiar with music theory are probably wondering "what about all of the accidentals?" In other words, if our scale represents all of the white keys on the piano, what about all of the black keys? This method can be used to incorporate all 12 tones, but for the purposes of simplicity and clarity, we're initially going to use only the 7 notes in a major scale. And for those of you solfege experts who are used to "fixed Do," this method is more akin to "moveable Do," with the 1 representing the tonic note in every key.

Chordal Numbers (I, II, III . . .)

Now that we have a simple language (numbers) to discuss melody, we need a language to discuss harmony.

First of all, it's important to note that Western Harmony is built upon triads. What is a triad? Three notes occurring at the same time, usually a third apart.

Side Note for theory buffs: Yes, chords can and often do become more complex, with 7ths, color tones, suspensions and the like, but almost every moment in a song can be reduced to a simple triad. Also, yes, the roman numerals are usually spelled in lower case, such as iii, when referring to minor chords, but I'm intentionally keeping this simple so people can focus on using their ear.

Every note of the scale, 1-7, can have a triad built upon it. To avoid confusion, we'll use roman numerals throughout this chapter when discussing chords: I, II, III, IV, V, VI, VII.

Example: the most commonly occurring chord in any song is the I (that being the roman numeral 1) chord, comprised of 1, 3 and 5 (a triad is built upon notes a third apart, so you skip a number when building them).

The second most common chords are the IV and V chords:

IV = 4, 6, 1

V = 5, 7, 2

Remember, after 7 comes 1, just as after Ti comes Do.

And that's it. That's all you need to know to start improvising harmony. The rest is already in your "ear" as we like to say. You've listened to a lifetime of music, and the rules of Western harmony are deeply imbedded in you such that you don't know you know them, any more than you know all of the rules of English grammar (or whatever language you learned as a child).

Three Chord Songs

Many of the greatest rock, pop and folks songs use only three chords, and those are usually I, IV and V. Before going any further, let's set up a couple simple guidelines to help us as we decide what notes to sing:

If you're singing harmony with someone else, you don't want to sing the same note, be it a unison or an octave.

Until you have three part harmony, doubling a note is a lost opportunity. Ideally you'll cover all 3 notes with three people, creating the fullest sound possible. Of course if you're improvising and you both move to the same note it's not a big deal; we're just outlining the best way to create the fullest harmonies possible.

Example: the song is on a I chord, and you have three people. Ideally your three singers will be singing 1, 3 and 5. If two people are singing 5 that means you'll be missing either a 1 or a 3, and the chord will sound somewhat empty.

If a chord changes and you can stay on the same note, stay.

Part of the act of improvisation, be it on stage as an actor or comedian, is to pay attention to what the other actors are doing, and have your lines make sense within the conversation. You take turns moving the story forward, and you don't make a move unnecessarily.

The same principle applies to improvised harmony. If a chord is changing, the people who need to move should move, and the people who can remain on the same note should remain. Otherwise, if they move, it creates confusion.

Example: if you're moving from a I to a IV chord, you will want to cover the chord factors 1, 3, 5 and then 1, 4, 6. When you're singing, unless you've discussed in advance who will move where, you want to rely on a common set of assumptions and the simplest logical decisions by everyone. Therefore:

    1 -> 1

    3 -> 4

    5 -> 6

Very simple. Now, let's say the person singing 1 moves jumps to 4. Where does that leave us?

    1 -> 4

    3 -> either 1 or 6

    5 -> either 1 or 6

. . . but how will they communicate to know which note to move to? By remaining on the same note, the first singer eliminates unnecessary confusion.

When moving, move as little as you need to, leaving space for the other singers.

When dealing with harmonies, you'll find you don't need to move very much, usually only a step in either direction. Occasionally you'll need to leap, but when you do, it shouldn't be far. Let's look again at the above example, of the I to IV chord:

You know that one of your singers will be staying on the same note:

1 -> 1

If you're on 5, you have 2 choices:

5 -> 4

or

5 -> 6

Your ear will be happy to move in either direction. Which should you pick? Here's where awareness of the other singers comes in handy. Your friend right now is on 3, so if you move:

5 -> 4

that forces

3 -> 6

leaping over you. There was nowhere else to go, as moving to the two closest chord factors (1 and 4) would have resulted in a doubling, and the chord would have lost a factor.

If this is getting confusing, don't worry. As Steve Martin said "Talking about music is like dancing about architecture." This is all far more intuitive when sung than when written.

You don't need to know music theory to sing harmony by ear. The above examples are not to get you to think about every note in terms of its scale and chord factor, but rather to help understand why you don't want to leap around and move when you don't have to. Of course, knowing theory, and which chord factor and scale factor your singing is valuable, it's just not necessary, especially when you're just getting started. Focus on listening, not thinking.

It's time to show how these principles work in practice, where they'll become more clear.

Three Chord Verse: Big Yellow Taxi

Joni Mitchell's classic song has been in the Top 40 several times over the years, most recently by The Counting Crows. Each version has it's own tempo, it's own key, its own nuances, but for our process none of that matters. The basic chord progression remains the same, and this process works regardless of key or tempo.

Improvising harmony is a bit like driving, in that you're either going to stay in your lane or you're going to move into another lane/turn. If you don't need to change, don't change. But this begs the question: when might you need to change? The answer: when the chords change. The lyrics in the first verse are:

"They paved paradise
And put up a parking lot
With a pink hotel, a boutique
And a swingin' hot spot"

Avoiding sheet music for the moment, consider where the chords change, in your mind. The chords change on syllables:

(They) PAVED paradise
And put up a parking LOT
With a PINK hotel, a BOUtique
And a swingin' HOT spot

When you're improvising by ear, you should pick a note, dive in, and when you hear the chord change stay on your note unless it doesn't fit in the basic chord, in which case you should move. To outline what that would look like, let me show you the basic chord progression:

IV – I – IV, V – I

The comma between the IV and V is merely to indicate that time passes more quickly there (Both chords happen in the same measure).

Before looking at a single written note, let's just pick a note, dive in and sing. Let's start on 1, which happens to be the same note as the word "They." You can sing 1 through the IV chord, through the I chord, through the next IV chord, but then you need to change when you get to the V chord.

When you hit the V chord, your choices are 5, 7, and 2. Which should you choose? Either 7 or 2 are next door. Let's choose 2, and then return to 1 for the last chord.

1 – 1 – 1, 2 - 1

Go find a recording of the song and try this. Start on the same note as the melody ("They . . .") on a simple vowel ("oo"), and hold that note all the way until the world "boutique" at which point you go up a step, then go back down on the word "hot." Simple.

Could you choose other paths? Sure.

If you start on 6, you'll want to move back down to 5 on the I chord, then back up to 6, then 7, then back down to 5. We'll call this "Harmony B" to differentiate it from your first path, which we'll call "Harmony A"

6 – 5 – 6, 7 - 5

If you start on 4, move down to 3, then back up to 4, then 5, then you can stay on 5, or if you're singing harmony with the two parts above, you'll hear the person above you move back down to 5 which will nudge you down to 3. Call it "Harmony C"

4 – 3 – 4, 5 - 3

If this is becoming a confusing string of numbers, using notation it looks something like this (based on the Joni Mitchell version):

Note that the Harmony C line is written an octave above the other three. That's fine. Generally speaking, you can layer harmonies on top of or below a melody, based on your vocal range. My only recommendation is that you not stack harmonies down too low, as they'll begin to get "muddy." If you generally keep your harmonies in the middle to upper middle part of your range, you will have an easier time tuning with others.

Simple held whole notes are fine, but in time you're going to want to add some rhythm. Will this change anything? Nope. You can sing any rhythm you'd like on your note.

---

* For reasons having to do with physics of harmonics, every note has overtones, and harmonies tune better when higher in your register, locked in to a pitch played by a low instrument, such as a bass.

Let's pick a fairly complex rhythm, based loosely on the guitar pattern, for Harmony A. You'll see that nothing changes melodically or harmonically. Harmony B isn't feeling quite as comfortable on her part yet, so she's going to sing ???, and Harmony C is going to stick with whole notes.

Fact is, you can sing any rhythm you'd like, and if your cohorts on the other parts sing different rhythms (or just hold a whole note) it'll all still work together. When everyone is on the same rhythm and/or the same syllable you'll have a more cohesive, unified sound, but there are times in contemporary a cappella when different rhythms and vowels are preferred because they create a more complex texture. You're improvising, sing anything you'd like.

Bass

One last thought before we move on: If you're a bass singer, you're likely used to singing the bass line, not an upper harmony part. That's absolutely fine. You should follow all of the principles above, with one important difference: you should sing the root of each chord (with occasional exception: if the bass is clearly on a different chord factor in the original song). You're already used to doing this, so it should be rather easy for you.

In this verse, if the chord progression is:

IV – I – IV, V – I

You should sing:

4 – 1 – 4, 5 – 1

Simple as that.

Upper voices shouldn't worry about doubling your chord factors, as it will inevitably happen from time to time, as you're leaping around based on the chord progression, and they're trying to not step on their neighbor's note. In time, if you find yourself improvising 2 part a cappella harmony and one person is a bass, the upper voice can learn to leap around to avoid doublings, but that's a skill acquired after you have lots of experience harmonizing by ear. For now, upper voices follow the rules above, basses sing the tonic.

Three Chord Chorus: Big Yellow Taxi

Now, let's jump to the chorus, and to show you that the specific recording doesn't effect our process, we'll now sing along to the Counting Crows version, which is in a different key and vocal range (neither of which matter, using this method).

What is the chord progression? Give it a listen and see if you can figure it out.

Let's start by singing a note and seeing when you need to move the note.

The lyric is:

> *"Don't it always seem to go*
> *That you don't know what you've got til it's gone*
> *They paved paradise*
> *Put up a parking lot"*

The chords feel like they change, more or less, on the following words:

> *DON'T it always SEEM to go*
> *That you DON'T know what you've got til it's GONE*
> *They PAVED paradise*
> *PUT up a parking LOT*

Try starting on 1, see how long you can hold it. Let's go back to a simple "oo" sound and whole notes (or as long a note as the harmony will allow). Looks like it works until the word "put," right? Move up to 2 or down to 7 for that note, then back to 1 on "lot" and you've got a harmony part that works well. You've probably also noticed the great descending line 1-7-6-5 on the words "Don't", "seem", "don't" and "gone." That works too, right?

But wait. You can't have both a 1 and a 7 on the word "seem" can you? There's no triad with both notes in it, which means we've moved beyond triads. Every note in this song is still 1, 2, 3, 4, 5, 6 and 7, but some chords have more than just 3 notes in them.

This isn't a problem. Your three chord song just turned into something more complex, but music doesn't always follow predictable rules or easy paths. Nonetheless, our system can still get us through this passage. In fact, we already have 2 harmonic lines we've sung, both of which work, and we know there must be more.

Try starting on the 5 and see where your ear takes you. Then try starting on the 3. And if you have a low enough voice, try singing the roots of the chords. With a little trial and error you'll likely arrive on the following, or something close to it:

Arranged by **DEKE SHARON**

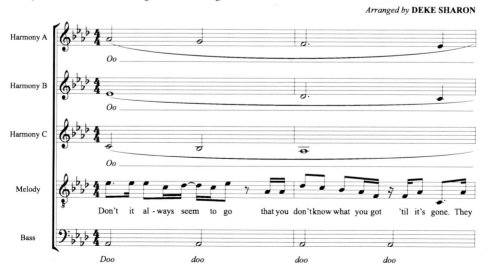

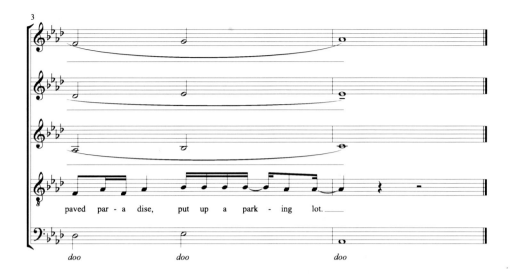

Since the melody gets pretty low, I've notated the harmonies above the melody, where they'll sound best.

Your first question is probably "are these the only notes that work?" and the answer to that is "no." When the chords get denser, you have more options. If you're an arranger working with few voices, you have to prioritize which notes to use and which to drop, but if you're improvising by ear for the first time, there is no such expectation.

Your second question might be "what ARE those chords in the first half of the chorus?" and the answer to that is I – V – IV – I, with a 1 in the bass throughout. The result is a chord progression that both moves and remains static, creating tension and resolution while remaining in the same place. None of this is very important to what you're doing, beyond giving you insight into the fact that anything can happen in a song, but if you follow your ear, and move when your note no longer fits because the chord changed, you'll soon become good at anticipating the chord changes and be able to sing along with the radio effortlessly.

Can you change the rhythms? Yes. In the third measure could everyone move down instead of up? Yes . . . although if you have someone singing a line similar to Harmony C, you'll hear them on the A and not want to bump them off his/her note. Could the last chord go down instead of up? Yes . . . but again, you don't want to bump the Harmony B singer off of the 5.

When you're arranging on paper, it's easy to move parts around, jump inversions, cross voices, and get fancy in other ways. However, when improvising harmony with other people, it's best to keep the melodic motion simple and predictable. If you want to get creative, play with vowels and rhythms and dynamics.

One last thought before we move past this song. There's a cool harmony that happens at the end of the verse: "ooh bop bop, ooh bop bop." What is that?

Start singing parts and see if you can figure it out. The top line moves from 7 to 6. The other parts don't move, do they? They sit on 5 and 3. That gives us:

Arranged by **DEKE SHARON**

Before moving on to the next song, if you're looking for more three chord songs to improvise along with before moving on, a simple internet search will bring up long lists of well known options. Choose a song or two that you know well. I recommend "Twist and Shout" or "Down On the Corner" as a good place to start, if you're familiar with them, as the background harmonies integrate lyrics.

> For more in-depth information about arranging, please see the book *A Cappella Arranging* by Dylan Bell and Deke Sharon. Published by Hal Leonard #00333442.

Four Chord Verse: Don't Stop Believin'

If the three chord song was the basis of early rock and roll, the four chord song is is the new standard of rock and pop music writing. In fact, it's so ubiquitous that there's a viral video (over 32 million views as of printing) by a comedy band "Axis of Awesome") that weaves together over 30 songs above the same four chord progression.

One of these songs, the first and perhaps best known is "Don't Stop Believin'" by the legendary San Francisco rock band Journey. It follows the ubiquitous chord pattern from first note to last chord: I-V-VI-IV (reminder for theory buffs: we're not writing minor chords in lower case, so "vi" is intentionally "VI"). Once you master this chord progression for one song, dozens of others will present as very easy .

We can start at the top of the song, before the melody comes in. You can clearly hear the piano part, and the highest note starts on 1, in steady quarter notes. It moves up to 2 for the second chord, then back down to 1 for the third and fourth chord.

1 – 2 – 1 - 1

So simple that I want you to avoid that, assume someone is singing that part, which we'll again call Harmony A and sing a harmony part just below it, Harmony B.

What chord factor would that start on? We're starting on a I chord, so our choices are 1 (which is the top voice), 3 and 5. Moving down from 1 the next note we hit is 5 so you should start there.

5 comes first, then when we move to the second chord, which is V, we should stay on the 5, right? Well, rules are made to be broken, and if you're trying to create a close harmony, this is a time when you should jump up to the 7 to say close to the top voice. If you're just singing two part harmony or singing alone you could certainly stay on the 5, but let's assume you're following the upper voice, and that upper voice is following the original. After that 7, you'll want to move down to the 6 , then stay on the 6 (since there's no reason to move):

5 – 7 – 6 – 6

Time for Harmony C: start on 3 (the only remaining chord factor), then keep the chord close by jumping up to 5, then down to 3, and up to 4:

3 – 5 – 3 – 4

If these numbers are confusing, perhaps sit at a piano and look at the notes, assuming 1 = C and so on up all the white notes on the keyboard (2 = D, 3 = E, etc). Sometimes voicings make much more sense when you're able to visualize them on a keyboard, or watch as one finger pushes another out of the way.

Basses: you're welcome to sing the root of each chord, but I think you'll find the opening bass melody far more enjoyable to sing, and it touches down on those roots, so you might as well give in and sing along as you likely already do. When improvising a cappella, feel free to sing along with the bass line at any time. Sometimes it's wooden, but sometimes it's melodic (as in the opening of this song), sometimes it's iconic ("Under Pressure"), and sometimes it's just fun ("U Can't Touch This"). The upper harmony parts have to be careful if they're hoping to create a cohesive unit, whereas you're much more free, so long as you establish the root of the chord as needed.

We'll keep the upper harmony parts on quarter notes, and since we're restriking the note we'll use "noo" instead of just "oo" for the upper voices. The bass, on the low melodic line, will sing "doo":

Arranged by **DEKE SHARON**

Eight Measure Pattern

As you're singing these parts along with the recording you might notice a slight variation in this four chord pattern: every other chord is slightly different from the third chord: a III instead of a VI. In other words, this isn't a four chord pattern, it's an eight chord pattern:

I – V – VI – IV – I – V – III – IV

Don't worry, this isn't a problem, is it? You just move your part as needed (in this case, the top two harmony parts need to change):

Arranged by **DEKE SHARON**

Why did the top two move down? Because the piano part moves down, and the top voice is following the piano part. Other voicings would work; I'm just expecting this is what would happen if you were singing along to the recording with friends.

Elaboration

So far so good. This simple pattern absolutely works, and would sound great. However, you're going to be singing this pattern over and over again for a while before the prechorus comes, as the harmonic progression doesn't change for over a minute, so you might want to vary it. Plus, you're likely missing the off-beat note played by the pianist's right thumb that keeps the pattern moving along.

You have several options here: the lowest voice could move down a chord factor on each off beat eighth note (which you'll see in the first measure below), it could restrike the same note on eighths having a similar effect (shown in the second measure), it could sing only on the offbeats (shown in the third measure), or if you're feeling particularly silly all four parts could hop down an inversion on each off beat, which I admit to having done more than once on stage with the House Jacks while taking requests (shown in the fourth measure):

There is no right or wrong choice, no canonical way to improvise harmony by ear. Your fundamental goal should be to cover the core chord factors and generally represent the overall character of the song. Beyond that, you can ornament your vocal line any way you'd like.

Melodic Trio & Repeated Lyric

If you've ever sung along with this song on the radio, which I'm guessing you have, you likely have encountered the chorus with its three part harmony. What should you do when you get to a passage in a song that has vocal harmony in the original? Incorporate it!

Getting into the harmony is usually easy: You just move from your background part, whatever it is, to the closest harmony part, which sometimes will be the melody. This isn't a problem if you're improvising three part harmony as the other two parts will cover the other parts of the harmony.

The difficult choice is how you should "dismount" from the harmony. Go back to the pattern you had before? Create a new pattern repeating the harmony you just sang? Create a new part that mimics the background instrumental parts in the original song? There is no perfect answer.

My recommendation, which is only one option but a solid one to agree upon with your cohorts, is if you enter a passage of a song with built in harmonies on some notes, continue a simple repeating lyrical and rhythmic pattern in the gaps between the lyrics. Why? Because the texture has changed so you should embrace the change and do something different, but there are so very many options that you should pick the easiest to remember and repeat.

So, in the case of this Don't Stop Believin' chorus, you have some harmonies built in ("Don't stop believin'" and "streetlights, people"), and some holes to fill. The easiest thing to agree on is to take the first lyric and repeat it on the new notes as the chords change, as you'll see in the example below:

You'll notice a couple of assumptions I've made: The bass line will remain the same as the introduction and verse (as it does in the original), but the vowel has changed to "da" which is louder, as the chorus wants to build, contrasting with the more quiet and restrained introduction, and the upper harmonies are an inversion or two higher than the introduction, which you may find happening as you move through the song and all want to increase the volume and impact of the repeating background part. Of course there are countless other options. This is in no way the "right answer" but rather one possible result of improvisation.

The simple repeated lyric as chorus texture works very well as variation from background syllables in songs spanning from "Stand By Me" to "Shake It Off". The more you improvise the more you'll want to start including lyrical components into your melodic and harmonic vocal tapestries.

I hope these examples have given you some insight into how you can improvise harmony by ear, alone or with friends, using a very simple numerical system and set of guidelines. Obviously there are many more complex chord progressions and harmonies than the ones we've presented, but once you have the basic principles down and begin to listen and trust your instincts, you should be able to tackle chromatic as well as diatonic chord factors. As with all forms of improvisation, you'll never be perfect, as you'll always make mistakes from time to time, but those mistakes will become less common, and your instincts more finely honed the more you "sing by the numbers."

VOX

Filming the Riff-Off in *Pitch Perfect 2*

A CAPPELLA IN THE MOVIES

- In *The Music Man* (1962) (both the stage version and the film), Professor Harold Hill teaches the four squabbling members of the school board to sing Barbershop. All of their performances from then on are a cappella. (In both the original production and the film, the School Board was played by the barbershop quartet the Buffalo Bills.)

- One of the most memorable movie scenes is the bar scene in *Top Gun* (1986), in which the characters Maverick (played by Tom Cruise) and Goose (played by Anthony Edwards) burst into an a cappella version of the song "You've Lost that Lovin' Feeling" in an attempt to get the attention of Charlotte "Charlie" Blackwood (played by Kelly McGillis).

- The dads in *3 Men and a Baby* (1987) (played by Tom Selleck, Ted Danson, and Steve Guttenberg) team up to sing "Goodnight Sweetheart" in an attempt to lull their baby girl to sleep.

- In *Scream 2* (1997), Jerry O'Connell's character Derek serenades Neve Campbell's character Sidney in the cafeteria by singing an a cappella version of the song "I Think I Love You" while the entire lunchroom claps along.

- In *My Best Friend's Wedding* (1997), George (played by Rupert Everett) serenades Julianne (played by Julia Roberts) with the tune "I Say a Little Prayer for You" in a crowded restaurant and is joined by the other guests at the table.

- In *Anchorman: The Legend of Ron Burgundy* (2004), the Channel 4 News Team spontaneously begin singing an a cappella version of the song "Afternoon Delight" as the character Ron Burgundy, played by Will Ferrell, tries to describe what true love is like.

- In *Wedding Crashers* (2005), you can hear a clip of The Swingle Singers "ba-ba"ing their way through Mozart's "Horn Concerto No. 4" in the background after the scene where the characters played by Vince Vaughn and Owen Wilson are running a divorce mediation.

- In *The Break-Up* (2006), one of the guests at a dinner party describes his love of singing with his a cappella group "The Tone Rangers," and then leads all the dinner party guests in an impromptu performance of the song "Owner of a Lonely Heart."

- In the movie *Good Luck Chuck* (2007), the character of Chuck (played by Dane Cook) hires an aging barbershop quartet to serenade Cam (played by Jessica Alba) Beyoncé's "Crazy In Love" before he jumps out of an oversized present in a penguin suit rapping to the same song.

- In *Step Brothers* (2008), there is a scene in the car where the character played by Adam Scott and his family hit every note in an a cappella version of the song "Sweet Child O Mine."

- In *The Other Guys* (2010), Will Ferrell's character, Detective Allen Gamble, joins a group of old-timers in singing a cappella snippets of some depressing songs.

- The film *Pitch Perfect* (2012) is about competitive college a cappella groups and competing in the ICCAs.

- In *Pitch Perfect 2* (2015) the Barden Bellas travel to Copenhagen for the A Cappella World Championship.

Bonner Jazz Choir

CHAPTER 13

ARRANGING WITH CONVICTION

By Deke Sharon

People often ask what they can do to perfect their arranging style. Are they using the right kind of chords? Should they consider other syllable sounds?

The fact is, the single most important factor in every a cappella arrangement has nothing to do with harmony, rhythm or music theory. The single most important factor can be summed up in a single word: conviction.

Arranging for a cappella is unlike any other form of arranging because the elements you're arranging aren't only people's voices but their emotions, their focus, their excitement, their attitude. Singers need to believe in the notes they're singing or it doesn't matter how brilliant you are as an arranger.

We've all heard amazing arrangements sound bad, but there are also very questionable arrangements that have sounded transcendent.

As an arranger you should think about "playing" your ensemble the same way a musician plays his instrument. "Playing" the ensemble isn't about manipulation, but rather the careful understanding of a group's proclivities, attitudes and opinions. Know where to push and where to pull, when to pull someone up and when to take someone down.

This, of course, isn't possible if you're arranging for a group you've never met who live several time zones away. However, you're likely arranging for groups you know, and when you are, you need to consider not only their voices but their desires, tastes, beliefs, hopes, and needs.

Consider an analogy from Dungeons and Dragons. In this game, there's a type of sorcerer called an illusionist who casts spells that appear but are ephemeral unless or until the person perceiving it believes it. Then it becomes real. If your enemy doesn't believe the goblin that appeared before him is real, it disappears. But if he does believe, then it's a real goblin. Arrangements work much the same way. If a group believes in a chart, they'll sing it with heart. If they don't, you're stuck with a long chain of notes and a bored audience.

There is no single way to guarantee a group will love your work, regardless of how excellent it might sound in your computer or how great it sounds when another group sings it. A personal example: I was commissioned to arrange "White Christmas" for The Nylons (one of the groups that inspired me to make a career of a cappella). I was honored and thrilled . . . until they summarily rejected the arrangement I presented to them. I had poured my heart and soul into that arrangement! It sat on the shelf until a year later, when I was asked by the Gas House Gang if I had any four-part male holiday songs they might like. I sent over the "White Christmas" chart, which they immediately recorded and put on their album. Now it's the single most performed arrangement of mine throughout the barbershop world. Once I published the song, it quickly became my most performed holiday arrangement, from middle school choirs to the LA Master Chorale.

What can you do to try to inspire the greatest level of conviction when groups are singing your arrangements? Here are a few suggestions:

Make Sure the Song Choice Suits Them

Sometimes singers love a song but it's not right for them, and sometimes a song would be perfect except that they just don't like it. Rehearsal time is precious and opinions coalesce quickly, so before you start, make sure you're set up for success with a song that they're excited about and will effectively make their own.

Present Your Vision Clearly

If you won't be running the rehearsals, be sure to indicate your thoughts about the arrangement. For a group who learns from sheet music, use dynamics markings and leave notes in the margin. If a group learns by ear, do your best to make it easy for them by producing midi files for them to listen to or (ideally) by singing the parts. Much will be made clear by your inflections.

Leave Some Space for Your Arrangement to Breathe

In other words, don't create something that's very challenging and delicate that can only be done under precisely controlled conditions. Don't require all singers to be in perfect health, with their very highest and very lowest notes intact, etc. Try to give your singers some wiggle room so that your vision will hold within a certain range of tempo or if the key is moved up or down a half step (groups do drift flat and sharp at times—it can't be avoided), and so on.

Encourage Some Changes

Give your singers an opportunity to make suggestions and incorporate them into the arrangement. This is best done if you are the person teaching the chart and if you have a section of the song that could go a couple of different directions. Ask for a group's suggestion about a vowel sound or the number of repeats at the end. Sometimes it won't matter to you but, by soliciting their opinion, you'll find they feel more ownership once their idea or suggestion is incorporated. It's simple psychology, and it works.

Remember that there are literally thousands of possible ways an arrangement can be altered and still be great, so you have some room to make changes.

Tonal Spectrum

Lose Some Battles

It's ok if you acquiesce sometimes and give in to a change you're not entirely happy with. If your ego is bruised at one point because the group doesn't love one of your favorite choices, just remember that they'll sing their preferred option far more convincingly. In the end, that will make the arrangement and performance better, and that's what matters overall. Your arrangement isn't what matters; their performance is what matters.

But Keep a Copy

Remember that you don't have to keep all of the changes that a single group makes. If you're convinced your ideas are sound, keep a version of your arrangement the way it is, and send it off to another group in the future to see if they're on board with your vision.

Ultimately, like a custom tailored suit, an arrangement's success is a careful balance between how your singers look and sound to others and how comfortable they are. The most beautiful jacket won't look good if the wearer is constricted or looks stiff, and sometimes that's a matter of how tight the suit is and other times it's purely a matter of how comfortable the wearer is.

Even if it pains you, sometimes your best move is to let the suit out a bit: have a happy client who proudly displays your work at every opportunity, resulting in more clients and more requests for your work, which eventually will be presented exactly the way you originally intended.

SoCal VoCals

CHAPTER 14
COMBAT READY ARRANGEMENTS

By Deke Sharon

Dear Arrangers,

Please sing your own arrangements.
On Stage. Repeatedly.

Sincerely,

Deke

. . . not clear? OK, I'll explain.

Since the tender age of 7, I've been performing in vocal groups in a variety of locations, in a variety of situations. Early in the morning, with a cold, after traveling all night, etc. I love gigging. It's in my blood, and I can't imagine ever stopping. Singing makes me whole, and a big part of my life's work is both to inspire others to sing and to create infrastructure, opportunities and materials that make that more possible for everyone.

And I would say my arrangements benefit from the experiences I have on stage and on the road. Learning not only what the voice can do at its best, but what it can do on balance, wherever, whenever.

As a cappella has expanded around the globe, I've seen a tremendous growth in the number of contemporary a cappella arrangers, both professional and casual. This makes me very happy, as a cappella needs many, many arrangers. If you'll allow a food analogy: if we want everyone to eat, we need lots and lots of chefs, cooking meals all around the globe. Big, extravagant meals and simple dishes. Banquets and snacks. As it should be.

However, I've seen a growing trend that I fear might be taking us off course a bit: big, lavish arrangements that are performable only under the most controlled conditions.

Perhaps the proliferation of multi-layered studio recordings and carefully edited in-studio YouTube videos have inspired and reinforced this ethic, with groups and solo singers trying to impress each other and a growing fan base with ever more dense and wide harmonies.

These ivory tower, crystal-delicate arrangements are indeed often beautiful when painstakingly recorded and edited, but undoubtedly difficult to sing live. There's a great tradition of dense, in-studio a cappella reaching back to The Singer's Unlimited, but remember that they were never particularly well known, appealing primarily to a rarified fan base of jazz musicians and close harmony vocalists.

A cappella may be its most technically impressive and flawless when recorded, but the fact is a cappella is most impactful and most powerful when performed live. The audience-performer connection is second to none, and I know everyone reading this can harken back to their most powerful, most life-changing a cappella memories, and by-in-large those will be either as an audience member or a singer.

To this end, we, as arrangers, need to make sure our arrangements are not only performable under ideal conditions, but under reasonable, real life conditions. An amazing arrangement that is largely unsingable isn't an amazing arrangement, as the arrangement isn't the point. The arrangement is merely the road map that connects an audience and a performer emotionally, experientially, spiritually. To continue the road map analogy, there might be a beautiful road through the mountains that's drivable under ideal conditions, but if it's often rained or snowed out and you need special tires, you're not likely to drive it often, and when you do it might not be the ideal experience you were hoping for.

These thoughts came to me while in the back of a van during an eight hour drive from Germany to Italy while suffering with a cold. Sound check upon arrival, workshop first thing in the morning, lots of singing all weekend. I didn't want to take the long and winding road during this journey, and when singing that weekend, I didn't want to have the show's most powerful moments reliant on the extremes of my vocal range and technique, achievable only under pristine conditions.

You know what's great? Whole notes. Some of the best choral moments ever written happen on the back of whole notes. And triads. A perfectly balanced triad is a beautiful thing. And it's not impossible to sing. In fact, most great choral music was not written to be supremely challenging, and those pieces that are written that way end up rarely being performed.

You know the expression "you don't go to war with the army you want, but instead with the army you have?" Same goes for a cappella.

So, what can you do to make your arrangements "combat ready?"

- Don't rely on extremes in vocal range. Your tenor may be able to chest a high B on a perfect day, but what can he do consistently? Same goes for your basses' lowest notes: just because they can sing a low C first thing Saturday morning doesn't mean they'll be able to do the same on Saturday night.

- Don't make arrangements any harder than they need to be. Sure, you need variety in arrangements, but make sure when there's variety it's something that will really change the experience for the audience. Otherwise keep it the same, or make it easy to remember ("oo" first verse, "oh" second verse, "ah" third verse). No need to spend any more time in rehearsal than absolutely necessary, and arrangements that are easier to learn and memorize end up being tighter on stage. Easier arrangements also allow for a larger repertoire.

- Make your arrangements fun to sing. Boring vocal lines or too much repetition will send your singers into "auto pilot," which will suck the life out of the performance. Weave in cool little bits, lyrics, and playful lines, especially in your bass lines. Basses most often get boring, repetitive parts.

- Limit yourself and your singers to a reasonable number of challenges. I speak from experience when I say that there are things I wanted on paper and in my head, and as soon as I had to sing them, I no longer wanted them. Some things are just too challenging on a daily basis, too hard to balance, too difficult to sing with repeated precision. This is not to say your arrangements should all be simple, but rather make them, for lack of a better term, "reliably singable."

- Stop trying to draw attention to yourself as an arranger. Great arrangements create great moments, but not moments that will take the audience or singers out of the emotional focus. If you're a movie director, you want beautiful shots, but not ones that take the audience out of the story repeatedly and make them think "wow, great cinematography," because every time an audience member goes "meta," it takes a while for them to get back to being fully immersed in the story. And when you're busy thinking about mechanics, you're usually not feeling.

- And, as I said in my brief letter earlier, join a group and go on a road trip singing your arrangements. Then, listen to show recordings and see if you like what you hear. It's always easy to blame the shortcomings of a performance on a group of singers, but my opinion is that the first place to assign blame is on the arrangement itself. A good arrangement sets a group up for success, knowing not only what they can do but what they will do.

A great strategy is one that will win a battle, not just look good on paper and appear clever, and a great arrangement is one that will win an audience, night after night.

Got it? Good. Now get back to the trenches!

The Sing-Off South Africa rehearsal

UCD Mix

CHAPTER 15
UNIVERSAL ARRANGEMENT CRITIQUE

By Deke Sharon

I'm frequently asked to look over an arrangement and offer my thoughts. I find a surprising number of my responses contain the same comments, the same thoughts. So I've decided to create a one-size-fits-all, universal arrangement critique. If you want to know what I probably would say about your arrangement, keep reading.

Boring Bass Line

Yes, the bass in most cases needs to hit the tonics of each chord, and, yes, he needs to let notes ring long enough for the upper voices to lock into his tuning. However, if your bass line is boring, your bass will be bored, and that will drag down the overall performance. Instead of a one measure repeated rhythmic figure, how about a four measure phrase? How about some melodic elements as opposed to a string of tonic notes? Perhaps a couple cool fills and stand out moments? Even Atlas was able to hand the earth over to Hercules for a spell.

Clunky Top Voice

Popular arranging isn't 18th century four-part writing, so you can break many of the "rules" you learned in theory class (with good reason, hopefully), but you must always remember that human perception still draws our attention to the highest voice we hear. Whatever that voice is—soprano, first tenor—it's going to be heard as a counter melody. You might have written your background voices and then flipped inversions, but that's not always workable. Write that top background part, then build your harmonies down from the top.

Improper Spacing

There's a reason so many arrangements have the bass down low with the other voices clustered over an octave above: it's because of the harmonic series. This gives your singers a chance to "attach" themselves to the harmonics your bass is casting. There are moments to disregard this voicing, but they're few and far between when you're arranging for live performances. A cappella is hard enough and tuning potentially problematic for many groups.

No Dynamics

Yes, popular music is compressed to death, and you're used to everything being the same volume. However, you're not on the radio. Sound only has four elements: Pitch (which combines to create melody and harmony), duration (which, with silence, becomes rhythm), timbre (all vocal sounds and colors), and loudness (which in contrast becomes dynamics) The best grade you're going to get on this test is a 75% if you eliminate one of the four. Pretty much every song should at least be able to span mezzo piano to forte, and many can (and should) go beyond.

No Build

Moreover, your audience would benefit from all the drama you can provide them, since your lead singer's last name isn't Springsteen. Start small, grow, pull back, build to a climax. Yes, even droning club remixes can be arranged with nuance and direction. A song's shape and growth is more than just dynamics; it's the combination of all of the elements of music reinforcing and underscoring the song's journey.

No Emotional Focus

This might be a result of a lack of emotional focus. Music is communication, and every song has a message, explicit or implicit, that your singers will reinforce. An arrangement is merely a road map which gives a group of singers a set of directions so they know how to collectively take the audience on a journey. If you don't have a feeling when you listen to a song, and you're not clear how and why and when your singers will be directing the audience's emotions, then you shouldn't be arranging this song, as you're handing them a speech without meaning, a movie without a plot.

Not Enough Breaths

And, to make sure they can remain lost in the fog of emotion without passing out, you need to make sure there are enough breaths throughout. Sing each line. If you're still not sure, remember that they're going to be on stage, perhaps nervous, perhaps moving. They'll need more air than you do now.

You're Trying Too Hard

Yes, we all want to be geniuses. But take a step back: you're not curing cancer; you're coming up with the right notes for some singers to share a song with some people. Take a deep breath, and stop trying to make every measure a masterpiece. Sometimes whole notes are exactly what the doctor ordered. Take some risks, have some clever and complicated moments, but don't overdo it. I don't think I can say it better than Steve Martin: "I believe entertainment can aspire to be art, and can become art, but if you set out to make art you're an idiot."

Listen To This

The frustrating thing about arranging is that it never sounds the way you think it will in your head. However, that's your problem, not the singer's problem. You're making a suit for them to wear, as opposed to them sculpting their bodies to fit your fabric. Go to a rehearsal, hear your arrangement, and start custom tailoring it as soon as you hear how it really sounds.

Arrange More

People cook thousands of meals before becoming great chefs. There's no shortcut. You might be on the fast track, with excellent skills and instincts, but you will still benefit from every new group and new song you encounter. I've arranged over 2,000 songs and I'm still learning. Frequency will bring fluency, which will bring an understanding of the inherent potential of the human voice, and, more importantly, your own style.

FUN FACTS

- Pop songstress Sara Bareilles can be heard singing her song "Gravity" with UCLA Awaken on BOCA 2004.
- Doo wop revivalists Sha Na Na was founded by members of the Columbia Kingsmen.
- SoVoSo was initially formed by members of Bobby McFerrin's Voicestra.
- The Real Group took their name from that venerable tome of jazz standards: The Real Book.
- Perhaps the most widely seen barbershop quartet of all time is the Buffalo Bills, featured in the movie *The Music Man.*
- Whether you are in California, Orlando, Hong Kong, or Tokyo, the barbershop quartet on Disney's Main Street is always called The Dapper Dans.
- The soaring Celtic harmonies of Anuna provided a sonic break between frenetic dance numbers in *Riverdance.*
- Pop iconoclast Bjork recorded an all a cappella album *Medulla* in 2004.
- Several of the members of Vox One are faculty members at the Berkelee College of Music in Boston.
- The House Dust is a Japanese tribute band that performs the original music of The House Jacks.
- The first all a cappella group to perform at the Grand Ole Opry was The EDLOS and they were the first to release an all country album *A Cappella Country.*
- Naturally 7 had a #1 radio hit in Germany with solo artist Sarah Connor: "Music Is The Key."
- Bobby McFerrin's "Don't Worry Be Happy" (1988) was the first a cappella track to hit #1 on the Billboard Hot 100.
- All 4 One's first pop hit was an a cappella remake of "So In Love."
- Boyz II Men had two top 40 a cappella hits: "Thank You" and "In The Still of the Night" (remade for *The Jacksons* miniseries).
- Huey Lewis and the News had a big radio hit with their a cappella version of Curtis Mayfield's "It's Alright."
- Richard Greene, founder and bass of The Bobs, recorded voiceovers for many years and is best known for singing the classic "Fall into the Gap." The Bobs is an acronym for "Best of Breed," a term taken from dog shows.

PREPARING AND PERFORMING

Eight Beat Measure

CHAPTER 16

SINGULARITY

By Deke Sharon

A cappella is unique as a performing art in that it is, in essence, the single most concentrated experience of personal expression possible:

- In theater, many people are expressing, but they're playing characters, each with his or her own set of emotions and motives.

- In dance, people express, but their bodies are the primary mode of expression, and as soon as there are more than a couple dancers the movement is highly choreographed, the vision of a single choreographer. Faces are sometimes toward the audience, but often not.

- In instrumental music there are many people expressing, but they're doing it through their instruments, sometimes hidden behind them or hunched over them. As a result, in a band or in a symphonic orchestra, rarely do you have even the majority of musicians looking out at the audience.

- In choral music there are many faces, more than in an a cappella group, but they're bringing to life the conductor's vision, usually looking either at the conductor or at sheet music.

Only in a cappella do you have the most expressive human feature—the face—engaged directly with the audience, each person expressing as themselves. This makes a cappella potentially the most compelling performing art, but only if it is done with a clarity of emotional expression.

For lack of a better term, I'm going to call this "a cappella singularity."

Singularity in a cappella occurs when the entirety of an a cappella group, be it 3 people or 30 people, are all sharing in the same emotional expression. Music is communication, and without a unified message the audience will be confused, distracted, disengaged.

There is no more expressive instrument than the human voice, and there is nothing more compelling than having multiple people express, openly and honestly, in confluence and concord. This can happen naturally, but it would be serendipitous and you should not leave this to chance. A great director, especially one working with young or amateur singers, will navigate this emotional process from song selection through performance.

DECISION

The first step to ensuring singularity of emotional expression is to choose a song that your group can properly and convincingly express. "Still Crazy After All These Years" is a fantastic song, but not for a middle school group. Moreover, your singers might want to sing the #1 song on the pop charts right now, but if it's not a message that you can express, then it would at best only be an exercise in having fun.

That said, don't underestimate the importance of having fun (provided the song's lyric and theme support it). In fact, the joy of singing is one of a cappella's greatest expressions, and is often all the message you need, especially when working with young singers. Choosing a song they love and helping them remain engaged throughout a performance is absolutely a worthy message.

As your group matures and your repertoire expands, "the joy of singing" will likely not be, and you'll want to say more. At this point, make sure that what you want to say is something you believably can say.

DISCUSSION

Once a song is chosen, unless the song's message and theme are incredibly clear (e.g. "Walking on Sunshine"), it's a good idea to take time before you start learning notes to discuss the song's lyric, message, perspective and context. Sometimes the lyric is all you need, sometimes the history of the song is valuable (who wrote it, when it debuted, what it meant at the time), sometimes your group's own situation—as a unit or as individuals—will provide additional insight and grounding. A song is a vehicle for expression—intellectual and emotional—and it's important that you all decide where you're going before you leave.

In some cases this discussion can be brief, when just a few words are needed to ensure everyone understands your collective approach to an obvious song. No need to belabor a point. At other times you will likely want to have your rehearsal become a time of openness and discovery, as you carefully guide your group through a difficult discussion about the loss of loved ones or the failure of relationships. The more you can get your singers to open up and share in the safety of your rehearsal room, the more they will all be able to express as a unit in front of an audience.

There may be tears, but this is the time for tears, as the transference of emotion between your singers creates a powerful shared experience that they can all draw upon when on stage or in the recording studio. I find that it can be very helpful to distill the discussion down to a few key words or a short phrase that encapsulates your newly shared focus, and those words can be recalled just before you perform the song on stage or in front of a microphone, especially in the middle of a set that has many varied emotional messages.

DIRECTION

Every choice you make as a music director should reinforce your group's emotional delivery of the song. Full stop. Nothing matters more.

Too often directors emphasize precision in vocal music, which stands to reason. Instruments are often designed to always be in tune (like a piano) and there's a long tradition in musical education circles to refer to the instrumentalists as "musicians" and the vocalists as "singers," casting the latter as second class. Moreover, there isn't an an experienced a cappella singer alive who hasn't heard "A cappella? You mean singing without music?" This malaprop belies a deeper prejudice against vocal music, and yet we should not allow it to sway us from our course.

Musae

If you have a conservatory degree you might be bothered by music that isn't exacting in its technical precision, but the fact is that almost all listeners choose music based on how it makes them feel. No one goes home and says "I want to listen to the most in-tune piece of music in this house," so you should not fetishize tuning as if it's a measure of your group's ultimate quality. This is not to say that tuning doesn't matter, but rather that it isn't the point. The point is expression and communication, and audiences prefer music sung with compunction and compassion over music sung with precision. As Ben Folds said on the first episode of the *The Sing-Off* (when referring to the Tufts Beelzebubs) that it wasn't perfect but he didn't care, he was making the exact same point: if you can make a listener feel something then they won't care if some of the edges are a bit rough. A passionate speech trumps a perfectly pronounced speech every time.

What does it mean to make choices based on the song's message? There is some interpretation here, based on your singers own technical ability and emotional expressiveness. Will a ballad work best if you start pianissimo? Usually, but not if your group unravels when it's singing that quietly, in which case piano will do just fine. Push your singers to their highest notes when the song's passion peaks, and dial back when appropriate.

To this end, you should definitely be making changes to any arrangement as you go. Arrangements aren't music, they're only a road map, and if you find a better way to your destination, take it.

Of course if a song is a duet/trio/quartet and the lead vocalists are expressing differing or competing messages in the process of the greater whole, that's as it should be (e.g. the '80s pop tune "Don't You Want Me Baby" or "Quartet" from *West Side Story*). The expression is complimentary, three dimensional, sides of the same coin.

While in rehearsal there will be times you stop and work on specific notes and chords, at which time you can loosen the emotional reigns, but once you start singing longer passages you should insist on emotion. Just as learning a song's dynamics as you learn the notes, so should you "learn" the emotion as well. It may not be easy, but the challenge of your singers repeatedly finding emotional honestly and expression is essential. This is a "muscle" they likely haven't spent much time exercising, but exercise it they must, as it needs to be strong and reliable upon performance. Like actors, without emotional focus their lines will be empty, hollow, pointless.

MOVEMENT

As in the medical profession, "First, do no harm."

Lest you think that every a cappella performance needs elaborate choreography, the most powerful and effective ICCA finals set I've ever seen was by Stanford Talisman in the mid-90s. The other groups ran around the stage energetically whereas Talisman walked out on stage, stood in an arc, and sang songs from the African Diaspora beautifully from the heart. In a way, they appeared as the adults, casting the other groups as children, as their collective honesty and clarity was both mature and timeless.

This is not to say that choreography is a hinderance, and when well used, especially in uptempo songs, it can reinforce the song's mood and message. If you're having fun, have fun! If you're being funky, be funky. Just as with the musical elements of your performance, take your cues from the song's emotion, and make sure every choice reinforces and underlines your message.

Just as with your musical choices, make sure your choreography is not only within their range of expression, but also doesn't distract or pull them away from the mission at hand. If they're focused too hard on being in the right place or staying in sync while executing a step their faces go to blank and work against your ultimate goal.

SYNTHESIS

You may be thinking "this is a complicated process" and you'd be right. You need to identify a song that will work, guide your group through the process of emotional discovery, make choices about the musical elements from this emotional perspective and insist your singers repeatedly deliver on the promise of the song emotionally, but when you do the end result will be nothing short of breathtaking.

Many a cappella groups have a couple of singers who "get it" every time, but that's not good enough. We're not satisfied with a couple bright lights in a string of dim or burned out bulbs. We want every face to be alive, every person committed to delivering the same unified message/feeling/experience to the audience.

Audiences are used to glam, glitz and glitter. Show business has become about creating spectacle instead of creating moments, and that is in part why a cappella is so popular now. Don't worry that you don't have huge projection screens or high tech bells and whistles because you have heart, and heart is what draws us all to the arts in the first place. We want to feel. Make people feel.

I'll leave you with my favorite Aesop's fable, one that I think best summarizes this principle: The Wind and the Sun made a bet that they could remove a man's coat. The wind went first, blowing and blustering, and yet everything he did left the man clutching his coat even tighter. Then the Sun came out from behind the clouds, gently shone on the man, and he took his coat off himself.

Be the Sun.

"I think there are rock stars within every subgenre, and for people who are obsessed with musical theater Sutton Foster and Audra MacDonald are like Beyoncé to them. I'm sure the a cappella world has their own version of that, and that exists in every geeky subculture."

— Anna Kendrick

"With the a cappella groups, every voice is like one string on a guitar, one note on the piano, or one cymbal, and you don't have the luxury of falling back on anything."

— Ben Folds

Cape Harmony

CHAPTER 17
EFFECTIVE WARM-UPS

By J.D. Frizzell

Every warm up routine should address the following:

1. Breathing

2. Phonation

3. Articulations

4. Dynamics

5. Range Extension

6. Intonation

7. Blend and Balance

I usually place my warm ups in this order, placing an attention-getter at the front and a smooth transition into sight-reading, theory, or the music to be rehearsed on the back end.

Well-planned and varied warm ups are essential to building an a cappella ensemble. Directors must be careful not to choose the same exercises every day without regard to the music to be sung or the current strengths and weaknesses of the singers.

My Favorite Attention-Getters:

Squash:

The director begins by performing a 4 beat pattern of one kinesthetic gesture. This can be clapping, snapping, patting your head, etc. The singers are instructed to be one movement behind the director (i.e. the director starts, then the singers start 4 beats thereafter). As the activity goes on, the director should increase the level of difficulty for by increasing the tempo, adding concurrent sounds like buzzing, sirens, animal noises, etc. Towards the end of the exercise, incorporate low, full breaths to provide a quick and seamless transition into stage 1—breathing.

Key to success: Start slowly and simply, like clapping quarter notes.

Dance Jam:

This is for the groggy, low energy Monday or the reward on Friday of a great week of rehearsing. The director plays an up-tempo song over speakers and begins leading a dance. The singers are instructed to mirror the director. Then, at some point, the director leaves the front and gets a volunteer to lead the dancing. When a singer is out of ideas or energy, she can leave the front and another singer must quickly take her place. I usually set a countdown rule wherein if someone doesn't replace the leader within 5 seconds, the game ends.

Key to success: Make sure the song is appropriate and be ready to quickly transition to avoid lack of focus.

Breathing

In for Four:

Have the singers place their hands at the bottom of their ribs, touching the thumbs to the ribs and the rest of the fingers on the stomach. Starting with a low, full diaphragmatic breath, inhale and gradually open up your hands. Exhale, pulling hands back towards the body. Then, say "In for four" and breathe in for four beats. Then say "Out for four" and exhale with the singers. Repeat this process in time without breaks, changing to "out for eight", "out for twelve", etc. I usually go up to sixteen or twenty. For variety, you can exhale on a hiss.

Key to success: Model well with your own breathing and keep a steady, moderate tempo.

Phonation

The Easy Open:

This warm up is great place to start. It has a three note range, improves unison tuning, and develops proper vowel placement. I choose different vowels on different days based on the literature I'm teaching. Often, I'll start with a closed hum. In addition, I will have students put a cup shaped hand on the side of their face to emulate resonating space.

Keys to success: Start at a B, C, or C sharp and don't go up past an initial note of A or A sharp.

The Placement Helper:

I often find that as I teach private voice lessons, brighter vowels like "Eee" are much easier for singers to place in a forward position with a raised soft palate. By combining a bright vowel with a closed mouth shape, the focus turns to the onset of the vowel each time. The end of the warm up exercise attempt is designed to transfer the placement of the brighter vowel to the darker one.

Key to success: Again, keep the key moderate—start at C sharp and end on F or G.

Articulation

The Hot Stove:

This is one of the best warm ups out there in my opinion, because it does so much at once. I first saw it in rehearsal with my choral mentor, Dr. Jeff Johnson at The University of Kentucky. Start by placing one hand palm up in front of you and start to lightly tap it with a finger of your other hand. Say, "Hot stove!" as you show the lightness and quickness with which you pull your finger away from your hand. Then you alternate to tapping the other hand, switching back and forth each time. Then sing this pattern:

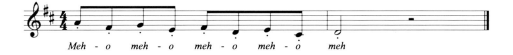

You can then change the articulation to legato by making your hands flat and change your alternation of hands to a smooth one. You can even alter the tempo and dynamics by going faster or slower and increasing or decreasing the size of your gesture. You can also add accents by using a big gesture on one beat followed by small gestures immediately after.

Key to success: Keep a moderate tempo and don't get too big with your gesture size.

Dynamics

One to Eight:

Place your hands together like a clap, directly in front of you. Build a chord, then start singing 1,2,3,4,5,6,7,8 as you expand your hands outward. Start at pianissimo at 1 and build to fortissimo at 8, then reverse the process.

Key to success: Make the singers do the kinesthetic gesture, too.

Range Extension

The Lip or Tongue Trill:

Slide up a perfect 5th and back down on a lip trill or (more advanced) tongue trill. Another benefit of this exercise is that it is not easy to do without substantial breath support. I'll often reinforce that support by having singers use the rib hand open and close from the "In for Four" warm up. This is also great for very quickly warming up your voice.

Key to success: Start in the middle of the range, B or C.

Zee Yah:

This extends the range without letting singers push their voices.

Key to success: When modeling the exercise, be sure to keep a light tone.

Intonation and Blend and Balance
(These can usually be done together)

Build A Chord, Any Chord:

Build a major chord that works for your particular voicing. For SATB groups, for example, I find that Basses on C sharp, Tenors on G sharp, Altos on C sharp, and sopranos on E sharp works well. For TTBB, C sharp for B2, D sharp for B1, E sharp for T2, and G sharp for T1. For SSA, C sharp for A, G sharp for S2, and E sharp for S1. Sing the chord on any open vowel. I usually begin with a closed vowel like "Oo" so singers can hear better. Instruct them to hold the chord, stagger breathing when necessary, and then point up and have them all go up a half step. Once that has tuned, go back down a half step. Then go down a half step and back up to the original chord. As your singers get better at this, isolate individual sections and move them around by half step.

Keys to success: Plan where you are going in advance to ensure success (i.e. don't end on a "weird" chord that doesn't sound "right").

Half Step Over Counts:

Point your two index fingers horizontally in front of you at each other. Sing a G on "loo." Then raise one hand up higher, maintaining a horizontal plane for your index finger, and sing a G sharp. Then go back down to G and even fingers. Have the singers repeat this process. Then, quickly slide your finger up and back down, sliding the note you sing from G to G sharp. Then go back down. Have singers repeat. As they get better at tuning, increase the difficulty by sliding through the half step over 2 beats, then 4 beats, then 6 beats, then 8 beats.

Key to success: Don't move on to a higher number of beats before singers can really do well where they currently are.

This is a small selection of the warm up exercises I use. Make sure you learn new ones all the time and keep them written down to provide variety and utility in rehearsals.

A CAPPELLA TV THEME SONGS AND COMMERCIALS

- Bobby McFerrin performed an a cappella version of the theme song for the opening credits of Season 4 of *The Cosby Show* in 1987.

- Rockapella sang the theme song from *Where In The World Is Carmen Sandiego?*

- The theme songs to *Mighty Mouse Playhouse* and *Mighty Mouse: The New Adventures* were both a cappella.

- In 2009, Toyota commissioned Petra Haden to perform three songs for television commercials for the third-generation Toyota Prius, including an a cappella version of the Bellamy Brothers 1970s song "Let Your Love Flow."

- Rockapella performed a Folgers commercial with the catchy jingle "The best part of waking up is Folgers in your cup!"

- Rhett Miller and the Old 97's performed the Chili's "Baby Back Ribs" a cappella jingle.

- Bobby McFerrin sang the music for a Cadbury chocolate commercial using the song "Thinking About Your Body" and substituting the word "chocolate" for "body."

- Rockapella was featured in a Taco Bell commercial in 1991 performing a song called "Rock Art Cups" advertising for cups featuring the artists MC Hammer, Bel Biv Devoe, George Michael, Diana Ross, and Scorpions.

- The House Jacks sang the "Monday Night Football Theme" with Hank Williams, Jr. for the 2011–2012 NFL season.

Ben Bram, A Cappella Academy

CHAPTER 18
TIPS, TIPS, TIPS!

Tips for Healthy Singing

Those who sing a cappella music must be aware of their instrument: their voice. We each only get one voice. The upside is that every person has a unique sound. The downside is that if we fail to care for our voice, we won't get another. In order to make sure you are taking good care of your instrument, remember the following common pitfalls and how to avoid them.

- Overuse/abuse of the *speaking* voice (your singing voice is the same voice, after all)

  ▷ Do not talk "on your fry" (that lazy, gravelly sound that Ke$ha made famous). Make sure you speak with a clear tone.

  ▷ Avoid the strain of talking over loud noises. Get closer to the listener or shut off any ambient sounds (like the radio or TV) if needed.

  ▷ Watch the sheer volume of speaking you do in a day. We all have to talk at school or work, on the phone, at home, etc. Watch your speech patterns and see where you can curb the amount of talking you do each day. Maybe some communication can be shifted to notes or email.

  ▷ Avoid screaming when at ball games, public events, etc. Screaming really taxes the voice. Consider a loud whistle and/or clapping instead.

- Overuse/abuse of the *singing* voice

  ▷ Don't sing too much. Singing is fun, and getting better requires practice. However, you can sing too much. There are physical limits, so when you feel fatigued, back off.

  ▷ Singing in the car can be bad, as there is so much road noise that we often oversing to hear ourselves. Our driving posture is also not conducive to good support.

  ▷ Don't sing outside your natural range. If you like a song and it's too high/low, change the key or pick another tune! If you are working on an especially high passage, give it time to work into your voice. Slamming high notes over and over won't do anything but wear you out.

▷ Sing without tension (well, without **bad** tension). You need to have tension in your breath mechanism to move enough air for singing. Tension in the shoulders, neck, jaw, etc. is not good. The muscles used to change pitch in the voice are not those on the outside of your neck. If you feel tightness, that's wrong.

▷ Don't oversing. Singing too loudly for too long can wear you out. If you have a microphone/sound system, let it do the work! Sing well and let the speakers fill the house.

• Dehydration – your body needs water to make the thin mucous that lubricates your vocal cords

▷ Drink water throughout the day. Take the number of pounds you weigh, and divide that in half. That's the number of ounces of water you should drink each day.

▷ Avoid habitual over-indulging in caffeinated or alcoholic drinks. A cup of coffee in the morning or a glass of wine at night is fine. Just make sure to increase your water intake to offset the diuretic effects.

▷ Voice teachers preach sayings like "pee pale" or "pee white, sing right." Your urine should be light in color or clear if you are fully hydrated.

• Lack of sleep

▷ Not much to say about this one except . . . get enough sleep! Sometimes you just have to put Netflix aside and hit the sheets. Tired bodies don't perform as well as rested ones.

▷ Remember that your body uses sleep time to repair itself—something we all need.

• Illness – even the common cold can affect your instrument

▷ When sick, your body will most likely thicken all of its mucous. This not only leads to a stuffy nose, but provides less lubrication for your vocal cords.

▷ Avoid clearing your throat! Coughing.

GOOD HABIT CHECKLIST

• Stay hydrated

• Get appropriate sleep

• Monitor your talking throughout the day to avoid overuse or strain

• Be mindful of your singing—don't abuse your voice oversinging or by singing out of range

• When fatigued or ill, don't whisper or talk on your fry—support, talk higher in pitch, and maintain vocal rest as much as possible

General Performance Tips

Any list of performance tips will have exceptions, just as you can find an exception to every rule. However, there are time-tested practices that have proven valuable for the vast majority of contemporary a cappella groups:

- Like a great actor doing eight shows a week on Broadway, you must experience your performance as something that's fresh, new, happening for the first time. Don't let the audience see any exhaustion, boredom or "auto pilot."

- Unless you're a choir, introduce the members of your ensemble to the audience throughout the show.

- During a performance try to find a way to show the range of your abilities—as individual singers and as a group. Show off special talents, set soloists up to sing their best songs, make everyone look their best and show variety so that the audience leaves impressed both by everyone's individual skill as well as your collective versatility.

- Have a core positioning on stage and build your stage pictures and choreography around that. Should a stage or radio station or other performing space be too small, you can always revert back to your core stance and know you'll sound good and everyone will be comfortable.

- Regarding your appearance: make sure your wardrobe and grooming fit your name, image and style. There's always room for variety but within your group there should be a clearly defined visual presentation to reinforce the musical one.

- If you're not dancers, don't dance. Much can be done with simple stage pictures and basic blocking.

- When constructing your set, start with a song that defines who you are—one of your best—then slowly increase the variety after establishing your core. Vary tempos and soloists, as juxtaposition creates energy and keeps the audience's attention. And save your best song for last, with one more great song up your sleeve if you get an encore.

- Only take an encore if it's genuine. Sometimes a show doesn't need one, and the audience is done after the last song. That's not a failure. Always better to leave people wanting more.

- When singing a background part, focus on and follow the soloist's lead. Make sure you're not upstaging him or her but rather supporting the mood, the lyrics, the energy.

- Believe in what you're doing. For instance, the difference between a tired joke or a gimmick and a successful show moment is in the delivery and the conviction. If you don't believe in what you're doing, do something else.

- Find a way to get the audience involved in your performance. People will want to clap along and sing along, but you have to find a safe and inviting way to bring them out of their shells and make them feel comfortable joining you.

- When a song is finished, hold the moment. Too many amateur groups immediately move into their next position, the soloists turning his back and shuffling back into the formation. You just shared something with the crowd. Let the moment linger, and let them show their appreciation.

- Never apologize on stage for mistakes. No one is perfect and the audience doesn't expect you to be. However, when you draw attention to an error, you're amplifying it. In fact, many people might have missed it. Audiences don't experience music the way performers do, and they don't know your arrangement they way you do. Let it go, move on, people will forget.

- Be sure to announce your web site, your social media sites, upcoming shows, albums and merchandise for sale. Ideally you would do this just before your last song so people are thinking about it as soon as you leave the stage.

- Be yourself. Granted, every performer is an amplified, exaggerated version of him or herself on stage, but there must be a kernel of truth behind each performance to

Tips for Achieving Blend

Like the Blue Angels flying in perfect formation, a group with a tight blend maneuvers through chords with a precision that borders on super-human.

The four elements of sound are at the foundation of a good blend:

Pitch

- If you've ever been in a choral rehearsal you know that pitch is probably the single most discussed element of any vocal performance. As soon as you have two singers on a single note you need to make sure they agree on the exact pitch or else their wave forms will create "beats." You can make sure your singers are aware of how this feels by having one of them hold a note as you start in unison and slowly slide up or down.

- Scooping up or down to a note (like a pop singer) can be ok if everyone does it precisely the same way. You don't want to remove all pop stylings from a pop melody or else your group will sound wooden. Just make sure they're agreed upon and consistent.

- Make sure vibrato is not undermining the tightness of your tuning. Whereas as little bit of vibrato "spinning" at the end of a long held note can be pleasing, if it's consistent and wide (like a operatic soloist) your choir might sound big but they won't sound tight. Straight tone singing should be your default technique.

- Once you've conquered unisons, lock your intervals, remembering that a piano is not in perfect tune. (if you aren't familiar with the compromises made to our 12 step system, search for "well-tempered tuning" or "well tempered" online.) Strive to lock your intervals cleanly so you hear overtones; the barbershop tradition reveres "ringing" chords so their organizations are a great source of tips and best practices.

Timbre

- Most instruments have a limited range of timbres, whereas the human voice is almost unlimited in it's timbral variety. To that end, we need to make sure our voices are all singing the same vowel (each of which has a different set of emphasized overtones). Listen to each singer's "oo" one at a time and identify whose vowel is brighter, taller, rounder, tighter (and so on) and find a tone that everyone can match. Do the same for your other core vowel sounds, and return to this exercise when you're hearing your singers disagree on a vowel. Only siblings match vowels and diphthongs effortlessly.

- Beyond simple vowels, the English language is filled with diphthongs, and truly great blend requires your singers to move through vowel changes together as well. Even a word as simple as "I" could need your attention, as it morphs from "ah" to "ee" or "low" as it moves from "oh" to "oo."

Loudness

- A chord can sound out of tune simply because the chord tones aren't balanced properly. If you're skeptical, have your singers sing a chord as you bring up and down the volume of different chord tones: the more complex the chord, the more fragile it's apparent tuning. Just as in a recipe, vocal blend requires the right amount of the right ingredients.

- For most harmonies, the tonic of the chord should be loudest, followed by the fifth and the third, with the seventh and other color notes quieter, especially if they're next to/in seconds with another core chord tone. Obviously the ratio of the notes and the number of singers you have on each note matters, so if the tonic is doubled at the octave, or you have twice as many sopranos as tenors, adjust accordingly (a good arrangement will have set you up for proper doublings and the like so hopefully any tweaking along these lines is minimal).

- Caveat: obviously the melody should always be predominant, so don't worry about balancing it against the other chord factors unless you're dealing with a close voiced homophonic piece, in which case the melody might occasionally need to back off a bit so as to not overwhelm a chord.

Duration

- Less important than the other three elements, duration is not entirely moot, as a group with sloppy attacks or uneven cutoffs will not sound tight. Before learning a piece of music figure out where everyone will breathe (if it's not apparent), and give longer chords a chance to ring. No piece of music is in perfect tune throughout, and much as a gymnast is criticized for a poor landing so will your group be if you're not ringing your big final chords.

Tips for Soloists

There's no one path to turning a solo into a great performance. Here are a few tips to help you on your way:

- Learn about and understand the song from all angles: the melodic shape, the harmonic progression, the lyrical nuances, the emotional core, the song's history, context, previous versions. Together these will help you make good choices about how to make the song your own.

- Consider creating a short phrase—just a few words—that summarizes your interpretation and direction of the song. Use that phrase to help trigger the appropriate emotion while you're on stage or in front of the microphone in the studio.

- Sing the song often—in different locations, in different moods, at different times of day—to see where your voice and sensibilities change.

- Play with different keys, tempos, harmonic changes, to make sure you have the right one for your voice and your interpretation of the song.

- Record yourself singing, live and/or in the studio, and listen to your performance both technically (tuning, phrasing) and experientially (emotion, feel) as well as watch yourself (look for tics, best moments, facial expressions, etc)

- If you plan to deviate from the original melody of the song (to do runs, add flashy high/low notes, etc.), do so more and more as the song develops. Don't use every trick in the book on the first chorus. Let the progression happen organically.

- If there's an improvisatory section (scat solo, vocal/instrumental solo), play with ideas in rehearsal, come up with a core shape, then build upon it live taking greater risks as you become more comfortable with the song.

- Make sure the movements you make in a song fit the mood, then commit to them (hesitation or half-hearted choreography can overwhelm your intended message and mood)

- Do not look at the floor or ceiling—sing to people in the audience, your fellow singers, or in rare cases a chosen spot in the distance.

- If you make a mistake, do not think about it—recover as soon as possible then throw yourself back into the mood of the song.

- Don't hesitate to sing with a lot of character; a cappella singers are trained to blend whereas a solo needs to stand out and draw attention.

- Just as actors are "in the moment" during a great performance, work on remaining focused and present while singing, and do your best to avoid "auto pilot".

- Remember that you have everyone's attention. That's a powerful situation. And remember that a stage is an amplifier or energy. Don't give a living room performance while you're in the spotlight.

- Don't try to copy the original artist. No one can be a better Whitney Houston than Whitney Houston, so don't try. Study, learn, and draw inspiration from others, but then sing with your own voice. Voices are like snowflakes: no two are alike! Therefore, no one can be a better you than YOU.

Don't forget to have fun! Unless it's a very serious or sad song, infuse each performance with your love of singing. That joy is one of the most compelling aspects of a cappella

Daughters of Triton

Semiscon Vocal Band

CHAPTER 19

MOVEMENT

Throughout history, each style of a cappella has had its own characteristic positioning on stage, be it the tight rows of a chapel choir, the "park and bark" on risers of choral music, the jubilant sway of gospel, the shoulder-to-shoulder barbershop wedge, doo wop's synchronous moves behind the lead singer, or the full dance moves of contemporary a cappella, as seen on *The Sing-Off* and *Pitch Perfect*. This chapter will help you find the proper placement and proximity on stage, married with the right level of movement for your singers.

Establish a common vocabulary

In order for movement plans to be properly taught and executed, it is important that your group members share an understanding of terms. The most common are:

- *Stage Left* – The performer's left-side stage area
- *Center Stage* – The center area of the stage
- *Stage Right* – The performer's right-side stage area
- *Downstage* – The "front" of the stage, closer to the audience
- *Upstage* – The "back" of the stage, farther from the audience
- *Outside* – refers to the area away from center stage. A singer's outside arm is their left arm if they are stage left, their right arm if they are stage right.
- *Inside* – refers to the area towards center stage. A singer's inside arm is their right arm if they are stage left, their left arm if they are stage right.
- *Reference position* – this is generally your "default" position, in which all singers are slightly angled toward center, as if making a subtle rainbow. This allows the singers to see the audience and still see each other.
- *Down the Tiles* – imagine you are in a room with a tile floor. "Down the Tiles" means that you face out so that your shoulders are perpendicular to the back wall. You are completely facing straight-on to the audience with no curve. A straight line of singers across the front of the stage would be considered facing "Down the Tiles."

Proximity and Shape

When considering the appropriate level of movement for your group, you'd be wise to heed the advice of the medical profession: "First, do no harm." There are myriad ways you can make a mess of your group's sound by simply placing your singers in the wrong formation.

First and foremost, your singers need to be able to hear each other. This can be especially problematic with young and inexperienced singers when moving from the safety of your rehearsal space where they are likely facing each other (and have a piano as a safety net) to a concert venue where they're facing the audience.

In the absence of other mitigating factors, we suggest:

- Keep your singers close together (no more than the width of one person in between).
- Place your bass singer(s) in the middle of the back row, making it easiest for all other singers to hear them.
- Place your singers in rows if you have more than eight people, with the back row(s) offset, so they can see between the members of the front row.
- Arc the line, so the people on the far ends can make eye contact with each other.
- Place the director on one end of the group, so he/she can cue when needed and even step to the middle if absolutely necessary. In this position, the director can spend the majority of the performance facing outward and focusing on performing instead of directing.

There are exceptions to all of the above, but for the most part these principles have proven themselves over time.

The proximity of singers is essential, so they can hear the sound coming from each other directly, over the sound that is bouncing off the walls. This will help both tuning and timing and is still helpful even when your group is singing with microphones and monitors. The one exception is if your group is using in-ear monitors, which applies to a very small percentage of professional groups, all of whom initially learned to listen and tune acoustically.

Ideally, your group will tune from the bottom up. The bass singers are likely the quietest of all the vocal lines, especially as an arrangement progresses and they're called upon to sing lower and lower in their range, getting quieter as they go. In contrast, the upper voices are all moving higher and higher, which forces them to sing louder. Luckily the basses are likely among the tallest members of the group, so it's not awkward to place them in the back row.

Additionally, when mixing recorded a cappella, the bass is usually treated as a unit, and is often reduced to a single track. Even when recording a collegiate a cappella group with a bass section, often only one voice is used, akin to a single bass guitar in a rock band. All of the other background textures (except for vocal percussion) are usually doubled. To this end, you can spread the sopranos, altos and tenors on both sides of the basses, giving your group a full, warm "chorusing effect," while the grounding bass line comes straight up the middle, just like a well mixed stereo recording.

As you know from weddings, clubs and fraternity parties, an empty dance floor is an awkward place— most people do not feel comfortable moving in such an exposed environment. The same goes for an a cappella group. If you have fifteen singers spread out in a single line, you'll likely see a measure of discomfort as they sing an up-tempo song: they will want to move but won't want to draw too much attention to themselves for fear they'll look out of place. This can be solved by placing them in two rows: seven in the front and eight in the back. Or, better yet, a deep arc of six in the front and nine in the back with a bigger space in front of the directors, who will be on the end in the back row. This "double U" is a very popular and effective formation for college groups, who then feel much more comfortable bobbing, dancing, and generally moving around to the music as they sing, just as one would be more comfortable dancing on a crowded dance floor. Plus, in such a tight formation, they'll all be able to hear each other very well.

This double arc is most effective if it's deep <u>and</u> if there is a clear sightline between the opposing sides of the group. This minimizes the potential for people on the ends to be either out of tune or out of rhythm with the singers on the far side. Just as importantly, it allows for great moments of eye contact and connection between singers. The greatest enemy on stage is "auto-pilot," the tendency for singers to lose focus and let their mind wander while they sing with vacant eyes and no emotion. Eye contact is the best antidote to auto pilot, as it allows for the singers to constantly engage each other, and then turn their focus and share that energy with the audience.

Falconize

Choral music often requires a director, who is facing the singers with her back to the audience. This tradition follows that of the classical orchestral idiom, with the conductor helping the ensemble navigate difficult tempo changes while providing a dynamic emotional narrative. However, chamber ensembles usually don't require a conductor, save for a countoff and cutoff from the pianist or violinist. Popular music in general does not have a conductor. As the director, get out of the way of your group as much as possible.

Why? Because a cappella is one of the most powerful forms of communication, and when there's a director standing in front of the group, the singers usually focus on that person instead of singing to the audience. Also, there's sometimes a lack of ownership on the part of the singers (which is exacerbated by the presence of sheet music on stage, which you should also avoid), who are followers more than leaders, infantry more than elite soldiers. You want every single set of eyes to be as engaged and engaging as possible, including your own if you're singing with the group. And you want to connect with the audience in the most powerful and emotional means possible, be the emotion joy, sorrow or reverence. Even classical a cappella groups such as the King's Singers and Chanticleer do not have their director stand with his back to the audience.

Staging

Although it won't be appropriate for all venues, it is generally a good idea to vary your group's formation during the course of a show.

Staging is as good a term as any for the general position of your group on stage, absent any specific movement or choreography, and should be considered even if you're not planning any unified movement during your songs. Some options include:

- Have your group enter or leave the performance space singing. This can be a simple song, a chant, or a repeated chorus.

- If appropriate to the music, break the ensemble into two or more sections, with them singing back and forth to/at each other

- Vary your position on stage. For instance, for a ballad, consider having the soloist stand downstage left with the other singers upstage right in an arc, to create more of a focus and sense of isolation for your lead singer, emphasizing the character of a heartfelt lyric.

- For a song without a soloist where the sections carry the melodic lines, consider grouping the sections together. For instance, all sopranos together on the left side. This way they can sing as a unit.

- Use the natural levels and characteristics of your performing space, be they steps up to a podium, a second floor balcony, etc. Vary the positioning as your venue varies. If the venue has no available levels, or if you just want more variety in your visual plan, you could also:

  ▷ Go down on one knee

  ▷ Go down on both knees

- ▷ Crouch

- ▷ Put one foot up on a stool or monitor

- ▷ Jump

- ▷ "Lay back" so that your weight sinks into your hips, making you slightly shorter

- ▷ Bend at the waist, then rise back to standing over a certain amount of counts

- Create shapes that emphasize a song's lyrics and mood. For instance, an inverted V could work for a song of isolation, or a straight line across the front of the stage for a song where every group member sings lyrics in a personal way. Remember these guidelines:

  - ▷ Louder, faster sections lend themselves to spreading out and coming downstage toward the audience

  - ▷ Softer, more intimate passages lend themselves to a tighter position that is more center stage and/or upstage

  - ▷ Singers who are linked with similar instruments should often stand together. You might have a "horn line" of singers together in one area, rhythm section (bass and drums) in another and the soloist up front. When the "instrumentation" changes, your position can change, too.

There are no rules, and few limitations beyond the need for your singers to hear each other. Set aside time before each performance during sound check to maximize your use of space, adjusting as needed.

Blocking

You might consider some unified movement during a song, especially if you're singing any up-tempo songs and/or popular music. How much movement should you consider? Well, that depends on several factors:

- the style of music

- audience expectation

- the movement ability and comfort of your singers

- the amount movement effects their ability to sing well

- the appropriateness of movement in small groups

Every style of music carries with it a collection of images, gathered from concerts, movies and music videos. Before making any decisions you should acquaint yourself with the artist and the song, if you haven't already.

There's a level of expectation that comes with singing certain popular music, especially dance music. If you sing "The Charleston" and nobody does the Charleston at any point during your performance, the audience will feel cheated. The same also goes for Michael Jackson's "Thriller," unless your arrangement has significantly changed the style and feel and even then people will likely want to see an appearance by some dancing zombies.

Before deciding exactly how you'll incorporate movement, you should assess your singers' ability to move while they sing. This can be done in rehearsal. Try swaying during a song or a simple step-touch move with the group standing in lines or in a circle. Everyone can move to some degree, but it might take a little practice to ingrain movement with the music in your less dexterous singers.

You might assume that movement will diminish your group's musical ability, but sometimes the reverse is true. A simple side-to-side movement or clapping can bring a gospel song to life and unify your singers' rhythmic accuracy. Stomping and clapping during "We Will Rock You" will likely increase your singers' energy and tone. Some songs can sound too "perfect" and want to have a little yell in them.

Almost every ensemble will have some singers who are more comfortable moving than others. To this end, it's sometimes best to have a select group step forward and dance, be it a gentle pas de deux during a love song, some stepping during a rhythmic R&B song, or a full dance break where some of your singers stop singing and dance, while the others provide a rhythmic bed.

You might want to utilize a choreographer to help you with blocking, or you may find plenty of creativity and aptitude within your own ranks. Remember, the goal is not necessarily to find the highest level of complexity at all times, but rather to find the right mix of moments, where movement accents and supports your performance without distracting or diminishing your musicality.

The Suspensions

Choreography

Although it's definitely not for all groups, there may be a time and a place for a fully choreographed number in your set. If you're not planning to do much dancing throughout the show, it's best to save your biggest movement for the closing number or encore, so that you don't have to follow it with a less impressive performance. It also means your singers will not spend the next song panting.

Unless you have an experienced choreographer in your ranks, you're best bet is to bring in someone from the outside and have them create something for your group. Make it clear to the choreographer how much experience your group has with dancing while singing and be sure that this person understands that the music comes first in a cappella. No one wants to hear a group sing while they're out of breath.

Alas there's no comprehensive checklist that we can provide, even having worked on hundreds of choreographed live a cappella performances on *The Sing-Off* with over 50 groups, as every group is very different in their flexibility, comfort and ability to integrate. However, we have seen a few common threads:

- Be sure to leave some "cushion" and not require movement to the outer limits of singers' abilities, as they'll likely be nervous during the performance, which will leave them with less oxygen during every breath.

- Make sure the movement compliments the music as opposed to stand in opposition. If everyone sings an anticipated note, it's likely not best to have them step on the following downbeat. Marry movement to music.

- This will sometimes mean different parts should physically move at different times, along with the music. Mold the choreography around the individual vocal lines when appropriate

- Vocal percussion and bass are sometimes too busy to allow for much movement. If so, have them stand off to the side as "the band" with any other similarly complex parts.

- The choreographic process will require some trial and error. Leave time for this, over more than one rehearsal period. Adjust as needed. If you feel stuck while rehearsing, ask the singers to try some moves of their own. You'll often find one singer who comes up with great stuff the others can copy. Similarly, you might find that many singers have certain movement patterns in common. Finding what the singers instinctively do, then enhancing that (rather than creating arbitrary choreography) will keep them looking natural on stage. It will also help them remember the plan better and feel great that they contributed.

- Always be aware of the positioning of singers (and monitors, if you're using them), reminding the choreographer that hearing the other voices is never optional.

- Listen to your singer's perspective. Some people need to be pushed before they realize what they're capable of physically, but after a few repetitions if something is too challenging or too taxing on the voice, it's better to simplify initially then expand as your singers are more comfortable and experienced.

- Unless a song is very serious, have fun. Often the reason people have come to see your group is not only to hear interpretations of various songs, but also experience the unique interconnectedness of a vocal ensemble, and the fun you have singing is often the most compelling aspect. That's a large part of why people love watching collegiate a cappella groups. Make sure the choreography doesn't take itself too seriously, embracing and reflecting the fun you're having singing.

Not every choreographer "gets it." Some expect too much of singers, others have difficulty letting the movement take a back seat to the music. However, many choreographers have a sensitivity to musical nuance and some are singers themselves. Work with different people until you find a great fit, and then build an ongoing relationship between your group and that person. They're worth their weight in gold.

Visual Rehearsal Tips

Now that you have some tools to begin crafting your visual plan, here are some ways to hone your product.

Video Review

Just like football players watch films, we should watch our performances. Either one song at a time, or sometimes a whole set (for flow, talking, singing, and visual elements) the video review is invaluable. Watch a performance and take notes. Have each singer share with the group one thing that looked great and one thing that needs improvement. Aren't we all our own worst critics?

Another video review tip is called *fast-forward*. Start the performance you wish to review, then put the playback on fast-forward. You'll either see the singers moving around the stage, changing positions, using their arms to create interest or you'll see a bunch of people who look like they are vibrating in place. If it becomes boring on fast-forward, why wouldn't it be boring in real time?

Imagineering

Once the plan is in place, there's great value in *imagineering*. This can be done in rehearsal or at home (or both). The goal is to have the entire group close their eyes and picture themselves on stage. Literally blow the pitch so everyone is imagineering in the right key. Tell them that they are to imagine (silently) the entire performance from start to finish. They should see all the visual plan happening perfectly. They should hear every sound perfectly in tune. How many singers were done at the same time? This process allows us to plant the seeds of perfect performance in our minds. If we can see it, if we can believe it—we can achieve it.

Silent Runs

Get on stage. Blow the pitch. Start the song . . . with no singing. Every singer must "mouth it" as if they are singing along with a track. Every move should be made. Replicate the performance as if someone is watching it on mute. When the singing is gone, the performance goes up. Immediately following the silent run, do it again with the same visual intensity, only adding the singing. This not only helps visuals, but helps timekeeping as well.

Still Shots

With today's digital cameras, this one is easier than ever. Run your song (or set), with an outside "helper" snapping one or two photos during each section of the performance. Immediately print the photos, then present them to the group to put in chronological order. Can it be done easily, or do all the pictures look roughly the same? Your visual plan needs variety, and this trick can force the issue.

One Man Out

Every so often, pick a singer to sit out in the audience for a performance. Not only will they be able to give some immediate feedback, they might be able to address some issues outside rehearsal in a more casual setting. Singers often "think they're doing it" until someone other than the music director says, "You're really not doing it," or "I see you trying, but it needs to be much bigger."

Two Crucial Concepts to Remember

#1 Break It All Down and Have Patience

It is important to remember that once your plan is in place, it must be polished until it sparkles. This will require a lot of attention to detail and tons of patience. Ultimately, you'll decide how clean is "clean enough," but remember that everything needs attention. Body posture, foot position, arm angles, head position, eye focus, and spatial relationships on stage are all items that need cleaning. You will need to isolate and examine each move beat by beat to make sure they all match. While this will take a lot of time, remember that as your singers grow more and more accustomed to this level of visual cleanliness, they will soon self-correct. As they grow as aware performers, the time required to clean their moves will lessen. Your group will also develop good visual instincts that will enhance any performance.

#2 Every Move Needs a Motivation

Every move must have a purpose that is motivated by the music. If your singers are merely executing choreography because someone said to do it, they will always look stilted and flat. Singers who move with purpose in order to express an emotion will always thrill an audience, even when their execution is not perfect. Remember "ya gotta have heart!" Audiences do not want to be impressed by perfection. They want to be moved. If they get both, so much the better.

Bare Naked Statues

CHAPTER 20
THE ART OF VOCAL PERCUSSION

By Nick Girard

One of the most important textural and musical elements of the contemporary a cappella sound is vocal percussion. A versatile addition to your vocal music, this technique can truly enhance your performance by breathing life, rhythm and energy into your arrangements. There are a multitude of styles and techniques that we'll explore together throughout this chapter and as we do, I can't stress this point enough: TAKE IT SLOWLY! Whether you're a complete beginner or a seasoned pro, your primary function remains the same: *keeping time*. The job of the drummer in any ensemble is to provide a rhythmic backbone that stays in-time. The techniques found in VP involve intricate mouth movements that put strain on your muscles in a whole new way and, just like a bodybuilder, you need to build those muscles carefully or you risk injury. As you learn these techniques, practice them slowly and methodically before you attempt to speed them up. And of course if something you're doing hurts (beyond normal muscle fatigue), STOP and consult an a cappella professional near you!

Vocal Percussion and Beatboxing

What is vocal percussion? Well, it's simple and . . . not so simple. Generally put, vocal percussion (VP) is the use of percussive sounds made with the mouth. That could mean anything from natural voiced, guttural or breath sounds all the way up to near-perfect instrument mimicry and absolutely everything in between. So, how can we keep track of stylistic variation across this discipline? Let's look at some common naming conventions:

- Mouth Drumming (MD) – a general term often used to describe ANY form of rhythm made with the mouth

- Human Rhythm (HR) – the use of simple, often speech-based sounds to create simple rhythmic elements

- Vocal Percussion (VP) – the use of refined sounds meant to replicate both the sonic footprint and the stylistic execution of an acoustic drumset.

- Beatboxing (BB) – a complex collection of human rhythm and vocal percussion sounds, as well as electronic and acoustic instrument mimicry which, when artfully combined, supplies all the necessary textures for a complete musical performance.

So, when is it appropriate to use VP and how do you choose which style to use? Good question. First and foremost, though we said earlier that VP can enhance your performance, it's also true that it can detract. Knowing whether it's appropriate for a given arrangement to have VP is important. This is somewhat subjective, but here are some helpful considerations.

- Is the song an upbeat, driving, rhythmic song or a slow, delicate, sweeping ballad?

  Answer: An upbeat, driving song is a perfect place for VP! The ballad . . . not so much.

- Is the arrangement very rhythmic and staccato or legato?

  Answer: A very rhythmic arrangement often doesn't 'need' VP, but adding it doesn't detract from the arrangement. An arrangement lacking in rhythmic elements will often be enhanced by the addition of VP.

- What should you do if the drum part is too difficult for your percussionist's ability level?

  Answer: It's not necessary to perfectly replicate the drums from the original recording. The most important thing is adding that rhythmic and textural element of the vocal drums. Depending on your percussionist's style, anything from simple HR sounds to advanced BB sounds can help augment the arrangement, if the performance is musical and appropriate for the song.

- Should we employ several percussionists to cover complex drum parts?

  Answer: It depends. Having multiple drummers can definitely expand the rhythmic palette for a song. The danger is keeping the groove tight across several performers. If, after careful rehearsal, the compound drum part grooves, then rock on! If, despite lots of practice, the groove never quite locks, then you're better off with one drummer doing less but doing it well.

The key to having effective VP in your repertoire boils down to solid, clean execution and appropriate performances. The first point is obvious—there's never a situation where you want the drums to be weak and sloppy. The second is a bit more subjective, but relatively straight-forward. A boisterous rock song won't be appropriately driven by light brushes on a jazz kit. Conversely, a sweet, gentle, mid-tempo song will be bombarded by the artillery of a beatbox arsenal. Ultimately, there are few places where VP absolutely shouldn't be used, as long as the drummer is letting appropriate sounds and musicality dictate his/her decisions.

Rival Schools

There are two general classifications of sounds in vocal drumming: "Breathing" and "Clicking." Within these two schools of sounds, variations of each drum sound can be made. For the most versatile vocal drum kit, you'll often use techniques from each school to make the same sound, under different circumstances. The more variety you have in your arsenal, the better you can customize your performance to enhance an arrangement.

- *Breathing* – using forced breath to create the sound by building air pressure within your mouth with either with your lips or tongue (or both). The pressurized air is then released with a very controlled explosion.

- *Clicking* – using suction in your mouth to create the sound by applying your tongue firmly against surfaces within the mouth and then aggressively releasing the tongue, creating a snapping sound. This technique can also be done with firmly pursed lips (think of a kissing noise). No breath is required to make Clicking sounds.

We won't cover the myriad techniques used to make each sound within each school but it's important to be aware of the different approaches. Each vocal drummer is different and will inevitably "personalize" each technique to best suit his/her instrument.

Keeping the Beat

So, before we get ahead of ourselves, let's take a look at what we're ultimately trying to achieve. In order to understand our job as a vocal percussionist, we need to understand a little bit more about rhythm and groove. Let's start at the beginning.

We can all count to four . . . and that's a great start! For the sake of ease, we'll work in 4/4 time for this explanation but of course this concept can be extrapolated to any time signature. Now, the time signature '4/4' denotes that there are 4 x quarter notes in a measure. So, when we count "one, two, three, four" we will have counted one measure's worth of quarter notes.

How can we explore more rhythmic complexity within this measure? For starters, let's subdivide the quarter notes into eighth notes. Within one measure, we count 8 x eighth notes. Now, instead of only having four rhythmic beats to play with in each measure, we have eight.

That's certainly an improvement! But we can do better, so let's repeat that process and divide the eighth notes (subdividing the quarter notes) into sixteenth notes. Now, within one measure, we have 16 x sixteenth notes, giving us 16 distinct rhythmic beats to use in each measure of our drum pattern. Given our purposes, this is a good place to stop as it affords us lots of flexibility without getting too carried away; this process could continue in perpetuity.

As we look at creating drum parts, we look back at our subdivision. The way we choose to utilize the beats within our subdivision is called "groove." Pop music (and indeed most music) follows this basic formula: The "downbeats" fall on beats 1 and 3 of each measure. These are the "heaviest" beats and fall on the "front" of the measure. Next, the "backbeats" fall on beats 2 and 4, are the "accent" beats and fall on the "back" of the measure. So, the simplest 4/4 groove is the following quarter-note subdivision:

downbeat   backbeat   downbeat   backbeat

For further complexity, we incorporate the eighth-note subdivision. These are the beats that fall in between the downbeats and backbeats and are known as "upbeats." Without altering our 4/4 groove but simply adding the upbeats, we get the following:

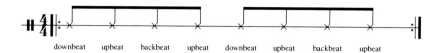

And lastly, incorporating the sixteenth-note subdivision which I'll call "splits" we get the following:

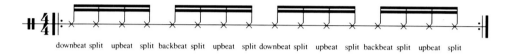

Does this organization make sense? Go through it a few times until you understand how the measure is being broken-up in each example. Got it? Great! For now, this is all we need to know to get started!

The Drumset

For our vocal percussion to function like drums in a pop song, we need to understand what comprises a typical drumset. Though it is possible to execute many more drum sounds than these, our primary focus will be on the six major drumset elements:

1. Bass Drum (kick drum) – the biggest and therefore deepest and loudest drum in the kit, struck by kicking a foot pedal.

2. Snare Drum – a shallow drum with wires called "snares" strapped to the bottom head to create a rattle when the drum is struck.

3. Cross-stick – a technique used on the snare drum where you strike the rim of the drum with your stick. Related to and often referred to as a "rimshot" or "rim click," though technically all three of these techniques are slightly different.

4. Hi-Hat (HH) – paired cymbals mounted to face one another on a spring-loaded stand which can be opened/closed by a foot pedal.

5. Tom-Toms (toms) – deep, tuned drums of varying sizes often used for fills or other supplemental purposes.

6. Crash Cymbal – bright, metal resonating disk used to punctuate musical moments.

7. Ride Cymbal – a darker, longer resonating cymbal used in lieu of the HH's for bright subdivision.

We will learn several techniques for making each of these 6 elements. But before we do that, let's just take our study groove one step further. First of all, what if we made the following equivalencies:

Downbeat = Kick Drum

Backbeat = Snare Drum

Now, let's apply that change to our quarter-note groove. We get the following:

And if we define **Upbeat = Hi-Hat** and apply that to our eighth-note groove, we get:

And if we define **Split** = **Hi-Hat** and apply that to our sixteenth-note groove, we get:

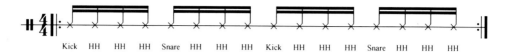

Kick HH HH HH Snare HH HH HH Kick HH HH HH Snare HH HH HH

Now we have drum grooves in quarter-, eighth- and sixteenth-note subdivision. And something very important to notice about this way of defining grooves—each beat of the subdivision only uses one drum sound. This is very convenient because as vocal drummers, we only have one mouth! Real drumset players can indeed make 4 (or more) sounds at the same time as they play with all four appendages, but as mouth drummers, we are largely limited to making one sound at a time. And speaking of those sounds, let's start learning some.

The Toolchest

Because I'm going to reference many different parts of the body throughout the next sections, I just want to provide you with a snapshot of the anatomical elements comprising your human drumset:

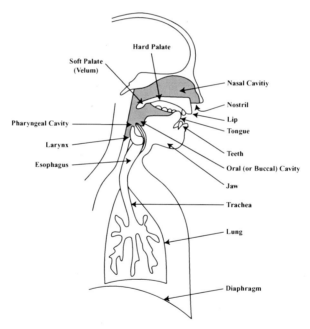

A schematic diagram of the human speech production mechanism.

In concert, all of these elements commonly used in speech and singing are employed for the creation of our drum sounds. As this is a new usage of our natural, organic instrument, it's important to be cognizant of which parts you're engaging in order to maximize efficiency and sound production.

Let's face it . . . there's no elegant way to make most of these sounds. You will be making some goofy faces and spitting on yourself for a while as you refine your technique. *Don't Worry About It!* Don't take yourself too seriously or you'll never get past the awkward stage of learning vocal percussion. Once again, I just want to reiterate that it's important to start learning these sounds slowly and gently. You will be using your breath and face muscles in a new way and it takes practice and training to build stamina and endurance. Now, with that said, let's get started!

The Kick Drum

The kick drum can be made either using the voice or by using a "plosive" or forced air. There are applications for both and we'll look at some of those. For the most part though, we're going to be focusing on the plosive kick for two reasons. First, since you're not using your voice, you avoid the risk of hurting it. Second, since this sound needs to be very low-pitched and you're not relying on your voice to generate it, your natural range doesn't have an impact on your ability to make the sound.

The Voiced Kick

We begin by saying "doo." Now, in the same way you might shout "DO IT!" at a sporting event, I want you to increase the pressure you apply to your hard palate with your tongue and let that word explode "DOO!" Do you notice how much more percussive that is than just saying "doo?" Practice until you get a feel for how to apply that pressure and execute that explosion. Remember to not pitch the word too low or else you'll tire (or even damage) your voice over time. Use a pitch that's low in your range but comfortable for you.

Next, to refine the sound, we're going to say the word "doop" where we use the "p" formation to close the lips. So, we're not saying "doo-puh" but "doo(p)." Once you get the feel for that, slowly eliminate the "oo" vowel sound until you're left with a voiced, almost humming sound. The resulting drum sound resembles the combination of letters "dp" and has a bright attack from the hard, glossy "d" sound and a snap at the finish from the "p."

The Plosive Kick

Let's begin by saying "boo." Now, like you're trying to scare someone at Halloween, shout "BOO!" Hear how percussive that word is? Let's augment that even more. By clamping your lips tightly shut you build back-pressure in your mouth. If you let the air explode through your tightly clenched lips, the resulting "b" sound will be much harder than you encounter in normal speech. Try that. Now, say "BOO!" again. Practice that until you can repeat that with same amount of pressure behind the "b" sound. Once you get that, you're going to eliminate the voiced part of the word and just whisper "boo" as hard as you were shouting it, just without the voice. Now comes the tricky part. You're going to practice minimizing how much vowel you're using until you end up with a sound that is mostly lip snap from the "b" sound. The vowel shaping still exists, but not really saying the "oo" vowel anymore. Instead, you're using a minimal exhaustion of air and using the vowel shaping to keep your larynx lowered, creating a deep resonating cavity to pitch your kick drum low. Play with your lip placement to find where you get the best snap (moving your upper lip slightly in front of or behind your bottom lip). Also, play with the vowel shaping to find where your drum resonates best. Everyone's instrument is a little different, so you'll have to adapt the technique to your anatomy in order to maximize the sound for you.

The Cross-Stick

As I mentioned earlier, the cross-stick is an application of the snare drum. We're starting with this sound because of its relative ease. It is a very functional backbeat sound and is much easier to learn than the snare, so it's a good place to start.

Begin by saying "cushion." Now, if we focus on the "c" and "sh" sounds and say this word putting tons of emphasis on these two sounds, we get "CuSHion." Repeat the syllable "CuSH" until you learn to control the attack of the "c" and the decay of the "sh." If you eliminate the vowel, you end up with a collection of consonants that resembles "ksh" and that is the basic cross-stick sound. Just as with the kick drum, there is some natural vowel shaping going on that alters the resonance of the cross-stick. Explore the variation in this sound by widening or darkening the implied vowel (KuSH, KiSH, KeSH, KaSH, etc.). Hear how the sound changes? Changing your jaw placement by slightly over- or under-biting will have an effect on the resonance as well. Play with all these attributes to make this sound your own!

The Clicking Cross-Stick

The cross-stick is a very effective sound generated using the Clicking school as well. This is a little hard to describe. You know the "tsk tsk tsk" sound we make when we see something that makes us think "well, serves him right!"? It's essentially that. The basic idea is to place the middle of your tongue firmly against your palate to create suction between the two. If you then pull the back of your tongue down off your palate, a snapping sound will occur. That's the click and the root of a lot of click-based sounds. With similar vowel shaping, mouth shape and jaw movement, you can make a variety of cross-stick sounds that require no air to make whatsoever.

The Hi-Hat

The hi-hat or "HH" is the easiest and arguably the most life-like of all the VP sounds. Consequently, it tends to be the most intuitive of all the sounds to learn. The trick to having really effective, musical hi-hats is practicing nuance and variation. You can improve the "feel" of a groove dramatically by employing super-musical hi-hats, so don't underestimate their power.

The hi-hat is basically just the sound of the letter "t." Be careful to not misinterpret what that means. It doesn't mean the letter "tee" but rather the sound made by the letter "t" when you say the word "tee." It's the flick of the tongue against the back of the teeth. There is a small, almost undetectable exhaustion of air associated with the sound. You'll notice that you can change how "bright" and "metallic" the sound is by playing with where your tongue strike is relative to your teeth, as well as how much saliva is present. I know that sounds gross . . . but that's just how it is. Explore that sound until it feels very comfortable and consistent.

The Open Hi-Hat

One of the cool attributes about the hi-hat is that it is a dynamic instrument, controlled by a pedal to close, slightly separate, or completely open the cymbals which comprise it. Essentially, the looser the hats are, the longer the decay is. The tightly closed hi-hat is made using the "t" sound as we learned above. The open hi-hat is made by saying "tss" meaning you put a long, hissing "s" sound after the "t." Practice the difference between the two sounds.

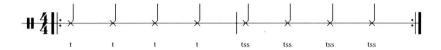

For the most life-like execution of the open hi-hat, you need to account for the sound made when the cymbals close again. That sound can be made by making a "sut" sound after an open HH sound. Practice the following pattern:

Hi-Hat Variations

For increased "feel" and nuance in your HH's, explore the following:

- ts = putting a short "s" sound at the end of the strike for a longer decay

- tf = putting a short "f" sound at the end of the strike for a longer, darker decay

- t-k = because saying many fast t's in a row requires a lot of coordination, alternating "t" and "k" can help to make very fast repeating HH's

- ti-ta = like the "t-k" variation, implying the vowels "tih" and "tah" in alternating HH's will slightly change the way the tongue hits the palate and help increase speed in quickly repeating patterns.

The Inward Hi-Hat

The first inward sound we've seen, this is especially helpful for eliminating the need for superfluous in-breaths. Instead of dropping your groove to breathe, just weave these inward HH's into your groove.

Place the tip of your tongue behind the center of your front teeth and suck in a short burst of air, as though you were hissing inwards on an "sss" sound. Now, start that sound by lightly tapping your tongue against the back of your teeth and practice shortening it, alternating between outward and inward HH's until they're indistinguishable from one another. Now that you have this inward sound, you can weave it into your grooves anywhere you need to breathe and you'll never need to stop drumming!

Inward Open Hi-Hats

Inward Open HH's can be done as well and are nice for "recovery breaths"—when you just need a long, steady in-breath. Make the same inward hissing sound but longer and with a slight volume swell. Remember to close to an outward "t" closed-HH for improved realism.

The Crash Cymbal

Another straight-forward sound, the crash cymbal is used as a bright accent for transitions and other musical moments. Think of it as your drumming exclamation point!

The sound on its own is made by combining "k" and "sh" where the "sh" decays for several seconds. If you imply the "i" vowel in your sound, it will have a brighter attack. Try it—"K(i) SSSHHH!" Some variations on this sound include:

- psh = has a slightly "grittier" attack

- tsh = has a smoother attack

- dsh = has a smooth, dark attack

A further variation is to cheat closer to an "s" sound rather than an "sh" sound. This will provide a brighter ring as the cymbal decays. For "fizzy" cymbals, try using an "f" sound.

An important detail about using the crash lies in understanding how a drummer would typically use this element. Perhaps counter-intuitively, the crash is *almost* always accompanied with a kick drum. Now, we are lucky as vocal percussionists because we can simulate this combination of sounds simply by starting with a kick drum and ending with a crash cymbal. This *composite* sound can be written with the letters "bsh" where the "b" represents the kick drum attack and the "sh" represents the decay of the crash cymbal. Practice so that you clearly get both the low-end attach from the kick drum and the high-end fizzle of the crash.

The Snare Drum

This is likely to be the most difficult percussion sound you learn. There are many subtleties to this sound and it takes quite a long time to develop the control needed to really effectively incorporate it into your grooves. All that to say, don't worry if this doesn't come naturally to you . . . it certainly didn't for me! I'm still exploring the myriad possibilities with this sound and I encourage you to dork out on this one too. Now, here's how it's done.

Some Helpful Insights

The snare drum is a very complex sound. It has a sharp, loud attack followed by a metallic fizzle (made by a series of small metal wires strapped to the bottom head of the drum). And if that weren't complex enough, the drum also has some "body" (meaning a deep resonance). The composite of these sounds takes some pretty fancy face-work! I'd like to present a couple different techniques for approaching this sound so we can find one that best suits you.

The PF Snare

This is the workhorse of the vocal snares. It's often the one that people learn first and it's a very functional sound. The basic idea is to use the explosion of the "P" sound and the decay of the "F" sound. Let's work through it together! Start by saying the word "puff." Now, in the same way that we tighten our lips to make our kick drum sound, build up some pressure and let that word explode "PUFF!" Repeat that until you really dial-in the explosion from the "P." Once you can do that consistently, remove your voice from the word. Hear how that sounds a little bit like a snare drum already? Now, remove the vowel entirely from the word until you have a sound that resembles the letters "PF." In order to effectively achieve this, you need to use more air pressure than when you just speak the word "puff." It will take some getting used to, generating this much pressure. It is a diaphragmatic exercise, meaning that you need to be supporting this explosion using your diaphragm, not just the nominal air stored in your mouth. Consequently, this will feel like a full-body workout for a while! Your abs will get tired, you will get a little light-headed and your lips and cheeks will ache. All of those things are normal and signs that you're on the right track. The key, of course, is to not do too much too soon—pace yourself—you're building new muscles and programming new muscle memory and that takes time.

The Finish Work

The best thing about this sound is how "big" it is and, in order to make the most of that attribute, you need to work out the resonance of the sound. As we said, the snap of this sound comes mainly from your lips make when the air passes through the "P" sound. And the decay comes from the fizzle as the air passes through the "F" sound. So, where does the resonance come from? The vowel shaping—exactly! The darker your vowel shape, the more resonance you'll get from the drum. You'll need to play around with this a bit because it's a bit tricky since you're not actually making any vowels when you make the sound! The principles are the same, you're just shaping air instead of speech. Try it! Move your larynx up and down and see how that changes the sound. Shift from "wide" to "tall" vowels and see what happens. Smile. Frown. These small shifts will change the resonance of your snare and, ultimately, you'll find a few shapes that work really well for you.

Variations

One you get the hang of all this, try experimenting with different decay sounds. You'll find some really cool variations by changing your "F" decay to an "SH" or a "CH." Another variation that is awesome, albeit hard to describe, is changing your decay to just air. Let me try to explain it. You know the sound you make when it's cold outside and you blow into your hands to warm them up? That dark "hoo" sound that almost resembles a whistle? It's that sound. Incorporate these into your technique to customize your snare drums.

Limitations

The big limitation with this snare sound is how cumbersome it is to make. It requires a lot of air and effort and is consequently a slow sound. You can't functionally make many of these sounds in a row without needing to breathe and it's hard to transition from this sound to other sounds nimbly. As I mentioned, this sound is great for situations where you need lots of volume but falls a bit short if nuance and agility is what you need.

The Poo Snare

Yeah, I know. Get the laughs out of the way now . . .

This is a very nimble snare drum and is also exceedingly versatile. It has a nice crack, great resonance and realistic decay. It takes less air to make this sound so it's much more agile than the PF snare, but with that comes a volume sacrifice, rendering it less functional in certain situations.

You start by saying the word "poo" . . . Seriously? I thought we got over that already!

Now, if you tighten your embouchure and let a quick burst of air through, you'll hear a tighter, snappier sound. That's what we want. Once you get the hang of that, whisper that sound and practice again until you have a nice tight sound that consistently starts with the same lip shape. You'll find this easier if you purse your lips a bit, like you would for a kiss. Once you get that, try using less and less active breath, relying more on the air that's stored in your cheeks. That's the secret to making this sound so nimble.

Variations

The resonance of this sound comes from the buzz your lips make when the air passes through them. Notice that if you make this sound with "heavy," lips, you end up with something that sounds a lot (if not exactly) like your kick drum! So, if you play with the lip tension, you can find several, in fact many embouchures that dramatically change the resonance of your snare drum. This is a very cool feature of this snare!

Limitations

Once again, the big one is volume. That doesn't mean that you can't make this snare louder by using more air and further refining the embouchure to accommodate that louder sound. But, the speed and agility are, largely, indirectly related to the volume so just know that the louder you are, the more cumbersome the sound becomes.

The Clap Snare

This is actually a variation on the Poo snare. It requires a very tight embouchure such that the drum has virtually no resonance at all. It resembles the sound of hand claps (hence the name) and is very high-pitched. Just as with the Poo snare, you start by pursing your lips, only this time much more tightly. Now, let a very small, quick blast of air through. The sound is made only by the high-pitched buzzing of your lips. Hear how that sounds a bit like hand claps? It also has a gritty, almost electronic sound which makes it suitable for a lot of hip hop and R&B beats.

The challenge with this sound is mastering the embouchure. It takes a while to find the right lip tension to make a consistent sound and because you're using so much lip tension, your face muscles will tire quickly, so endurance will take some training.

Limitations

This sound has somewhat specific uses and therefore less a utility sound but rather a speciality sound. Listen to a lot of drum beats to develop the intuition for when this sound is appropriate.

The Inward-K Snare

This is one of the more common beatboxing sounds and is very functional while also being extremely helpful for breath management. Because you make this sound breathing in, using this sound for your snares will all but eliminate your need to breathe during your grooves. Here's how this works.

Recall my description of the Clicking Cross-Stick. We're going to activate the Inward-K the same way. Start with the middle of your tongue pressed firmly against your palate to create suction. Now, suck air in, past the sides of your tongue—press your tongue tighter against your palate until you hear a slurping sound. That sound that you're generating along the sides of your tongue is what we're going to learn to control for this sound. Practice making this sound, moving your tongue around to find some good placements where you get a nice, loud slurp.

To make the snare itself, you're going to suck one quick burst of air in while simultaneously dropping the back of your tongue off your palate. This will make a "K" sound and is the basic sound we're after. Now, this being your first explosive inward sound, be aware that you are likely to have a few "miss-hits," suck the air down the wrong tube and end up coughing a bit. This is an inevitable part of the process, as is tiring out your tongue and cheek muscles, so just remember to pace yourself.

The Finish Work

Refining your slurp-to-air ratio is the primary challenge in polishing this sound. Once you have the musculature to consistently make the sound, the next step is determining how much decay you want and how bright you want it to be. This is a function of how much air you suck in after the sound is made and on what shape your mouth is in. You'll find that you can alter both the decay and the resonance by changing your vowel just as we saw with the Cross-Stick. Experiment to find what works best for you!

Limitations

Even at its best, this sound doesn't have a ton of body, so some implementations of this sound may be problematic. The other big one is breath management. If you do too many of these snares in a row and haven't done enough outward sounds to exhaust some of the air you've taken in, you will end up overloaded with breath and need to get rid of some air somehow and this could negatively effect your groove.

Tom-Toms

Toms are typically used for fills, though they can also be used in drum patterns. Toms are pitched drums and are normally tuned in 4th's. It's not necessary that your toms be in the key of each song, though sometimes it's a nice touch. A drumset can have several (sometimes MANY) toms but personally, incorporating more than three into your vocal kit can be very cumbersome. That doesn't mean there are never applications for more, but I think three is a good starting point.

Toms are actually quite difficult to perfect. They need to strike a delicate balance between being percussive while also having pitch and tone. Like many VP sounds, the basic tom is fairly easy.

You begin by making your voiced kick sound, "Doo." Only with toms, you want to maintain an even, constant pitch. Ultimately, your three toms should cover almost an octave (2 intervals of a fourth), so start high enough that the lowest (biggest) tom is low but not as low as your kick. The other characteristic of the tom is that it rings longer than the other drums on your kit and has a steady decay. You may find that closing the sound on an "m" such as "Doom" helps control your pitch and decay. Practice each tom separately, focusing on the percussive attack, even pitch and decay of the drum. Once you feel comfortable with each drum separately, begin combining them into a simple "high-middle-low" pattern. From there, you can start creating more elaborate tom patterns for use in fills or grooves.

Variations

Like many of the vocal percussion sounds, altering the vowel can change the resonance or color of your drum. This is especially true with toms, as they have the most vocal resonance of almost any drum sound you'll make. Try altering your vowel to change the color of your toms. Even more precisely, try opening your vowel as your tom gets larger (lower in pitch) to help simulate the increased resonance of the larger drum.

For complex and/or fast patterns, try alternating starting your toms with a "d" and a "b"

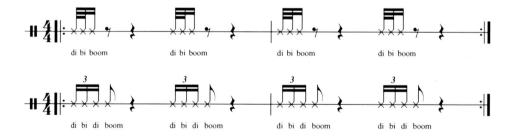

Brushes

An application of the snare drum, this is a useful sound for jazz or for songs where gentle percussion is appropriate. The characteristic thing about brushes is that they play continuously, typically in a swirling pattern. The result is a consistent sound with accents to define the groove. Let's look at how to do this, keeping in mind the biggest challenge: breathing!

Make a continuous "F" sound. That's the basis of the brushes. Now, there are two accents for brushes, the weighted swirl and the tap. To make the swirl, you simply accent the "F" sound itself. The tap is made by adding a small "T" sound. The resulting pattern looks like this:

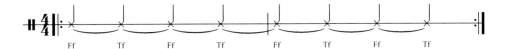

To further the complexity of this technique, add the rest of your drum kit to your brush groove. To do this, simply add the continuous "F" sound to your voiced kick and cross-stick. The result is:

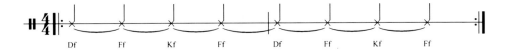

Mixing up where the accents fall adds further complexity to your grooves. Try some of these grooves:

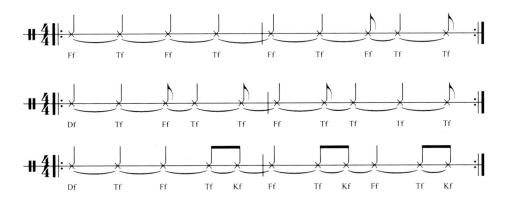

The most challenging thing about brushes is the breathing, in that you . . . can't, really. Because your sound is a constant, outward "F" sound, there are no in-built places to breathe. You need to just find musical moments to drop a hit to breathe or find a spot to sneak an inward sound. With practice, you'll soon master this versatile technique and really add some musical dimension to your jazz repertoire!

More Groove Variations

After extensive practice, your drum sounds will be honed and polished to near perfection and, thus, you're ready to learn how to construct some more interesting grooves. The possibilities here are literally endless, so let's just practice a few to further develop our coordination. Additionally, we'll develop some notation which is helpful for communicating and teaching these patterns.

B = kick drum, PF = snare, K = cross-stick, t = HH, tss = Open HH, Ksh = Crash*

---

* a left-pointing arrow represents an inward sound

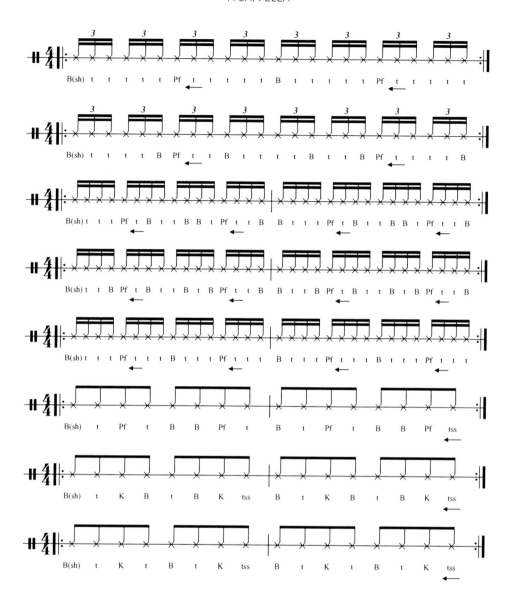

Step Up to the Mic

Vocal percussion's awesome power is truly unleashed through a microphone. The flexibility afforded to you by allowing your sounds to all be controlled and quiet is a dream come true, particularly when drumming for an entire show. Let's take a look at some of the adaptations we need to make when shifting from acoustic to mic'd VP.

Beyond keeping good time, the most important thing about acoustic VP is volume. With the microphone, volume is no longer an issue. Instead, the most important thing becomes consistency. Because your sounds are all being amplified now, it's critical that each drum is controlled, polished and has the same sonic footprint. Each kick, snare, HH, etc. should sound "identical" to the last (barring intentional variation). Practice such that your performance is dynamically consistent. This affords the sound engineer maximum control of how your drums sit in the mix. If your drums are wildly uncontrolled, the engineer will have to keep you quiet in the mix for fear of clipping and/or feedback (or compress you beyond recognition).

Extended Mic Technique

Imagine that your breath is beating the mic diaphragm just as a stick beats the head of a drum. How you utilize the mic has a drastic effect on how the microphone interprets your sounds. As such, here are some helpful techniques for learning to get the most out of your microphone.

Proximity Effect

The closer you get to the diaphragm, the more low-end you'll make. For your standard kit, the closer you stay to the grill of the mic, the better. This will give your kick lots of low-end and, as long as your snare drum is controlled, will provide nice body for your snare. Your HH's should be light enough to not incite much (if any) low-end, so the close proximity shouldn't negatively effect the brightness of your hardware. If you're doing lots of HH's or brushes, you may find that going slightly "off-axis" with the mic results in a more consistent sound for you. Off-axis means that instead of drumming directly into the mic, you tilt the mic slightly so that your air passes slight *across* the mic. This minimizes how much air hits the diaphragm directly and makes for crisper sounds when lots of high-end is needed.

Cupping

Vocal percussion is one of the few useful applications of microphone cupping. The idea is that you wrap your hand around the globe of the microphone, enhancing the proximity effect, narrowing the pickup pattern, as well as altering the frequency response of the mic. With the midrange enhanced, the sonic result is a louder, "grittier" output which can serve your drums very well, particularly for beatboxing techniques. There are limitations to this technique though. Cupping effectively works as a bandpass filter, meaning it minimizes the low-end and high-end from the output. Your kick will have more "punch" but less rumble. More problematic is that your high-end brightness will all but disappear. So, if your technique relies heavily on using the nuances of the entire frequency range, cupping might not be for you.

You can (and should) experiment with cupping to see what works best for your technique. Try varying your grip: cover the entire globe, half the globe, a quarter . . . each will have a different effect on your drum kit. And, feel free to mix up your grip to best suit each application.

full cup

half cup

quarter cup

Effects For Your Drums

You will need to tweak your EQ in order to get the most out of your amplification. Some typical EQ adjustments for drums are:

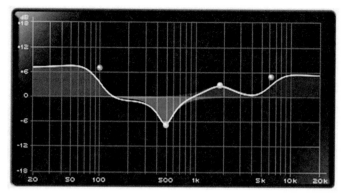

example parametric EQ for Vocal Percussion

- Boosting the low-end for thump

- Cutting some low-mid's for clarity

- Boosting the mid's for punch

- Boosting the high-end for brightness

Compression can also be very helpful in giving your drums more punch as well as help control their dynamics for easier mixing. Your settings will require some experimentation and may vary in different performance settings, but as a starting point, consider the following:

- Start with a medium ratio

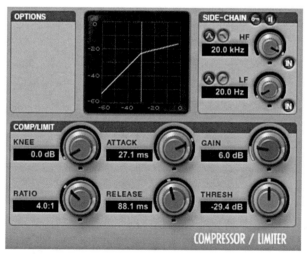

example compression for vocal percussion

- Set the threshold such that the dynamics are controlled but not squashed

- Set the attack early, but not so early that you start losing the detail of your hits

- Set the release as fast as possible while still maintaining control

- Increase the gain to make up for any lost volume

For a detailed explanation of EQ'ing and compressing drums, review the "Live Sound" chapter of this book.

The Long and Winding Road

Now that you've mastered the sounds and grooves, what's next for you? Vocal percussion is an ever-evolving art form. Each practitioner has a different instrument to work with and thus has something new to offer the VP-sphere. It's important that you continue to experiment and grow. Keep refining your sounds. Learn new sounds. Create new grooves. There's no "right" way to mouth drum, so if you create something that sounds cool and serves your music, use it! And lastly, don't be afraid to ask questions; there are a lot of great VP's in the world and I'm willing to bet they'll all love to talk shop with you!

Summary

- Take your time and be patient as you learn these techniques

- Have fun with the process, it's inherently goofy at first!

- Understand how to subdivide time and how that relates to grooves

- Perfect the basics of each sound in your vocal drum kit

- Modify each of your sounds to suit your style

- Try creating your own sounds!

- Work on incorporating your own style/sounds into your patterns

- Spend time working with a mic to further develop your style

- Always continue to learn, share and teach!

Robert Dietz, The Funx

CHAPTER 21

CONTEMPORARY A CAPPELLA COACHING TOOLS

By Deke Sharon

I looked at the clinician list for BOSS 2013 and thought "Holy moly! There are dozens if not hundreds of contemporary a cappella coaches now!" So encouraging, so exciting!

Alas, there's literally no training program for coaches, no formal pedagogy. I assume they're all just sharing the lessons they've learned as singers and directors, as I do.

To that end, I'd like to share with them, and with you, a few of the hard-leaned lessons and perspectives I've assimilated over 20+ years of working with groups. No need for me to mention the obvious musical techniques (tuning a chord, blending vowels, etc.), as that's easy to find. Instead, I offer a few thoughts to help round out a coach's approach, technique and toolkit:

The Big Picture

Music is communication, and as each piece of music has a particular message and mood, the myriad decisions there are to make around a particular song and arrangement should all point to the song's central emotional focus. This is easy to conceptualize, but I find it alarming how often directors lose sight of this fact. Why did you choose this move? Why are you singing this chord in this way? "Because it looks/sounds good" or "because I like it" are not acceptable answers, especially in light of a young director's desire for perfection above (more on this later).

If I'm working with a group and I feel nothing when they've sung the song for me, my very first act is to make sure the group both understands the song's meaning and has a clear emotional goal for the song. If it's not clear, we discuss the lyrics, and I invite the singers to discuss their own related experiences and feelings. At the end of such a discussion, it's very helpful to summarize in a few words, like "big crazy circus" or "gentle melancholy stream." The specific words will be a trigger, something the director can mention when playing the pitch, just before starting the song, to help the group focus it's emotional delivery.

Show AND Tell

There's an oft-spoken adage in writing—"show, don't tell"—that definitely carries an important message: use words to create a feeling rather than simply state what a character feels. Expanding this idea into coaching, I urge you not only to explain to your group how they should feel, but to reflect that feeling in your own tone of voice, your own gestures, your own mood. Create the moment yourself as you're urging your singers to find it. In essence, you're called upon to act while you direct, just as you're asking your singers to do the same when they sing. Wave your arms and jump around, slump your shoulders and speak more quietly . . . whatever it takes. Change the mood in the room to reflect the song, and help your singers find the moment.

Fear of Imperfection

Everyone wants to be great, and everyone wants to be right. In music, the default is to focus on the elements that are easily measured and graded: tuning and rhythmic precision. Those are important elements of a group's musical performance, but an over-emphasis on them can seriously skew perspective. If a group is thinking about the notes and rhythms, then they're essentially singing about nothing, having turned the song into a dull exercise in musical execution. I've seen too many directors spend the vast majority of their rehearsals on tuning, the results of which are largely lost on the audience, as only a trained musician will care about the frequency of audible overtones in a particular piece of music.

Think of it this way: if you're coaching an individual to give a speech, would you spend most of your time on diction? Probably not. You'd make sure the words were pronounced correctly, but you'd think about the emotional impact first and foremost. Do you believe the speaker? Are the points well made? Are you convinced? Excited? Don't let precision destroy passion. You may find yourself working with the group's director more than anyone else on this point.

Moreover, there will be tradeoffs, and you should be willing to make them. A big stage picture might sacrifice tuning for a moment, but have a larger impact on the audience's experience of a piece of music. Go for it. Perfect tuning isn't and never will be the point of a piece of music (especially since there's no such thing as perfect tuning in our Western musical system!) Don't sacrifice "musicality" willy-nilly, but neither should you be a slave to it.

The 90% Problem

Fact is, no matter how good a group is, you're going to spend almost all of your time focusing on problems and fixes. It's the nature of coaching, the nature of directing. This can have a chilling effect, as a group that is working with you for a short while might have the impression that they're not doing a very good job since you're constantly harping on them, delivering a litany of things they can do better. If a group's 95% of the way to perfection, you'll still spend 95% of the time focusing on the 5% that needs fixing . . . which can create the impression that they're only 5% of the way to their goal.

The only thing you can do is to mention this fact directly, and offer significant ongoing encouragement, so the group realizes how much they're doing well. People thrive on positive feedback (so long as it's genuine), and delivering compliments alongside the suggested changes will help correct this imbalance.

The Unspoken Message

You're coaching a men's college a cappella group, and they're singing a song about driving fast, or hanging out with friends in the summertime, or trying to find the right girl. Focus on the message, make sure they're on point . . . but realize there's usually a deeper message conveyed by a group, especially a collegiate a cappella group. That message is: we're young, we're happy, and we're having fun.

Trite? Not at all. It's a deep celebration of life, and I'd argue there's no single more powerful message for a bunch of college guys to share, because it's true, and it's universal. You can and should make choices reflecting the song's lyrics, but you should also reflect who the singers are and where they are in their lives. This goes for every group of people you work with. The subtext in every DeltaCappella performance is, roughly "look at our group: men aged 20-75, from all corners and strata of Memphis' diverse community, coming together to create something, and loving it." You might think it obvious, but there is no organization in the city that so powerfully and effectively delivers that message, while delivering it in such an entertaining manner. A rather socially and racially segregated Southern city has their poster children for the future, spreading and showing harmony through harmony in the most literal sense.

Help a group find its larger message, and weave it into their performance and presentation. Don't be didactic. There's no need to be. The joy of singing and the power of music will bring people along effortlessly.

MPact

Encourage Dialogue

The older I get, the more I realize how little I know, how much there is to learn from others, and how complicated communication can be. Before starting, I make sure the group knows I welcome comments, questions, and dissent. If someone thinks an idea is stupid, I want them to say "that's stupid!" so I either have to defend my suggestion to their satisfaction, or come up with an alternative. A great coaching session is a dialogue between singers and coach, with ideas presented, considered, molded to fit a group's sound and personality. It keeps me on my toes, and ultimately ensures a more deeply rewarding experience for us all.

Change Anything

A chord isn't working in an arrangement? Change it. Don't like where the sopranos are standing? Move them. The group's making too much sound for a passage? Drop down to one on a part. Nothing is off the table, and nothing is sacred, especially in a coaching session. If you have a big, bold, potentially crazy idea you should most certainly try it, and sometimes it won't work. Good! The group will see you take a risk, fail, and rebound, which is exactly what you're asking them to do.

Remember: contemporary a cappella is young, even while a cappella is old. Every year popular music changes, and a cappella along with it. We're constantly testing and trying, changing and growing. As such, you will not always be right, and things you suggest will not always work. That's not a problem. The only problem would be to assume you always know best, or that one particular approach/technique will always work. Stay young and hungry, with open eyes and ears, and you'll learn as much from your session as the singers do.

Have Fun

There are times when gratification needs to be delayed, when a chord needs to be laboriously worked and reworked, but those moments are few and far between. Music is fun, singing is fun, a cappella is fun, and rehearsal really should be fun. As such, make your coaching sessions fun. Smile, laugh, crack jokes, don't take yourself too seriously. Bring your love of a cappella to bear. Get excited. Be stupid. Tell stories about stupid mistakes you've made. Remember that the singers will likely be a bit scared and worried about being judged. Remind them that you're not there to judge them, but rather to help them reach their greatest potential. Remind them that they can throw out all your ideas as soon as you leave, so it can't hurt to jump in with both feet and try them. Have fun, and one way or another make sure the singers are having fun.

CELEBRITIES WHO SANG COLLEGIATE A CAPPELLA

Sara Bareilles
UCLA Awaken

Mayim Bialik
UCLA Shir Bruin

Jessica Biel
Rejected by the Tufts Amalgamates
because her voice didn't blend

Andy Bowers (NPR)
Yale's Society of Orpheus & Bacchus

Laurie Dhue (FOX News, Bill O'Reilly,
has a segment "The Dhue Point")
University of North Carolina at Chapel Hill

Loreleis Kurt Eichenwald (New York Times)
Swarthmore College 16 Feet

Peter Gallagher
Tufts Beezlebubs

Art Garfunkel
Columbia University Kingsmen

Lauren Graham
Barnard Metrotones

Anne Hathaway
Vassar's Measure 4 Measure

Ed Helms
Oberlin College Obertones

Rashida Jones
Harvard Opportunes

Mindy Kaling
Dartmouth Rockapellas

Dave Karger (*Entertainment Weekly*)
Duke

John Legend
University of Pennsylvania Counterparts

Ryan Leslie
Harvard's Krokrodiloes

Debra Messing
Rejected by an a cappella group

Wentworth Miller
Princeton Tigertones

Masi Oka (*Heroes*)
Brown University The Bear Necessities

Diane Sawyer
Wellesley College Blue Notes

Brooke Shields
Rejected by an a cappella group

Mira Sorvino
Harvard-Radcliffe Veritones

Aisha Tyler
Dartmouth Rockapellas

James Van Der Beek,
Drew University 36 Madison Ave.

Forte

CHAPTER 22

THE LAST PERFORMANCE

By Ben Spalding

I'll never forget the last performance of the 2011–2012 school year with my group Forte. It was the most meaningful performance of any group that I have ever directed. Forte is the top all a cappella ensemble at Centerville High School where I am the choir director. The 2011-2012 school year was the year that Forte started to get on the map and we started to make a name for ourselves. This particular group really helped pave the way for members that would wear purple and call themselves members of Forte for years to come. When I first took over as the choir director at Centerville, I would have never dreamed that I would get the opportunity to work with so many special people. As I looked up at Forte performing for the last time that night, the culmination of the work of the prior two years when I took over at Centerville really started to hit me. I had never been as moved by a performance as I was at that moment. I looked up and the kids were performing in the gym in front of our entire school, principals, our superintendent, and many important members of the community and I cried uncontrollably.

For this particular performance, Forte only sang one number, but you could feel that the kids wanted this moment to last forever. I watched the kids perform with the energy and passion that they had become accustomed to when performing as a member of Forte and I reminisced about the year. This was the group that went to Lexington, Kentucky to win first place in a regional competition against eleven other schools and got to open up for The House Jacks as a result. This was the group that won their regional division at the International Championships of High School A Cappella and advanced as one of the top ten a cappella groups in the country to the finals in New York City and then placed 2nd overall in the country placing runner up to a Performing Arts School from Oakland, California. This was also the group that composed and recorded ten original songs. This group exceeded every hope and dream I could have imagined for them. Their last performance brought every emotion and every memory back from the past two years and the emotion just rolled down my face. The kids aren't supposed to see me like this, but I just couldn't help it. We all knew we had something special and when you feel that, nothing else matters. As the kids walked off the stage in the gym with an audience of around 3,000 students and adults, they saw me break down for the first time. I'll never forget the way that those kids made me feel and what we accomplished as a cohesive unit.

Because of those kids and so many others I have encountered in my career, my life has been changed forever and there's no looking back. I've found my home away from home and I want to share that "home" with anyone willing to read this book. I want to share my passion for contemporary a cappella and express how it has changed my life. A few years ago I actually quit my profession. I turned in my resignation and was about to walk away from teaching. There were many factors that led me down that path and I am not going to go into them here because truthfully they don't really matter now anyway. I think back on that single day, moment, and decision. What if I stuck to that? What if I wasn't teaching anymore and never got to have the opportunities that I've had? I can't imagine how different my life would be! Luckily, something deep inside me was telling me that I shouldn't do it. I couldn't walk away from teaching. All I know is that right after I made the worst decision of my life, I very quickly turned around and made the best decision of my life—to withdraw my resignation and continue teaching.

Let me stop right here and give you some background into how I came to love a cappella. When I was in college, I was a member of a men's a cappella group the AcoUstiKats at the University of Kentucky (yes the same group that was featured years later on *The Sing-Off*). I truly loved performing with that group. I loved the fun atmosphere and appreciated the musical talent that it took to create the perfect blend and that there was no hiding behind accompaniment. What I appreciated most was how much the audience was always engaged and seemed to always genuinely love the performances. I knew then that I would find a way to incorporate a cappella into all my jobs in the future. For my first few teaching jobs the only feasible way to do this was to create extracurricular after school a cappella groups. It was extra hours and work for me outside of my already demanding schedule, but it was worth it. The kids really came alive when performing a cappella music. They loved it and it really helped further foster their love and appreciation for music. My passion for a cappella music continued to grow as I witnessed how inspired the kids were by it.

When fate brought me in my career to Centerville High School, my life changed forever. First I must say, that I was extremely blessed to get a choral director job in a school district where the Fine Arts are well supported by the administration and the community. There is no substitute for that support. When I took over, Forte was a small chamber choir that was already in existence at the high school and I knew that group would be the perfect group to transform into a pure a cappella ensemble. I started this process as soon as I took the job and that first year was the most challenging as I worked to mold this group into my vision of what I knew it could be. That first group will always have a special place in my heart as the ones who accepted my vision and jumped right in with me not knowing what they were getting into. But it was that second year that I directed Forte when things really came together and the fruits of our labor really came into being as I mentioned earlier.

It is not the success that moved me to tears on that last performance that night; although, I was incredibly proud of all the things that group had accomplished. It was the feeling that those kids truly loved what they were doing and their lives would be forever changed because of what they had experienced being a part of that group and I knew they all felt that and I had a hand in that. It was during that performance that I knew I had made the right decision to continue teaching and I knew I had gotten my passion back and would never lose it again. I knew that everything I had gone through was worthwhile and I was so grateful to have been given the opportunities that I had been given. I knew I was so blessed to be able to have the job I did and be able to share my love of a cappella music with the world and have a vehicle in Forte to do just that. I have been rewarded in ways I never even imagined. So I challenge you to open your heart to the a cappella world and see how it changes your life. I really hope this book opens your eyes to all things a cappella and you get inspired!

Deke, Liz Banks, and the new Treblemakers

TECHNOLOGY

Mr. Tim

CHAPTER 23
LIVE SOUND

By Nick Girard

Live sound is both an art and a technical behemoth. One could write volumes on the topic and indeed many people have. This chapter is intended to provide you with a general overview, the basic information needed to ensure that your group sounds its best when performing using amplification. There are a myriad ways to approach live sound and the explanations below are meant to function merely as a guideline. Every sound engineer has his or her own style and process. In many cases, there is no right way to achieve a goal. Often times, the right answer is simply the one that sounds the best.

The Venue

The first thing you must familiarize yourself with when considering amplification is the space where you'll be singing. The size, shape, number and placement of seats, treatments on the walls, floor and ceiling . . . these all affect the choices you'll make. For theaters and well-funded professional venues, acoustical engineers perform a thorough analysis of the space to determine what treatments are needed, the best seating configuration, the specifications for the sound system as well as optimizing that system specifically to the room. These venues are often wonderful places to run live sound, because all the hard work has been done for you!

So, let's then assume that you're presented with the opposite case: an empty room with no sound system and you need to design a system that can provide adequate sound for your show. The first consideration is size. How big is this room and how many people are likely to attend the show? How high are the ceilings? Or, is it an outdoor venue? These all dictate how powerful your sound system will need to be.

The next consideration is the layout of the show. How will the production be staged and how will the seating be arranged? These will impact what speaker configuration you'll require. You need to make sure that everyone in the audience can hear the show as well as be certain that the performers can hear themselves. In addition to the physical layout of the space, the nature of your group's aesthetic is also a determining factor of your speaker configuration. Is your group an all-female ensemble whose repertoire is choral in nature, therefore not engaging the ultra-low subharmonic frequencies? Conversely, does your group's sound rely heavily on thunderously low bass and huge vocal percussion? These two groups would demand very different sound systems. Whether you're renting or purchasing gear, it's best to know what your specifications are.

Lastly, there will be a variety of accessories required to build your sound system. The layout and size of the space will dictate the requirements of these accessories. Things like speaker stands, number and length of cables, location of power and extension cords, adaptors, tables, mic stands . . . these are all very important to your setup as well. Make sure you think ahead and have all the things that you need (and a few extra to be safe)!

Now that you have an idea of what you require from your sound system, let's choose one that suits your needs.

The PA

The PA (Public Address) system is what you'll need to amplify your sound. It is comprised of the signal device(s) (in our case, the microphones), a mixing console, an amplifier, and speakers. The basic technical function of the PA is simple: The microphone turns your voice into an electronic signal which is sent to the mixing console. The signal is then sent to the amplifier where it is boosted. The amplified signal is then sent to the speakers for broadcast. Every element of this signal chain is important in the process of amplifying your sound. We'll discuss microphones a little bit later, so for now let's learn about the amplifier, the console and the speakers.

The Amp

The power amplifier is the piece of equipment responsible for how much "power" your PA has. Measured in watts, the more powerful the amp, the more sound you can send to the speakers. It's very important that you use an amp that has sufficient wattage for the space in which you're working. You're better off having a bigger system as pushing the limits of a small system will result in poor sound quality. Consult a pro audio representative to determine what size system you need for your space, but a general guideline can be found in the table below.

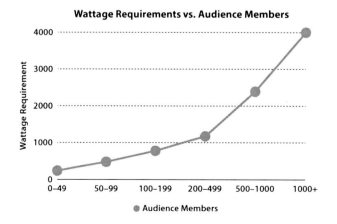

Audience Members	Wattage Requirements
0–49	250
50–99	500
100–199	800
200–499	1200
500–1000	2400
1000+	4000

The Console

There are countless mixing consoles on the market. They all serve the same basic function: to balance and shape the sounds you're sending to the speakers. There are two types of consoles: powered and unpowered. Powered mixers are all-in-one units that contain both an amplifier and a mixing console. These units can be an easy solution for small, simple live sound applications. In my experience though, their limitations render them less than ideal for mixing an a cappella group. We'll revisit mixing consoles a little later in this chapter for more in-depth information.

The Speaker

The speakers are the final piece of your live sound arsenal. They broadcast the sound to your audience. Because music broadcast requires the entire audible frequency spectrum, you need to use "full-range" speakers.

Now that we understand the function of each element of the PA, let's learn more about the specifics of each one to better inform the specifications of our system.

The Speakers

The typical full-range speaker is actually comprised of three separate, smaller speakers:

- Woofer: for low frequencies
- Horn: for mid frequencies
- Tweeter: for high frequencies

Together, these three speakers provide full, even sound across the entire audible frequency spectrum. They are typically contained within a cabinet or box and the cabinet will have a wattage rating. The rating will tell you how much power you can send to the speaker before damaging it. You therefore need to be certain that you've chosen an amp and speakers that have the same power capacities.

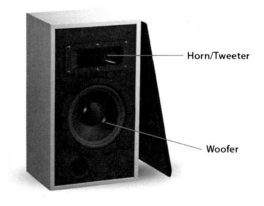

Horn/Tweeter

Woofer

Sub-Woofers

If your group requires lots of deep bass, then you'll want to add a sub-woofer to your speaker system. This speaker is designed to handle the ultra-low frequency content found in a kick drum or deep bass (especially if a subharmonic generator or octave pedal is being used). In order to effectively add a sub-woofer to the system, you need to use a "cross-over," a device that sends all the low content below a certain frequency to the sub-woofer instead of the woofer in your full-range cabinet. The typical cross-over frequency range is between 80Hz–120Hz.

Passive vs. Active Speakers

There are two types of speakers, passive and active. Passive speakers require the use of an external power amplifier as we've described thus far. Active speakers, however, have their own built-in amplifier and can seriously simplify your sound setup. Though limited in their power capabilities, active speakers can be a great solution for a traveling sound system. Similarly, active sub-woofers typically have a built-in cross-over, thus eliminating yet another piece of gear from your kit.

Monitors

When you sing acoustically, it's very easy to hear what you're doing and make adjustments in tuning and balance. That process becomes increasingly difficult when amplification is involved because the speakers are often broadcasting so much sound into the hall that the performers can no longer clearly hear what they're singing on stage. Monitors are a separate set of speakers, the primary purpose of which is to broadcast sound to the performers. This way, each performer can hear him/herself and is thus equipped to make adjustments. There are several types of monitors:

- Wedges: a full-range floor cabinet designed in a "wedge" shape to broadcast the sound up (and backward) towards the performers. This design minimizes how much the audience hears the monitors' output.

- Side-fills: a separate pair of speakers that are positioned in the wings, aimed inward toward center-upstage. For small stages, these are typically unnecessary and compound feedback problems.

- In-Ear Monitors (IEM's): a wireless system that sends the monitor feed directly into earbud headphones. This is the most consistent method for monitoring as your listening experience will be more consistent from venue to venue.

Monitors, like your main speakers, can be either passive or active. If you're using passive monitors, you'll need additional amps to power those.

A HELPFUL HINT

Although monitors are immensely helpful for hearing yourself on stage, it takes a while to get accustomed to hearing yourself through multiple layers of amplification. You are no longer listening and tuning to the sound coming out of your mouth, but rather to sound coming at you from the floor. And, this is especially true with in-ear monitors. Practicing with the monitors as much as possible will increase your comfort level with this new listening environment.

The Mixing Console

This is where the magic happens! Also known as the *desk* or *board*, this is the central hub used to control what the audience hears. Though there are countless consoles on the market, they all share the same basic functions.

- Input/Output (I/O): multiple input channels allow for multiple signal devices to be connected to the PA. The "main output" of the mixer is the final signal sent to your Amplifier (or powered speakers).

- Gain-Staging: Gain is, simply stated, how "loud" a signal is. It's measured in the logarithmic unit known as decibels (dB) where 0dB = line, nominal or "unity" signal level. Gain-Staging is an essential step for ensuring a good final mix. This is the process of establishing a maximum input volume for each singer to prevent any distortion of the input signal. If a singer's input gain is too high, they will distort their channel going into the board and no matter how quietly you send their output to the speakers, their voice will sound distorted. You also run the risk of damaging the electronics in your board, so make sure that everyone has a safe input gain!

- Balance: using either faders or knobs, the mixing console allows you to control how much of each channel gets sent to the main output. This allows you to "mix" your output, making sure that each voice is heard at the appropriate volume.

- Equalization (EQ): a way of enhancing the overall sound of a channel's output by manipulating the frequencies of that channel. You can cut (reduce) unwanted frequencies to make the sound clearer as well as boost certain frequencies to further enhance and shape the final output sound. We'll revisit EQ a bit later to learn more specifics.

- Auxiliary Sends/Returns (aux-send, -return): most mixers will have at least one aux-send and return. These are a secondary I/O path used for routing effects and most commonly, your monitors. They allow you to send signal from each channel to the monitors, effects device, etc. and then loop those back into the main mix. Aux-sends are either pre- or post-fader meaning that the amount of gain you send is either independent or dependent of the gain you're sending to the main output. Monitors are typically sent pre-fader, as your monitor mix needs are not necessarily the same as your house mix needs.

- Inserts: yet another I/O path generally used exclusively for effects. Using an "insert cable" or "tip/ring cable" the insert jack is a closed loop (both input and output) and allows you to apply an effect (or chain of effects called a "side-chain") to that particular channel. Common effects would be additional equalizers, compressors/limiters, delays and reverb.

There are two types of mixing consoles, *Analog* and *Digital*.

- Analog boards are relatively simple to navigate. Everything you need is physically in front of you in the form of a jack, knob, fader, switch, etc. These desks generally have a limited number of features and few, if any "on-board" effects (effects built into the board itself). Any additional EQ, compression, delay, reverb, etc. will need to be added to your setup with physical effects units. These boards were the industry standard for years and are still very effective. These can be a great, cost-effective solution for your mixing needs, once you acquire all the gear necessary to achieve your goals.

- Digital boards are much more complex than their analog counterparts . . . and their price tag follows suit. However, most if not all the functions you'll need are built into the board itself, including a multitude of effects. The board is controlled by a computer processor so you have access to many more features than an analog board of equivalent size. The only catch is that you have to master the interface to efficiently make the most of the console, which can take some time. Digital boards are becoming more affordable and are slowly becoming the standard for all sorts of live sound solutions.

The most important considerations when choosing a console are size, function and sound quality. You need a board that has enough input channels to run all the microphones you'll need. They are typically sold in units of 8 (8-channel, 16-, 32-). Be sure you have all the inputs you require while at the same time keeping the board small enough that it doesn't become cumbersome to transport and/or operate. Next, based on what other functionality you require for your mixes, choose a board that allows you to perform all the functions you need. This includes how many bands of channel EQ you need (3 is the recommended minimum, Low, Mid, High), how many aux-sends you need for your monitors and effects and whether you need or want on-board effects. Lastly, how clean the console's processing is can dramatically affect the sound quality of your mix. Read reviews of the console before purchasing or renting to make sure it comes highly recommended.

Microphones

A microphone (mic) is a device that takes an acoustic signal (your singing) and converts that into an electronic signal that can then be manipulated and sent through the PA. There are many different options when picking microphones and understanding what you need the mic to do will help ensure that you make good selections for your needs.

- Dynamic: these are the standard handheld stage mics because they are simple, durable, and forgiving. They are a passive device so they don't require any power. Dynamic mics have a close-range pattern, meaning you have to have the mic close to the sound source to acquire a strong input signal. Because of this, dynamic mics are best suited for individual handheld use and not for "area-mic" applications where you set the mic far from the group to amplify the ensemble.

- Condenser: these mics are much more sensitive than dynamics. Unlike their passive counterpart, condensers require power to operate. This power, known as "phantom power" is a 48-volt signal that charges a capacitor inside the microphone's diaphragm (the membrane where the air pressure from the voice is converted into electric signal). This design results in a much more sensitive device which makes condensers well suited for use as area mics as they can pick up a strong signal from a great distance. However, this increase in sensitivity brings with it an increased risk for feedback (the overloading of frequencies), so your EQ and gain-staging must be carefully treated when using these microphones. There are also handheld applications of the condenser mic which can be very helpful for both the performer and sound engineer when employed correctly.

Microphones come in both wired and wireless constructions. Let's look at the pros and cons of each.

Wired

- **Pro:** these mics are simple, reliable, and require little-to-no maintenance. You simply plug these mics into the console and you're ready to go! Wired microphones are also very durable, which makes them an excellent choice for frequent use and for traveling. Good wired mics have a consistent, clean, and full sound and are very affordable.

- **Con:** having so many mic cables on the stage can be very cumbersome while performing. Doing lots of choreography that requires people crossing one another renders your mic cables into a big pile of spaghetti on stage! This makes setup and teardown time consuming and can seriously restrict the flexibility of your performance.

Wireless

- **Pro:** these mics are free to roam about the stage and enable lots of flexibility in your performance. Chosen wisely, you can still achieve a nice clean, full sound from your wireless.

- **Con:** the mics themselves require maintenance. Each handheld uses batteries, so you'll need to have batteries with you at all times. The mics are a 2-part unit: the mic itself (the transmitter) and the receiver, the device that sends the signal to the console. The transmitter uses radio frequencies (rF) to send the signal to the receiver and the receiver is then connected to the console using microphone cables (XLR). The radio frequencies used by the microphones can reap havoc on your sound quality and will often need to be manipulated at each venue to ensure you have no interference issues. Lower-quality wireless have frequency restrictions which can be a big issue, particularly performing in cities where lots of frequencies are being used. Also, lower-quality mics often don't sound as clean due to how the signal is being transmitted. High-quality wireless have many options for frequency selection as well as cleaner, more full-range transmission, but they are very expensive.

In the end, the most important thing when selecting your microphones is choosing the best tool for your needs. Often, a combination of dynamics, condensers, wired and wireless mics will be the best way to balance your needs with your budget.

Ok, now we understand the sound system and its components. Let's learn how to set the system up and mix your show!

The Setup

Depending on the components of your system, the specifics of your setup will change. As a general overview, it should look something like this.

- Place your "mains" or "front of house" (F.O.H.) speakers at the front of the stage. Make sure they are set at a comfortable height for the audience to hear their unobstructed output. Tilt the speakers inward a few degrees towards the middle of the audience as this will help keep the sound even throughout the venue. Do not place speaker cabinets directly on the stage if you can avoid it. Subwoofers should be placed on the floor in front of the stage and your mains should be on stands, either on stage or just in front. Connect your speakers using the appropriate cabling to the amplifier(s) or mixing console (if the speakers are powered).

- Locate your mixing console in the center of the room, halfway into the audience (if possible) as this is the ideal location for listening. Connect your speakers to the main outputs Left and Right on your console. Be sure to have your main output running through a dual 31-band graphic EQ . . . I'll explain this in a bit. Also, set up any outboard effects you may have.

- Place your monitors on stage. The location will depend on your performance configuration, but the goal is to set them up such that everyone on stage can hear themselves for accurate monitoring. Connect your monitors to either the amplifier and/or to the appropriate aux-send on the mixing desk. You'll find that running each monitor through a graphic EQ will also be helpful.

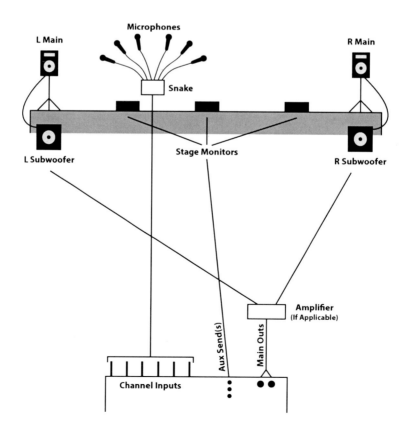

- Connect your microphones to your console. If the desk is far from the stage, a "snake" or "multi-core" will be a helpful way to limit how much cabling you need. The snake is a long bundle of cables that has a "patch bay" at the end—this will let you connect all the channels at the board, run the snake to the stage and then plug your mics into the snake's patch bay. It's a much cleaner way to travel long distances with cables. Once the mics are connected, turn all the channels on and just test that you're getting clean sound from each mic. That is called your "line-check."

That's it, in a nutshell.

Ringing the Room

Before you can mix, you need to flatten the natural EQ in the space. This is CRITICAL to achieving a good mix and yet it's the most commonly skipped step in the whole process! You've connected a dual 31-band EQ to your main speakers and this is the device you'll use to neutralize the EQ in the room. This takes a lot of practice and good critical ears, so don't worry if you don't excel at this right away!

- Connect a playback device such as an mp3 player to your console either using the tape-in jacks (RCA-⅛") or a stereo XLR-⅛" cable.

- Choose a song that you're very accustomed to, one that has nice clear, full-range sound. You want to be able to clearly hear the lows, highs and a nicely balanced mid-range.

- Play that song through the PA and listen to how it sounds.

- Using the 31-band EQ, you're going to evaluate whether each of the 31 frequencies creates issues in the room. You need to make sure you're adjusting both sides of the EQ together, otherwise the Left and Right speakers won't sound the same and that will be jarring to the listener as well as create potential phase and feedback issues. Now, go through each frequency on the EQ and find any that feed back by pushing the fader all the way up. If it does, you'll hear a loud humming, ringing or screeching sound. THAT'S BAD! Push that fader down until you hear the sound become more clear. Then, continue along the graphic EQ repeating that process for each frequency. Once you're done this, and it may take a few passes to dial-in, you should notice the song sounding much more clean than prior to EQ'ing. That means you've neutralized the room and you're ready to start EQ'ing microphones. If you attempted to EQ the mics before ringing the room, every mic would feedback at the "bad" frequencies that you found, making it virtually impossible to get a clear mix.

Ringing the Monitors

Repeat the process above for each monitor mix. This can be tricky as it often involves needing two people, one listening to the monitor output on stage and one by the board manipulating the EQ. If you have a digital board, it's possible to setup a LAN (Local Area Network) with a standard router and use a tablet to control the EQ from stage, eliminating the need for the second person.

Functionally, you'll be asking for something sonically different from your monitors versus your F.O.H. sound. Generally speaking, you won't need the same bass response from your monitors. Often, you can cut the bass content below around 80Hz as it's not helpful for tuning. Similarly, you won't likely need anything above 10kHz so you can cut that too. Lastly, you might choose to cut some of the low-mid's as those tend to obscure the midrange frequencies most helpful for tuning. Make these adjustments sparingly at first (if at all) and then revisit this stage during soundcheck based on the needs of the performers.

Gain-Staging

Each microphone will need to have its input gain set before EQ'ing can happen. To set the input gain, have each singer sing into his/her mic as loud as they will be singing in the concert. Activate the "solo" function on the current channel (this will ensure that only the solo'd channel will be sent to the output). Turn the gain on that channel up or down such that the output meter on the board doesn't "clip" (reads past "0" thus overloading the output, typically denoted by red on the meter) when the singer is singing his/her loudest. It's imperative that no one clips in order to have nice, clean sound while mixing.

Clipping the Mic

Wireless mics often come with a built-in "pad" which allows you to attenuate or limit the amount of sound the mic itself is picking up. A particularly loud singer or vocal percussionist can clip the microphone receiver, thus sending distorted sound to the mixing console. It's important that the signal be clean at every step of the process so if you notice the receiver clipping for a given singer, engage the pad on their microphone.

Mic Technique

The purpose of mic technique is simply to maintain a similar input signal while performing across your entire dynamic range. It's very important that each singer practices good mic technique at all times. The distance between the microphone and the singer's mouth differs slightly depending on their performance style and function. As a general rule, follow these guidelines:

- Vocal Percussion: The mic should be as close to the mouth as possible. It's very common for your lips to touch the grill of the mic. Also, depending on your drumming technique, "cupping the mic" or covering some or all of the grill with your hand can help with the sound of your drums. Just be aware that cupping will minimize the low- and high-end in your sound, so use this technique appropriately.

- Vocal Bass: The mic should be as close to the mouth as possible. This incites a physical phenomenon known as "proximity effect" which boosts the amount of low-end in your sound—this is GREAT for bass! Also, depending on your sound production technique, keeping the mic raised just slightly towards your nose can help enhance resonance as well. Cupping the mic can also be used for bass, but again, this technique needs to be used appropriately as it will change your EQ profile significantly!

- Vocals: The mic distance will vary depending on whether you're using a dynamic or condenser mic. For dynamics, you must keep the mic close to your mouth—approximately 1"–2" from your mouth is a good starting point. If you put the mic too close, the proximity effect will kick-in and change the nature of your sound, which is not ideal (unless you're intentionally doing so for effect). When you sing something VERY loud, you can (and should) increase the distance of the mic from your mouth to make sure you don't clip. But, don't pull off too far as dynamic mics have limited range. Only pull-off as far as necessary to keep from clipping (usually not more than 6"). Condenser mics are much more sensitive and thus you have more flexibility with how far you can be from the mic. It's best to experiment with your mic technique distances during sound check. Cupping the mic is almost never appropriate for vocals as it drastically changes your EQ profile as well as your gain.

EQ'ing the Microphones

This also takes practice and familiarity with the EQ on your board. The basic principle is to find the frequencies that are obscuring the clarity of the singer's voice, and cutting those so that the voice sounds clear and natural, just as they sound without the sound system. It's a simple concept that can be quite frustrating at times! Here's some more information about how EQ works.

- A High-Pass Filter (HPF) is an EQ that "rolls off" all the low-end below a certain frequency, typically around 80Hz, meaning that it only allows the frequencies above 80 Hz to pass through it. Use this on your vocalists but not on your drums or bass singer. You want to make sure your rhythm section has plenty of bass, but you won't need those frequencies in the upper voice channels (baritone-soprano). Digital HPFs are often adjustable which can be very helpful for more nuanced sound design.

- There are 3 basic types of EQ on most consoles:

  ▷ Low-Shelf: allows you to add or subtract low end. Will include all the frequencies starting as low as your system will go to around 60–120Hz, depending on the EQ.

  ▷ Sweepable Parametric: allows you to control 2–3 parameters of the EQ band.

    » Frequency: choose which frequency is being manipulated

    » Gain: increase or decrease that frequency

    » Q: vary how wide you are spanning the frequency (typically digital only)

  ▷ High-Shelf: allows you to add or subtract high end. Will include all the frequencies starting at around 10–12kHz, depending on your EQ, to as high as your system will go.

Ideally, you'll have a high-pass filter, a low-shelf, 2–3 bands of parametric and a high-shelf. With this many bands of EQ, you can make anything sound good. If you don't have this many bands, then you'll have to make some compromises, but can still clean up each singer's voice considerably. You may find, on occasion, that the most helpful way to clean up a singer's voice is to boost certain frequencies, as opposed to cutting. Boosting mid's and high-mid's (1–5kHz) will add clarity and presence to the voice and when faced with a difficult room, is often the best way to mitigate muddy low's and low-mid's. Boosting the high-shelf can often help with presence in particularly dark spaces as well.

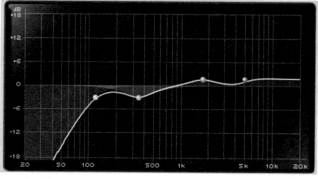

example EQ for vocals

This process is the same for every vocal microphone, regardless of its eventual function (vocal bass, backing vocals, lead vocals). Once this process is done, you then move ahead with "sound designing" the rhythm section mics.

Condenser Pairs

When you're using a pair of (or several) condensers for area-mic'ing an ensemble, the process is slightly different. First of all, because you're using condensers, remember that you need *Phantom Power* so be certain that you have that switched 'ON' for each condenser channel.

Set your mics up onstage. There are several configurations that tend to work well as depicted in the figure below. Now, with the condensers on an empty stage, turn the gain up for each mic until you hear them start to feed back. Adjust the channel EQ such that the mics aren't naturally feeding back anymore (or as best you can). Once you find a setting where you can keep the mic's turned up pretty "hot" without feedback, you're ready to move ahead to soundcheck.

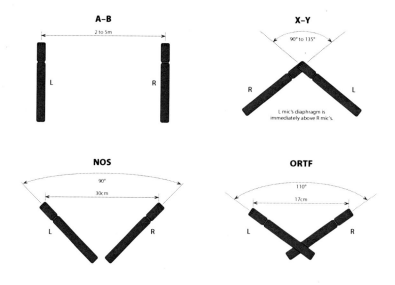

It's important to note that you don't have the ability to push the volume on area mic's like you do with handheld dynamic mics. Area mic's offer gentle reinforcement only, so go easy on them. If you find that you're not getting a mix that's loud or punchy enough, you might want to consider adding some handhelds to your setup.

EQ'ing Vocal Percussion

Vocal percussion requires some different EQ treatment than your vocal mics, as it serves a different mix function than your voices do. While it's still important to have a clean channel with no "mud," ultimately you'll be using a more aggressive approach to the EQ since your vocal drums utilize a broader frequency range than your singers do. Let's dissect the drum kit and see how to sound design each element thereof.

- The Kick Drum: Have the performer repeatedly make his/her kick drum sound. Sweep through the low-mid's until you find the frequency that makes the drum sound BAD and cut that frequency until it sounds clean (typically somewhere between 300–700Hz). Next, boost the low-end with either the low-shelf, a parametric EQ or a combination of the two until the drum has lots of low-end thump, but not so much that it's out of control. Remember, it's not a beatboxing competition, your drums need to sit in the final mix appropriately so don't overdo it! It's VERY IMPORTANT that your drum channel is being sent to the subwoofer (if you have one in your PA) to ensure the fullest low-end. Lastly, boosting the high-mids (typically somewhere between 2–5kHz) can help enhance the attack of the kick drum.

- The Snare Drum: Have the performer repeatedly make his/her snare drum sound. Adjust the mid's and high-mid's (parametric EQ's) to make the snare drum pop without sounding too boomy or too thin. Make your adjustments sparingly so as to not alter your kick drum sound too much.

- The Hardware (Hi-hats, cymbals, etc.): Have the performer make a variety of hi-hat and cymbal sounds. Adjust the high-end (parametric EQ, high-shelf or a combination thereof) until the hardware sounds bright without being harsh.

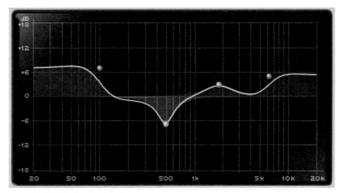

example EQ for Vocal Percussion

Fine Tuning

Have the performer loop a groove which incorporates his/her entire kit. Listen to the drums and make any adjustments to the EQ necessary so that the drums are full, warm and balanced. Sometimes it's very difficult (or virtually impossible) to get each element of the drum set to pop the way you want. You need to compromise until you find a functional EQ. Also, be aware that if the performer doesn't have clean, distinguishable sounds, there's nothing you can do with EQ to rectify that. You can only enhance what is coming into the microphone, you're not a sonic magician!

Advanced EQ Technique

It can be very helpful to split the VP channel into two parallel channels (either with a "direct out" into a second channel input, with a "Y" cable which splits your single XLR input into two XLR inputs, or by "soft-patching" in your digital console). This will allow you to shape the low-end and high-end of the drums separately which, depending on the percussionist's technique, can help provide added clarity to his/her drum kit.

EQ'ing Vocal Bass

Some added tips for shaping your bass sound. Now, remember to clean the "mud" from the channel just as you would any other vocal mic. You don't want to have any resonant frequencies feeding back in your bass. Once that's done, let's give the bass a bit more oomph!

Note: it's best, from a mixing perspective, to treat one bass singer as the "primary bass" used in the mix. The additional basses should certainly be used, but depending on your desired ensemble sound, EQ'd slightly differently so as to not overwhelm the low-end in your mix.

- Low-End: Make sure that the bass channel is assigned to the subwoofer (if applicable). Next, while the bass singer loops a bassline, boost the low-end using the low-shelf until you've added some extra body to the sound. You may find it helpful to use a combination of the low-shelf and a parametric EQ to best boost the low-end. But remember, just as with the kick drum, you don't need the bass to be thunderously big, it just needs to function sonically in the bass frequencies. It's important to keep your bass controlled, as it can consume your entire mix if you let it run wild!

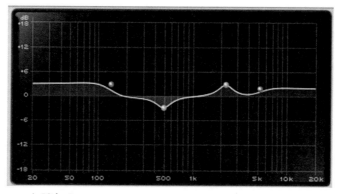

example EQ for Bass

- Clarity: Make any necessary adjustments to the low-mid's and mid-range to make the bass sound deep and full without losing the singer's voice. Boosting the mid-range (approx. 1–3kHz) can help with the presence of the bass and boosting the high-end (approx. 5–8kHz) can help bring out the articulation.

Subharmonic Effect

Depending on what style bass aesthetic you're after, you may find it useful to employ a subharmonic effect to your bass. This effect will add the frequency one octave below the note your bass sings. There are many different products that will achieve this effect and they all differ slightly in terms of interface and function, however the basic concept is the same. To learn how to best connect your "subharm" or "octave pedal" to your bass channel, read your owner's manual and follow the suggestions listed therein.

Subharm effects have the following two basic parameters:

- Level of natural signal
- Level of octave effect

The trick to utilizing this effect well is blending the octave and natural bass such that you have the added "weight" and frequencies of the lower octave but the articulation of the natural signal. This can be done artfully, whether you want to hear mostly subharm for a totally effected sound, or just to help even out the low-end but maintain a very natural sound. This is (largely) achieved by manipulating the low-mid's and mid's to blend the upper-harmonics of the two signals. This will allow the low- and high-end to come through while minimizing the artifacts of the effect itself, which tend to sound "electronic" and are neither sonically pleasing nor useful.

There is no one setting to achieve the right blend of natural and effected sound. There are so many variables involved in sound designing your subharm that you'll need to make changes at every gig. But with time and mastery of the process, you'll quickly learn to get a great bass sound at every show!

Sound Check

Now that you have all the mics sounding great, you're ready to soundcheck the group and get your mix levels set for the show!

The most important thing to remember while mixing: don't overload the output. Watch the output meter and make sure that you're not clipping. If you are, you need to send less level to the output (lower your channel faders a little). If you find that your mix isn't loud enough, you need to turn up your amps (or speaker gain on active speakers).

If you have the time during soundcheck, endeavor to check each song. It will help to know what to expect from each song throughout the performance. With that in mind, you'll need to find some good baseline levels. Let's look at how to do that.

Console Organization

It's very helpful to have an organizational scheme while you mix. Using board tape (or any tape you can affix to the console), label each channel with either a singer's name (if that serves as a descriptor for you) or with whatever label helps you identify that channel's role in the mix. If you can, group like-things on the board—it will make mixing much more intuitive. For example, organizing the board in the following way is one effective layout:

Channel 1: Bass (primary)

Channel 2: Bass 2

Channel 3: Bass 3

Channel 4: Tenor 1

Channel 5: Tenor 2

Channel 6: Tenor 3

Channel 7: Alto 1

Channel 8: Alto 2

Channel 9: Alto 3

Channel 10: Soprano 1

Channel 11: Soprano 2

Channel 12: Soprano 3

Channel 13: Vocal Percussion

This layout allows you to identify each voice part clearly along the length of the board. If you need to make adjustments to the alto part in a song, you know exactly where to find the alto singers without scrambling around the board looking for individual mics. Another useful layout is to have the mics in numerical order as they appear on stage from, say, left to right. Or, using a color-coded system on the mics and the board correspondingly. Ultimately, the best layout is the one that allows you to find your mics the quickest. Don't undervalue the need for "house keeping," live mixing is a stressful, fast-paced job and the more intuitively you understand your board, the better equipped you are to make adjustments quickly and effectively. Lastly, have a method for taking notes on each song. Channel levels, who's singing the lead vocal, so-and-so has switched to alto on this song, etc . . . all of these details will help you when it comes time to mix the show. You only have one chance to get the mix right so the more info you have, the better!

Mixing the Rhythm Section

Have your vocal percussionist and your bassist loop a groove. Ideally, it'll be something loud and punchy as that will be more illustrative for this process. First, with the drums and bass looping, check the input levels for each channel and adjust as necessary. It's quite common for people to perform louder than they soundcheck, so it's a good idea to keep an eye on input levels during this stage (and especially during the show when adrenaline is pumping!). Next, make any necessary adjustments to the EQ so that you can hear the drums and the bass clearly. Here's a quick checklist to follow:

- Low-End: Make sure that you're not overloading the low-end. You want the bass and the kick drum to be nice and low, but you want to make sure that together they're not overwhelming the mix or one another.

- Drum Clarity: Listen to the drums and make sure that you can clearly hear each element of the drum kit. It's important that the frequency range is clear and present. If one element is not present in the mix, adjust the EQ slightly until you can clear-up the whole kit.

- Bass Clarity: As above, listen to the bass and make any necessary adjustments to the EQ so that you can hear the bass clearly and it sounds warm, deep and full.

Submixing the Backing Vocals

Whether you're going to physically group the voice parts on the board or not, it's useful to do a quick submix of the backing vocals. Have each singer for a certain voice part sing a section of the song and adjust their levels to balance each singer in the section. Repeat that process for each voice part. Ideally, you'll be able to do this for each song and just make a note of the levels for each track to use during the show. This method will help simplify the complicated task of mixing the backing vocals.

Monitor Mix

Once you have your general levels set for your "band," it's time to make sure that everyone on stage can hear themselves clearly. Regardless of which type (or combination) of monitors you're using, the process is basically the same.

Each monitor mix will be fed using a separate pre-fader aux-send. For each track that you want heard through a given monitor mix, increase the aux-send fader level on that channel until that signal is heard clearly through the monitors. A good place to start when setting monitor levels is to set all the channels equally across all the monitors and then make adjustments as subtly as possible to individual channels, compensating for varied input gains, singing technique and musical function. This is also the time to revisit your monitor EQ. The lower you can keep your overall monitor level, the better, both for feedback issues as well as minimizing the effect the monitor output has on your F.O.H. mix.

A USEFUL TIP

Getting closer to your mic will help your voice be heard more clearly through the monitors; this is counterintuitive to most singers who tend to timidly pull off their mic when they can't themselves.

Remind your singers that they can use the monitor mix to make their own balance adjustments. Your monitor mix can become an arms race, so shy away from just turning people up in the monitors unnecessarily, lest your monitors become an unmitigated feedback disaster!

Remember, listening through monitors is very unnatural at first and it takes practice. The more time you dedicate to acclimating to this new listening environment, the more nuanced you can be with your mix and this will help both your singers on stage as well as your mixing engineer.

Putting the Mix Together

Now, the moment of truth! Have the group start a song, preferably something loud. For now, have the lead vocalist sit out as you're going to be spending a bit of time working on the backing vocalists or "the band." Adjust your track levels so that you can hear each element of the arrangement clearly and balanced while not clipping the output. In general, having the bass and drums just a little louder than the other arrangement elements, particularly on an upbeat, rhythmic tune will help. Once you have the arrangement sounding good, have your lead vocalist sing. Make sure that you have enough headroom to push the lead vocal loud enough that it can be heard over the arrangement. Generally, the lead should be the focal point of a performance. If you find that you can't hear the lead without pushing it past the point of clipping, turn everything else down (evenly across the board, so that your relative levels remain unchanged). Of course, throughout this process, you need to make sure that everyone is practicing good mic technique!

Again, ideally, you'll be able to do this process for every song so that you can set levels for the whole set and not have to worry about any surprises once the show starts. The more information you have about each song, the easier time you'll have mixing. Be thorough and take good notes that you can easily refer to during the show so that you're not caught off-guard. And most importantly, be attentive while you're mixing. You can rest assured that the moment you look away from the show, something important will happen!

The Main Event

It's show time! Get comfy and stay focused because this is the moment of truth. Everyone in the audience is going to experience the concert through your fingertips, so . . . no pressure!

Your primary objective: create a comfortable yet exciting, dynamic listening experience for the audience. If you've done all your setup and soundcheck effectively, this should be pretty straightforward. Let's assume the best-case scenario and then discuss some troubleshooting techniques later. Here are some important mixing mantras:

Keep Your Eye On The Ball: You have lots of things to pay attention to. You need to stay focused. You aren't there to *watch* the show. You are the single thing standing between the performers and the audience. In a way, and certainly sonically speaking, you ARE the show. Remember: CONSTANT VIGILANCE.

Keep Your Eye On The Prize: You've spent hours painstakingly working out the tiniest sonic details. And everyone in the audience will be thankful for that work . . . they just won't know it! But, everyone in the audience will notice if they can't hear someone's solo, if a mic is accidentally muted or if the beatboxing comes screaming through the mix like a fighter jet. The point is, don't sweat the little details now—the time for that has passed. Have fun with the show and make sure all the important things are attended to. Chances are, you will miss lots of tiny details. That's ok. The important thing is that everyone in the audience enjoys the show.

A Balanced Mix Is A Happy Mix: The rhythm section needs to be clear and driving. The arrangement needs to be tucked-in nicely so all the harmony and texture is represented. And most importantly, all the solo moments need to be front-and-center for the audience to hear. As you make changes, remember to make them gradually and subtly. The more nuanced you can be with your mixing the more natural an experience you'll create for the audience.

Effects

Once you master the basics of mixing, there are a few additional tools that can really help your mix both functionally and aesthetically. Let's learn the basics of a few of these tools.

Compressors and Limiters

As the name suggests, a compressor takes the amplitude of a given signal and compresses it, meaning makes the soft's louder and the loud's softer—essentially making the sound a more consistent, steady volume. You can imagine that this can be very helpful for mixing, because you don't need to worry about anything being wildly soft of loud. Compressors have the following parameters:

- Ratio: How much you're compressing the sound

- Threshold: How loud the signal has to be before the compressor engages

- Attack: How long after the threshold has been reached before the compressor engages

- Release: How long the signal remains compressed after the compressor has engaged

- Gain: "Make-Up Gain" to compensate for any loss of overall volume due to compression

- Knee (optional): How drastically or gradually the compressor engages

Limiters are a type of compressor. Their primary difference is that they only address the loud's of a given signal, not the soft's. Essentially, they just prevent a signal from clipping by rounding-off any peak over a certain volume. Limiters are very useful for controlling your vocal channels as they allow the singers' dynamics to translate, while safeguarding from the occasional wild outburst.

Compressors and limiters are typically connected to your rig using an *INSERT*. If you're inserting a physical piece of gear, you'll need an "insert cable." If you're using a digital board with onboard compression, you simple enable the compressor for the selected channel.

Compression is a very powerful tool for shaping bass and drums as they tend to be very dynamic. By adjusting the parameters artfully, you can perform very nuanced shaping of the channel's sound, particularly when used in conjunction with EQ. Here are some helpful hints:

Compressing Bass

Ratio: Keep a fairly low ratio (~3:1). You want to compress the sound while still maintaining its dynamic range. You'll need to experiment to see exactly what setting works best.

Threshold: You'll need to play with this. The lower the threshold, the more often the compressor will kick-on. This will impact your EQ, so be aware of that. Find a setting that helps make the bass more consistent.

Attack: You want to set this such that the attacks feel even. You don't want to set it so slow that the huge attacks slide past the compressor, but you also don't want it so fast that all the attacks disappear.

Release: Set the release fast enough that you can hear all the nuance of the bassline without losing control of the dynamics. If you set it too fast, you'll hear random loud attacks and if you set it too slow, you'll miss a bunch of attacks as they're getting squashed by the compressor.

Gain: Use this to recover any lost gain due to the compression.

Knee: Adjusting this can help with the nuance of how the attacks get treated. A softer knee will make the compressor engage gradually and can help maintain the dynamics of the attacks. If your bass is very aggressive, a hard knee will make the compressor control the attacks with equivalent aggression.

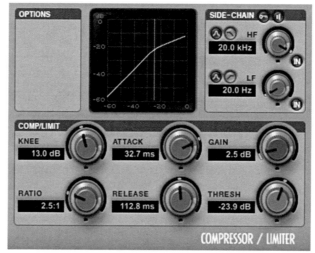

example compression for bass

Compressing Vocal Percussion

Ratio: Start with a medium ratio (~4:1). Depending on the drummer's technique, you'll want decent control of the dynamics, while still allowing for some nuance to translate. You'll need to experiment to see exactly what setting works best.

Threshold: You'll need to play with this. The lower the threshold, the more often the compressor will kick-on. This will impact your EQ, so be aware of that. Find a setting that helps make the drums more consistent.

Attack: You want to set this such that the attacks feel even. Set it fast enough that all the big attacks are under control but not so fast that the little nuance hits disappear.

Release: Set the release as fast as you can to capture all the nuance of the drums while not losing control of them at any point.

Gain: Use this to recover any lost gain due to the compression.

Knee: In general, you'd want this set fairly hard for drums. Of course, experiment and use what sounds best.

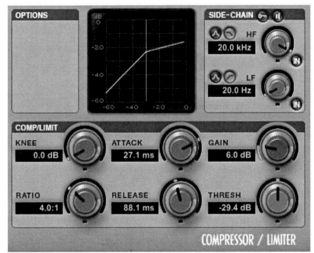

example compression for drums

Reverb

Reverb is another effect used to add space or dimension to your mix. Like when you sing in a big stone cathedral and the sound dissipates over several seconds . . . that's reverb. Generally speaking, reverb can help make a very dead, dry room sound more interesting by adding some depth and ring which can be very helpful for your mix's "definition" meaning how *dry* (clear) or *wet* (distant) certain elements sound. Let's see how reverb works.

- Algorithm: The type of reverb you're using (plate, spring, hall, cathedral, etc.). Each has its own characteristics and thus will be geared towards certain implementations.

- Size: How spacious the reverb is, typically mimicking the size of a room.

- Decay: How long the reverb rings.

- Mix: The balance of how much of the reverb you hear versus the original signal.

When using reverb, remember to match the type of reverb with the style of music you're mixing. You wouldn't want to use a large cathedral reverb for a group singing all upbeat pop songs. But, it would certainly sound nice on some legato choir pieces! One common mistake is to use too much reverb. It does sound really cool, but if you use too much reverb, the mix will be too wet and no one will be able to hear any detail in the mix so use it appropriately.

Reverb is best employed using an aux-send/return. Read the manual on your console to learn how to hook up effects using your aux's. The nice thing about this setup is that it allows you to adjust how much each channel is being sent to the reverb. With that in mind, let's look at some tricks for using reverb to help shape your mix.

Definition

Set your send levels on all your channels equally. You should hear a nice balance of dry and effected (reverb'd) vocals. Now, remember how we said earlier that we want the drums and bass to cut a little more than the other background parts? Turn the reverb send down on the bass and drum channels (especially the kick channel if your drums are split). Hear how they cut through the mix better? The rhythm section is more dry than the vocals so those elements become more clearly defined.

EQ'ing the Verb

Every piece of gear that you add to your signal chain imparts its own sonic signature. Additionally, by using the aux-send setup for your reverb, you're creating a second "copy" (if you will) of your mix to be played through the reverb. Any EQ issues that might exist will be accentuated now that you've duplicated those signals. If you have the ability (whether by connecting an EQ in-series after your physical reverb unit or via your digital console) to EQ your reverb, you will have a much easier time working with the effect. The goal of EQ'ing the verb is to eliminate any unwanted mud while keeping the gloss and wetness of the effect.

Delay

Mostly an aesthetic effect, delay adds an echo to a signal and can breathe a lot of life and excitement into your mix. Delay's can vary greatly in their parameters, but let's look at the basic concept in its most simple form.

- Delay Time: This is where you set the tempo at which the echo repeats. "Tap Delays" allow you to physically tap the tempo of the song, setting the delay time dynamically.

- Decay: How long the delay will repeat before fading away.

- Mix: The balance between the delay effect and the original signal.

You need to use discretion when implementing delays. They can have a negative effect on your mix's musical function as your adding a new musical texture to the mix. Now, artistic situations aside, you typically won't want any delays on your bass or drums. If you have your backgrounds going through a delay (set up with an aux-send/return again), you want to make sure that the delay isn't imparting any negative rhythmic information into the arrangement. Less is more here. Also, just as with the reverb, making sure the EQ of the delay makes for a pleasant addition to the mix and doesn't obscure anything is critical to a successful implementation.

The one place where you can be a bit more liberal with the effect is on the lead vocal. It's an age-old practice to put a delay on the lead vocal and it does make for a cool mood. Just be appropriate with the effect; it should function as "the cherry on top" and not interfere with the function of the lead.

Troubleshooting

No amount of preparation or experience can prevent issues 100% of the time and that's ok, as long as you're thinking quickly on your feet and able to make adjustments. Here are some common issues and some considerations for resolving them.

- *I don't hear any sound.* Make sure that everything is powered "ON" (speakers, amps, console, effects, etc.) and that all the cables are still attached to the right inputs/outputs. Next, make sure the mics are all "ON" and unmuted. Finally, double check that your channel outputs are assigned to the right path. There are often buttons on the console that define which output path the channel runs down. Make sure the channels are assigned to the correct path (main, submix 1, submix 2, etc.).

- *There are feedback problems.* First, check that none of the channels are clipping. If they are, lower the input gain for any overdriven channels. Next, check if the output is clipping. If so, lower all the faders evenly across the board so that you stop overdriving the output. Third, if the feedback persists, it's likely an EQ issue. You'll need to find the channel where the feedback is coming from and modify its EQ to stop overloading that frequency. If many channels are feeding back on the same frequency, you can make a change to the F.O.H. EQ for global adjustment.

- *I can't hear the lead vocal.* If you can't correct this with simple volume adjustment, then you'll have to modify the EQ on the channel to make the lead cut through the mix better. Try sweeping through the mid's until you find the frequency that helps the lead's voice cut through.

- *The bass sounds low but I can't hear any notes.* Remember that the part of the bass that contains most of the pitch content isn't the really low stuff, but the low-mid's. Try sweeping from ~200–500Hz. If that doesn't help, sweep through the mid's ~1–3kHz to help the bass cut through better.

- *I can't hear all the detail of the arrangement and the solo at the same time.* No, you can't . . . you need to remember that you're mixing an ensemble comprised of all the same instrument . . .

there's nothing inherently different about your backing instruments from your soloists. The lead vocal is the most important part, so err on the side of making that audible over the arrangement. If you're using a reverb, try making the lead more dry to help it cut through.

- *The singers can't hear themselves on stage*: Send them more level to the monitors. If the monitors start feeding back, try repositioning the monitors—it's very common that the monitor cabinets end up aiming the sound either too low or too high for the singers to hear their output. Try putting a block of wood under the front of each wedge cabinet. Finally, try removing some of the low-mid's from the monitor EQ. The content that lives between 200–500Hz often obscures the useful "tuning" frequencies which range closer to 1–2.5kHz. You may also find it helpful to cut some of the high-end (>10kHz, as this doesn't help you tune but is prone to feeding back).

Summary

- Understand the room
- Choose an adequate sound system
- Set up your gear
- Ring the room
- Ring the monitors
- Line-check the mics
- Label your console for efficient mixing
- Soundcheck the mics
- Soundcheck your rhythm section
- Submix your background vocals
- Set your monitor mix
- Soundcheck a song
- Design your aesthetic effects (reverb, delay, etc.)
- Soundcheck as many songs as time allows, taking detailed notes
- Showtime—stay alert and HAVE FUN!

Voicebox

Vox Machina

CHAPTER 24

LIVE LOOPING

By Jacob Reske

Live looping is one of the most exciting techniques to emerge for live production in the last few decades. Already, we are seeing totally new genres pop up, where solo singers and beatboxers layer and repurpose their voices as instruments in creative ways. But these tools are still new, and we've only scratched the surface of their power for creating and improvising music. Live looping is just the next step toward something greater: live production.[1] The dream of being able to create, sample, and modify sound on the spot is one that many musicians are exploring, and it could change the way that we approach the creative process.

Right now there is a lot of potential. Twenty years after the loop pedal's commercial debut, and live looping is on the cusp of a kind of musical renaissance.[2] A quick look at the Billboard Top 100, and you see some familiar faces in the scene: Ed Sheeran, Kimbra, Imogen Heap, and many others all openly use looping as a key component to both songwriting and performance. In a recent video, Ed Sheeran shares that his most recent album "was all written around the loop pedal. And most of it recorded with the loop pedal."[3] Listen to any of these artists' albums, and the musical fingerprints that looping encourages can be found on nearly every song.

Even more so, looping has thrived as a tool to expand solo performance. The looper has enabled a whole new class of musicians to grow and emerge as headliners: professional beatboxers. Solo acts like Dub FX and Kid Beyond have completely transformed the way beatboxing can be presented in a live context. Nothing is off-limits: loopers, octavizers and heavy effects are used freely, and everything is created on the spot. Often, these artists deliberately plan nothing beforehand. They place emphasis on looping as an enabler of improvisation. Prominent looping artist and beatboxer Beardyman has openly praised the looper as a tool for creating music on the spot.[4] With a few taps, Beardyman can recreate the instruments and songs in his head before he forgets them. For songwriters and producers, the potential here is huge. A looper can act as a musical sketchbook—a way to jot down ideas, vary them, and (most importantly) keep them playing while you write.

Even more portentous is the way that these artists' fans talk about looping music. Ed Sheeran's fans don't classify him as a "live looping" artist. They see the looper as a tool; an instrument that the artist uses for composition and performance. They get to glimpse into the songwriting process and see the song being constructed, part by part, right before their eyes. In addition, the audience instinctively knows that live looping is a challenge because things could go wrong at any moment. That tension can add an extra level of energy and excitement to an artist's performance.

Live looping and a cappella music

One by one, every genre and instrument has seen a rekindled interest using loop pedals. That's one of the greatest things about live looping: it's instrument (and genre) agnostic. Anyone, from a solo guitarist to a 30-person choir, can use loopers as tools for composition. Of course, soloists have the most to gain from this way of working; a few loops later, and a single performer can create a whole band by themselves, with no other accompaniment. With a bit of thought and preparation, however, any group (and instrument) can find ways to use these tools to their advantage.

But live looping has always had a very special relationship with vocal music. Some of the biggest advocates of the art form at the moment are singers and beatboxers.[5] They're the ones who are constantly searching for solutions to new problems—expanding the arsenal of sounds that their voices alone can produce. There is an active conversation between a cappella musicians and live looping artists, as one informs and inspires the other. And there's a good reason for that: a cappella is an art form that is constantly interested in re-contextualizing the human voice. For that reason, I think that there may be no better genre with which to explore and extend the implications of these ideas.

"But, in a larger ensemble, what's the point?" you might ask. A 16-person a cappella group, for example, never runs into the same problems that a solo artist might. These groups have plenty of capable voices to go around; they don't need a looping pedal to add rhythm sections or harmonic complexity. Introducing more elements might even be overwhelming to the listener. I often get comments along the lines of, "Why not just add more singers, rather than looping a smaller ensemble?" and "If the same arrangement can be done simply with more voices, rather than introducing loops, why bother?"

Here is another common concern: songs that use looping can be repetitive and structurally stiff. If a looped phrase is played back for the entire song, with no variation, things can get boring quickly. With a traditional rhythm section, on the other hand, it's very easy to introduce variation and transition. Most looping hardware has a difficult time making transitions sound fluid. Song sections are another big problem; as a solo artist, how do you create contrasting sections, if it takes four loops to build each section when you perform live?

These critiques should be explored further. With one performer, the case for using live looping makes sense for a technical reason: there just aren't enough performers onstage to make every element of most songs. If loopers were only capable of repeating phrases (and nothing else), there wouldn't be many uses for them in a larger ensemble.

But these ideas are so much more than that. On a computer, live looping is just another entry point for recording and sampling musical material, live and in a performance. Once you have that, anything goes. You could take a recorded phrase and chop it up, then reintroduce it as something completely new. This kind of variation can add musical nuance and character to the rest of your song. It also highlights the close relationship that looping has with sampling; a practice that has made waves in almost every musical genre today. In part because of the limitations above, this relationship has yet to be fully explored.

But let's not get too far ahead of ourselves. To understand how looping can enhance a performance creatively and technically, we have to identify some of the basic building blocks, the tropes of a looping performance that you'll consistently hear. Let's dissect these tropes to find their origin, how they are used well, and where they can be either helpful or constricting from an artistic standpoint.

The Basics

Every performance with a looper has two basic components: recording and playback. The order usually goes like this: the performer records a phrase of a certain length, defines consistent start and endpoints, and hears it played back exactly as it was recorded. If this seems intuitive, it's because these steps are incredibly common; they are embedded in the workflow of almost all loopers used today.

Even though this seems like a simple process, it requires the performer to make several decisions before the performance even begins. How long will this loop have to be? Does it play for the entire song, or will it start and stop throughout? Does the phrase start on a downbeat, or a pickup measure? How will the performer trigger the looper to toggle between record and playback? More to the point: do they even have enough hands free to trigger the loop at all? For singers, this isn't usually a problem, but many instrumentalists have to consider this.

The biggest questions that have to be solved revolve around timing. In this chapter, I will often refer to a musical phrase's **internal clock**—where the phrase's musical downbeat lies in real time, and how that downbeat relates to the clock of the rest of the song. In a typical live looping performance, the performer records a single loop at the beginning of the song, and its endpoints define the loop's **period** for the rest of the song. All the material that follows, including future loops, refer to that loop's internal clock for starting and stopping. But what if you want the looper to follow a different internal clock, for a tempo change, or to sync with another instrument or player? In the simplest situation (with just one performer) these questions are easy to solve. But these early questions compound on themselves by adding more loops and performers who need to sync with the looper.

What about the content of the loop itself? Will it remain the same throughout the song, or will it be modified during the performance? Will it be shortened, chopped up, or change in pitch as the song goes on? What kind of effects do you want to add to the loop? Will you ever need to replace elements in the loop as the song goes on? There's one more vital question, and it's not one that many solo loop artists have to consider. Where is the looped material coming from? A solo vocalist might only have one source for looping, but an a cappella group could get very creative by changing the source of the loop. You could loop a single singer or vocal percussionist, a part or rhythm section, or the entire group itself.

Some of these questions do not have easy answers. To talk about effects and audio sources requires you to get pretty deep in hardware and audio routing. While some people (like me) could have fun spending all day on problems like those, you're forgiven if you get frustrated or just want to get on to making music. This is the state of live looping today; there is no "one size fits all" solution for every musician. Every looping device has different answers to the questions I posed above, and these answers reflect a way of making music that the hardware (or software) designer intended.

Many simple hardware loopers, like the popular **Line 6 DL4** for example, don't allow you to create loops longer than 14 seconds. The design places emphasis on loop effects, like delay (after all, it is a delay pedal first). **TC-Helicon** makes a series of touch-based loopers; each loop is recorded to separate, independent channels with their own set of effects. Then again, since it's hardware, you're limited by the set of features inside the box. Sometimes, software loopers offer a plethora of features to cover every possible use-case, but they aren't as easy to use out of the box as their hardware cousins. **Ableton Live**, for example, arguably has two different looper interfaces, each designed for two totally different purposes. The whole program could be used as one very flexible (but complicated) global-clocked live looper (more on that later). Or you could just use the included "Looper" audio effect, which works much more like a traditional analog tape looper.

If all this sounds confusing, it's because (at the moment) it is. As of this writing, there is no single looping device, hardware or software, that I can confidently say is both intuitive and extensible for every live musician's needs. But there are patterns that emerge in these devices, and it is important to understand them before knowing what works best for your performance or group. To help explain these concepts, it would be helpful to start small. We'll first look at the concepts that the most basic looping devices have in common, and how they work in practice. After that, we'll build on up.

Single channel (Overdub-based) loopers

Single channel loopers are the most common way to use looping in live performance, and they are the most basic unit in any looping system. If you've ever seen a solo singer loop themselves live, you're likely familiar with the concepts in these loopers. These devices usually have three modes: **record, overdub,** and **playback.** In **record** mode, a single tap will start recording audio;

another tap will set the endpoint of the loop. Depending on the hardware, the looper will next go into **playback** mode: where the loop will repeat from the beginning, over and over, until it is told to stop. Sometimes, the next tap will trigger **overdub** mode: playback, but the looper continues recording over the existing loop. Recording in overdub mode will continue to add incoming audio to the loop, writing on top of the loop that has already been recorded for the length of the first phrase. Another button will start and stop the loop from the top.

These concepts are our starting point; they are the way that almost every looper operates, and they're taken directly from the ideas of analog tape recording. The best thing about this approach is that it's both simple and ubiquitous. There are hundreds of hardware and software loopers out there, many of them free, that follow this exact approach. If you haven't played with a looper before, try downloading a free one to your computer or smartphone. Practice singing into the looper while toggling the record/overdub/playback buttons. Often, you can control these three modes by pressing just one button! The simplicity of these devices can be very helpful– especially for singers or instrumentalists who have their hands full. The one-button approach makes it a good starting point for most performers, because it manages to be both intuitive and versatile.

As you practice, you'll start to notice some of the challenges that artists who use these devices have to deal with. You'll probably notice that toggling the start and endpoints of the loop (in time with your singing) is harder than you originally thought. Since those two button presses define the strict length of the phrase, they have to line up precisely with the musical phrase that you want to loop. Staying in time, especially for the first loop, is very important; since those two endpoints are your only reference points, slowing down or speeding up the tempo can lead to big problems when you start to overdub. Solving these two problems requires practice. Mastery of both your own tempo and the tempo of the looper, its internal clock and yours, is what makes a live looping performance appear seamless. Once you get the basics down, this kind of looping can be endlessly fun. Start with a beat (percussion), overdub with a rhythm part or two, and you've got a whole band to back you up.

As long as your song sticks to the basic form that these loopers require, you're golden. But, as you might have already noticed, this workflow does have its limitations. Most hardware loopers, for example, use **destructive overdub**: meaning an overdub loop will always record on top of the base loop, and there's no way to separate the two after the fact. The implication of this isn't immediately obvious, but here's an example where destructive overdub becomes constricting. Suppose you record a 4-bar beatbox loop, then overdub with a 4-bar baseline, then a 4-bar harmony part. Now you have phrases 1, 2, and 3 as a single 4-bar loop. Now say that, in a new section of the song, you wanted to cut away to just Phrase 2 (the bassline). On loopers that use destructive overdub, you can't. All three phrases have become permanently merged.

Here's another example: suppose you sing an 8-bar bassline to start your new song. You're ready to add a loop of beatboxing, but the part is simple; it repeats after two bars, not eight. You'd love to record the percussion in 2 bars to get to the meat of the song faster. With single loopers, however, you can't. Every subsequent loop has to be exactly 8 bars. This problem becomes compounded as your first loop gets more complicated, since the song takes that much longer to add every part you want. On the flipside, your first loop has to be as long as the most complicated (longest) element in your song. The shorter that first loop is, the less variation you can have in the single loop.

I believe that these two limitations are the biggest factors that determine the song structure and musical tropes in live looping. When you can only add to a loop, rather than subtract, it's hard for your song to go in any direction but bigger and more complicated. If every phrase has to be the same length as your initial loop, you'll have a long lead-time before you can get to the meat of the song (especially if you're performing as a solo vocalist). Consider a song (as before) that has the following: an eight bar bassline, two bars of repeating percussion, and a four bar rhythm section that is made up of two voices in harmony. In a single looper, all of these loops have to be recorded as eight bar phrases. If our tempo is 120 beats per minute, every bar will be two seconds long, and each of our phrases will be 16 seconds. Just looping these four phrases alone (perfectly, with no interruptions) will take 1:04. That's over a minute of adding before your audience can hear the solo! Much of that time could have been cut down if our looper allowed phrases of variable length.

In the digital world, you might think that these limitations are old hat. Surprisingly, this basic single-looper structure is by far and away the most common interface for looping, both in hardware and software. Part of this may be due to how easy it is to pick up and use single loopers with no experience. But some of the biggest names in hardware and software use this model as their basic unit. Almost every looper app on mobile (Android/iOS) uses this format. The ideas of destructive overdubbing and a static loop length are so widespread that their musical fingerprints can be found everywhere in live looping performances.

But we want to go further than that. We want use live looping in other song structures, other than just additive ones. Eventually, we want to see if we can use these techniques in an ensemble setting, especially with an a cappella group. The limitations of single loopers will only become more more obvious when we add more complexity. What other tools can we use besides these?

Parallel (multi-channel) loopers

Thankfully, loopers have evolved. One great way to overcome both problems above is for your looper to be a series of multiple (independent) loopers, each of them containers for recording different musical phrases. On some devices, using this technique is called "phrase looping." The key thing to realize is that these loopers are just extensions of the single case above. They work in the same way, but having more containers gives us far more flexibility. Some of these devices will have four, eight, or even sixteen channels for independent loops. The more channels, the more options you have.

Let's revisit our previous example. Say you record an eight bar bass line as one loop. With a single/overdub-based looper, you could overdub the percussion on top of the first loop, as before, but then you wouldn't be able separate them later. They will always have to play together. With multiple loopers, you have options. Instead, you can now loop the percussion on a separate channel, and record that as a two bar phrase, rather than eight. With two independent loopers, we've solved two problems right away: we can play one phrase without the other, and we don't need each loop to repeat with the same period. Clearly, this way is much more flexible.

There are other big advantages to this approach, though some of them might not be immediately obvious. With just a four-channel looper, you can start to group parts by their musical role in the song. You could have one channel for all your percussion loops; another for a harmony section; another for backing vocals. You could overdub all the notes of a chord into one looper, so it functions like a pad or rhythm guitar in your song. Writing, improvising, and performing in this way starts to feel closer to the way a band would compose: adding and subtracting elements as groups, and using them as larger, macro-level building blocks in a song.

But we've just started exploring the potential of splitting musical material into separate loops. An independent, four-channel looper starts to feel a lot like the live version of a four-track recorder. Many multi-channel loopers will let you adjust different elements of these channels independently. You could change the relative volume of each channel, or add an octave effect to the bass channel while keeping your percussion track clean. With **post-loop effects**, we can start to treat each loop channel even more like separate musical elements. This is where live looping starts to meet live production. The tools that you can use today to modify the voice are the same tools that producers of pop, EDM and hip hop use with instruments today. They're also the tools that are found everywhere in modern a cappella recordings. Now, with separate channels, you can start to use these same tools and effects live.

Of course, adding independent loopers can add complexity. The biggest problem has to do with timing. As before, each single looper has its own **internal clock**, and it is very important that the clocks for all loopers run in sync to each other. If they didn't, the distance between the start and endpoints (or **period**) of any two loopers might be slightly off from each other, causing the loops to slowly move out of sync as time goes on. Different loopers (hardware and software) approach this problem differently. In the **master clock** approach, the start and endpoints of one looper define the basic unit of time. All other loopers act as "slaves," starting and stopping in sync to that loop's clock. Here's an example: suppose you record a two bar loop that repeats exactly every five seconds. When you press "record" on any other looper, it will start as soon as the master loop completes one period. Switching the loop to "playback" will stop recording as soon as the master loop completes one period as well. In technical terms, this means that every new loop's **period** will be a multiple of the master loop's period.

Another popular approach is the **global clock** method. These loopers do not have a hierarchy, where one looper defines the clock for all the others. Instead, they all reference their internal clock from the same place, usually a running metronome, or an external instrument. This means that every looper that you use will create loops that are in time with this metronome. This is called a **quantized looper**; it will only ever create loops that are synced with an external clock and tempo. Specifically, the **period** of every loop will be directly related to the global tempo. This also means that anyone who uses a quantized looper has to have some reference to the external tempo for the beginning of the performance. For a solo looping artist, this might mean that there's a metronome playing in their ear, letting them sync their phrases with the looper's clock at all times.

All of this might sound pretty technical, but these distinctions can make a big difference. Like our single looper case, the timing relationships between each looper will inevitably shape the phrases of music you compose with them. Let's give an example: With a parallel looper synced with a **master clock**, you need to listen to your first loop over and over to hear the tempo and position of your master clock. For this reason, you'll probably want your first loop to be a rhythm track, like a vocal percussion track. This is the same as the single looper case; since your first loop defines the strict start and endpoints, it had better be a pretty rhythmic part (so that you know where the loop position is at any moment).

With a **global clocked** looper, you don't have that limitation; the global metronome is always playing in your ear, telling you where you are for every bar. Now, your first loop can be more interesting. You could make your first loop a less rhythmic part, or start midway through the bar. But there's one big disadvantage to the global approach: since the loops are all **quantized** (to a bar, for example), your songs have to be a little less flexible. You'll have to define the tempo of your global clock beforehand, and you really can't do much outside of that grid. This approach requires more setup, and the constant metronome can make your songs and transitions pretty rigid. For that reason, many live looping beatboxers prefer software and hardware they can define the tempo on the fly with a master clocked looper, not a global one.

Some more advanced software loopers even let you switch between these modes fluidly, even back to loopers whose clocks aren't synced at all. Imagine this situation: you want your loops to transition fluidly from one song to another, but they're at very different tempi. In this situation, you could introduce another loop that becomes *another* master clock for a different set of loops. Or you could start to make music that isn't totally periodic, that is not every looped phrase lines up every time. This kind of control is incredibly powerful, but mastering it for performance is not easy. Just wrapping your head around multi-clocked looping requires an incredible level of patience and hours of practice. Hey, we never said this kind of live performance would be easy.

Looping with a group (and multiple live loopers)

So far, I've only given examples of *solo* live looping: looping a single voice, with one performer and one controller. We've already seen that there are many different ways to approach this problem: from a single analog looper all the way up to a complex multitrack approach, with internal clocks that can switch in and out of sync. In the end, the approach you use comes down to what you prioritize most in your performance: simplicity and improvisation on the one hand, and creative flexibility on the other.

But this is a book about a cappella, where the focus is on the ensemble; what happens when you scale up to more than one voice? How do these concepts work if you incorporate live looping in an ensemble setting, or when more than one singer has the ability to loop at any time? What creative possibilities emerge with this new ability, and what are some of the added challenges of this approach?

These are exciting questions to ask, because the idea of group-based, live looping and production is a very new one. And, as we'll start to see, a lot of the creative limitations of (solo) live looping start to disappear when you add just one more voice to the mix. Let's go back to our earlier example and see what happens when we perform our song with two singers who can loop, rather than one. If you remember, our example song has an eight bar bass line, two bars of repeated drums, an 8-bar doubled rhythm section that makes up the chord, and a live solo. Right from the beginning, our options for the arrangement's form get much more interesting. We no longer have to stick to adding these parts sequentially– bass, then drums, then rhythm twice, then solo. The soloist could start the song off from the top, while the other singer adds each looped part sequentially. Or one singer could record our eight bar bass line, while the other simultaneously lays down the shorter phrases, like the drums and rhythm parts.

Another huge advantage with multiple live loopers is that song sections work more naturally. Parts that often change between sections (like the bass) can now be sung live on top of the solo, rather than looped (and "given away" to the audience) beforehand. In some ways, looping with an ensemble gives you the best of both worlds: you get the creative options that a looper affords you, but you don't have to stick to the strict song structure that solo looping often requires. Another exciting possibility is the ability to loop many singers at the same time and treat it as a single phrase. Imagine your group singing the chords of a chorus, looping it back as a single phrase, and transforming it into something new. I haven't seen many groups, in or out of a cappella, that do this kind of looping, but it could introduce a whole new way to use looping as a musical tool. It feels a lot like the musical practice of **sampling**: a production technique taking sections of recordings and repurposing them as instruments or musical material. In many ways, sampling has defined the sonic landscape of modern music, making its way from hip hop to R&B, pop, and EDM. The techniques of sampling and live looping are very close cousins, and it will be exciting to see how their paths cross further. Many hip hop and EDM producers sample choirs and a cappella groups wholesale and re-contextualize them in new music. What's to say that an a cappella group couldn't sample itself live, in the same way?

Of course, all of this comes with a word of caution. As we saw in the single looper case, one of the dangers of live looping is that it can lead to arrangements that add more often than they subtract. With multiple loopers (and multiple performers using them), that danger becomes even more pressing. Say you have an ensemble and setup where five singers have the ability to add loops at once, at any time. Make an arrangement where each of them contributes just three loops, and that's fifteen repeating parts; your song will start to feel pretty crowded. A multi-looper approach also introduces a new danger: it is very easy for your audience to lose the connection between the material they hear and the performer who is creating it. For a solo live looping artist, this isn't a big problem. It's easy for the audience to understand what's going on, because there is only one focal point: the soloist who is recording each loop. Just add one more person into the mix, and things become more difficult to follow. Add too many loops (and too many people using them at once), and this visual disconnect becomes greater: what you see being performed is only a small fraction of what you hear.

These are good concerns to have, and it speaks to one of the earlier questions I mentioned about using looping with voices in an ensemble setting. If you already have a group that can sing many parts at once, why complicate the texture further by adding loops? What benefits do you gain, other than just having more stuff going on? I think that the best advice for looping in this manner is that great power requires great responsibility. Like any technique, live looping is a tool. A way to expand the musical and timbral options that you have, both in your arrangement and performance. It isn't the act of looping itself that makes for a good piece of live music, but how they serve the story that you tell (and the emotions that you can evoke) using it. Used too much, and these tools begin to lose their meaning.

This goes for live looping in a solo setting as much as with an ensemble. If your only goal is to add more and more material—to show the audience how much you can do with live looping— your end musical product won't be very interesting. A song that just adds loops over and over might be effective in showing off this technique, but it doesn't accomplish much else. The most artful uses of looping today are by artists who use it in different degrees of moderation, as a means to an end, but not the end itself. There is definitely a time and a place to blow your audience's mind and show off a rich, full texture of dozens of parts. But this is just one musical story that can be told using looping, and there are many, many others.

I think that having more of these tools at your disposal, and a larger ensemble with which to use them, only gives you more options to use them subtly. We've talked about how having a parallel looper allows a solo artist to escape from the rigid structure that a single looper demands, or how having just two looping artists (rather than one) can eliminate many of the big restrictions that these tools have on song form. Give these tools to a group of singers, and it becomes just another tool in your musical arsenal. Telling a story that you perhaps couldn't otherwise tell. Think about the looper as an instrument in your ensemble, a tool for songwriting. Identify what you want to accomplish musically, and use it as a means to that end.

Case study: a.squared, and ensemble looping using Ableton Live

In this section, I will show one way to use looping in practice in a vocal music group. You're going to see some of the challenges of looping with an a cappella group, as well as some of our solutions that we've found along the way. A.squared is a new vocal music group that uses ensemble looping as a core component. We use a specific workflow in Ableton Live, a program for live performance and production. With this setup, any one of our singers can loop or sample their own voices, in sync with each other, in real time. I'll explain our approach to ensemble-based looping, and the basics of how our system works right now. Though the concepts in this chapter are pretty common to any looping system, the technology is all pretty new. So, who knows? In a few years, we could be using a completely different system, or a different way of working.

As mentioned earlier, however, this is not a one-size-fits-all approach. In my research for this chapter, I discovered that there are almost as many hardware and software platforms for live looping as there are professional live loopers. Everyone's system is different. We are at a point where the features of most looping platforms lag far behind their potential. At some point, many live looping artists hit a wall, and they often choose to invent their own solution. Some solo acts, like Ed Sheeran, commission heavily customized hardware, designed exclusively for their style.[6] Others, such as beatboxer (and former member of The House Jacks) Kid Beyond, use custom workflows and heavily mapped controllers in Ableton Live.[7] Even Ableton itself was created by live musicians: Gerhard Behles and Robert Henke, of the electronic duo Monolake.[8] They built their first version out of a need to have tools to perform their compositions live; tools that did not exist in any other music programs at the time.[9]

Possibly the most extreme case of this level of customization is Beardyman, a live performing artist who has created his own, elaborate live production software.[10] In workshops and interviews, Beardyman has expressed a common sentiment among professional vocal artists: dissatisfaction with both the lack of features on looping hardware and the lack of stability in looping software.[11] He and a group of programmers chose to build new software and workflow with very specific hardware. Together, they make up the Beardytron 5000.[12] With hundreds of features unmatched by almost every looping platform out there, it is probably the most advanced live looping and production system today– and the only person who uses it is Beardyman himself.[13] This sort of do-it-yourself attitude reflects how brand-new these concepts are to digital (and vocal) music making, and how they could change the way that we approach live production when they become more accessible. Leading the push are the live performers who, at some point, ran into a wall—wanting to do something live that just wasn't possible out of the box—and found a way to get around it.

I formed a.squared to explore how live production and looping could be done with an ensemble of singers. I started to notice that recorded a cappella has quickly become an art form of its own. Many of the techniques that a cappella producers use today parallel changes and techniques happening in all types of music production, and they're very exciting ones. There are some seriously cool ways that you can sample and modify sound today. Live looping and production offer a way to interact with those ideas more directly: at a show, in front of an audience. The basic question we asked was this: what kind of music do you make when you use these techniques as a central idea?

Using Ableton *Live* as a Parallel Looper

With a.squared, we use Ableton Live as our looping and production platform. Together with the computer, it is the brain of a.squared. Nothing happens outside of it; every note that we sing is processed in the computer and is available for us to manipulate live.

To help follow along, in Appendix A I've provided a link to download an example session of a.squared's workflow.[14] This session will open in any version of Live 8 or later.

When you open Ableton Live, you'll be greeted by its distinctive Session View: a grid pattern of cells. The axes of this grid are **tracks** and **scenes**, respectively. Tracks are the way that Live divides up channels of sound, by person and by instrument. The number of active tracks increases and

a.squared

decreases as the song goes on. Some of them take sound from one singer live and are used for looping. Other tracks take their input from multiple singers at once, or even the entire song itself. On the other end, **scenes** are units of time. They represent a small, repeating section of the song, from sixteen bars to four bars to a very small moment. So now, we have a file that is is broken up into small sections of looping parts—clips—one per track per scene. This creates a sort of "grid" of clips, where the tracks are the columns and the scenes are the rows.

Start to think about this in the big picture. Each track takes input from one singer (or many), and each has a series of containers (on the scene axis) that can record and play back periodic clips of sound. Sounds a lot like a looper, no? In fact, that's one way to use Ableton; each track can record and play back one of these looped clips at a time. Which singer is being looped, and ultimately, who controls them, is up to you. But the groundwork is there: with more controllers, as many performers as you like could all be controlling one session of Ableton Live, looping themselves in sync at once.

To use our earlier terms, I would classify this workflow in Ableton as a **parallel looper** that can be used with an ensemble. Each track is like a single looper, able to record and launch looping clips. By default, you can't overdub loops in a single track, but that's almost for the better; as I mentioned before, overdub-based loopers have their own problems. When we need this feature, we make tracks that each contain Ableton's "Looper" device. Now, things work as intended. Each track has a fully functional single looper on each track. Live is also **global clocked looper** by default. Everything, from clips of sound to loops to program changes, has to start and stop in time with a pre-defined grid.

We use this program and method for a number of reasons. The biggest reason is latency: the delay in time it takes for audio to get from the singer's microphones to the monitors onstage, so they hear what they're singing. The latency varies by track. A track with no effects on it has roughly 3.5 milliseconds of latency, which is about the amount of time it takes for sound to travel 1.2 meters (pretty fast). But a track that has more intense effects on it, like a vocal harmonizer, for example, might have up to 15 milliseconds of latency. This would mean that our bass would hear his own effected voice up to 15 milliseconds late, if his voice has effects on it. Hearing sound at a delay makes looping almost impossible, since humans are very bad at adjusting their timing by something large and arbitrary like 10 milliseconds.

Ableton's solution is to use global quantization. That way, loops will always be the right length relative to each other, and relative to the program. But, as covered earlier, the disadvantage is that every singer has to hear the program's global clock at the same time. This is why we use a metronome in the performance. Of course, this approach means that a lot has to be planned out beforehand, and the relationship between internal clocks can't change. It doesn't lend itself well to a workflow that is improvisatory, in the same way that many other loopers do. But the big advantage is that every looper is guaranteed to be totally in sync from singer to singer, and periodic with relation to the tempo.

No matter what, though, there is latency, and the singers have to constantly adjust for that. In fact, much of the skill and practice we devote in rehearsals is to practicing making entrances come in "on time" to the audience. You have to train yourself to account for the delay in the program, since everything you hear is slightly behind. That is one of the inherent challenges of a.squared, and one that we need a lot of time to practice and perfect. A metronome gives the performers a consistent marker with which to time themselves.

There's one other, big advantage to the global clocked approach: many loops and instructions be started and stopped at the same time. When we get to a certain section of a song. a four bar loop, for example. we might want as few as one or as many as 30 instructions to happen at once. These can be little changes, like turning off a track that is no longer in use, or large changes like turning on a big effect for our bassist. Pressing 30 buttons at the same time is very cumbersome, which is where scenes come in. **Scenes** are basically a row of the grid. A single button that can trigger all the instructions in that row to happen at once. You don't have to have every instruction triggered by scenes, but it helps for the bigger moments in the arrangement. To move between sections of the song, even small sections, you have to trigger these scenes with a controller. You can use the computer, but we like to use touch controllers in performance, because they're more visual for the audience.

In practice, this means that one person can control all of the individual loops, or every performer can control them individually. We often have one person controlling the arrangement and loops from one central controller. That way, the other singers can focus on performing and giving it their all. Sometimes, though, having each performer control their own loops and effects gives you more flexibility, and it lends itself better to improvisation. Both options are good for different reasons, and we use both fluidly in performance. That's the great thing about the software approach: how you choose to divvy the work is ultimately up to you.

What's next?

By now, I hope that you're as excited as I am to see where this is all headed. Right now, you can pick up a single loop pedal (or download any of several free apps) that lets you start writing and improvising with your voice right away. Chances are, you'll write, record, and perform in a very different way than you might without the looper. These tools invite you to think non-linearly. The basic ideas of the single, overdub-based looper will inform the way that you approach songwriting and arranging. Best of all, the barrier to entry to explore this art has never been lower. It's never been easier to get started.

But we've only just started to tap the potential and artistry that these techniques can produce, and the future they envision for live production. I would love to see musicians of all types, especially ensembles, have versions of these tools that have these advanced creative features, but are still easy to use. The truth is: modifying digital sound in real time is still a relatively new idea. The singers and vocal groups who are using these techniques have to spend a lot of time and effort practicing this new art. My group, a.squared, spent about a year and a half testing different systems before we settled on the one that we use today. Most live looping artists will tell you a similar story.

Once you get over that technical hurdle, though, there's no limit to what kind of music you can make live with the voice. New techniques have emerged that let loopers go beyond the limits that hardware units have traditionally had. And there's much, much more left to explore creatively in this space, especially for vocal music. This music is nonlinear, improvised, and it takes a lot of practice to master. So play around with these ideas. Identify what looping could accomplish creatively for your performance, your arrangement, or your group. You might discover, as so many other singers and beatboxers have, that it unlocks a new way of making music.

MORE FUN FACTS

- Take 6 creates all of their complex harmonic arrangements by ear, never using sheet music.

- The first (and perhaps most prescient) solo contemporary a cappella album was Todd Rundgren's *A Cappella* (1985).

- Vox Audio (originally called Toxic Audio) first performed at the Orlando Fringe festival and then spent many years at Disney World before making it to Off-Broadway with their show *Loud Mouth*.

- Return 2 Zero performs year-round at Disney World's MGM Studios as Four for a Dollar.

- The Singers Unlimited got their first big break from jazz pianist Oscar Peterson.

- The Persuasions got their first big break from progressive rocker Frank Zappa.

- Straight No Chaser inked a record deal with Atlantic after a song from their decade-old performance became an internet sensation.

- Comedy a cappella group Minimum Wage starred in their own Off-Off-Broadway production in 2008.

- M-pact was formed near Denver, moved to Seattle for a decade, and recently relocated to Los Angeles.

- Beatboxer/live looper Kid Beyond (Andrew Chaikin) originally performed in the House Jacks and before that the Brown Jabberwocks.

- Hookslide's Jon Pilat is a one-man rhythm section, singing the bass line and vocal percussion parts simultaneously.

- The Flying Pickets had a huge international radio hit in the 1980's with an a cappella remake of the Yaz song "Only You."

- The biggest radio hit by the Blenders? Novelty song "McDonald's Girl."

- Ball in the House is named after a line in a Brady Bunch episode.

- Rockapella's first big break came from movie director Spike Lee's decision to include them in the "Do It A Cappella" PBS special.

- Vocal percussionist Wes Carroll does not use his voice at all when doing percussion.

- The House Jacks, based in San Francisco, was the first a cappella group with a full-time dedicated vocal percussionist.

- The Nylons were formed by four actors in the back room of a Toronto deli. Thirty years later, they are still touring the world.

OneVoice

CHAPTER 25
EFFECTS (FX) PEDALS

By Christopher Given Harrison

How and Why Do I Use FX Pedals?

FX pedals further the character, depth, contrast, and originality of your arrangements and performances. They are by no means a crutch, or some substitute for musicality. They are creative tools that allow one to expand upon the statement already being made with the interpretation of the music.

Let's say your group performs a piece from the era of early rock'n'roll—perhaps an Elvis song. Your lead singer will probably put on at least a hint of an Elvis impression, manipulating his or her vowels to sit in the back of the mouth, slurring certain consonants, etc. The point of this is to take the listener back to the "Sun Records" trademark sound. You know what could take them just that much further? A hint of slap-back delay on the lead (which you can hear on just about everything from that era) and a nice, round, quiet octavizer on the bass for that upright "rock-a-billy" sound.

Or you're performing something modern, such as Beyonce's "Halo." You can dial in the same long ballad-timed-delays ("far away echo" sounds that occur in time with the music) that can be heard on the studio track, as well as a little synth bass to beef up the low end of the choruses. The charisma and chops of your lead singer and the musical precision of your hard-working background vocals are still the elements that make or break the performance. The FX can be the gloss coating that allows us to depart from where we are and further immerse ourselves in the journey of the performance.

Definitions of FX Pedals

While there are (of course) many exceptions, FX pedals tend to do one or more of three specific jobs:

- Accentuation: coloring the sound to make it more distinct or interesting
- Extension: reaching beyond the natural limitations of the human voice
- Clean-up: improving the clarity or effectiveness of the sound

Examples of Accentuation Pedals

Distortion/Overdrive

Literally overloads the signal path. This can sound like anything from a broken speaker to an electric guitar solo from the glam-rock era.

Flanger/Phaser/Chorus

Takes one voice, splits it into two, gently manipulates the copy, and plays both simultaneously.

Tremolo

Quick and consistent volume fluctuation of the voice. Imagine vibrato, but rather than the pitch bending slightly up and down at high speeds, the *volume* fluxes up and down at high speeds.

Delay (short, such as "slap-back")

Makes a copy of the incoming sound and plays it back a fraction of a second later, one or more times.

If any of these or the following descriptions leave you wondering what they actually sound like, take a quick spin on YouTube. Search any of these terms and watch about five pedal demonstrations. By the fifth one, you'll get the gist of what the pedal does.

Examples of Extension Pedals

Octavizer

Duplicates the incoming voice one (or several) octave lower.

Harmonizer

Splits the incoming voice into multiple voices in intervals specified by the user.

Looper

Records a long segment of the incoming voice (four or eight bars, for example) and plays it back in a repeating loop.

Delay (long)

Like the loop station, plays back a copy of the incoming voice several seconds later, but unlike the loop station, the repeating voice dies away gradually.

Examples of Extension Pedals

EQ

Allows volume control over specific frequency ranges of the voice (like on a car's sound system).

Noise Suppression/Gate

Cuts the voice out entirely when it comes through at or below a designated level (absolutely necessary when using distortion and overdrive FX to prevent feedback).

Compression

A full explanation of this pedal's operations would be rather lengthy. In short, a compressor shrinks the distance between the sound's quietest and loudest volume levels. It can help a quiet voice cut through a loud background.

The extension pedals are slightly more inconspicuous while in action. It's easier to hear what they do when you switch them off, rather than listening for their effect while they're on.

Which Pedals Should I Get *and* Where Should I Get Them?

In general, I make a blanket recommendation of BOSS pedals to get you started. The sound quality is great, the construction is durable so they tend to last a while, they are functionally reliable (some cheaper FX units have discrepancies in the production of the effected sound), and they can be purchased rather inexpensively through second-hand channels like craigslist.org or in the used section of amazon.com. But in case you'd like specific recommendations across the board, here is a list:

Distortion
BOSS DS-1: Simple, classic, and cheap.

Overdrive
Ibanez TS9 "Tube Screamer": Classic, not as cheap.

Flanger
BOSS BF-3: Lots of variety and pretty color.

Phaser
MXR Phase 90: Simple, effective, and cheap.

Chorus
BOSS CE-5: Lots of variety, but boring color.

Tremolo
Electro-Harmonix Stereo Pulsar: Lots of control and in stereo!

Delay
MXR M169 Carbon Copy Analog Delay: Simple.
Line 6 DL4: Insanely awesome and complicated.

Octavizer
BOSS OC-2: Creates single and double octaves. Awesome, but hard to find.
EBS Octabass: Very smooth, but one octave only.

Harmonizer

Digitech Harmony Man: Can split incoming voice into two additional voices up to one octave above or below, and in a variety of ways.

Digitech Whammy: Creates one additional voice and allows for glissando and pitch bending.

Looper

Digitech Jamman Series:

Jamman Solo: Standard "single" size, 35 minutes of recording time, and computer "sync"-able.

Jamman Stereo: 35 minutes of recording time (or 16 hours on SD card) and computer "sync"-able.

EQ

BOSS GE-7: Simple, durable, and effective.

Noise Suppressor

BOSS NS-2: Simple, durable, and effective.

Compressor

MXR DynaComp: Simple, effective, and cheap.

To begin, I'd suggest getting an octavizer, delay, and flanger, phaser, or chorus. You can experiment with any of these without too much danger of feedback or loud blasts of sound. This is a must at the beginning of your pedal journey since the very best way to learn to fully utilize FX pedals is to play around with them for hours! The delay and flanger/phaser/chorus you'll likely use on your lead singer, or a "guitar solo," and the octavizer you'll likely use on your most reliable and pitch-accurate bass singer. Because almost all pedals have a quarter-inch input and the microphone you're using almost certainly has an XLR output, you'll need an impedance converter. These are usually about $15. Get a "Whirlwind Little IMP Low to High Impedance Matcher."

Here's the order of your chain:

Microphone → XLR cable → Impedance Converter → Pedal → ¼-inch Cable → Amp

Start on your own. Plug in, switch on, and just sing whatever comes to mind while fiddling with the various knobs on the pedal. Pretty quickly you'll discover settings that you don't like (or that are sonically annoying) and settings that you do like—sounds you think are cool and that you'd like to use. Keep a notebook handy and make a note of the position of the dials when you like the way something sounds.

Once you have a collection of favorite settings, invite another set of ears that you trust to come listen to you sing through the pedal. Outsider perspective is endlessly valuable. Your inclination will likely be to push an effect a little harder than necessary so you can hear it clearly while you're singing. Your second set of ears will help you more accurately calibrate your setting. If you don't want to invite someone else to listen, record yourself and listen back. Adjust your favorite settings accordingly. By doing all this, you're establishing a good starting place for your ensemble's integration of pedal usage.

I've Mastered the Octave, Delay, and Flanger.I Want More . . .

Distortion/Overdrive

This is fantastically fun whenever covering a song with an actual electric guitar solo, especially when the singer is female. If they work at it, it'll sound almost indistinguishable from an actual electric guitar!

Note: When using any type of distortion or overdrive with a microphone, you *must* also use a noise suppressor or gate. Otherwise, you'll fill your whole world with screaming feedback.

Here's how to rig it up (using the BOSS NS-2 noise suppressor):

Microphone → XLR cable → Impedance Converter → NS-2 Input → ¼-inch Cable from NS-2 Send → Distortion Pedal Input → ¼-inch Cable from Distortion Pedal Output → NS-2 Return → ¼-inch Cable from NS-2 Output → Amp

Here's how to safely start playing to find your settings:

- On the distortion pedal, turn the knob labeled "level" or "output" all the way down (to the left).

- On the noise suppressor, turn the "mute/reduction" knob to the "mute" setting (pointing straight up to 12:00). Turn the "threshold" knob all the way up and the "decay" knob all the way down. Tap the pedal so that the little red light is off (turning it on will mute everything entirely).

- Tap the distortion pedal until the little red light is on, and then very slowly begin creeping the "output" knob to the right while you sing intothe microphone.

- Once you have a quiet or manageable sound coming through, feel free to safely play with the knobs marked "drive," "tone," "color," etc. to find your desired sound. Add some long delay and go Hendrix!

Harmonizer

This can be especially useful if your ensemble is small and you'd like to thicken the inner parts, or if you're covering something modern in the electro-vein of Imogen Heap (because of its digital vocodery timbre).

Here's how to rig it up (using the Digitech Harmony Man):

Microphone → XLR cable → Impedance Converter → Harmony Man "guitar clean input" → ¼-inch Cable from Output Left (mono) → Amp

Here's how to start:

- Set the "mix" knob to 12:00. This will give you an equal amount of fundamental tone and harmonized tones.

- Roll both "voice" knobs (labeled "voice 1" and "voice 2") to the right until simple single digits appear. These single digits refer to the number of half-steps above or below the incoming voice that you'd like the pedal to generate new voices.

- Start out with a major triad. Set "voice 1" to "4" and "voice 2" to "7" (four half-steps for a major third and seven half-steps for a perfect fifth).

- Click the left pedal (harmony on/off) to make sure the effect is activated.

- Sing through like this a while. Play with other intervallic variations.

- When you find one you'd like to keep, tap the "store" button twice.

- The right pedal controls which "page" you're on. There are four "pages" that you can scroll through by taping the right pedal, each with their own customizable setting (unfortunately, you can only scroll through them forward). So let's say you want your singer to be able to jump back and forth between major and minor triads. Set the voices on page one to "4" and "7," the voices on page two to "3" and "7," page three the same as page one, and page four the same as page two.

The majority of the other functions provided by this pedal rely on incoming sounds to be in concert pitch, thus making them very tricky to use in the context of a cappella because of the likelihood of drifting tonic. It can be done, of course, but it is no easy feat.

Looper

This is an absolute lifesaver for any group that can't spare their beatboxer's voice, but still needs his or her beats!

Here's how to rig it up (using the Digitech Jamman Stereo):

Microphone → XLR Cable → Jamman Stereo XLR Mic input →
¼-inch Cable from Left Mono Out → Amp

Here's how to start:

- Turn all four small knobs all the way to the left: loop level, rhythm level, mic level, and instrumental (inst.) level.

- Turn the one large knob to the right until the digital read says "20" (each one of these numbers is a separate "tape loop" upon which you can record and layer sounds). The first 13 or so are occupied with obnoxious demo loops. You can delete them later if you like.

- Sing into the mic and slowly turn the "mic level" knob to the right until you get a reasonable volume coming through the amp and the little green light just to the left of the digital read is glowing.

▷ **Note:** If the green light turns yellow or red, you're overloading the signal inside the pedal and should turn your "mic level" back to the left until your loudest singing or beatboxing only turns the light green. If the sound from the amp is still too quiet, give yourself more volume from the amp.

- Once you've found your ideal "mic level," adjust the "loop level" knob to match it. For example, if the "mic level" is at about 11:00, set the "loop level" at about 11:00.

- Practice performing a simple two-bar loop a few times.

- When it feels steady, hit the lower left silver button on the downbeat of your performed loop. This is going to record your performance. When you get to the end of your loop and are about to begin again, hit the same silver button on the same downbeat. Try to think of hitting the button as part of the musical performance. The more musical you are in your operation of the looper pedal, the closer to perfect the loop length will be.

  ▷ So it goes: (button! - 2 - 3 - 4 - 1 - 2 - 3 - 4 - button!).

- The pedal will go straight from recording your loop to playing it back in time. If the loop is imperfect or you'd like to try again, click the lower right silver button to stop the loop.

- The quickest way to delete what you've recorded is to turn the larger knob one click to left, then one click back to the right again.

- Once you've recorded a loop that is to your liking, you can layer on top of it by clicking the lower left silver knob again while the loop is still playing, putting the pedal in "overdub" mode.

- To review, the lower left silver button functions are:

  ▷ First click = record.

  ▷ Second click = playback.

  ▷ Third click = overdub.

  ▷ All of the following clicks will toggle back and forth between playback and overdub.

- If you'd like to save your loop, slowly push the "store" button twice. Your loop will remain on that "page" (we'll call the glowing numbers on the digital read "pages") until you delete it.

- You can delete your loop by slowly pressing the "delete" button twice.

Multi-FX Pedal

If you love any or all of the single FX pedals you've explored thus far and are certain you'd like a great many more, you can save a lot of money and physical space by going with a multi-FX pedal (my personal favorite at the moment is the Line 6: M9). A multi-FX pedal contains digital emulations of sometimes hundreds of classic FX pedals. The possible combinations are endless! If you've understood and successfully navigated your pedal experience thus far, you'll explore multi-FX pedals with ease.

Summary

- *Always* use a noise suppressor or gate with distortion/overdrive pedals.

- When stringing together a series of pedals that include a delay pedal, it is best to put the delay pedal at the end of the chain. When a delay pedal is placed before certain FX pedals (especially an octavizer or harmonizer), it can hinder their ability to function.

- When initially exploring the delay pedal, be careful not to turn the knob labeled "feedback" or "repeat" too far to the right. This is the one situation in which you can accidentally generate loud feedback with a delay pedal.

- Some octavizers create an unwanted "scary" sound in the higher frequencies. An EQ pedal can be used to remove (or at least reduce) the presence of these sounds by pulling the higher frequency bands down. Place the EQ pedal after the octavizer in your pedal chain.

- Some octavizers tend to track certain vowels better than others. If your octavizer is glitching at all, experiment with different vowels until you find one that causes the pedal to glitch the least. In the sections of arrangements where you plan to use the octave pedal, change all vowels to the one you find works best with the pedal (this applies only to the pedal user, of course).

Metro

Arora

*"I played piano back in my elementary school days
and I sang a cappella back in college."*

—Masi Oka

MAKING A NAME

Brick City Singers

CHAPTER 26

PUBLICITY AND PROMOTION

The hope of every young professional group is to one day have an entire promotion machine at their fingertips. Until then, there are several steps any group can take to maximize their publicity without a publicist

Web Site

Even if it's only a simple site using a free web hosting service's template, you must have a web site. You can upgrade over time but be sure to list basic information about your group such as a biography (for both fans and the media), a list of upcoming (and perhaps past) appearances, a list of group members, examples of your music (live concert or rehearsal footage is fine if you don't have an album or video yet) and your contact information. Keep this up to date when you add concerts, change members, and have new audio, video and/or photos.

Social Media

Make sure you have an account for your group with the major social media machines (currently Facebook and Twitter are the largest but that may change). Announce the accounts at concerts and stay active posting (ideally) weekly with information about rehearsals, new songs you're learning, upcoming concerts, etc. You want to keep your fans informed and excited about upcoming appearances.

Kaleidoscope

Local Listings and Calendars

If you're a scholastic group, be sure to take full advantage of your school newsletter, emails, and announcements. If you're a regional group, get to know your local news outlets and web sites, and be sure to let them know when you have upcoming concerts, public events and auditions. A good relationship with the local media can be more valuable than a paid publicist, as eventually you might become the focus of an article.

Printed Materials

If you have a big upcoming show, consider printing postcards and handing them out at local appearances beforehand. If you're on a campus, perhaps printing posters will be cost effective, especially if you have many places in the area you can post them. If you have a steady gig at a local eatery or theater, consider printing rack cards and distributing them to local hotels. Of course the most valuable printed material of all is your business card, which you and all members should have on their person at all times.

Naughty Scotty and Octapella

Appearances

There are always locations who are looking for good entertainment and are willing to help you promote an upcoming concert or album. Radio shows love having a cappella groups on the air because they can perform live in the studio. Television shows that feature local acts, such as local morning television shows, also appreciate a cappella groups, especially if you have a timely performance (Danny Boy for St. Patrick's Day, etc). Baseball and other sports have an endless need for National Anthem performances, and sometimes teams will let you do a song before the game starts, during half time, or even the seventh-inning stretch. Sometimes national touring acts need an opening act, so getting to know the theater directors and local producers in your area is a good move.

Some of these appearances might be short, but there's nothing better than a teaser performance to get people excited about your group.

By combining any or all of these ideas you can start to generate some buzz about your group and build a loyal following. No matter what method you use, remember that your fans will ultimately be your best promotional tool!

Vocalocity (Israel)

The CompanY

CHAPTER 27

RECORDING

By Bill Hare

The time has finally arrived for your group to leave something for the ages, but just how *do* you make an album that stands out among all the others—especially if you've never been anywhere near a recording studio? In this chapter, we will break down the process of recording into its smaller parts, de-mystifying the illusion that you are competing against perfect-sounding groups who just walked up to some microphones and pressed the "record" button. That's *just* what they want you to think!

We'll get into much more detail later in this chapter, but a quick basic breakdown of the process looks something like this:

The first step in making a recording comes well before you step up to the microphone. **Pre-production** is basically lining up your ducks for the adventure ahead; setting your goals, fine-tuning your arrangements, scheduling, researching and contacting any outside people or companies that will be involved in the process, and so forth.

Once your group has educated yourselves (and hopefully gained a clearer picture of your own goals and vision in the process), the next step is **tracking**. This is the part where the *recording* light actually comes on. The illusion is that the group just sings their songs, perfectly. The reality is much more like making a movie, where tiny scenes are worked on meticulously, sometimes for only a few seconds of screen time, but that attention to detail is worth it—as long as the big picture is always kept in mind as well.

After all that work, you will have amassed a large number of little pieces of audio. There might be several different approaches to the same ten seconds of the lead vocal; do you want that little riff at the end of the first verse, or do you want to keep it simple, letting things build later in the song? Maybe the group tried some takes of the bridge in head voice and some in chest voice on all the background parts. The chords seem reasonably in-tune, but could land a bit better. The groove is *okay*, but doesn't get your toes tapping. Good **editing** is the next stop on our journey, and this crucial step is often not given the importance it should have. A strong edit will make all of these choices flow in what appears to be a deliberate and cohesive work, even though during the recording process it was a game of options.

A strong edit also makes way for a better and faster **mix**, as it frees that process from having to also try to force square pegs into round holes. The strong edit allows the mix process to concentrate on making the good stuff *better*. Mixing is an amazingly open-ended and creative process, where the song can take new directions and transform into a new piece of art.

Mastering is the final piece in this puzzle, where the mixed song is then given a final polish, making it bigger, wider, more impactful, and more consistent across various stereo systems, headphones, speakers, over the radio, and so forth.

Let's look at each of these steps again, in a bit more detail:

Pre-Production

Many people mistakenly think of pre-production strictly in an inward sense, basically defining it as follows:

"be as prepared as possible"

"know your parts cold"

"tweak the arrangement to make it perfect"

and a plethora of other "us" statements.

The opportunity that is so tragically missed in many recordings is the *outward* side of pre-production; basically, "what has everyone else done before us, and how can we set ourselves apart?" Also of much value is learning from the mistakes of others, saving you the time and expense of duplicating those mistakes.

Listen to the recordings of other groups similar to yours. It's the *only* way that you can be sure that you won't come across as the annoying kid who thinks his drawing of a house with the sun in the corner is the most original and artistic work that has ever graced the planet. Yes, his parents put it on their refrigerator and told him he was going to be the world's best artist someday, but until he goes into other houses and looks at other refrigerators, he won't know that he's just adding yet another nearly carbon-copy version to the pile, right down to the 4-pane windows and curlicue smoke coming out of the chimney.

Many groups think they are being "cutting edge" when they do a certain song, only to find out after they release it that it was last year's most overdone track, evoking eye rolls to those already in the know. A very small amount of time spent on research could have strengthened the album. It would also prove to be a great investment compared to the many hours of woodshedding yet another version of a song that 50 other groups have already done, frankly, better. Ignorance is bliss, at least until your album is reviewed.

Another important question to answer for yourself before going into production is this: What are your goals for this album (or EP or single)? There is no wrong answer to this question, but the answer can greatly impact the way you move forward.

If your group decides the album is just for friends/family/fans, as well as having something to sell after shows just to help pay expenses, you can ignore much of what this chapter has to say. Don't spend too much, just aim to make something representative of how the group sounds on a good day. No trickery or high art, just something for the parents to "stick to their refrigerators." Go ahead and make that 51st version of the current hit song that every other group is doing, and let your weakest singers have solos, especially if it's their last year in the group. Seriously, this is a fine approach as long as it is truly your goal—what we would call a "Yearbook Album." Make yourself happy with it, and your demographic of people who know the group will love it. The rest of the world probably won't care to hear it, but that's not necessarily not a bad thing, since it's not really for the rest of the world.

Deke and Rebel Wilson recording her solos for *Pitch Perfect 2*

The opposite end of this spectrum is for the group that wants to get out on the playground and fight for dominance. If good reviews, awards, compilation placements, and broader sales are the goals your group agrees upon, you need to also understand, to help achieve these goals, it's going to take money, quality equipment, checking some egos at the door while letting stronger egos shine, and most likely hiring skilled help from outside the group. This is why there are record producers, not only in A cappella, but on every other serious recorded work since the beginning of recording itself. Producers are the equivalent of coaches/managers of a sports team, hired to turn a ragtag bunch of amateurs (or professionals for that matter) into a winning force. A record producer has the benefit of having been through this process hundreds or thousands of times, and learning from many failures as well as successes.

As you do your research listening to other groups' recordings, take special note of the things you like and don't like about each album or song. Note how well they were reviewed or awarded, the good and bad buzz about them in discussion groups, who tracked (recorded) it, who edited it, who mixed it, who mastered it, etc.

Just as Woody Allen and Steven Spielberg are both great directors, their moviemaking styles and end results are very different from each other. Finding a good match to your group is key, so this research will be well worth the effort. There are many ways to hybridize this process between your own labor and skilled outside labor, depending on your budget, amount of free time, willingness to learn, etc. It's helpful to discuss your specific goals with people who have been through this process before, be they the ones you are potentially hiring to help you reach your goals, alumni of your own group, or simply friends in other groups who have been through the process before.

There are, of course, many *levels of in-between* to the above answers, and some of the limitations will simply be made for you: What one group spends on an album might be twice what another can afford; one group might have all their members excited, involved and enthusiastic, while another group might have trouble getting a number of their members to simply show up for recording sessions. Before starting to record, make sure the whole group is aware of as much of this as possible, and discuss all of these levels of commitment, finances, goals, and dreams as they relate to your own group and the individuals within. If you do this, as well as educating yourselves as to how others did it, your road will be much smoother. However, this is also the point where you may discover that everyone in the group has a very different opinion of what they like and what they don't.

Live Sound/Arrangements vs. Recorded Sound/Arrangements

You may have been singing your arrangements for some time now. They work for your group, and the audience seems to love them. But are they enough to stand up on their own, without your choreography, charm, and good looks?

This may be the first of many times in this process that you're going to have to honestly confront yourself and your peers, not to mention the arranger; try to step out of your own shoes, your own voices, your own egos for a moment and figure out what may be missing for the end listener. Much of the stimuli the audience usually gets from your live show will be gone in the *audio-only* version of your songs, leaving holes in the story you were telling in other ways.

What a group *sounds* like live and what the group is live are usually two different beasts entirely. An a cappella show is an *event* in real time in a real space that includes both the group and the audience. Sticking earbuds into your head and listening to that same arrangement while you do the dishes is a completely different picture of it. If you are one of the few who have seen this group perform live multiple times, you might have a slight advantage standing there listening while doing the dishes, remembering how cute a certain member of the group was, the humorous acting out of a song's lyrics, their choreography, or the sound that filled the room that night pushed by thousands of watts of amplification; but using this theory, we would have to trust each listener to fill in the gaps based on their own experience. Do you trust them to do that, or do you want to have control of how the story is told?

Anyone who has heard a good radio drama knows that settings, images, feelings, and more can be filled in by virtue of a little extra dialogue and sound effects; compared to the same story being told on TV, where they can just *show* you the context. In our case, that dialogue can be musical and sonic rather than words. Someone watching your live show can look at your vocal percussionist flailing his arms like he's playing a drum set and say "wow, that guy sounds just like a drummer." The same listener, if she hasn't seen your percussionist's antics, can't form that picture in her mind; and she might just hear a lot of spitting!

This doesn't mean you have to completely re-write your arrangement before you can even start recording. If there are some obvious things, such as the extra note you've always wished you could add to the chord, or the section you wanted to fill with some lush "oohs" behind the rest of the parts, by all means, write them in. Use this as your foundation, and when you are done laying this foundation, take the time to listen objectively in order to judge whether you think this will stand on its own. Chances are, more layers will be needed to complete the picture. You might even remove some of your layers that work well live, layers that could be replaced with something more daring or fragile under the recording microscope.

This, the spontaneous creativity of adding parts "on the fly," will likely be the part of the process you will remember most fondly years after the album comes out. Think like a painter, brushing a few strokes, taking a step back, contemplating what she sees, and finding the places that need to be filled in. She might try something, paint over it, and try something else, but eventually she'll come up with something that might even surprise herself. A bit of spontaneity can add a lot of freshness to a planned-out piece of art—so in that planning, leave yourself some blank canvas for these inspired (and fun) moments.

Tracking (Recording)

Are you ready? Don't worry, hardly anyone else is either, even professional groups starting their tenth album; this is the point where you will jump into the pool, anyway, and just start swimming. Just like that cold swimming pool, getting started is the hardest part, and as you warm up to it, the swimming gets easier and more fun.

As with building anything, you should start with a sketch that will guide you through the process. The basic "scaffold" of almost any contemporary a cappella recording will actually be an instrumental MIDI track to keep the singers on pitch, as well as a click or rhythm part to keep things in the groove. This idea might seem counterintuitive at first, as many groups feel that it might make them sound stiff or unnatural. The thing to keep in mind here is that this is just the foundation of the building, and it needs to be as solid as possible. No one else sees the foundation, just the nice stuff built on top of it and the nicely formed walls once the scaffolding is taken down. Build your foundation, then the detail work can begin!

Some groups are tempted to forgo the use of an instrumental track and, instead, use a live recording of themselves they can follow because they are afraid of "losing the live feel." This is almost never a good idea, even for the best groups in the world. It does seem like a good idea until you actually try it. The key is to be able to sing *around* your cue track, rather than be a slave to it.

The cue track can be a piano playing the chords in the background or the actual notes of the arrangement itself, taken from the output of your computer-notated score (which also helps in learning parts in the studio). Don't distract the singers by trying to be creative with the orchestration sounds in this cue track, but rather, just feed all notes to a basic piano sound. This will keep the pitch center narrower as well, so that people singing along with string pads don't just choose any center in the 20-cent wide window of many of those sounds. A percussive attack like those on a piano will also be more rhythmically easy to follow than other sounds with a slower envelope of attack.

On top of this, a click track will be your *conductor*. It's best subdivided into a groove of some kind, rather than just a quarter-note count (as some people think of the "classic" click track). This can be a simple programmed drum machine beat. Or you could just use sixteenth-note high hats with the strongest accents on the quarter note beats, a slightly softer accent on the eighth notes in between, and even softer on the 2nd and 4th sixteenth notes between those. This will help to keep people in a tighter groove, rather than pushing and pulling against the relatively long gaps of a straight count. (The exact settings for this will vary greatly depending on tempo, feel, etc. In very fast tempos, for example, an eighth note click will suffice). This rhythmic guide can also be swung to any degree, so make sure the feel is just right.

Eight Beat Measure

Starting with your vocal percussion and building on that is a viable option as well, but you will need to schedule it accordingly, setting some time aside between recording your vocal percussionist and any other tracks. You will of course still need the click track options noted above to keep your vocal percussionist locked to the tempo, but you will also need to edit that track into a final groove since this is what the rhythmic feel of the other parts will be referencing. More on this later in the chapter.

One other option—if your group is recording a cover song, the original version can also be used as a guide. The original file can be manipulated somewhat to change the key and tempo, within reason.

The most important point in any of these methods is that your recording platform (usually some type of Digital Audio Workstation, hereafter abbreviated as DAW) should be locked to the tempo of the song—even if that tempo is fluid.

Yes, it *is* quite possible and common to have a guide track with ritards, accellerandos, meter and tempo changes, and fermatas. In these cases, especially, it is valuable to have subdivided beats to help "gear" everybody to the same reference point, rather than a bunch of guesses that will feel uncomfortable to both the singer and the listener. Every program handles this differently, but just the knowledge that it's available to you (and commonly used on the albums that you admire) is the first step. Also, most notation programs in which you are writing your arrangements have these *tempo maps* built in anyway, and can be exported to the DAW directly in seconds, keeping studio setup time to a minimum. Most notation programs have a feature in which you can play the audio of the arrangement. If you can manipulate the feel and tempo(s) to match the way you want to sing the song (in other words, if you can comfortably sing along to the playback and it feels right), then you've succeeded. If you are still having difficulty, ask someone more familiar with MIDI sequencing for help using that toolset. Getting this right will be well worth it as you go through the various phases of the recording and mixing processes.

Using the notation program to create the cue also has other benefits, one of which is that the measure numbers showing on your computer screen match those on the printed paper (provided that the score is written out linearly, rather than having repeats, D.S., Coda, etc.). Even if the score is written out traditionally with repeats and such, this can be easily rectified by just changing the numbering on the paper score with a pencil (or directly within the notation program if it allows such editing). Let's say that measures 9 to 16 repeat; in that case, you can double-number those measures—Measures 1 to 8 remain the same, measure 9 becomes 9/17, measure 10 becomes 10/18, and so on. After the repeat, what was previously measure 17 simply becomes measure 25 and we move on from there, double-numbering (or sometimes in the case of a D.S. or multiple repeats triple-numbering) any repeated parts, until the end of the song.

Almost all notation programs can be exported as a MIDI file, and this is the file that will translate to the recording software to create the tempo maps and cue file.

One thing to note—rather than cram the very first note "against the left wall" of the session, make sure you leave room for a count-in, initial breath, etc. The first note shouldn't sound like it was a surprise to either the listener or the artist. There are many ways to deal with this, such as adding a "measure 0" to the arrangement or moving all of the MIDI to start at measure two of the session, and either re-number the bars in the DAW or re-number the bars on your printed arrangement. As long as the goal is met that the measure numbers line up between the recorder and the printed music sheet, and there is a least one measure buffer in front of the song start, you are golden.

A big reason for making these numbers match is because it makes for much quicker communication between the producer, engineer and singer for the days, weeks or months they will be working on this track; the engineer doesn't need to be reading the sheet music, but can still just say "we're going to cut in at measure 71" just by looking at the counter of the DAW rather than some vague statement such as "start singing two-thirds of the way through that verse where you do that little riff thingy," to which the singer will invariably reply with "where?" and another few minutes will go by until it is figured out. Multiply this scenario many, many times, and that adds up to a lot of time which is either taken from your own schedule or paid for in hourly studio charges.

Now that you have your roadmap, you can start your trip. As you start recording, you need to first make sure the singer gets out of his own way by assigning *someone else* to do the thinking for him. If you leave every performance decision to the (internally-focused) singer, you'll never get "out of here." Having someone to direct the singer to best fit in with the big picture, to say when a take is "good enough," to help guide him through rough spots, to find the right emotion and character for a given phrase or sound is key to getting a better performance, faster.

This isn't as daunting of a task as it sounds. Recalling the statement at the beginning of this chapter about making a movie in tiny pieces—one of the biggest mistakes people make is trying to do too much at once, losing both the detail and the big picture in one shot. It's much more efficient to work on one phrase over and over, rather than singing the whole song, or even just the chorus, and making slightly different mistakes each time. Rather than take your chances with 100 notes, just concentrate on 10 or 20, get them to feel good, and move on.

Before you do move on, though, do one more pass of those few notes on a second channel. (Each singer should have two channels.) Double-tracking is a common technique that dates back to the 1960s that smoothes out each performance considerably. It also gives much better stereo image options later on in the mix. At first glance, you might think it's twice the work to get two good passes rather than one; however, more often than not, once the singer gets it right, they will immediately get it right again.

Going back to the movie metaphor, you don't need to start filming at the beginning nor with the main character. All that will be filled in eventually. If you want to start with an alto, doing the chorus, that's fine. Just make sure you keep track of what has and hasn't been done!

If you like, you can also lay down a "scratch" lead vocal, to mark where you are in the lyrics. A scratch lead vocal can also make the singers more comfortable than just hearing the parts being plunked out by a piano in their headphones. There will be a lot of time where you DON'T want to hear this vocal as well, such as when micromanaging the same two seconds over and over in one of the background parts, or when the scratch vocal is getting in the way of the tuning and rhythm of the singers. For the first part of building this foundation, we want to stay "within the lines" as much as possible and get freer as we build up.

After you get started, you'll find you can start to collect tracks fast and furiously. Keep things moving, don't let the singer obsess on a part or try to "produce" her own performance; the best tracks come when the singer is not thinking about the technical things or which multi-note run to try on the next single-syllable word. Try to keep the bigger picture in mind as you guide the vocalist through, keeping the mood, intensity, story and character as main objectives, and not nit-picking every pitch, attack or cut off like a school choir director. If the singer, music

Hailee Steinfeld recording for *Pitch Perfect 2*

director or producer starts prioritizing technical building blocks over appropriate performance, the battle is lost before it is begun.

Sometimes you *will* run into those road blocks where a part is so difficult (or requires more air than the singer has lung capacity, or was simply learned incorrectly originally) that the process needs to be broken down into an even smaller chunk. At these times, recording in a loop, rather than linearly, can get you through those rough patches quickly and painlessly. For example, let's say a part calls for a fast run that needs to be very accurate in the middle of a longer phrase. Rather than take your chances trying to happen onto it each take in the middle of an 8-bar phrase, just work on that measure or two. The worry of the problem few notes might also be taking away from the bars around it, so another benefit of this is to tell the singer not to worry about the hard part, that you are just getting the parts around it for now.

Often, just the psychology of telling the singer that you're just "marking" the difficult part for now and you will go back to work on it specifically will solve the problem anyway. If not, you can quickly micromanage that second or two of acrobatics via intense repetition.

All DAWs have the *loop mode* mentioned above, where a set number of bars play over and over (while simultaneously recording), allowing the singer to practice and perfect, staying in the groove, and, more importantly, not stopping between takes to let them dwell on The Universe. After several (or eight or thirty) loops through these few seconds, the singer builds a muscle memory as well as an understanding of the notes/rhythms and easily nails the formerly "difficult" part, sometimes as a call and response with another singer who might be able to demonstrate the part in a way the main singer can understand.

If they *don't* nail it after awhile, instead of getting frustrated (and letting the singer get frustrated as well), just move on, make a note that you need to come back to it later, and get the rest of that track done. It may be that you come back to it at the end of the session weeks later, after the singer woodsheds on it, or even have someone else with a similar voice sing those few notes. In the big picture, this sort of stuff doesn't have to be traumatic—just make sure it gets done eventually. It's a good idea to keep a running of list of "loose ends."

A big time saver that might spark more philosophical discussion: if verse one has the same basic building blocks for a lot of the background parts, there is nothing wrong with using the same utilitarian background parts used on verse one again in verse two. Save the time rather than doing redundant work. There will be other things, such as the lead vocal, new auxiliary parts, and so forth, that will make verse two different enough that no one in the world will know several of the background parts have been used previously. Record smart, and you'll have more time to record better.

While in this philosophical discussion, here's another thing to consider: in your group, whose voice do you blend best with? Trick question—the answer is almost always "your own." Sometimes when doing certain layers within an arrangement where a few voices make up one instrument, say a guitar, organ, or just a nice "ooo" background vocal, don't be afraid to try having one singer do *all* the parts of that particular instrument. In other words, a single person can sing the three "ja-jeng" guitar parts, doubling, thus occupying six channels just for this part. This will help separate layers in the mix tonally later on, as well as keep syllables, attacks, releases, and tone very consistent.

Recording Vocal Percussion

Vocal percussion (usually abbreviated as "VP") is one of the defining aspects of contemporary a cappella and one of the most open-ended parts of the recording process. The point at which groups start recording their percussion parts in this process varies quite a bit, especially compared with mainstream recording; if you decide to start with the drums (as an instrumental pop recording almost always would), your main goal should be to make a track that is appropriate to the song, as well as something the rest of the group can comfortably groove with. Unfortuntately, trying to show off beatboxing skills usually results in unusable tracks and wasted time. This track would also have to be heavily edited before any of the singers start recording against it, making sure every single hit is in place, very consistent, and appropriate in each attack. This makes for an excellent foundation to sing against when done right . . . or a regrettable idea when done wrong.

There are few things worse than trying to record on top of the unstable foundation of an inappropriate or non-grooving VP track; problems will start compounding on top of each other right away. If the vocal percussion tracks are going to be heard by the singers while tracking, you MUST be absolutely sure that every hit is exactly where it should be, that the degree of swing is correct, and that it works in a complimentary way with the arrangement. There are many approaches to making a solid VP track in the studio. However, this can become one of the most political and philosophical discussions your group will have in the recording process.

The harsh reality is that only a *tiny handful* of vocal percussionists have the ability to *truly* hold a groove, with correct "pocket" or feel, with consistent and appropriate sounds, as well as working musically within the song itself. We're talking maybe a few dozen on the planet, so we'll assume that your vocal percussionist is not among them, no matter what his or her friends say.

This doesn't mean they aren't at least functional—or even impressive—in a live setting, but you most likely do not want to put them under the recording microscope as far as real-time performance is concerned. Of course, you should *record* what your percussionist does live (for political reasons if nothing else), but it won't necessarily resemble what the end result will be. We call this the "spit" track in the a cappella production world.

You may have noticed that so far we have not discussed any specific pieces of recording gear or software that are used in these processes. To keep the information in this book relevant for as many years as possible, suffice it to say that microphones, preamps, interfaces, software, and other specific equipment involved come and go fairly quickly, and current information is readily available elsewhere about this universal aspect.

Installing and learning the equipment is not difficult, it's how you approach making music with it that is the important part. Recording VP is divergent enough to make an exception here and discuss the unique issues in trying to capture these odd human sounds with a microphone.

First off, the moisture (spit) and air pressure involved in making these sounds can be harmful or fatal to sensitive microphones, especially side-address condenser mics, which are most likely what you are using to collect the rest of the vocals. If you just have the one condenser microphone, you can protect it by putting multiple pop screens (at least two) in front of it to slow down the airflow in stages. Another option is to simply have a more robust (or disposable) microphone specifically for recording VP. A dynamic mic such as a Shure SM58 or equivalent can take a lot of pounding, though a handheld condenser such as a Shure Beta 87 or Rode NT3 can give you more clarity. A foam windscreen will give these mics a longer life, but they will eventually become "sacrificial lambs" due to the unique abuse VP incurs. The good news is that they are relatively inexpensive and should last at least a few years under moderate use.

There are many ways to approach getting the performance down, but in most cases the micromanaging style of the vocal parts recording won't apply to VP. If your group's percussionist is not among the very best of the very best, the approach below will be the best use of time in 99% of cases.

Fire Drill

At any point during the process where you find you have a few minutes, you can just record a couple passes of your percussionist going through the song, showing his or her ideas. This can just be muted, put away for editing at a later time. While such a seemingly uncaring approach may sound counterintuitive for such an important part of your project, keep in mind that the modern sound of recorded vocal percussion is more a result of editing than performance. Don't spend *too* much time on this, unless you are absolutely sure your VP is in the top 1%.

Also, on another channel to be put aside for later, it is usually a good idea to have individual sounds from your percussionist that can be used as "samples" if needed. A few crash cymbals that are allowed to ring out rather than abruptly stop at the next beat as is necessary in live performance; kicks, snares, and toms done individually that aren't immediately coming from or going into different sounds. Collecting these individual sounds gives your percussionist a chance to concentrate on just getting the best sounds, not worrying about making different sounds rapidly. These tracks can either be sequenced into a new groove or laid against an edited version of the "spit" track, combining human feel with consistent sounds.

Much of the time, especially when the notated parts are a transcription of an existing song, the percussionist's ideas or abilities will not match the original drummer's placements. This mostly comes down to whether your vocal percussionist actually *thinks* like a drummer, and, unfortunately, only a small percentage actually do.

In most cases, decisions have to be made whether to change the *performance intent* of the vocal percussionist in editing. Most performers don't seem to have a problem with this, as it makes the overall arrangement make much more sense, and it would be what the percussionist would want to sound like anyway in a perfect world.

Time for the lead vocal—or is it?

Looking over all of these fragments we have amassed, we see that there is already quite a mess to clean up—and we haven't gotten to the lead vocal yet. It may be difficult to get the lead singer to be inspired over parts that still need help in tuning and articulation, or to get her excited when verse and chorus backgrounds that were recorded in one place still haven't been put into their repeated areas. At this juncture you should probably start making the tracks ready to *inspire* a good lead vocal performance. While it is possible to record the lead vocal at any point during the process, it's usually better to have this final piece of the puzzle (which is usually the central point the listener focuses on) relate to the actual parts that will be backing said lead vocal in the final version. This just might be the time to do the first major edit, instead of more recording.

'Round Midnight

Editing

There are quite a few different skill sets in the overall process of making a great recording, and hardly anyone has all of them. A good editor can make all of your fragments into a professional-sounding track, as well as shave hours off of an expensive mixer's time to get a better result, faster.

In the world of a cappella production, the people who have shown themselves to be the best editors are in high demand and well-respected for their musicianship and vision. Most mixer/

producers, as well as DIY groups, have found that sending their work out to be edited (usually at less than half the hourly rate of a top mixing-engineer) is a win-win situation for everybody.

A good editor should first and foremost be a great musician, with the ears and musical sensitivity/chops to be able to translate your tracks into tight, complete, and flowing performances. They also need to know the technology very well and be able to equally interface between the tools and the music. Lastly, they usually know the particular specifications each mixing engineer needs to be as efficient as possible.

Of course, those groups on a *very* tight budget can also do this part themselves, but before we get into that, let's look at some reasons why it is recommended to have this done professionally:

You have just finished a ton of work recording your group, and a break from the songs will help keep you inspired for the next steps.

You have already spent dozens of hours to get the takes recorded, and you'll spend many more doing the editing because you are so close to it. An outside editor will take care of everything much quicker, without the bias of emotional attachment, and also be able to hear your singers from a real-world perspective.

Editing is a relatively cheap process. If you are going to have your tracks mixed by a professional who charges twice what the editor does, then a good edit will probably pay for itself a few times over. Even if you are going to try your hand at mixing yourself, it's still a good idea to have someone else tune up your tracks.

A professional editor is likely to have the more comprehensive and expensive tools that will make the job sound better, in a fraction of the time. They also have the experience to make the edit sound natural rather than mechanical and processed. This skill usually takes years to learn, because there is a lot of cumulative effect involved that isn't apparent when you're working on a channel at a time.

If you are planning to send your songs to be mixed by one or more of the top A cappella engineer/producers, a professional editor knows the specifications of layout and organization that each of these people need to be most efficient.

If you're still not convinced, then we'll move on to what you will need to do this yourself.

The basic elements of editing include optimizing the pitch, rhythms, subtle and not-so-subtle groove adjustments, drum sequencing, vocal attacks, cutoffs, dynamic ramps, and many other details. On top of that, you will need to give the mixer as much control over the individual percussion sounds as possible, all while not overdoing it to the point where things sound unnatural and robotic.

To do this yourself, you must have total confidence in your musical, arranging, and drumming abilities, as well as comfort with your software and workflow. Your ears should always be your final gauge, even if things don't quite "look" right.

Your visual guide is called the "grid," basically vertical lines where each subdivision falls on the tempo map. These subdivisions can be set as fine or as course as you need, from straight quarter notes to triplet 32nds or beyond. Each grid line identifies a certain point in musical time, so you'll know exactly where to find the third 16th note of beat two of measure 74.

But just because you *know* exactly where that beat is doesn't mean that you are going to line up your samples, attacks, and releases surgically to that line. Having everything "perfect" means that it's going to have a very mechanical sound to it, taking all perception of humanity away. *Quantization* is the act of automatically "snapping" all events to the grid, an "event" being any sound that happens in a linear fashion, say a high hat, snare, and kick drum. Most programs will let you choose to what degree of rigidity it quantizes, say within 5%, so things are just *closer to* rather than *exactly on* the line. This leaves you with a bit of natural error that can appear more "human."

Sometimes, as in the case of laying better-sounding samples alongside a quantized spit track, you'll want to put everything right on the grid just to get it assembled and hitting together. Then you can take all of the parts together and do the opposite of quantization, which is *randomization*. This works the same way in the degree of distance from the line, the difference being that the events are each starting from right on the line (sounding mechanical) and being allowed to randomly drift within a set amount.

Quantization can also apply to pitch, automatically taking each note and tuning it to the closest semitone or scale note value. This is even more dangerous in "roboticizing" a voice in that it can remove all of the natural ways that singers get from note-to-note (portamento, stylistic scoops, etc.), as well as add an unnatural, "perfect" temperament that sounds less like voices and more like a synthesizer. Just as in rhythmic quantization, the degree of correction can be expressed as a percentage to make the effect less mechanical. The difference here is that there are many more parameters to pitch-based correction than rhythmic-based correction, which primarily looks at when a signal simply starts and stops rather than all of the musical nuances of pitch, tone, and inflection. A machine doesn't understand the emotional intent, stylistic variations, or chordal movements of a performance, so this part of the edit can make or break the track in terms of its "listenability."

The better way to correct pitch is to keep it under human control, listening for the parts that need to be left alone as well as those needing help, editing with both the eyes and ears. There are, and will continue to be, a myriad of choices of programs for this, but the basic concept is the same; notes can be moved as a whole in their natural shape or can be re-shaped to the whim of the human editor. This takes a lot of practice to make sound natural, but can also be used for many other unnatural effects, as well as adding or rearranging notes that were never sung in the first place.

Here we can get into another political debate over arrangement and performance "integrity," but the main goal here is to optimize what the listener's experience is going to be, and if the arrangement/performance is not doing that on its own, there is a lot of help to be had in the editing stage. Many a great recording only came to life *after* all of the recording had been done, and a strong, musical editor filled in all of the holes.

To go back to the movie analogy yet again, there may be some great writers and great actors (and maybe some weak links) working on a movie, but the job of making sure all the parts work with each other in a relevant way falls upon a good director and editor who can see everything in perspective. Starting to see a pattern here?

Now that you've cleaned things up and have put all the repeated sections where they belong, the song should be sounding pretty good to your ears. If it sounds mechanical, overly tuned, or too much the opposite, you might want to go back and loosen or tighten up in places. If you're generally happy with the raw result (remember this will shine much more when mixed and mastered), it's finally time to start thinking about the lead vocal(s) that will be the centerpiece of the song.

You can either start with the tracks dry and unmixed, or you can add a bit of flair to inspire the lead vocalist further. Sometimes a track will actually be sent to a professional mixer at this point to start working up the mix, resulting in a roughly-mixed version for the lead vocalist to sing over. The leads are sung to this more-inspiring track, then sent back to the mixer to finish the mix from that halfway point.

The Lead Vocal

This is probably the most critical channel of the tracks that make up the song, as it is where most listeners will focus their attention. Your lead singer will need to really understand what she is singing about or come up with a new twist of her own, but words simply put on pitches won't do. Many amateur singers do just that, even if they feel like they are putting 110% into their performance. Instead, get them into the right mood for the song, give them things to think about that don't have anything to do with singing, but everything to do with feeling.

If it's a sad song, try darkening the room and have the lead think of something that could bring him to tears. The 1973 Song of the Year Grammy winner was for a song that used this exact motivation. Roberta Flack's moving performance of "The First Time Ever I Saw Your Face" made many people ask her who she was singing about. Her cat had been run over by a car just days before, and she used that heartbreak to drive the song home.

For a bouncy song, make the studio a party atmosphere. Bring in flashing colored lights. Fill the room with balloons, stuffed animals, or tacos—whatever makes the singer happy. Creating a vibe is key to avoiding the "empty words and melody" trap.

For an epic song, tell the singer to imagine that he or she is singing from a mountaintop to the throngs below. Or, if they are near a window, point out something or someone in the distance, tell them to ignore the microphone, and sing to that distant object.

Use your imagination and creativity to set the vibe, or different vibes/scenes throughout the song. A little psychology and role-playing goes a long way in getting a singer to connect with a lyric, rather than just mindlessly singing the part they learned by rote.

Maccabeats

One point to make here is that due to the nature of many a cappella arrangements, the harmonies that compliment the lead vocal may have already been written in to another line already recorded. The phrasing of the background harmonies might be a bit stiff or distracting to the lead singer, so rather than force the lead into their phrasing (after all, the harmonies are supposed to sound like they are following the lead), you might want to temporarily mute them in those sections. It could be just fine as well, so maybe try a "test pass" first. (Always record your "test passes," though, because you might catch an amazing performance when the singer has his guard down.)

If the singer is feeling it and getting into the "zone," leave him alone and let him go. Do several takes all the way through the song, telling him not to stop if he makes a mistake, and just collect four or five run-throughs. Make notes along the way, and if there are some rough spots that happened on the run-throughs, work on those in more of a micromanaged way, while at the same time trying to keep the singer in the vibe rather than thinking about notes and rhythms.

After working your singer through the rough spots, give him a couple more passes through the whole song and send him on his way. Try to avoid playbacks, as this will just put the singer back into his "music" head, and the vibe will be lost. If a singer insists on a playback, try to remember which take was the overall best and play it back for him. He will probably obsess on that note that was flubbed in the bridge, but remind him that the final take will be made up from all of the best parts, and some of those exist on other channels. If he says he knows he can do it better, give him one or two more chances to prove it, but don't fall into the trap of getting fifty takes of almost the exact same performance. If things are on the upswing, keep going, but once they plateau, try not to waste any more time. Especially if you are paying for that time by the hour.

This doesn't mean the lead is done—hopefully she is, but the lead vocal is important enough to come back to later if improvement can be made. Obsessing on it too much in one sitting can be counterproductive—the best takes tend to be the earlier ones in a lot of cases anyway. Make some notes on the settings and position of the mic and preamp in case you need to revisit a few phrases, but for now you can start compiling the best take out of the various versions you've just laid down.

First, make sure the person who sang the song is nowhere near the studio when you do this, as she will hear it differently than every other single person on the planet. Listen to just one phrase, then listen to all of the other takes of that phrase, and pick the best one. Try to listen for character and feel, as well as appropriate emotional connection to the lyric, before listening for things like pitch and rhythm. The best take of this line will be put on a new channel called the "comp" (compilation) track. Go to the second line of the song and repeat this process until you get to the end. Take special care to make sure the phrasing and attitude work between the chosen edits.

At some points, you may want to pick out two takes, doubling certain sections such as the chorus or bridge for effect. If the song is a cover, listen to the original and see if and where the lead vocal doubles. There was probably a good reason that was done in the first place, and there's nothing wrong with duplicating a good idea. If the song is original, listen through the song and ask yourself "Would a double serve this song/lyric well in certain places?"

As with the background tracks, pitch can be corrected and timing can be shifted on the lead vocal. Just be careful not to overdo the editing, as the lead vocal is usually quite a bit more exposed than the backing tracks.

Now everything is comped, tuned, and in place. You can hear everything in full context for the first time. That second tenor part that was really bugging you last week isn't even a blip on your radar anymore, now that the lead vocal is in there. As we touched on earlier, check the written-in harmonies against the newly-born lead vocal. Are they fitting in context, emotion, phrasing? If not, it might be a good idea to just record those sections again, so the harmonies can match the lead vocal and not the other way around. These re-recorded harmonies can also be put on new channels, so they can be treated differently from the arranged parts and be more connected to the lead vocal both sonically and emotionally.

The song at this point finally has its full shape and context, so make sure everything is working together. This would also be the time to play it for some people outside of the group to get some opinions that are not biased by over-familiarity with the arrangements and voices, as you and your group certainly are by now. Don't pay too much heed to individual comments as much as several people noticing the same things.

You've gotten your notes, may have taken out a distracting drum-fill or two, recut a few lines of the lead vocal, and are ready to send the session off to mix!

Mixing

The mix is an art in itself, and can't really be taught in a book. Many years of practice, making horrible mistakes, is essential. Each channel that has been recorded and each individual sound in the vocal percussion will now get its own treatment, which in turn affects how all the other tracks are treated. With each change made, a thousand new options open; finding one correct path is not the goal. In fact, sometimes what seems like the wrong path will actually be what is eventually best for the song. Willingness to experiment, make mistakes, sometimes EMBRACE said mistakes, sometimes backtrack, and eventually find the best combination of genius and mishap is key, as well as realizing this point before you overwork it.

Just as in the section about editing, the same holds true about professional experience: a professional mixing engineer has been through this process thousands of times over the years and has already learned to navigate the thousands of choices, as well as avoid the pitfalls. Just as you probably wouldn't want a heart transplant from someone who has never performed one before, it might not be the best idea to mix your own album. However, there is much less risk of dying from mixing your own album than an amateur heart transplant, so if you have the time and determination and have survived the previous steps on your own, there is no reason not to try your own hand at it. The worst that can happen is you end up sending the tracks to a professional mixer anyway.

A whole book can be written on just this part of the process (and many have been), but we'll try to break it down to just a few pages here.

Before we get into the technical matters, we need to define what makes a mix work. The art of mixing involves blending the tracks enough to not distract the listener from the song itself, yet at the same time keep important events or textures distinct enough from each other to create depth and musical interplay. On top of this, the mix has to convey the correct attitude, appropriate aggression or subtlety, and many other details. And ALL of that needs to support the lead vocal without pulling the listener in too many directions at once.

A contemporary a cappella mix is approached much like an instrumental mix, as the genres of music performed are the same for the most part. In cover songs, much of the time the textures are directly brought over into the arrangement, so those three previously-mentioned "ja-jeng" guitar parts will be kept distinct as a group. Or a signature backup vocal part that everyone knows from the original will stand out from the rest of the "a cappella-ized" arrangement in a different way.

In the mix, these combined sections (made up of a few or hundreds of voices each) will be given their own space, be it a narrow part of the frequency spectrum, or physically somewhere left or right of center in the stereo field. There are also many other ways to make it distinct from other parts. You immediately hear the difference between a guitar, piano, and horns when played on those instruments, but you are working with voices no matter what, so helping them occupy the space that the instruments naturally would can help bring the intent to life, such as running the guitars through a guitar amplifier or digital simulator of a guitar amp. Even running these vocal guitars clean, without heavy overdrive and distortion, can make a difference, as it sounds more like the vocals are coming through a separate speaker before being mixed back in to the overall track.

The "Big Picture" of a mix is made up of many smaller pictures, each of which is made up of many individual parts itself. The mix is the piece of the overall process that has the potential to change things the most, as you are revisiting each and every channel that has been recorded and finding its final place and character in the mix.

Mixing will also be the most emotional and political part of the album project. By this point you most likely have learned that not everyone in your group agrees with the direction things are

Key of She

going. The mix will disturb this balance even more, where some people in the group will love the way something is sounding, and others will be threatening to leave the group unless it's changed. Even a relatively natural mix will sound quite foreign to many within the group, as they have a very unique perspective as to what things sound like inside their head as they themselves are singing these same songs in a live setting. Each will have a different opinion, and be quite vocal about it.

So, how can you keep everyone happy? The answer is; you can't. If you take your favorite albums of all time, a cappella or not, it's almost a guarantee that some members of those groups couldn't even listen to those albums objectively for many years after they were released. Understanding that is half the battle. More important is how the people outside your group perceive your work. The Beatles are the most successful band in history, universally loved, with a body of work that holds strong half a century after the fact. Does it matter to the billions of people who have heard their music that John Lennon was dissatisfied with nearly every record they made? No. Had he been able to have the power to make it all sound correct to his own ears, the result would have been a completely different body of work with an unknown outcome. The point is, they finished the work anyway, the world loved it, and they moved on.

If you are going to have this mix be a complete democracy, the overall vision will most likely become blurred as each member is placated. Go back and have the discussion again about goals and aims from the pre-production days of the album. Have you held true to those? When you again listen to the other groups' albums that achieved the pinnacles you are shooting for, do they sound that much better or different? Sometimes just re-assessing the original goals will help bring more of the group to the center.

Some groups, however, suspend all democracy at this point and put all of the decisions into a trusted set of hands, be that someone inside the group or a producer who has seen these inter-group struggles in 99% (well . . . let's be honest . . . 100%) of the thousands of projects they have worked on. In the college world, the Tufts' Beelzebubs have for many years put out consistently excellent albums, and NO member of the group (save for the music directors) heard ANY mixes before the album was actually released and the group members were tearing the cellophane off of the new CDs at the same time as the rest of the world.

That "rest of the world" is quite an important demographic, as the immediate positive feedback usually quells any concerns the group members had (about something they can't do anything about anyway, since it's already done.) However, these outsiders can be very useful for perspective if you are staying on the democratic route. The group itself is generally so internally-focused that it becomes impossible to hear what the end result will sound like to the rest of the world. They know every part of the arrangement, so they can't really hear the overall sound without gravitating back to the individual lines that make up the outer shell that 99% of the rest of the world will hear. Each singer is intimately aware of each of the other singers' (and their own) voices, so they focus on "Fred" or "Wendy" rather than the way they'd listen to a group of singers they don't know.

When sending preliminary mixes to friends, relatives, and peers for evaluation and comments, be sure to keep in mind where their focus might lie. If one of these people happens to be an arranger, they might be focusing on that aspect and come back with notes on the arrangement. This isn't what you are looking for . . . what percentage, of everyone who will listen to this album, is an arranger anyway? This is why you must get a good cross-section of commentary, which in numbers should far outnumber your group, to help dilute or strengthen individual opinions. If three members of your group think an effect on a certain part sticks out too much, but none of the thirty outside ears mention it, then it's most likely not a problem. On the other hand, what if no one in your group noticed that the lyrics are incomprehensible in the second verse (because they are so familiar with the arrangement that they are easily able to fill in those blanks), yet most of the outsiders mention that they didn't understand the words? Probably something to address. Just as great movie directors will change the way a movie ends based on screenings for old ladies in Peoria, having a pulse on the outside world's reaction to your work while you still have time to change things is the best insurance for success you can have.

Now that we've discussed all of the esoteric and political topics, what are the tools to put together a good mix? The basic building blocks for shaping a sound are *Equalization* (hereafter referred to as *EQ*), and *Compression*.

Like the tone controls on your car stereo, EQ can be used in wide swaths to make a signal brighter or darker, but can also be used in very narrow notches to surgically bring out an aspect of a certain sound (such as the "crack" of the snare while leaving the end "ffff" sound intact), or to take annoying nasal frequencies out of certain singers. It can also be used to keep voices from interfering with each other in the middle frequencies where basses and sopranos alike both live. Even though, in context with everything else, your ear might tell you the upper parts are full-range, you would most likely be surprised to hear what many upper-range voices sound like if just played solo from an a cappella mix; sometimes it sounds as if the voices are coming through a telephone, but when in context with everything else, your ears can't tell that all of the thickness is gone from those parts. If those upper parts were left intact, you WOULD hear something—a great buildup of muddiness in the midrange. The takeaway from all of this is that each sound in and of itself should not be optimized to sound great on its own—the sounds need to compliment each other or get out of the way to make the whole puzzle fit together.

Compression is the next shaping of the sound. Basically, a compressor limits the range of dynamics. "But aren't dynamics a GOOD thing?" you ask. Well, yes and no. The dynamics will still be there, just less intense, and the tonal energy behind them will be left intact. The ear will still perceive them, but they will be much more under control during the mix so they don't keep disappearing then popping back out too loud behind all of the other parts going on. Multiply this by 100 or so channels, and you will see why you would want to control this range, even if by a small amount. Compression also affects the apparent energy of a track and, in skilled hands, can be used to make a weaker performance sound more confident and forceful. Or it can be used to just control quick spikes or valleys in volume where the singer has less control of his voice.

For vocal percussion, compression is one of the key tools in shaping the attacks and releases of various parts of the drum kit, such as kick (bass) drum, snare, and toms. Depending on how fast the compression starts working or releases (these are adjustable parameters), as well as the degree of the compression, you can shape all of these mouth sounds into fairly realistic drum sounds.

After each track is put under control with these building blocks, you can start looking for groupings and placements of these individual parts.

Building up the drum tracks, you can fairly easily get a huge low-end sound on the kick drum. However, when you hear your bass singer, there appears to be a huge chasm between the bottom end of the vocal bass and the large booming sound of the kick drum created by the (non-vocal) puff of air hitting the mic diaphragm. To fill this gap, enter the octave-dropped bass (or Überbass), one of the more-debated topics in groups, forums, workshops, and reviews. Used correctly, the Überbass can be very effective in filling in that unused space or just silly-sounding when used incorrectly.

There are many ways to drop that octave, but most have the same result on their own: a very alien tone with many audio artifacts. Luckily, you only need a *tiny* bit of the frequency spectrum to add to the bottom of your real bass tracks. Using a *Low-Pass Filter* (basically an EQ that gets rid of any frequencies ABOVE a certain setting), you can cut off everything above 90 Hertz or so, just leaving the very bottom thumping part, which automatically gets rid of all of that alien sound. Just a little bit of this track between the kick drum and bass can be all of the "glue" that's needed to make a song sound naturally thick and beefy, or it can also be turned up to heavy unnatural levels to make an a cappella club track that will make any room shake.

Gathering up some of the other obvious building blocks that make up a rhythm section, such as those "ja-jeng" guitar parts, they can now be combined into one event, balanced out, and treated as a whole. In this case the engineer might thin the whole group out and add another aggressive compressor or run it all through a guitar amp simulator.

Ball in the House

Some of the background "ooh" and "ahh" parts might now be a bit too static in contrast, as everything else is getting bigger around them and *modulating* them somehow such as running them through an organ rotating speaker (also known as a "Leslie"), or other moving effects such as phase sweeps, tremolos, or any of a thousand other "ear candy" toys may be advisable. On the other hand, the contrast of the pure vocals against the affected parts might be what it needs. Each track or grouping presents a thousand opportunities, and sometimes doing nothing is as effective as using the wildest new effect.

All of these events should sound as if they are taking place in a space (or various spaces), rather than the uncomfortable position of hundreds of mouths very close to the listener's ears. *Spatial effects* such as *Reverberation, Ambience,* and *Delay* help create these layers of distance, rather than everything coming from the same point. *Reverberation* (or *Reverb*) is the effect of being in a large room, which carries the tone after someone stops singing as well as creating pleasing effects of letting notes wash over each other slightly. *Ambience* is basically a shorter version of reverb, where you can hear the sounds bounce off the walls but the tone doesn't carry on. This is better for things like percussion, where you want things to stay distinct but still fill a room. *Delay* is a distinct echo, which is sometimes musically timed as well. If you listen to almost any pop record made after 1955, you should be able to identify these elements right away.

The lead vocal will ride on top of this menagerie, tamed also with all of the above elements. Before processing the lead vocal of a cover song, listen to the original and see how the rest of the world is used to hearing it. If the your singer is performing the song similarly to the original artist on the record, you can complete the effect by using roughly the same combinations of tools that were used on the original. If going another direction, feel free to make your own space.

As stated a few times earlier in this chapter, with thousands of choices presented thousands of times, no two mixes done by two different mixers will be alike. There is no right answer or no single best path to take, but hopefully a little light was shed here to start you on that path. Once you've survived this ordeal, it's smooth sailing from here!

Mastering

One last step, and the job is complete. Mastering is the final polish to the created mix or collection of mixes. If you are just doing one song, mastering is just that—an optimization of what is already there in the mix, just shinier and bigger! For an album, it becomes much more complex: just as mixing pulled all of those individual parts together to create a song, mastering pulls all of those songs together to create an album. Using some of the basic elements of mixing (compression and EQ, as well as a few other black arts techniques beyond the scope of this book), the songs take on a new life as they are worked into shape to find the best combination of optimization and cooperation with the other songs on the album. This is hardly ever a do-it-yourself process—a very accurate, purpose-built room as well as specialized equipment and different skill set is needed. However, the process itself only requires several hours from beginning to end for a whole album, so it is a reasonable expense. It also serves as a final inspection from another professional, ensuring that your album is going out into the world the best it can be.

The art of mastering includes getting an album of unrelated songs and textures to sit together and have some sort of flow or arc. The spacing between songs, relative levels, darkness, brightness, and a myriad of other parameters under the mastering engineer's skilled hand will give your album that final sheen and cohesiveness that has been evading you up until now. The mastering engineer should also be able to provide you with the latest types of file sets that correspond to the ever-changing norm of requirements as technology and standards dictate.

Congratulations on finishing your album—now it's time to get it out there!

The Hawkettes

Off the Beat

CHAPTER 28

WHY BOCA?

By Deke Sharon

"What is BOCA," you ask?

Sit down, kiddies, and let me tell you the story from the olden days:

The year was 1994, and the contemporary a cappella movement was young.

Adam Farb, a member of the Brown Derbies, had just graduated college and contacted me because he was interested in making a career of a cappella. I had several ideas bouncing around in my head that I shared with him, and the one that showed immediate promise was an annual collegiate a cappella compilation album.

It bears noting that CASA was born, in part, from a mailing list compiled and carefully updated by Rex Solomon, a former Brandeis student who loved a cappella so much that he contacted collegiate groups every year or two to purchase their latest album. This was hard work, as no central database existed, so he created his own. So it's not an exaggeration to say that CASA's foundations were laid in part by the desire for collegiate a cappella recordings.

Moreover, it was near impossible to find a cappella music anywhere those days. Record stores didn't have an a cappella section, so Take 6, The Nylons and the King's Singers were usually found in gospel, pop and classical respectively, if they were to be found at all. One of my personal hobbies since high school was to scour the racks for hard to find a cappella and vocal music, which was all the more difficult because a list of a cappella groups or albums didn't exist either. When I came across an album called "Montezuma's Revenge" in a used CD store in SF one summer in 1990 (?), I had to purchase it guessing it was a cappella, and only upon opening and listening at home did I realize I'd stumbled on what would become an historic Dutch group.

Needle, meet haystack.

Anyhoo, you can imagine how hard it was to find collegiate a cappella. Moreover, much of it was, how shall I say it—pretty terrible. There were so many versions of "Only You" by the Flying Pickets that Rex filled one 90-minute cassette with them—and then another 60-minute one.

Many albums sounded like they were recorded in a wind tunnel (usually the school chapel), with a couple of hastily erected mics, as the group sang once through their entire repertoire. In essence, albums were often just aural yearbooks, a memento for members, fans and parents. Hardly the stuff of legend.

But, occasionally I'd come across a great track or album, and I wanted to share these with the world. There was a market, I was certain of it, but how to reach it. And how to make the project financially worthwhile for the person who was going to take the time to chase down all the albums, handle distribution, etc.

The idea for the logistics came from a project I worked on with Danny Lichtenfeld, a fellow Tufts Beelzebub, during the 1989-1990 year. We had a great group and wanted to make an album, but the Bubs only made studio albums every other year (they were expensive, and logistically difficult). What about a live album? But would it sell well? Would it sound good enough? The Bubs were known for our albums, and we didn't want to put something out of lesser quality, so a full live album didn't make sense.

But what about a live concert album with other groups? They could sell the album as well. We found four other great groups, invited them to perform on Friday and Saturday night, taped both shows, and each group picked their favorite four tracks, resulting in a 20-track album. The other groups would pitch in to cover the cost, and get copies of the album that they could sell on their own campuses: and thus the Beelzebub Winter Invitational was born.

We got a great price on duplication, the location for free, an alum to record us . . . and before we knew it, our costs had dropped such that we were making a profit on the CD before we pressed it, and that's with the other groups getting the CDs for a great price as well. Win-win.

Plus, back in 1994, there wasn't a single mail order catalog that specialized in contemporary a cappella back in those days, so we'd just figured out a clever way to get our CD sold on four different college campuses.

Expand this model to include studio tracks by 18 different groups on 18 different campuses, and you have a direct distribution model that is promoting groups to college students and other groups across the nation, while promoting collegiate a cappella in general. Charge a small amount ($5 or $6 a CD), and require a minimum purchase (a meager 50 CDs or so, easy for any college group to sell), and groups have a built in $300-$500 profit as soon as they sell that batch. Very easy for most groups, and yes, we had plenty of reorders. Everyone makes money.

We did indeed require groups to purchase CDs. Why? Because we didn't want any group to be the one to say "we want to be promoted on other campuses, but we don't want to promote anyone here." The model only works if everyone's participating. To date, I don't know of any group turning down the offer (one group from Yale did pass the first year, but gladly signed up for the second BOCA the following year), because it makes sense.

My wife, Katy, came up with the name. Rather inspired, I must say. Stands the test of time: a topical acronym that makes sense, is easy to pronounce and easy to remember. (BOHSA, bless its heart, is the clumsy younger sister with a speech impediment.)

I did expect groups to want to be on BOCA, but I didn't expect it to be as big a deal as it has become. It was always intended to be a promotional tool for the community, rather than an award. Each year, I find myself explaining this fact, along with the caveat that the songs are chosen to appeal to the casual music listener, not a cappella insiders. All of the "rules" we have used (trying to include new groups when possible, not repeating songs, variety of sounds and styles) are all to this end. When accused of not being "fair," I try to politely remind people that it's better to think of it as my mix tape than the Grammys* (the CARAS were established for that purpose).

Since the beginning, any collegiate recording has been accepted. Some years we've only allowed albums that are on records (because the point is to promote a group's completed recording), but now with digital downloads, EPs, partial albums released . . . we're back to considering anything.

Who is "we?" Well, Adam Farb and I chose the tracks for several years, until he sold it to Don Gooding (along with the ICCAs), who oversaw it until he retired and sold both to Amanda Newman, who owns and runs Varsity Vocals to this day.

Speaking of the present day, one might think BOCA is no longer needed. It certainly doesn't fill as large a need as it once did, what with group web sites, digital downloads, RARB, CASA.ORG, Mouthoff and the like. And yet, I like to think it still has a purpose, providing busy fans an annual collegiate a cappella compilation of quality while giving groups a little feather in their caps.

And one day, if it fades into obscurity, it'll go back to being what it basically was initially: my annual collegiate a cappella mix tape. Wait, you don't know what a mix tape is? Oh boy. We'll save that history lesson for another time!

Take 7

CHAPTER 29

ONLINE DISTRIBUTION

By Peter Hollens

I believe the future is here. An artist can use YouTube to distribute a single or music video, license it on Loudr, distribute it on dozens of platforms and get support making consistent content on Patreon[*]. The only thing a label can offer beyond this model is radio airplay and $$.

Any artist with the drive, talent and the know-how to create their own content can make a living doing what they love, which means more music, more art, more inspiration, and more people on this Earth doing what they were meant to do: create and inspire!

We all saw what Macklemore & Ryan Lewis did with their recent album. Thanks to internet sites like Loudr and Patreon, we all can create content, distribute it and support it ourselves. No exclusive contracts, no one taking a percentage and most importantly, no longer do we need anyone to tell us that our music is good enough to be heard.

If you are an independent musician or group, you should do whatever you can to prevent people's hands from reaching into your pocket. Pay your production teams by the hour and keep 100% of the backend. Use crowd-funding to help pay your production costs. Push your audience to the places on the internet that give you back the most money and support you as an INDEPENDENT musician and creator.

By the way, these platforms aren't secrets. They are available, and you should be using them. If you are an independent musician or creator and you aren't using these sites to help make a living, you are missing out. Both Loudr and Patreon were created by musicians for musicians (and other creators). In addition, consider using websites like Tubular Labs and Epoxy. Both of these allow you to learn how to process and understand any and all analytical data, and respond and engage with your audience. MSCLVR is another site that gives value back to the creator. In essence, it is an iTunes "shortener" that pays you a percentage of each purchase that you drive to iTunes. It also gives great analytics about each click.

---

[*] All websites referenced are listed in Appendix A

While we're at it, if you aren't on Twitter, Facebook, YouTube, Instagram, and Tumblr engaging and answering your supporters, you are doing something wrong. These people are sharing your music, and paying you to make content. The least you can do as an artist is make sure to talk to as many of your supporters as you can. Engage. Be genuine. Be who you are and you will have a better chance of succeeding.

While you are listening, don't allow anyone to take a huge piece of your revenue stream unless they are offering you more value than they are taking from you. They didn't create your audience, your brand, they didn't develop YOUR talent—don't give them your money. Don't sign contracts with people or companies you don't know well. This includes virtually all members of your team: multi-channel networks, labels, managers, agents, and anyone that wants a slice of what you create. Learn how to do it yourself, and eventually the offers these other people bring will be worth it. I have created a FAQ on my website (www.peterhollens.com/faqs) that is updated frequently with new companies and products that help musicians succeed.

Peter Hollens

How Do I start?

Here is the workflow I use and recommend for new artists. Remember, the goal is to create a community of people who enjoy your work:

1. Create content that is genuine to who you are as an artist. Basically, what you LOVE to do, and what you are best at.

2. Utilize your social circle or social media influence to financially support the creation of your content with a crowd-funding platform. For example, Patreon, created by Jack Conte of Pomplamoose, is an incredible fundraising platform. Make sure that you have multiple streams of income to sustain your creation.

3. If you are doing covers, license your content. The best way is by using Loudr. You can also distribute with them, but there are dozens of companies that do this as well such as: CDBaby, DistroKid, MondoTunes, and Tunecore.

4. Stay informed! One of my favorite digital resources is Ari Herstand's site, Aristake.

Advantages of Independent Distribution

Independent music distribution has become much easier as artist-created platforms have grown up to fulfill the traditional services provided by record labels.

Take Loudr for example. Rather than being a music store, Loudr allows customers to pay what they want for an artist's music. In return, the customer gets lossless-quality audio, meaning the exact sound of the studio-mastered version—not the excessively edited mp3 version sold by most sites. Loudr also takes care of collaborative splits and all licensing. They pay monthly with up-to-the-minute sales information on the backend dashboard giving you 100% transparency!

One of the other benefits of direct artist-to-fan platforms is the lower overhead. It's pretty well known that iTunes, Amazon, Google Play, and all the big boys take a big chunk of each sale. You can offer your music for less on Loudr and still end up making more money from each sale. Loudr integrates beautifully with YouTube videos, and you can bundle different albums and singles together right on an album page, which helps your supporters find your music and encourages them to get multiple albums at once.

It's also cool that your supporters know that they're supporting you directly. I've been pleasantly shocked by how generous some people have been (I received upwards of $190 for a single once!) and it literally keeps me going.

Summary

These are the platforms that I currently use, in order of what I recommend:

- Patreon

    ▷ Consistent funding of your work whether per creation or per month

    ▷ Gives you the ability to have your own consistent salary

- Loudr

    ▷ Lossless format

    ▷ Pay what you want

    ▷ Highest percentage to artist

- Patreon

    ▷ Create a mailing list to keep your supporters informed

    ▷ Sell physical albums

    ▷ Sell other physical merchandise, such as signed CDs and t-shirts

- iTunes

    ▷ Integration with ecosystem

- Google Play, Amazon

    ▷ A lot of consumers in their ecosystem

- •Spotify, Apple Music, Pandora, Rdio

    ▷ Use all streaming sites! Having your music accessible is important, even if it pays less at certain sites.

I currently use every distribution platform I can find because I want my music to be accessible to everyone all over the world.

SHARING YOUR VIDEOS ON FACEBOOK

So, you're ready to share a video on YouTube and make money from the ads, but Facebook doesn't seem to be sharing it with your audience?

What's really happening: Facebook has an algorhythm with regard to posts. Facebook first features posts with videos uploaded directly to Facebook (native Facebook uploads). Next to be featured are posts with images uploaded directly to Facebook. Then regular posts with three lines or less and, finally, posts with YouTube video links. Your YouTube video link is initially getting suppressed in your audience's feeds because it is the lowest in priority.

Here are some recommendations on working around this problem.

1. Make an image/snapshot/screengrab of the video that is catchy or matches the video's thumbnail. This image file should be large, as in good quality. With a little more effort, you could make a short video-teaser or a snippet of your full-length video.

2. Create a Facebook post.

3. The FIRST thing you should do to this new Facebook post is upload that image. Or, for better results, upload the video teaser and at the end have a text that says "Click, " or "Watch" for the full video. This call to action will then send people your full video on YouTube.

4. Change the URL. Take the URL of the YouTube video and "disguise" it through a URL shortener, like bitly.com. I recommend doing this with a playlist, so after the first video it automatically starts a long list of your videos. This will increase watchtime on your YouTube channel as your next video in the playlist will automatically start after the first one ends.

5. Write the text in your Facebook post and paste in the shortened URL for the video or playlist.

Important: You have to upload the photo first so that it registers as a photo. You can't post the link first because Facebook will recognize it as a YouTube video, even if it's shortened through bitly.com.

INCREASE YOUR VIEWERSHIP AND EARNINGS

Now that your YouTube post has top priority in Facebook feeds, there are still other ways to increase the number of views you receive. For any post, as more engagement occurs, the more exposure that post will get. Facebook "Shares" are the most influential way to increase exposure, so make sure to share your post with as many people as possible. Comments are the second most influential way to increase viewership and Facebook "Likes" are the third.

Ads equal money. Getting a viewer to click on a link that launches the YouTube player in a new window is the best way to earn money because YouTube can serve all available ad formats on its own watch page. In contrast, if the video appears within the Facebook feed (an embedded view), there is no ability for YouTube to serve companion display ads. While Facebook is currently working on a monetization model for creators, it has not been released to the public and most likely will be a few years behind YouTube.

The bitly.com URL shortener tip described earlier ensures you earn as much as you can because it launches a new YouTube watch page window.

INSIGHTS

Plumbers of Rome

CHAPTER 30

TOUGH LOVE FOR A TOUGH MARKET

By Deke Sharon

This is a love letter—a tough love letter—to professional a cappella groups and musicians. Everyone in a cappella is so nice that I'm going to take a minute to hold up a mirror and be "that guy."

By the way, if you're a casual singer, have a CAL group, or don't consider yourself professional, this is most certainly not for you. Keep singing, having fun, spreading harmony through harmony. There is absolutely nothing wrong with a cappella as a hobby and avocation. In fact, the world would be a far better place if there were many more people and many more groups like you. Carry on!

As for the rest of you . . .

1) Nobody Cares

How many fans does your group have on Facebook? Take a long look at that number, then go to the Facebook pages of all of your favorite bands. Uh oh.

You performed at an a cappella festival this year, and had some fun doing a couple high school and college gigs last month? Fun, but if your group disappeared next month, how many people would be asking about you?

If you want fans to love you, and you want your music to matter beyond friends and family, you need to step up your game. More gigs, more videos, more tracks. You're not working hard enough. Until you have done over 250 gigs in a calendar year, you're not really hitting the pavement. Yup, it can be done. In fact, I've done it. Exhausting, and in the end you're humbled, but likely have some numbers that will make people in the general music industry begin to take you seriously.

You're not so much about touring, and prefer to make videos? That's fine, but there are fourteen-year-old kids in the Philippines making music videos with more hits than yours. Step up your game: more heart, more flash, more creativity, more cleverness, more . . . more. Make a video a week for a year. If Peter Hollens is making more videos than you, then you're not making enough videos.

You're more about recording? I have three words for you: Free, Track, Tuesday. We'll talk in 52 weeks.

That's all there is. Take your pick.

2) You Don't Care

Did you lose sleep over your latest recording? Either by staying up all night working on it, or better yet lying awake at four am the next night, worried if it's the absolute best it can be? If not, you're approaching your job with the same nonchalance as a middle manager working at a cardboard box distribution warehouse.

But wait: you're working as hard as you should have to work, as hard as you worked in school, and you're just not getting results, not getting A's like you used to, not at the top like you've always been? That's called grade inflation and entitlement. You might never have really worked hard. You might be a member of the "entitlement generation." Who knows, who cares? Just pick up a shovel and start digging, and don't stop until people start writing newspaper articles about your ditch. Which they may never do. But you keep digging anyway. Every day.

Did you spend more time looking at Facebook or working on your a cappella career today? Yesterday? Did you coach at the local high school for free, send off some arrangements to a group in South America as a gift, and volunteer for CASA, or did you spend another day waiting for the phone to ring and your email box to fill up?

Blue Jupiter

Wanting to be successful and popular is meaningless. Everyone wants that. And a million dollars. Make that a billion. Desire is meaningless, beyond its ability to motivate. That's not caring about your music, that's caring about yourself. Narcissism.

Here's the bottom line: a real, full time job is between 45–80 hours a week. If you are not working that hard at a cappella, day in, day out, for several years, then you have absolutely no right to expect anything. You start at the bottom like everyone, and shed blood, sweat and tears. For years. Then maybe you'll have some real success.

It doesn't work any other way. ESPECIALLY in a cappella.

3) Your Music Is Irrelevant

The statement above should sting immediately. Because it does for every single professional musician. Daily. Constant concern about the nature of art and commerce, and where they/you fit in. Even if your music matters today, tomorrow your music will have mattered yesterday, and you have to start all over again.

The problem for most a cappella musicians is that they're not fundamentally concerned about their musical relevance. I've seen too many people laugh about how there are far too many versions of "Fix You," and then turn around and record "Firework." If you're not part of the solution, you're part of the problem.

Are you singing songs because you like them or because you're saying something? Are you picking your tunes because they'll help you land a corporate gig or because they'll touch someone's heart? I'm all about people making money, selling albums, cashing checks, but that's commerce, and based on replicating someone else's relevance for people who can't afford the real thing.

Yeah, I said it: you're singing Michael Bublé covers of Frank Sinatra tunes to people who can't watch Frank because he's dead and can't afford Michael Bublé tickets. Ouch.

Start with one song. One powerful song. Might have been done before, or maybe you have a friend who is a songwriter. One amazing song that doesn't sound like anyone else. It sounds like you.

And then do it again a hundred times, as it might take that many before one clicks. You were kinda hoping that first one would be enough, weren't you?

4) There's No Extra Credit

You will get no brownie points for anything. No one cares how hard you work, or how many hours you log working on an arrangement or a recording. Zero. There's a recession and all pity parties have been cancelled.

You do get karma credit for working with students, and giving away arrangements to new groups. You get credit for volunteering with CASA or another great organization, but I should be clear: you don't get to walk in the door and do the coolest job. But none of this makes you a more popular musician. It just makes you a better person.

5) You'll Probably Fail

Whatever reasonably high goal you set for yourself, you'll probably fail. So, set another. That'll probably not work out as well. Welcome to reality.

I'd venture to guess that 90% of the things I initially set out to do haven't worked out as planned. And I consider myself extremely lucky having had a 10% success rate.

Yeah, I said it: luck. That's the most important thing, after hard work. In order of importance: hard work, luck, talent. Talent on its own is useless.

So you'll spend the next decade busting your ass (if you're doing it right), and maybe, just maybe, have enough to show for it that you felt it was worth it.

Fact is, if you do it right, you will have plenty to show for it, because a cappella is young, and the

Wise Guys

tree is still ripe with low hanging fruit. But it's only available to people who get up early and stay up late, as the really easy fruit has all been picked. Better yet, plant more trees. Even better yet, teach others to plant trees.

It may not be clear, but I'm saying all of this because I care. I love a cappella, as we all do, and want to see us make gains that make last year look like a quiet prelude. Let's talk again after we're filling stadiums and have another string of top ten hits.

How amazing would it be if we had all 5,000 graduating collegiate a cappella singers continue in some way, starting groups, joining groups, singing in retirement homes, filling every farmer's market and local TV station with their song. And the music that would be made by the best of the best?!?

This is nothing, our numbers are miniscule. Imagine if we had 100 times as many pro a cappella musicians. 1,000 times . . . but only if they really put their back in their work. A bunch of slackers will only water down the impact, filling the bandwidth with self-absorbed mediocrity . . .

Actually, you know what? I take it back. Go back to Facebook, to YouTube. Get out of the way so that the real musicians don't have to climb over you. Do ten arrangements a year, and 27 gigs, and make a video, and make sure to check your Facebook profile every day to see how many people liked them! Ooh, you got a new friend! She's kinda cute too! Click on her profile and check out her photos . . .

Ok, we got rid of those people. If you've read this entire chapter then you're left. There aren't many of you. That's OK. We only really need a few!

A LITTLE A CAPPELLA HISTORY

- The South African Mbube tradition (Ladysmith Black Mambazo, et al.) was born from a single song: "The Lion Sleeps Tonight."

- Madrigals, barbershop, and doo wop were all the contemporary a cappella of their day.

- Many classic doo-wop groups and songs were originally a cappella, but the record companies always added instruments for radio.

- The first contemporary a cappella conference, the A Cappella Summit, was held in Marin, CA, in 1993. Today there are many such events around the globe.

- Deke Sharon created CASA: The Contemporary A cappella Society of America in his college dorm room at Tufts University.

- The Yale Whiffenpoofs, the first collegiate a cappella group, was formed in 1909. Modern a cappella is 100 years old!

- Legendary music producer Brian Eno sings a cappella every week and considers it essential to good health and happiness.

- Many American Idol finalists have a cappella backgrounds including Blake Lewis and Justin Guarini.

- Although there are many variations, the proper spelling is "two p's, two l's, two words": a cappella.

- Yale University does not have any fraternities or sororities; instead they have as many as 20 a cappella groups each year.

- Bobby McFerrin's hit song "Don't Worry, Be Happy" was used in George H. W. Bush's 1988 U.S. presidential election as Bush's 1988 official presidential campaign song, without Bobby McFerrin's permission or endorsement. In reaction, Bobby McFerrin publicly protested that particular use of his song, including stating that he was going to vote against Bush, and he completely dropped the song from his own performance repertoire, to make the point even clearer.

PFC

CHAPTER 31

ALL YOU NEED TO DO

By Deke Sharon

One of my least favorite phrases in the English language is "All you need to do is . . ."

Example: how many of you have had a relative or (usually older) friend alert you to the success of Jonathan Coulton? Never heard of him? Look him up online and read his amazing story.

If you don't have time to research him, here's the gist: he quit his job, wrote a song a week, and started making real money without a record label.

Now, it's certainly sweet when a relative informs you that there's someone else in the music industry who has had unconventional success, and advice is always appreciated, if misdirected. But "See? All you have to do is . . ." is simply annoying.

For every Jonathan Coulton there are thousands of struggling musicians posting songs and videos with nowhere near the level of success. Analyze at will, the clear takeaway is that it's not all you have to do.

The most epic version of this I've ever experienced was from the father of a good friend. A very successful inventor and entrepreneur, he has a fast talking, no nonsense demeanor with a healthy dose of "if you're not with me, you're against me. In fact, you're an idiot" in his tone.

"Deke, I've got it. You want to be rich? Famous?"

"Yeah, sure. Why not. What's your plan?"

"Don't make fun of me, I'm serious. This is the big one. This could make you a household name."

"I'm all ears."

"I don't think you're ready. This is huge. THE big idea. Guaranteed worldwide fame and fortune. Are you ready? I don't think you're ready"

"I'm ready!"

"Ok. Here it is: write a new Happy Birthday!"

"Wait . . . what?"

"Yeah—the current one sucks, and everyone sings it. Just write a better one, and everyone will love you for it, and sing it everywhere, and it'll be in movies . . ."

<silence>

Right. I told him there's a "distribution problem," hoping to explain it in his language, but to no avail. He still must think I don't want to be famous. Oh well. I'm happy to have any of you run with this ball, and if you hit it big, I expect nothing more than a nice steak dinner.

So, it's really never "that easy." Especially in music. If it were, everyone would be doing it, right?

Moreover, I think it's extremely disingenuous when you hear the words "Anyone can do _____."

Nothing could be more foolish.

I recall having a meal with the 1996 Olympic gold women's softball team, shortly after their win, with a member who was writing a book.

She was espousing the frequent byline of the successful, which is "I was successful, look at me, you can do it, too!"

I haven't had dinner with Donald Trump or anyone else of his ilk, so this was my chance . . .

"Really, it could have been anyone on this team! I made my dream come true, and so could they."

"Wait . . . you're saying anyone? Poor crippled kids in Mexico City . . ."

"Yup! All they have to do is want it hard enough . . ."

"Wanting it has nothing to do with it, beyond motivation. It's all about hard work . . . and opportunity . . . then still plenty of people will fail."

"I disagree. I won the Olympics, and so can anybody."

"Actually, no. Only a few people will earn a gold medal in the Olympics, and the rest will lose. It is a zero-sum game in the extreme. In fact, it's a big negative sum game. You won, and many, many people lost, some of whom might have worked harder than you, or wanted it more . . ."

And so the conversation went, neither of us gaining any ground. I haven't read her book, but I assume it includes the same meaningless platitudes that we're all served regularly.

I'm no celebrity, and my success meager by our country's bombastic standards, but I'd like to do my best to break the cycle, and stop the madness. Some random thoughts:

- Your successes in life will neither come easily nor will they have been inevitable. If they were easy or inevitable, they were not successes; they were lucky breaks.

- You will have peers who will want it more, or work harder, and you might prevail, with your talent, skill set and work ethic. If you do, be gracious, and know that their success does not equate to your failure. If anything, they likely just made your success more possible by increasing the market. At least in a cappella. Especially in a cappella.

- Perhaps at times you'll be met with failure, only to see another succeed. One to whom you compare yourself favorably, perhaps very favorably. Perhaps one who does not deserve the success at all, by your calculus. This is where you're stung by the simple fact that life is unfair. Sometimes wildly unfair. Be gracious, as you may be the next guy who finds success without deserving it as much as another.

- Those who are overnight successes (and they are far fewer than they seem) rarely either appreciate or maintain their status. Former child stars are some of the most unhappy people on the planet. And those in a cappella who may seem to be overnight successes have still spent years honing their skills. A cappella is impossible without years of practice.

- Those who do succeed will find the story of their success distilled into an easily digestible paragraph. I see it happening for/to myself, and I have great ambivalence around it, as it makes for a good myth, yet I cannot let myself forget the truth, which is a far messier reality, a shade of gray that would take volumes to fully explain. And is, by in large, for all intents and purposes, boring.

I say all of this because I want to make clear: life is messy, life is nonsensical, life does not happen in easily digestible paragraphs. That's mythology. Don't believe it.

Your relatives and friends will forward you links and send you newspaper clippings, all well meaning, hoping to help you find success. Read the articles, then read between the lines, knowing that it's not so simple, the success wasn't that easy, and as such it parallels your own journey.

And then know that "all you need to do" is wake up tomorrow, wash your hair, and make some kick-ass music.

Lather, rinse, repeat.

Fermata Nowhere

CHAPTER 32

SO, YOU WANNA TOUR THE WORLD?

By Deke Sharon

As I write this chapter, I'm riding in a van racing across Switzerland to our next House Jacks concert, and I know what you want to ask:

"How can my group tour overseas?!?"

Well, obviously there are no guaranteed methods or procedures I can offer, but there are a few specific steps you can take:

First, you need a great recording and probably even more important, a great video.

Next, try to get an agent overseas. There is no better way to tour a foreign country than to have someone in that country organizing concerts, hotels, transportation, etc. You may well have to strike a deal to break even on your first trip(s) to the country, but together you're working toward a greater goal and it is always better to have someone say "these guys are amazing!" than you saying "we're amazing!" (and if it's in the local language, even better).

How do you find an agent? Well, search the web, and vocal groups' web sites for starters. Whereas it is possible to contact agents that have other similar a cappella groups on their roster, you'll find most agencies are not looking for duplicates, so you might do well to find one with a very different group, or perhaps no a cappella group at all. Obviously at this point you see the incredible importance of a great video, as you'll at best have 30 seconds to convince them you're worth their time.

It's also important for you to contact friends, family and business associates, wherever they may be. Often a first gig results from an existing relationship. Hand out lots of tickets, send around lots of CDs, and make sure to speak with everyone you know about potential gigs, agents, opportunities.

If you're not successful in finding an agent, which is likely the case for many of you (as they're often most interested in your group only once they've seen you live), your next best bet is to find some kind of anchor date to get your group into the country, around which you can build some additional dates to make your own first tour. For this, a cappella festivals are a great possibility (again, do a web search, or check out other a cappella groups' calendars to see where they've played), as are choral/vocal festivals and general festivals (which tend to be organized by theme or musical style, so if you're a jazz group, look for jazz festivals, etc.).

VPS Kek

What you want from a festival is airfare and an audience primarily, so don't be pushy about your fee after covering expenses. Remember, you contacted them. Be friendly and accommodating, realizing you're using them to get to the country, and from there you can:

Contact local groups and ambassadors to set up additional gigs. They will likely not pay enough money to cover airfare on their own, they'll certainly at least pay for your ground transport, hotel and meal, which is why having a good anchor date is key. You can search the acapedia for groups in a particular region, and then start writing those emails!

And be sure to post on rarb.org and or write a blog on casa.org letting people you're looking for gigs and hosts in a specific country. You'll find the international a cappella community to be very friendly and willing to help with advice. Oh, and don't only ask for help. Be prepared to offer it when you hear from someone who is looking to come to your country. Sharing the stage with them at a concert in one of your favorite venues, along with a split of the door and a couch to crash on can quickly turn into a reciprocal offer in their country.

If you're willing to invest a little of your own money, you can always fly yourself to a competition (like the Harmony Sweepstakes in America) or a vocal music festival, using the experience to make fans and friends, and perhaps an agent. There's no guarantee you'll make your money back in future touring, but if you're interested as much in the travel and experience as well as how it bolsters your resume back home ("international touring sensation . . .") then it can be money well spent. A vacation you can write off.

Now, a tiny bit of potentially helpful perspective:

The US is the #1 music market in the world, and is a great place to tour, but know that our country is wide and vast in contrast to Europe (making driving sometimes impossible) and that our music market is hungry for "world" music, but our fellow countrymen aren't too likely to spend money to hear American pop tunes in foreign accents (to be blunt). Bring to the US something you can't easily find in the US.

Also, I find many a cappella groups outside the US believe our country to be filled with a cappella groups and fans. Fact is, a cappella is a small niche market in the US, and Americans are notoriously difficult to get off their couches and into clubs or theaters to hear a band they don't know. Pairing with American groups that have an audience is a great way to make new fans here.

Japan is the #2 music market in the world, and a cappella has taken root there recently in a way reminiscent of American the early '90s: most a cappella comes in the form of male close harmony pop ballads (imagine a finger-snappin' Boyz II Men-esque slow song in Japanese). This doesn't negate the possibility for other a cappella groups there, but it is good to know the predominant flavor.

When it comes to Japan, an agent or contact within the country is essential, as Japanese business practices are more formal and nuanced than most Westerners are able to navigate without experience.

Germany is #3, and perhaps the single country in the world responsible for supporting the most full-time professional a cappella groups. The Comedian Harmonists (imagine the Kings Singers in the 1930s, with a piano) were the Beatles of their day, having created a culture of vocal harmony and a cappella that pervades the music scene. Add to that a densely populated country centered around cities and towns all with small and large theaters, a populace that is happy to go see whatever act is playing their local theater, and state sponsorship of the arts, and you have the "perfekt sturm," as it were.

Find our for yourself what other countries have great a cappella happening. I'll give you one more: Singapore. Amazing. One of the most vibrant a cappella scenes in the world. Go there.

Happy trails!

INTERNATIONAL FESTIVALS AND COMPETITIONS
AS OF OCTOBER, 2015

EUROPE

January

Lievekamp A Cappella Evening, Oss (NED)
www.lievekamp.nl

London A Cappella Festival (UK)
www.londonacappellafestival.co.uk

VocCologne, Köln (GER)
http://voccologne.hfmt-koeln.de

February

International Gdansk Choral Festival (POL)
www.gdanskfestival.pl/

BALK Festival Oost, Ulft (NED)
www.facebook.com/events/411284685597983/

March

The Voice Festival (UK)
www.thevoicefestival.co.uk

Total Choral – Pop/Jazz Chor-Festival, Berlin (GER)
www.totalchoral.de

A Cappella Rorschach (SWI)
www.acappella-rorschach.ch

EverySing! Festival, Ville de Montlouis-sur-Loire (FRA)
www.cepravoi.fr/pages/everysing

April

Prague Aca Fest 2013 (CZE)
www.pragueacappellafestival.cz

April–May

Internationaler Chorwettbewerb & Festival, Bad Ischl (AUT)
www.chorwettbewerb.at

A Cappella Woche Hannover (GER)
www.acappellawoche.com

Aarhus Vocal Festival (DEN)
www.aavf.dk

May

Wetterauer Musik Sommer Akademie – Festivokal (GER)
www.festivokal.de

A Cappella Festival Appenzell (SWI)
www.acappella-appenzell.ch

May–June

Festival für Vokalmusik Leipzig (GER)
www.a-cappella-festival.de

May–July

Stimmakrobaten Festival (GER)
www.stimmakrobaten.de

June

Tampere Vocal Music Festival and Competition (FIN)
www.tamperemusicfestivals.fi/vocal/vocal2011/?lang=en

Vocaal Festival Amusing Hengelo (NED)
www.amusing-hengelo.nl

Chortreffen Ibbenbüren (GER)
www.chortreffen.com

Sing a cappella Festival and Workshop Day (UK)
www.singacappella.org

Odense Vokal Festival, Odense (DEN)
www.odensevokalfestival.dk

Hofkonzerte – A cappella, Winterthur (SWI)
www.obertor.ch

Solevoci A-Cappella International Contest and Festival, Varese (ITA)
www.solevocifestival.it

July

vokal total, 14th International A Cappella Competition, Graz (AUT)
www.vokal.at

June–August

Crest Jazz Vocal Festival, Crest (FRA)
www.crestjazzvocal.com

August

XXI Choralies, Vaison-la-Romaine (FRA)
www.choralies.fr

Ohrid Choir Festival (Macedonia)
www.ohridchoirfestival.com

Nuits des choeurs / Stemmen onder de Sterren, Braine-l'Alleud (BEL)
www.nuitdeschoeurs.be

Vocal Pop & Jazz Days, Oberhausen (GER)
www.vpjd.nl

September

BerVokal – A Cappella Pop Festival, Berlin (GER)
www.bervokal.de

chor.com, Dortmund (GER)
www.chor.com

September–October

Acappellica, Hamburg (GER)
www.acappellica.de

sangeslust, Bayreuth (GER)
www.sangeslust.com

October

Festival Espoochor, Espoo (FIN)
www.festivals.fi/festivaalit/ooppera_ja_kuoro/88/?/eng

October–November

Voice Mania, Vienna (AUT)
www.voicemania.at

Polyfollia International Summer Festival, Saint-Lo (FRA)
www.polyfollia.org

Polyfollia World Showcase and Marketplace for Choral Singing, Saint-Lo (FRA)
www.polyfollia.org

November

Tonart-Festival Ilmenau (GER)
www.tonart-festival.de

BALK Top Festival, Rotterdam (NED)
www.balknet.nl

October–December

Vokal Total, Munich (GER)
www.spectaculum-mundi.de/index.php?vokal_total_programm

No future dates announced yet for the following European events:

Vocal Jazz Summit, Mainz (GER)
www.vocal-jazz-summit.de

Vokalarm, Trondheim (NOR)
http://vokalarm.no

The Real Group Festival, Stockholm (SWE)
www.therealacademy.se

Vocal Marathon, Rijeka (CRO)
www.vocalmarathon.com

VocalZone, Kiev (UKR)

Fool Moon International A Cappella Festival (HUN)
http://acappella.hu

Zoom+ Festival, Trnva (Slovakia)
www.zoomplus.sk

A Cappella Open, Moscow (RUS)
http://acappella-moscow.com

Voxon A Cappella Festival, Bleiburg (AUT)
www.voxon-festival.com

Sparkassen A Cappella Festival im Westfalenpark, Dortmund (GER)
www.dortmund.de/de/freizeit_und_kultur/westfalenpark_dortmund/westfalenpark_vk/event.jsp?eid=181953

Stemvork Festival, Torhout (BEL)
www.stemvork.eu

NORTH AMERICA

February

Los Angeles A Cappella Festival, Los Angeles, CA
http://www.la-af.com

Mile High Vocal Jam, Denver, CO
http://mhvj.org

NE Voices, Wilmington, MA
http://ne-voices.com

February–May

Harmony Sweepstakes A Cappella Festival, CA
http://harmony-sweepstakes.com

March

Sing Strong, Reston, VA
http://dc.singstrong.org

Sing Strong, Skokie, IL
http://chicago.singstrong.org

Texas A Cappella Calebration, San Antonio, TX
http://acappellacelebration.com

April

Boston Sings [BOSS], Boston, MA
http://bostonsings.com

ICCA and ICHSA Finals, NY
www.varsityvocals.com

Montreacappella, Montreal, QC, Canada
www.mtlacappella.com

VoiceJam A Cappella Festival, AK
http://waltonartscenter.org/voicejam-2015

May

Toronto Vocal Arts, Toronto, Canada
http://torontovocalartsfestival.com/

June

Camp Acappella, OH
http://www.campacappella.com

Summer

VoCALnation, Philadelphia, PA
http://vocal-nation.com

Fall

AcappellaFest, Chicago, IL
http://acappellafest.com/

SoJam, Raleigh, NC
http://sojam.net

Voices Aca-West:
West Coast A Cappella Festival
University of San Francisco
www.usfca.edu

ASIA

March

Youth Voices – Vocal Music Fest, Singapore (SIN)
www.a-cappella.org.sg

March–April

Hong Kong International A Cappella Festival (Hong Kong)
http://acappella.hkfyg.org.hk/chi/index.html

April

Spring Vocal Festival, Taipei (Taiwan)
www.tcmc.org.tw

FAN – Festival of A Cappella Nagoya (JAP)
http://fan.go2.jp/

June

Yamanashi A Cappella Summit, Yamanashi (JAP)

July

National A Cappella Championships, Singapore (SIN)
www.a-cappella.org.sg

Shanghai Children A Cappella Camp, Shanghai (CHI)

Shanghai A Cappella Camp, Shanghai (CHI)

Shanghai A Cappella Festival, Shanghai (CHI)
http://www.cjchtart.com/

August

Vocal Asia Festival, Yaoyuan (Taiwan)

Kanazawa A Cappella Town, Kanazawa (Japan)

October

A Cappella Society's International A Cappella Festival (Singapore)
www.a-cappella.org.sg

Taiwan International Contemporary A Cappella Festival, Taipei (Taiwan)
http://festival.tcmc.org.tw

November

Asia A Cappella Festival, Hong Kong
www.cashk.org

No future dates announced yet for the following Asian events:

**International A Cappella Summit Forum
(Taipei, Taiwan) – bi-annual**
www.vocalasia.com

AUSTRALIA

May

**Get Vocal – Melbourne Vocal Music Festival
(AUS)**
www.vocalaustralia.com

July

Festival of Voices in Tasmania (AUS)
https://festivalofvoices.com

AFRICA

No future dates announced yet

**Namibia International Vocal Festival,
Windhoek (Namibia)**
www.facebook.com/pages/Namibia-Vocal-
Festival/273174429407585?sk=wall

One Note Stand

CHAPTER 33

FAILURE IS YOUR FRIEND

By Deke Sharon

There are times in life to play it safe. I'm sure you can think of several.

Music is not one of them.

So many groups singing so many arrangements that mimic the original: same key, same tempo, same feel, same inversions . . . yawn. Yeah, sure, sometimes is fine . . . but always?

Take a risk. A big risk. This means sometimes you'll win big, and sometimes you'll fail.

That's right, I want you to fail.

Let me start by saying I want my children to fail. Over and over again. In countless big and small ways. If they're running out the door and I see their homework sitting on the table, not only won't I drive it to school later, I'll be glad they forgot it. Because next time they'll remember. Or not, but eventually they will. Failure is an excellent teacher.

What will you learn? You'll learn how to push your limits as an arranger/director, your singer's limits, and perhaps even your audience's limits. You'll learn what works and what doesn't. You'll learn how to take something and improve on it. You'll learn how to arrange, not just transcribe. You'll learn how to perform, not just replicate. And what will happen? Your worst nightmare: some people will hate it.

My daughter wrote a Christmas song in December and boldly announced to her class she was performing it at recess the next day. When she approached me nervously wondering what to do if some kids make fun of her, I told her bluntly: "That's what happens when you perform. Someone will always hate it. That's how it works. Don't worry about it."

I offer the same time-tested advice to you. Put yourself out there. And if you start going far enough, you'll start hearing negative feedback.

The critical response only means you're actually doing something. Now, I'm not suggesting that every bit of negative feedback is useless or petty. Some of it is great advice. Take it, learn from it, and use the rest to thicken your skin. Because you're going to hear a whole lot more hatred if you're doing it right.

Why? Because the opposite of love isn't hate, it's indifference.

Think about that for a second, because it's not what you usually hear, but it's true. Great art elicits a great reaction one way or another. People love it or hate it. It grabs you and won't let you go. Some people are shocked by this and don't like it, but it means the art is working. It's working on the mind, on the heart, on the soul. Great music makes you care. Mediocre music . . . click.

I'll go one step further: I like bad art much more than mediocre art. Bad art makes me cringe, makes me smile, makes me think. In fact, my high school buddies used to make mixed tapes for each other in High School and College lovingly entitled "Tape from Hell." Mr. T rapping, the Air Canada Steel Drum orchestra (brrrrrr!), the Shaggs. Our belief was and is that horrible music is actually great, and the worst music is what we deem "low mediocre." Low mediocre is your worst enemy. It lulls you into a sense of complacency when in fact you should be shocked into action. That meager applause you hear after a song? That's the audience's way of saying "that's nice." The way your grandmother says "that's nice."

Nice is third grade holiday concerts. Nice is the prize you get when you lose the game show. Nice should never be enough for you. Don't you want to touch people's hearts, grab their souls, and take them on a wild roller coaster ride through truth and beauty? Or at least you did, when you started.

Dig down deep, speak truth to power, face your fears and write about the journey. Tell me something I've never heard before, show me you care.

And to do this, you must fail. Miserably sometimes.

Do you fear failure? You shouldn't. You should fear mediocrity and complacency. That's what's holding you back.

Failure is your friend.

AN ASSORTMENT OF AMUSING A CAPPELLA GROUP NAMES

Alfred University: Sexy Pitches

American University: On a Sensual Note

American University: Treble in Paradise

Appalachian State University: What's Yer Pleasure

Arcadia University: A Little Knight Music

Arizona State University: Priority Male

Bard College Orapelicans

Berklee College of Music: Pitch Slapped

Boston University: Aural Fixation

Boston University: Chordially Yours

Bowling Green state University: HeeBee BGs

Brandeis University: Jewish Fella a Cappella

Brandeis University: Manginah

Brandeis University: Shirley Tempos

Cardozo School of Law: Acapellates

College of William and Mary: Cleftomaniacs

College Wooster: Merry Kuween of Skots

Concordia College: Six Appeal

Conneticut College: ConnChords

Dartmouth College: Decibelles

Duke University School of Law: Public Hearing

George Washington University: Sons of Pitch

Gettysburg College: Four Scores

Harvard University Law School: Scales of Justice

Harvard University: Din and Tonics

Haverford College: Ford S-Chords

Hofstra University: HOFBEATS

Ithaca College: Ithacappella

Kirkwood Community College: Jazz Transit

Lafayette College: Chorduroys

Le College Lionel-Groulx: Lionel-Groove Sexapella

Liberty University: Minor Prophets

McGill University: Tonal Ecstasy

MIT: Chorallaries

MIT: Logarhythms

MIT: Syncopasian (all Asian group)

Mt. San Antonio College: Fermata Nowhere

Nazareth College: Fermata Thin Air

New York Medical College: Arrhythmias

Northwestern University School of Law: Habeas Chorus

Ohio State University: Buck That!

Ohio University: Tempo Tantrums

Penn State University: Blue in the Face

Rice University: Lager Rhythms

Rutgers University: Deep Treble

Seton Hall University School of Law: EsqChoir

St. Mary's College of Maryland: Interchorus

SUNY Purchase College: Choral Pleasure

Temple University: Owlcappellas

University of Central Florida: Crescendudes

University of Central Florida: So Noted

University of Chicago: Ransom Notes

University of Chicago: Rhythm and Jews

University of Chicago: Unaccompanied Women

University of Colorado: Idiosingcrasies

University of Connecticut: Conn-Men

University of Hartford: Mouth Noise

University of Kentucky: AcoUstiKats

University of Kentucky: Paws and Listen

University of Mary Washington: One Note Stand

University of Michigan: Compulsive Lyres

University of North Carolina Chapel Hill: The Clef Hangers

University of Pennsylvania: Quaker Notes

University of South Carolina : Cockappella

University of Virginia School of Medicine: Spinal Chords

Wesleyan University: Mazeltones

Whitman College: The Testostertones

Moosebutter

CHAPTER 34

IN DEFENSE OF IMPERFECTION

By Deke Sharon

When I started this Mr. Toad's Wild Ride of a career in a cappella 21 years ago, there is one statement I thought I'd never hear myself say:

"People in a cappella have become too concerned with tuning."

It's easy to get people to agree with this statement nowadays, with so much pitch correction in recordings, but that's not what I'm talking about. I'm talking about too much focus on tuning during live performances. And I'm not talking about the use of live pitch correction. I think I just heard most of you jump off the bandwagon.

Let me explain.

A cappella is the oldest music, and throughout history has incorporated musical styles, both secular and popular. Most recently, that which we currently term "contemporary a cappella" is incorporating an ever-widening variety of musical traditions and styles—bluegrass, jazz, pop, R&B, hip-hop, soul, reggae, gospel—you name it.

None of these put a particular emphasis on tuning to the extent that it alters the style and presentation of the music. You can argue that it's easier to tune when you have a keyboard or fretted guitar in the mix, but as soon as you get one string out of tune, mix in a fiddle or trombone, anything can happen. It only takes one note for a chord to be askew.

Perhaps it's the prevalence of pitch correction in recordings and pop music, but groups seem ever-concerned with their pitch, and moreover judge other groups as if tuning is the point. It has never been the point. Wanna know what happens if you make it the point?

Exhibit A: Barbershop

Backstory: Over a century ago, "barbershop" (which didn't yet have that name) was largely improvised. In fact, it was created by and initially popularized by African Americans. Some guys standing around, jamming on the pop tunes of the day. Same as now, right? Yup. And, for the record, so was doo-wop, circa 1950. Same as it ever was.

Much later, in 1938, when OC Cash formed SPEBSQSA (now the Barbershop Harmony Society), he was trying to revitalize a musical style that had come and gone. It would be as if someone started the Doo Wop Harmony Society fifty years later, so, now. This was a noble act that has immortalized him in the annals of vocal harmony. As well it should.

However, over time, the music shifted. Changed. It went from guys hanging out with friends and singing the old songs in the old way to a codified form with guidelines and rules, perhaps in large part due to the increasing importance of the organization's annual competitions. Groups were judged, and judges needed criteria. This makes sense, as the organization's historical mission couldn't allow unlimited flexibility in all musical choices (lest the P in SPEBSQSA—preservation—be discarded).

AcoUstiKats

However now, over 100 years later, our barbershop has become its own style, with a litany of rules for acceptable chords and chord voicings, with the emphasis during performance on "ringing" chord after chord. Tuning.

Judges are trained to judge like each other, and coaches "teach to the test" when working with groups, all aiming at a specific aesthetic, with tuning a significant (albeit not only) priority. The music has gone from loose to tight, the sound from improvisatory to highly scripted, and the performances from natural to highly stylized. And, perhaps as a result, the organization has been shrinking rather significantly for the past 20 years . . . even as a cappella in general has exploded in popularity.*

Now, I wasn't around in 1890, so I'm just surmising, but my instinct tells me the music was more loose, less concerned with overtones. Music is communication, not some kind of Olympic sport, and all that should matter is how you make the audience feel.

You don't agree with me? Modern social science does.

Take, for instance, the fact that people do not make decisions with their minds. They make them with their hearts, and then they justify them intellectually. That's been proven time and again, and is at the core of everything from political campaigns to grocery store product placement.

To bring it closer to home, do you remember when Ben Folds said to the Beelzebubs in The Sing-Off Season One: "There were some tuning issues, but I didn't care!" That's exactly what I'm talking about. Do you know who else doesn't care? You don't care. Do you hate all Motown music? Most likely not. But the vocals are well outside what would be considered "in tune" nowadays. And they're beautiful. And real.

Moreover, if you're focusing primarily on tuning on stage, you're not performing and you're not communicating. You're manufacturing sound.

People love it when the House Jacks perform and we improvise a pop song. They don't care if it's perfect. And think of your own shows—sometimes the screeching high notes and rumbling low notes that made the audience go nuts were not in perfect tune, but they got a much bigger response than that delicate passage you worked hours on.

To be clear: I'm not chastising anyone, perhaps the Real Group, for their excellent tuning. It's a wonderful thing. But neither am I going to dock the Persuasions for having a wider bandwidth. There's not only room for both, we need both. And, in both cases, the groups have a lot of heart in their music. That's what connects with people, most of all.

Which all brings it back to you:

- Are you a studio editor, making a living "cleaning" tracks? First of all, don't tune everything. Some things sound better raw and untuned. Secondly, when you are tuning leads, back way off. Let the notes take a little time before they lock in, and leave some moments imperfect. Far more emotional impact in many cases.

- Are you a singer? Yes, work on your pitch, but don't go out on stage thinking about it. If you're thinking about tuning while performing then you're giving the audience a very cold, calculated performance. Channel the emotion and trust your training. When you're saying something, SAY something, and don't worry about your pronunciation.

- Are you a music director? Drill fundamentals in rehearsal, and make performing about the big picture. Get your singers into an emotive space instead of a perfectionistic one before they march on stage, and if you're conducting do everything in your power to keep their focus on the song's message and not worrying if you're going to chastise them on Monday at rehearsal.

The Leading Tones

- Are you a judge, perhaps of competitions, or recordings? Don't get caught up in the idea that the more precise group is the better group. It isn't. The better group is the one that makes you leap out of your seat. The audience favorite. They might be the most technically accomplished, but they might not. Please don't reinforce the notion that technical proficiency equals excellence, because groups will chase that trophy all the way down whichever path you open. Are you an arranger? I've said it once, I'll say it again: arrangements are roadmaps to help singers communicate with an audience. Every time you choose something that's technically difficult for a student group, it had better be in service of the singer's emotional delivery, because if you're just showing off, you're selfishly making the arrangement about yourself and are in effect forcing the group to focus on their technique rather than the mood, and it often backfires. Stretch them in a way that pushes them to higher emotional impact. Oh, and stack your chords ala the harmonic series (big gaps on the bottom, smaller ones on top) to make it easier for them to tune, so they can spend less time worrying about locking chords.

- Are you an a cappella insider? I'm guessing the answer is "yes" if you're reading this. OK, let me level with you, because I'm one of you. We like our 13th chords, and we love to hate the same ol' songs sung the same ol' way. And we should be pushing our own to pioneer, with original arrangements, original sounds, original songs. But we also need to lose any snobbery we have toward groups that are less than perfectly polished. There is only one Bobby McFerrin, and the rest of us are at least three solo albums and a minor 11th behind him. There is no perfect. Ever. And if that's what you're striving for, or what you look for in groups, you're missing the point. There are things a cappella does extremely well—like intimate, honest audience-performer connection. And there are ways in which a cappella has a harder time, and tuning is high on that list.

Recent articles have been written about individuals and success, trying to find the best way to maximize both happiness and productivity in the workplace. Our parents were taught to strive to be good at everything, and to spend their time working on the subjects in which they had the most difficulty. Modern studies have found exactly the opposite to be a far more effective path: focus your time and energy on your strengths, and let people who are good in other ways help you.

So, don't worry about being "pitch perfect." Instead, focus on being the best you can be!

*A note to my Barber-shoppin' friends—those that remain after the paragraphs above: I love barbershop music, and started my first quartet as a barber pole cat back in High School. I think the tradition is superlative, and there is much that all styles of a cappella can and should learn from you and yours. But maybe you should loosen some of the regulations and minutia, and instead create some different criteria: Who can create the most viral video? Who can get the biggest response from a theater full of non-barbershop insiders? Any art form that caters primarily to its own will find itself dying off. There's nothing whatsoever wrong with music from 100+ years ago. People listen to classical music every day. But remember that they listen to it because of how it makes them feel. That's all there is, in the end.

Vocalosity

The Current

CHAPTER 35
DON'T BE THAT GUY

By Deke Sharon

Centuries ago, most people never travelled or lived more than three miles from their birthplace. You'd grow up in town, have a crush on the farmer's daughter down the lane, get married, build a barn nearby, and the next generation was born.

Then people started to move to cities, came in contact with many more people, more potential spouses to choose from. People's perception of beauty changed, grew, expanded, perhaps grew more refined. Then came print, then photos, and now the Internet, skewing everyone's perception of beauty toward an impossible ideal.

Recently it appears Jennifer Lawrence is the standard, but that will change quickly enough. What doesn't change is that the vast majority of the world's males are being raised on and expecting a level of beauty that even the most beautiful people can't maintain. Photos are photo-shopped to perfection, videos edited with great care, images carefully managed. All eroding our ability to appreciate the beauty around us.

It's natural to want the best, but we have a problem when our image of beauty is effectively impossible to recreate in reality.

Crazy, right? You know people who are obsessed with celebrities, but you're not. You see lots of beautiful people every day and you appreciate more than a narrow band of socially accepted physical attributes. You have not been ruined. Good.

Except, if you're reading this, I'll bet you do have a strain of elitism that runs deep, and is difficult to shake: you think most a cappella groups suck.

That's right, dear reader. I'm calling you out.

Now, you wouldn't say that most women are ugly, because you don't think so, and you don't expect every woman to grace the cover of a magazine. But you think most a cappella groups are, well, ugly, and you're quick to point out the slightest deficiency, measuring them against an almost impossible ideal in your head that's a combination of the Real Group's effortless tuning,

Naturally 7's funkiness, Take 6's harmonic complexity and Pentatonix's effortless video image, and you're just getting started.

Fact is: your ideal group doesn't exist. You can't pick and choose the perfect quarterback based on elements of the greats from the past, so you shouldn't create an ideal standard that's not achievable in vocal music either. Plus considering the amount of careful editing and tuning that goes on behind the scenes, I'd venture to say your expectations have been distilled, via auto-tune, into the impossible.

This incredibly high standard can serve one purpose: to motivate you to achieve it with your own group . . . but even then I think we can both agree you aren't making music that lives up to your stratospheric expectations, and probably can't.

So all you're doing is making yourself miserable. It's as if you couldn't stand to eat a meal unless it was cooked by Thomas Keller or one of his kin. Otherwise, it's just not worth eating. But you have to eat. And you love a cappella, so you are going to continue to listen to it. And be frequently disappointed.

Truth be told, I'm not that worried about you alone. I'd like your standards to be more aligned with reality, but not specifically for you—for everyone else. For the community. To continue my analogy, you're that guy with impossible standards. Whatever. That's your problem, so long as it doesn't affect the women around you.

And I fear that it does.

Anytime you're picking apart group after group at a festival, you're only undermining other people's enjoyment of them. "Isn't she beautiful?" "Well, actually, her teeth are kinda crooked and she's a bit overweight. Plus I heard that last year . . ."

If you don't think this has an effect, you're wrong. Our community is small, tight knit, and ripples become waves. You can lift each other up, or bring each other down. Show by show, snarky comment by snarky comment.

Moreover, if you keep this up, you're less likely to continue singing long-term. If you can't meet your own standards, why date? Why sing? Because it's good. And I'll bet you're good, if you love a cappella enough to read this. Groups need you, and you need a group. And people need your music, because unlike you most a cappella makes them smile, even if it's not in perfect tune, even if it's a simple arrangement of an oft-sung song.

And there's little better you can do in this world than make other people smile.

Speaking of groups: remember that community group you turned your nose up at the last festival? They really needed your applause, your smile, your reassuring words. They respect you, and they worked hard for this performance. No, they're not the King's Singers, but I think we've established you're not either. There's plenty to enjoy about them, plenty to admire, if you can listen beyond your melodyne-addled standards. That farmer's daughter is just as cute as she ever was. Can you see past Jennifer Lawrence?

It used to be, long ago, that we all sang around the campfire with our village. We all sang around the spinet with our family. We all used to carol in the neighborhood. That's how music worked, how singing worked. Everyone.

What we do is very, very difficult. It requires far more precision, knowledge and nuance than most people have via today's standard music education. People join groups, learn a difficult skill and do their best. Very few of them are genius. The rest are, well, normal. And beautiful, in their own way.

We all want to spread harmony through harmony and the only way that's going to happen is face-to-face, one by one.

Find that beauty. See that beauty. Support that beauty.

Don't be that guy.

New World

Lost and Sound

CHAPTER 36

HOW TO BE AN A CAPPELLA GENIUS

By Deke Sharon

What would you say if I told you that genius is within your reach?

Seriously. The latest research shows that genius is not magic, and not primarily talent. It's primarily the result of carefully focused work.

People ask me all the time how to make a career in a cappella. Well, that now seems closer than ever, if you're willing to put in the time. I recall crossing paths with a young, eager kid a decade ago who wanted more than anything to be a professional a cappella singer, and just read yesterday, on RARB, that he's going to be performing with Bobby McFerrin across Europe next month. At the time, he had meager beatboxing skills and little knowledge, but a huge desire. He turned that desire into a decade of listening, learning, studying, practicing, and now he's an amazing professional beatboxer.

So, if you're serious, and really want to make a career of a cappella, here's what you do:

- Start singing as much as you can, wherever you can. If you're in elementary or high school right now, join every chorus and musical theater production you can. You need to train your muscles to sing on pitch on demand, learn repertoire, learn to blend. It might not be a cappella, but it's hugely helpful.

- If you're in college, in addition to singing in the university choir, join a contemporary a cappella group. There isn't one? Start one. And as soon as you can, audition to be the group's music director. President looks good on your resume and business manager will be helpful down the road in getting gigs, but music director is without a doubt the center of the action. You learn how to run rehearsals, deal with sensitive musical issues, choose repertoire, direct a group. What you don't know, you'll quickly learn (by fire!).

Motive

And if you've graduated already, you could always go back to school for a masters degree in music, at a school with a couple of great collegiate groups. Many groups admit grad students, who sometimes have a significant impact on the group (in some cases they get a PhD, allowing for a longer-than-undergrad-four-year tenure). Collegiate a cappella is serious business nowadays, with six-figure budgets, world famous albums, and rapidly increasing media exposure. Consider it the minor leagues.

- At the same time, learn music. Most of all, learn music theory. Your eyes might glaze over at the notion of diminished chords and plagal cadences, but believe me, you'll find it helpful down the road. Understanding chords, intervals, and form is integral to arranging and composing. You will use all of it. And if you have room in your schedule, take some music history classes as well.

- Listen, listen, listen. Get your hands on every award winning a cappella CD you can, and learn them all by heart to the point that you can sing along with any part. I hadn't heard "One Size Fits All" for at least a decade, but at a recent Nylons concert I stood in the back and quietly sang along with every song. Make this music your music, so that it's in your bones. And if there's a specific style that appeals to you more than others, great. Focus on it. Become an expert in that specific style: every group, every album, every arrangement of a specific song.

- Speaking of arrangements, crack open your laptop and arrange. Don't know notation? See step #3 and learn it quickly. Then start by transcribing existing arrangements and studying published arrangements. How can you tell bad from good? Simple: the ones you like are good. The ones that sound good to you are good. Learn to arrange a song just like them, and then arrange another. Ray Charles started his career by imitating Nat King Cole and Charles Brown, and he learned to play all their songs in every key, phrasing them just like the masters.

- Graduated and ready for the big world? Excellent. Find an existing group and join it, or start your own group. Or two groups. Or six. Tim Jones is one of the most successful a cappella businessmen in the Midwest, and he's not resting on his laurels.

The music industry is notoriously difficult, so you'll have to work harder, stay up later, underbid, sweat, toil. Remember, the current theory of genius is that it's hard, focused work, which means you can do it, but you have to do it. The harder you work, the luckier you are.

In the van this afternoon, I could hear Jake drumming away, coming up with cool new patterns grooves for his drum solo tonight, which will continue to be different from every other night. He saw a group back in 1994 (the House Jacks, ironically enough), and decided to start a vocal band (kickshaw), then joined M-Pact, toured the world, and now he's a Jack. He's one of the best vocal percussionists in the world, doing it professionally, and yet he's still honing his craft, learning from other drummers' YouTube videos, pushing himself to be better.

It doesn't end, for anyone. Tiger Woods can stop trying to improve on his historic career as the widely lauded greatest golfer ever, but the motivation that brought him this far continues unabated, and that is what keeps him great. A genius, if you will.

If this all sounds incredibly daunting, that's OK. Not everyone needs to devote their life to a cappella. I believe everyone should sing, and casual recreational singing is a wonderful thing.

But if that is not enough for you, it's empowering to know that genius is within your reach— if you start now.

"We didn't realize there were that many boy bands until we started touring in Europe. I don't think we were ever affected by it since a lot of the groups in Europe didn't really sing live, but we did and would perform a cappella as well."

—A.J. McLean

Delilah

CHAPTER 37

ON MYTHS AND LEGENDS

By Deke Sharon

In most fields, having a community that's relatively very educated and Western-minded leads to an increased level of productivity and success. However, the current contemporary a cappella movement, largely born out of East Coast elite collegiate a cappella circles, might also be hindered by the very same element and perspective. When it comes to science, math and medicine, an exacting precision is essential. In the fields of economics and law, great consideration, research and care are all needed before action is taken.

Not so in music.

You cannot get better at performing by thinking about it. You cannot become a better singer by studying vocal pedagogy texts. Cerebral pursuits are without a doubt valuable, but the average Ivy League grad is likely already as cerebral as she needs to be to embark on an a cappella career. There's a deep, strong current that runs beneath our best Universities, and after drinking four years from the aquifer, we graduate a class of young, eager minds who all share a common perception: the belief that they are excellent.

Personal mythologies are essential to us all, bolstering our resolve in difficult times, and allowing us to forge our own paths when prudence suggests the road more travelled. But the myths have changed over the generations, and there seems to be an increased belief in one's current self as the core mythology as opposed to the belief in one's self in the future.

And what's so important about this seemingly minor distinction? The fact that beginnings are ugly, and messy, and imperfect. When you start an a cappella group, you're likely rather lousy, and you need to crawl and scrape your way just to get up to mediocrity. This is a very difficult road for young a cappella singers, raised on a steady diet of Take 6 and Naturally 7.

I saw Naturally 7 when they first competed in the Harmony Sweepstakes. Guess what? I was not impressed. At all. Imagine a Take 6 knockoff with 7 guys: a little stiff on stage, muddy tuning, no clear emotional or musical focus, nothing new or particularly compelling.

Now they're one of the preeminent pop/R&B a cappella groups in the world.

Out of Range

The problem is not a lack of goal, vision, or desire for excellence. The problem is an understanding of and persistence trudging through the marshes and the weeds. It's a long, difficult march, and while you're on the path, you not only know you're not great, you can likely hear your peers' low voices as they analyze your imperfections, just as you analyze others. And yourself.

If your personal mythology is that you're somehow inherently great, the constant reminder of your own shortcomings and your group's distance from the upper tiers of a cappella's elite can be daunting, frustrating, and ultimately irreconcilable. I don't know how many groups and singers we lose, but a brief scan of the Harmony Sweepstakes website shows a road paved by many young groups with high hopes . . . that no longer exist.

Legends are made, not born. When you see Straight No Chaser or Pentatonix, you do not know the extreme effort behind their seemingly effortless rise into the public eye. Both have a work ethic that is second to none. They're proud of their success, but realize the elements of luck and timing, and do not take it for granted. You should not either.

There is no guarantee of excellent, but there is a guarantee of mediocrity. You must pass through the trials of self-doubt and question your own abilities. Perhaps for years. This might not be something that young, recently graduated collegiate a cappella singers are good at doing, but they will have to learn how. There is no other way.

We all need myths to create legend—they just need to be the right myths.

Miyake

Haley Klima, Touch of Class

CHAPTER 38
A CAPPELLA FOREVER

By Deke Sharon

I recently flew to Nashville to visit Barbershop Harmony Headquarters, where a few arrangers (including Kirby Shaw and David Wright) are meeting to consider the future of barbershop arrangement publication. The BHS (formerly SPEBSQSA) is in a difficult situation as a preservation society: they must constantly determine what elements of their style are intractable, to preserve their style and heritage, while allowing for some change and growth to appeal to new generations of singers.

This is not a problem for contemporary a cappella. If we stay the course.

How can I be so sure?

Style

From the beginning, CASA (Contemporary A Cappella Society of America) was formed to foster and promote all styles of a cappella music (yes, including barbershop), which it does in both formal ways (like the CARAs, with many different stylistic categories that change over time) and informal ones (inviting a variety of groups to participate in CASA events each year).

Infrastructure

The Barbershop Harmony Society (BHS)is closely tied to all "chapters," meaning there's great central control over the style, the organization, the direction of the form. CASA couldn't be less involved in group's artistic choices, doesn't publish sheet music, has no parameters for group size or configuration for membership.

Rules

BHS has very strict rules governing the chords, the progressions, the songs that can be sung at a competition. This all makes sense, given the need to preserve a style. Compare that with the Harmony Sweepstakes, which has two categories: Music and Performance, each worth up to 50 points.

SPARK

When you judge the Harmony Sweepstakes, you choose the group you thought was best, which is decidedly imprecise (different judges would give different results, as opposed to barbershop judges who all must attend a training program to ensure their scores are aligned with other judges), but also decidedly alive and easily able to change and grow as the style changes and grows.

Youth

Much of the sound and style of contemporary a cappella is driven and informed by scholastic groups. For the past couple of decades it has been collegiate groups, but increasingly high school groups are taking center stage. And unlike choral groups of the past, many of these ensembles don't rely on printed, published sheet music for their repertoire, instead choosing to write or commission their own custom tailored arrangements, the majority of which are current hit songs. If the above points don't convince you, this most certainly should, as every four years we have an entirely new batch of young singers who are looking to impress their peers by singing the biggest radio hits, and our style will continue to morph and grow alongside popular music as a result.

This is not to say that popular music will not also be influenced by a cappella, the way it has been by barbershop, and doo-wop, and mbube, and madrigals (long ago), and is once again now. This is just to reinforce the fact that we couldn't codify and calcify a specific style of contemporary a cappella even if we wanted to. The ever-growing legions of scholastic a cappella singers would immediately rebel and find a new sound.

History

When people think of contemporary a cappella now, they might have a specific sound in mind, but I posit that your average a cappella radio playlist already spans decades of change and variety. Not convinced? Compare:

- the proto-contemporary sound of the Nylons, who bridged the gap from doo-wop into the modern with pre-vocal percussion programmed drums

- the early '90s throwback close harmony R&B style that brought a cappella to the airwaves, by groups like Boyz II Men, Az Yet and Shai

- the complex yet still vocal mid-'90s collegiate a cappella sound that's been so successful for Straight No Chaser

- the now classic contemporary vocal band sound that remains popular in male quintets, from Rockapella to The Exchange

- the modern quintet sound with a more pop/electronica underpinning, ala Pentatonix

- the marriage of technology and voice, as demonstrated by Postyr and Sonos

. . . and the list goes on.

Compare this to the street corner/doo wop sound, which is a fairly narrow bandwidth: soaring lead vocal, bouncing bass line, and two to three part background harmonies trading between lyrics and open vowels. That's a snapshot in time, a lovely yet specific sound that did not move forward along with popular music.

If you think any of this is by happy accident, you should know it is not. The intention in choosing the word "Contemporary" to replace "Collegiate" as the "C" in the CAN ("Collegiate A Cappella News": the newsletter that spawned CASA) was specifically so that the wave of interest in a cappella in the early 90s ("Don't Worry, Be Happy") would not become tethered to a moment in history. And by helping to create several awards, contests, events and organizations not all under the same umbrella, my hope was that this decentralized community would always have to respond to the artistic choices made by groups, as opposed to dictate them.

Contemporary a cappella forever!

So far, so good.

Postlog: With 75 years of history, I'm not worried about the Barbershoppers one bit. I'm already shopping for a straw hat to wear to their 100-year celebration.

FUN FACTS ABOUT *PITCH PERFECT*

The Riff-Off

Ester Dean (Cynthia Dean) is an accomplished song writer in her first acting role. She has written or co-written songs for Rihanna, Britney Spears, Usher, Christina Aguilera, Ciara, Katy Perry, Selena Gomez, and Nicki Minaj. During the Riff-Off, she sings Rihanna's "S&M," which she actually co-wrote.

In the Riff-Off scene, one of the categories is "Songs Ruined By Glee (2009)." Anna Camp (Aubrey) guest starred in *Glee*: "Sectionals" (2009).

The riff-off scene originally had 17 songs instead of eight, but clearing that many songs would not fit in the movie's budget.

The riff-off scene was shot at 3 a.m. in an old, empty outdoor pool in early winter.

People

In the movie Anna Kendrick (Beca) and Skylar Astin (Jesse) are the romantic leads, but in real life, after *Pitch Perfect*, Skylar Astin and Anna Camp (Aubrey) started dating.

Adam DeVine's (Bumper) real-life girlfriend was Kelly Jakle (Jessica). She is an experienced a cappella singer and was a contestant on *The Sing-Off*. She also was an actual ICCA winner in 2008 and 2010 with the SoCal Vocals from the University of Southern California.

Ben Bram, who was part of the music team, was also a member of the SoCal Vocals when they won those titles in 2008 and 2010.

The Announcers

The role of Gail (one of the announcers) was originally written for Kristen Wiig, but she declined due to scheduling conflicts. Elizabeth Banks, one of the film's producers, eventually took the role. Amy Poehler was also considered for the role. "Fat Amy" is actually based off of a nickname Poehler called herself while pregnant.

Elizabeth Banks and John Michael Higgins, who played the announcers, filmed all of their scenes in one day. The duo based their performances off of John Michael Higgins' announcer character in *Best in Show* (2000). John Michael Higgins is an experienced vocal harmony singer and connoisseur, with a large collection of 20th century close harmony recordings.

Improvisation

Brittany Snow (Chloe) has said that Rebel Wilson (Fat Amy) improvised most of her lines. She would go off on long tangents that would have everyone cracking up in the cast and crew.

The story line between Bumper and Fat Amy was not in the original script. Adam DeVine (Bumper) and Rebel Wilson (Fat Amy) would improvise a lot during their scenes together and Devine would often try to kiss Wilson. They ended up making up a back-story for their two characters. The filmmakers thought the relationship between the two was funny and ended up keeping some of the scenes in the film—though according to the two actors, there was a lot that was cut out.

"Cups"

Anna Kendrick (Beca) learned her audition song from a viral video. "When I'm Gone," was written by A.P. Carter and first recorded The Carter Family. It was first combined with a children's rhythmic percussion game played with drinking cups by the British group Lulu and the Lampshades in 2009. Anna Kendrick learned about the song and decided to include it in her audition. She is quoted as saying "Originally that scene was going to be like 'I'm a Little Tea Cup' or something. It was supposed to be weird and funny and the second that they saw me do that, they were like, 'OK. That's your audition song.'"

In the United States, the version of the song from the movie debuted on the Billboard Hot 100 at number 93 for the week ending January 12, 2013. By its 32nd week on that chart, it had climbed to number 6 for the week ending August 17, 2013.

Oops!

Adam DeVine (Bumper) accidentally hit a cameraman with one of the burritos he had to throw out of the bus while shooting the gas station scene. Devine is quoted as saying "Yeah, it was when I was supposed to throw a burrito at Rebel, and he said to aim for him, thinking I wouldn't hit him, and I pegged him right in the face."

Lost in Translation?

Anna Kendrick (Beca) claims in the movie that Vader (as in Darth Vader) means "father" in German, but it does not. It does mean 'father' in Netherlands Dutch. In the German version of the film this was changed to say that Vader means 'father' in Netherlands Dutch.

Harry Potter

While Anna Kendrick (Beca) is attending the college activities fair and checking out the booth for the DJs (Deaf Jews), there are students playing a game of Quidditch (from the *Harry Potter* books and movies) in the background. Players are straddling broomsticks and you can even hear one player shouting "Pass the Quaffle! I'm open!"

The Campus Radio Station

When Anna Kendrick (Beca) enters the campus radio station for the first time, DJ Luke (Freddie Stroma) is heard saying the radio station is "95.7 WBUJ" along with the slogan "Music for the Independent Mind." But the station's frequency is written on the outside window as 85.7. "Music for the Independent Mind" is the slogan of the Emerson College radio station 88.9 WERS. The "All A Cappella" radio show airs on WERS every Sunday afternoon.

Cast Connections

Anna Kendrick (Beca) and Skylar Astin (Jesse) both have a connection to Stagedoor Manor, a prestigious performing arts camp in upstate New York. Skylar Astin attended the camp for multiple years and appeared in the documentary *Stagedoor* (2006). Anna Kendrick starred in *Camp* (2003) which was based on and filmed at Stagedoor Manor.

Auditions

Everyone in the cast had to successfully sing a song to audition for the movie. Rebel Wilson (Fat Amy) sang Lady Gaga's "Edge of Glory." The screenwriter actually asked Rebel to audition for the film through Facebook. Adam DeVine (Bumper) thought he was auditioning for a baseball movie and so on a whim he belted out the *Full House* theme song.

To prepare for the movie, the cast attended a month-long "A Cappella Bootcamp" in Baton Rouge prior to the start of filming. The Treblemakers, many of who were college a cappella singers, learned quickly and were better than the Bellas until the end of the month, causing much concern.

Pitch Perfect & *Pitch Perfect 2* are Box Office Hits!

Pitch Perfect debuted on just 335 screens and earned $5.1 million before slowly expanding into wide release. It expanded to 2,770 screens the next weekend and earned another $14 million. It ended up earning $65 million domestic and $115 million worldwide. In addition, it is the #3 grossing music comedy and the #11 grossing college comedy of all time.

Pitch Perfect 2 earned $27.8 million in its opening day (including $4.6 million in Thursday screenings) and ended its opening weekend with a gross of $69.2 million—the biggest opening weekend ever for a musical! For comparison, there are three musicals (*Les Miserables, Hairspray,* and *Mamma Mia!*) that opened with $27 million over their entire opening weekends. Other musicals faired better but did not come close to the success of *Pitch Perfect 2* including *The Muppets* ($29 million), *Into the Woods* ($31 million), *Enchanted* ($34 million) and *High School Musical 3* ($42 million) notching higher weekend debuts for a musical. More importantly, *Pitch Perfect 2* out-grossed the original film's entire domestic gross in just one weekend! To date it has earned earning $175 million domestic and $268 million worldwide. In addition, it is the #1 grossing music comedy and the #3 grossing college comedy of all time.

Anna Concepcion, VXN

CHAPTER 39

SO WHAT CAN I DO?

By Deke Sharon

Chapter 30, "Tough Love For a Tough Market, " was a little harsh. Intentionally so. Everyone in a cappella is nice, which is wonderful, but not always effective.

So, you want to be full-time, you want to do more. But what can you do?

1) Start A Group

I can think of exactly two people who have full time careers in a cappella who did not start out singing, and neither of them is exclusive to a cappella. Everyone else came up through the collegiate (or other) ranks, and is at heart a singer. And yet less than 1% of college grads keep singing a cappella. Why be one of them?

Moreover, a group is an income source, once you get it going. You'll meet people, show off your arranging skills, have someone to record, and so on. It all works together.

Yes, it's a lot of work to start a group. No, you won't start out great. Yes, you need to wallow in mediocrity for a while. Makes you a better coach, better arranger, better producer. Armchair quarterbacks are cheap. Show me, and everyone else, what you can do, blending passion and technique.

The good news is that the world, especially America, is in need of more great, young professional groups. Entire states have almost no a cappella representation, and few areas with groups have more than one or two. Plus, there are many great singers out there, bored and frustrated. They're never going to start a group on their own. They need a leader.

2) Schoolhouse: Rock!

Unless you're living in Boston or New York City, chances are there is a great need in your area for a cappella knowledge and opportunities. Local schools, especially high schools, are likely in desperate need of vocal opportunities for students. So, start an after school group, either at a single school, or at a central location that draws from many schools, ala Til Dawn.

You might not make any money at all at first, but eventually paid gigs will come, and parents will likely pay for an after school program once they see how great it can be. Moreover, you'll have just created another income source for yourself: one that will continue as long as you want it to.

The local college doesn't have an a cappella group? Help them get one started. The junior high wants to do a couple pop songs? Help them out for a day or two. Sometimes you'll get paid, sometimes you won't . . . but until you're working 50 hours a week on paid projects, pro bono is better than becoming a pro at Halo.

3) Build a Local Network

Maybe there is a private school with a proto-collegiate style group, and a barbershop chorus, and a classical ensemble that flirts with King's Singers pop charts, and so on. They all want gigs, they all want a community, but they're largely on their own. You can change that.

Be the nexus of all things a cappella in your area. Volunteer to be a CASA ambassador for your region, or if that's too much of a commitment right away, start by creating an informal Saturday or Sunday afternoon gathering where the groups meet and sing for each other. Maybe offer a free workshop, or free arrangement that you'll teach. Bring cookies. People like cookies. Be friendly, call groups, see what they need, find a way to get them together, and before you know it you'll find yourself working with one, promoting another, and the person that outsiders call when they want to know about a cappella in your area. You want to be that person.

4) Create Casual Singing Opportunities

Everyone wants to sing, or at least almost everyone, yet few people have an outlet.

Perhaps start a CAL group that meets regularly once a week. Kinda casual, kinda pro. Immediate circle of friends, some income from gigs, and a good time in general.

Perhaps start a casual singing opportunity on the weekends. "Sunday Sing" once a month. Two hours, provide sheet music, give people a chance to show up and sing some a cappella. Promote it in local community calendars (newspaper, web sites, radio, TV), and people will definitely come. Maybe after a time or two you can put out a hat for donations, and within a couple months there's a small fee to participate to cover costs and your time. If people will pay $12 to see a mediocre movie, they'll gladly pay $5 each to spend the afternoon singing.

5) Record Regional Groups

The business model for professional a cappella engineers has shifted over the years from "one stop shop" to more of a pyramid, where the top tier folks are spending most of their time mixing, and another group of young eager future producers spend most of their time editing (a polite way of saying "fixing the rhythm and tuning") in their own homes.

What is left is a need for tracking engineers: folks who know how to operate a pro-tools (or other) rig, and get great performances out of amateur singers. You can't just walk in the door and do this without experience, but learning how isn't too difficult and can be done in a week (Bill Hare and I teach "Soup to Nuts," Freddie Feldman and Dave Brown teach "A Cappella Boot Camp") and provide a source of income with minimal expense.

Upside: the more groups you have coached, networked with and founded, the more work you'll have. You're beginning to see a trend, right?

6) The More You Do, The More You'll Be Able To Do

When people ask me how I made a career of a cappella happen, especially in the early days, I came upon an analogy: the water skeeter. They can do the impossible: they somehow stand on water.

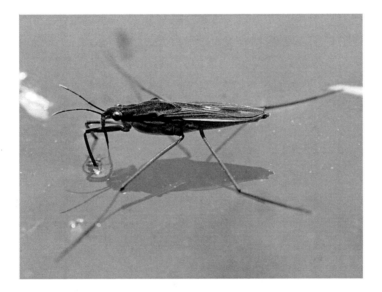

They're able to support themselves on water by never putting too much weight on any leg. Is this making sense? Do a little arranging, a little performing, a little production, a little recording, a little coaching. You get the idea. One month it'll be one thing, another month another. Do it for twenty years, and perhaps you'll find yourself making a television show one month, writing a book the next, making a movie the next, on an international concert tour the next. Stranger things have happened (but not much stranger). By the way, you might think I'm stupid for explaining all of this. Why would I want to motivate and train my competition?

Answer: You're absolutely right! What was I thinking?!? So stupid. Enough of the free advice. Go away, kids! Shoo! Get off my lawn! Grandpa's tired of your broken pitch pipes and discarded Chloroseptic bottles!

Real answer: we're all in this together, and there's plenty of room at the salad bar for everyone. Moreover, until we have too many amazing a cappella groups glutting the airwaves and media, our work is not done.

I still provide free advice, send arrangements for free from time to time (especially in "a cappella developing" areas, like South America and Africa), and generally spend time doing things that create community but have little or no direct benefit to my pocketbook: Writing a blog, making a podcast, recording videos, and so on. You get the idea. Do something, and then when you're tired or frustrated or unmotivated, do something else. Sometimes alone, sometimes with others.

You absolutely can make a full time career of a cappella, but it won't be traditional, and it won't be the same every month. Or day. Or hour. But it will be fun. Exhausting, and fulfilling, and frustrating—and fun.

Range

G-E-T VocalPoint

COMPETITIONS

Forte

CHAPTER 40

COMPETITIONS

Before we get started, we want to make one thing clear: we think that formal competitions within any art form are fundamentally silly. Why? Because you can measure science and math and you can have direct competition in a sporting event, but the arts are fundamentally subjective.

Do you think Beethoven's 9th Symphony is the greatest symphony ever written? Some critics do, and some casual listeners do . . . but others don't. Still others feel the addition of the chorus in the final movement was a gimmick that ultimately wasn't successful. Who is right and who is wrong? That is the wrong question, because there isn't a definitive answer.

Why do competitions seem to be such a significant part of the a cappella world (or show choir, marching band, etc.)? Because competitions get recognized. They draw attention in the form of viewers, listeners, fans and critics. Competitions draw a crowd, which is why they appear to be a central tenet of contemporary a cappella. The fact is that fewer than 10% of collegiate groups compete annually. The number is far lower for high school groups (less than 1%) and professional or recreational post-collegiate groups (similarly insignificant). Whether or not a group competes, it's impossible to deny the fact that competitions, both live and televised, have had a serious impact on the contemporary a cappella community.

This chapter describes some of the bigger, better-known competitions for a cappella groups, including the ICCA and ICHSA, The Harmony Sweepstakes A Cappella Festival, and *The Sing-Off*. We'll give you our top tips for competing successfully. We'll also give additional advice specific to certain competitions and hear from experts like Andrea Newman and Dave Brown.

ICCA – The "Pitch Perfect" Competition & ICHSA

For the past 20 years, the International Championships of Collegiate A Cappella has helped to define a cappella groups across the country. That's right, let's face it, most of you non-aca people just heard about this competition in the movie *Pitch Perfect*. So yeah, it's a real competition, and the movie was based off of this real competition that has been taking place for two decades.

The International Championships of Collegiate A Cappella is commonly referred to as the ICCA. Since it began, the ICCA has been a major element in the collegiate a cappella community, drawing both new and established groups into a quest to achieve a cappella glory. Similar to the ICCA, the International Competition of High School A Cappella (ICHSA) is the high school version of the competition. The ICCA and the ICHSA are produced by an organization called Varsity Vocals and they are the only tournaments that showcase the art of student a cappella singing. They are dedicated to providing top-notch a cappella groups with valuable feedback from highly qualified judges. Participants have the opportunity to showcase their talent to an international audience and develop relationships with each other, cultivating the art of a cappella singing and a lifelong love of music.

The ICCA was developed by Deke Sharon and Adam Farb, who was a member of the Brown Derbies, the a cappella group at Brown University. Adam absolutely loved being a member of that group. He loved it so much that, after graduating, he moved to the San Francisco Bay area to make a career in a cappella music. Once there, he contacted Deke to brainstorm ideas on how to make that happen. He and Deke put their heads together and created a national tournament-style competition of collegiate a cappella based on basketball's March Madness called the National Championship of Collegiate A Cappella, or "N-double-C-A" which was a tongue in cheek reference to the "N-C-double-A".

The very first competition was held in 1996. There were five regional competitions and a final competition held at Carnegie Hall, which was the venue for the finals for most of the 1990's.

In the early years, Adam pretty much did it all. He drove or flew to each event and personally handled or oversaw all of the organizing, managing, and hosting. It was a huge commitment and after a few exhausting years, he made the decision to sell the rights to the event to Don Gooding in 1999.

To give you a little background about Don . . . he sang in the Yale Society of Orpheus and Bacchus (he directed them his junior year) and sang in the Yale Whiffenpoofs of 1980. He founded Primarily A Cappella in January 1992 and then he bought out the "money" partner in Contemporary A Cappella Publishing in 1997. In 1998, he founded A-Cappella.com and then he bought what became Varsity Vocals from Adam Farb the following year.

Don describes his role in Varsity Vocals as the "patient money"—seeing that there was long-term potential and working to help realize that potential. He hired Jessika Diamond and then Amanda (then Grish) Newman to manage the ICCA. The ICCA had been losing money and Don needed to fix that.

An important turning point for the ICCA occurred when Amanda Newman took over. Amanda was the business manager and choreographer for the University of Illinois a cappella group No Strings Attached. She joined the Varsity Vocals team in 2002 and spent a year working for Jessika Diamond as the ICCA Midwest Producer before becoming Executive Director of the company.

Having a singer's background, Amanda quickly realized that groups were more than willing to pay a lot more to participate in a competition of this caliber. She raised fees and immediately brought financial stability to the ICCA.

Don's wife, Kate, loved the college a cappella scene and thought there ought to be something for high school students so she got the International Championship of High School A Cappella (ICHSA) off the ground. The high school competition occurred for the first time in 2006 with five regions and a small following and has grown exponentially since that time.

Each year, the competition takes place from January through April. Groups submit videos to audition and then they are selected to participate in regionals. Over the years, the regions have changed. Currently for the ICCA there are in seven regions: Great Lakes, West, Midwest, South, Mid-Atlantic, Northeast, and International. Each region holds several quarterfinal events. The top two college groups at each quarterfinal advance to college semifinals. The winner of each semifinal then advances to the final round. As for the ICHSA there are in eleven regions: East Coast, Great Lakes, New England, Midwest, South, Southwest, Mid-Atlantic, Northeast, Northwest, Ohio Valley, and Wisconsin. For this competition, only the top high school group advances to the semifinals and then the winner of each semifinal is then invited to participate in the finals. The final round for both competitions is held in New York City, where the groups compete for the coveted title of Grand Champion.

The current ICCA and ICHSA competitions are the result of a collaborative effort. Many people made contributions over the years and a fair amount of experimentation took place to get all of the pieces to work. Like several other a cappella phenomena, ICCA and ICHSA have created an exciting cycle: the competitions stimulate improvements in groups and encourage new groups to form, which make the event better and stimulate even more improvement and growth. And, of course, the excellence encouraged by Varsity Vocals has led to a huge increase in fans of contemporary a cappella as a whole.

The Harmony Sweepstakes A Cappella Festival

The Harmony Sweepstakes A Cappella Festival is the premier American showcase for vocal harmony music. It started back in 1984 and showcases vocal groups from around the country and overseas performing all styles of a cappella music including doo-wop, barbershop, gospel, jazz, and contemporary. It is a celebration of the human voice and was the inspiration for *The Sing-Off*.

The event started out as a weekly sing-a-long at the British Mayflower Pub in San Rafael, California. The participants formed the Mayflower Community Chorus because they enjoyed singing together and they held regular concerts/performances (that chorus still exists today). Several members ended up forming smaller a cappella ensembles and that is when one of the members, Lisa Collins, came up with the idea to start a competition for the a cappella groups. For the first few years the competition was part of the annual In Performance at Forrest Meadows performing arts series at Dominican University.

After a few years of attending the event, the English-born theatrical producer John Neal approached Lisa with that idea that they use his expertise as a producer and further develop the competition by expanding it to other cities and making it a national event. They immediately became partners and other cites were added and the venue for the National Finals was moved to the larger Marin Veteran's Auditorium.

Over the next few years the showcase grew in popularity and groups from overseas also started participating. Today the annual national competition draws from hundreds of vocal groups from around the country that compete in regional competitions in seven cities: New York, Boston, Los Angeles, Washington DC, Portland/Seattle, San Francisco, and Chicago. The winner of each regional is flown to San Rafael, California to compete in the National Finals in early May in front of a sold-out house and celebrity judges. The winner is crowned the Grand National Champion.

Many of the groups featured in the showcase have gone on and had successful careers and some have even landed recording contracts. After 30 plus years of competition the majority of national champions still continue to perform in some form or other.

The Sing-Off – The Televised Competition

The Sing-Off is a reality television show that first aired on NBC on December 14, 2009. The premise of *The Sing-Off* is to pit a cappella groups against each other in competition, eliminating groups each episode until a winner is crowned. The winner receives a cash prize as well as a recording contract.

The Sing-Off has had five seasons, each with a different amount of episodes and groups. The first two seasons were short, holiday replacement seasons containing eight and then ten groups. By the third season, the show had grown in popularity and NBC took a chance on a full third season with sixteen groups. Unfortunately, the ratings were not as high in this format, which lead to a yearlong hiatus and as a result, most people assumed the show had been cancelled for good. In a surprise move, *The Sing-Off* returned later for a fourth season, albeit back to a shorter holiday schedule. The fifth season was actually only a single episode—a holiday special.

The Sing-Off has also had international success with other versions around the world including *The Sing-Off Netherlands* and *The Sing-Off China*. The table below summarizes the American seasons, their winners, and other notable groups that were featured on the show.

Season	# of episodes	# of groups	Winner	Second	Third
1	4	8	Nota	Tufts Beelzebubs	Voices of Lee
2	5	10	Committed	Street Corner Symphony	The Backbeats
3	11	16	Pentatonix	Dartmouth Aires	Urban Method
4	7	10	Home Free	Ten	Vocal Rush
5	1	6	Vanderbilt Melodores	The Exchange	Traces

Of particular note is the success of the Season Three winner, Pentatonix. This group, more than any other group in recent history, has brought a cappella into the mainstream. They built an enormous following using viral videos, then parlayed that success into an RCA record contract. Their Christmas album, "That's Christmas to Me," was the highest-charting Christmas album for a group since 1962. Their success continues to climb, so we can only speculate as to what heights they have reached as you read this book.

Additional Competitions

In addition to what has already been mentioned, there are many single event competitions that have a long tradition and following. The Silver Chord Bowl has been held for decades in New England, bringing together six different collegiate groups for a single night. The Contemporary A Cappella Society (CASA) hosts SoJam, which is a weekend-long a cappella festival in North Carolina that is jam-packed with concerts, competitions, master classes and hands-on workshops led by some of the biggest names in vocal music. VoiceJam is a contemporary voacl harmony showcase in Arkansas that features regional, national, and international a cappella ensembles. The Los Angeles A Cappella Festival is a competition that pits high school and collegiate groups against each other (don't be worried about an unfair fight: in 2013, high school groups took first and second place!). The University of San Francisco ASUSF Voices hosts Aca-West, an a cappella festival, which consists of workshops and a concert featuring multiple a cappella groups. None of these competitions have much of a prize beyond bragging rights, but that is prize enough! The contestants and audience all embrace the events as an opportunity to draw a large crowd, have fun, and share the love and enthusiasm for a cappella music.

Beyond the contemporary a cappella community, you will find many vocal music competitions, especially in barbershop circles. The Barbershop Harmony Society, Sweet Adelines International, and Harmony Incorporated all have annual conferences centered around their international competitions. These draw thousands of attendees, with choruses and quartets who have met a series of challenges at the local, stage and regional level to make it to the top competition.

Competition Tips

So now that you have read about all the amazing competitions/showcases there are out there for a cappella enthusiasts you obviously want to get in on the action . . . so here are some tips for competing.

Have Fun

This is first on the list because it's the single most important thing a group can do on stage. All of the a cappella competitions are for amateur groups, and, at its root, the word "amateur" means "for the love of." Let your love of singing shine while you're on stage. If you smile, genuinely smile; you'll have the audience with you.

Judges have seen many performers in many situations and they can tell if you're pretending. Don't pretend to have fun; genuinely enjoy yourself, live in the moment, and have fun! Smile, relax, let loose, and "ride the wave" of the experience. Whatever happens will happen, and it would be a shame if you left the show having lost AND having had a bad time. Have a good time and you will be a winner even if you don't get a prize.

There are many reasons to enter a competition that don't involve winning including getting exposure, meeting and seeing other groups, and setting a performance goal. You should sing because you love to sing and share music with other people. If you are on stage primarily to win, it will quite possibly show through in your performance.

Be Prepared

Having fun on stage doesn't mean "winging it." If you're prepared, that means that you already did the hard work and now you can relax. There are too many people who wait until the last moment to perfect everything. This is not smart. Before the show you want to be relaxed with your mind clear—not worrying about lyrics, notes, cut-offs. Have your music be "second nature;" not something you have to concentrate on and worry about.

Do your homework and know what is being asked of you during the competition: how long you should sing, what kind of music you should present, and who else will be there. Learn all you can about the event and then plan your performance accordingly. If all else is equal, it's often the group that is more knowledgeable and made their performance decisions based on better information that will win.

Do Not Play to the Judges

They don't matter. They're not going to even smile—they're working, focusing on every detail, taking notes, trying to remember it all, and comparing it to everything else that happened. Forget them completely.

Play to the general audience. Make them smile, laugh, cry, gasp, and applaud wildly. If you win over the audience, you usually win over the judges as well, as the audience will sweep them up in a tide of clapping, laughter, and singing along. It's impossible to deny the force of a mob and, moreover, judges realize the supreme importance of connecting with the crowd.

Plus, in the end, it doesn't matter what the judges think, but it does matter what the audience thinks—they're the ones who will buy tickets and albums in the future.

Emotions

Consider the emotional focus of each song and make your musical decisions based on it. Too often groups spend most of their rehearsal time on details without having a reason for those details, other than the laws of music theory and the principles they were taught in chorus. Tuning is nice, but making an audience feel something is much more important. Dynamics, tempo, pacing . . . all roads should lead to the same emotional place and your decisions about what to do in measure 23 should have the same overriding priority.

Generate emotional energy within yourselves and then share it with the audience. Sometimes the audience is polite and quiet. You have to generate the energy because they will not give you more than you initially give them. Look at the other members of your group and your director (if you have one) to generate smiles and excitement and then look out into the audience and share it with them. If your energy drops, look back at your other group members.

Avoid "auto-pilot." All of us as performers know what it is like to perform and be engaged and what it is like to be thinking about something else. When you're on "auto-pilot," your face loses expression and your eyes glaze over. Competitions are short and intense—remain in the moment and focused throughout.

Solo, Solo, Solo

Never underestimate the importance of a powerful soloist that can wow the audience and really draw them in. A captivating soloist can draw attention away from the small imperfections and can really empower the rest of the group. Enough said.

Forgive and Forget

Yes, your alto sings the bridge out of tune sometimes, maybe even all the time. Fine. But don't shoot her that glance or bristle when she does. Accept that we're all imperfect and the nature of a live performance is rife with imperfection. Everyone expects this, including the audience and the judges. However, when you let the imperfections affect your performance and/or make them apparent, you're pulling the audience out of the emotional journey they're on and pointing an enormous arrow at a flaw. It's as if, when watching a movie, you hear a voiceover from the director stating "So sorry! I know this scene is a bit dimly lit! I did the best I could." All of a sudden the moment is broken. This includes apologizing in any way for a solo, be it coughing, rubbing your chest, straining your neck, or any of the other insecurities that overtake singers. Just do it and stand by it.

Segues

It might seem like a little thing, but the space between songs matters and very few groups pay attention to it. From the way you move onto the stage and get your pitch until the first note of the song, that time matters. In the same way, the space between songs matters.

If you're not sure what to do, here are some suggestions:

- When the last note has been cut off, hold the moment! Do not turn away. Let the chord ring in the hall and savor the mood for a second . . . or even a couple of seconds, if it's a heartfelt ballad.

- Next, when you relax your muscles at the end of a song, acknowledge the audience response. Smile, nod, whatever—especially the soloist. It's rude for a soloist to turn and disappear as soon as a song is done.

- While the soloist acknowledges the audience the background singers should all be moving into their next positions. Also the person who will deliver the next spoken introduction should be moving to the front of the stage to speak as the applause dies down. No dead space! No silence!

- If you're not planning to have anyone speak, give the pitch during the applause and try to get the music happening before it ends so there's a seamless flow. If someone is speaking, then practice having him or her do this while the music comes up under him or her. This can make a big difference.

- As soon as the music starts, have the speaker finish up and move back into the group. As focus on the speaker dissolves, the audience should see the rest of the group completely focused on the mood of the next song, whatever it is. Then the soloist can step forward already riding an emotional wave.

- It's not hard to make this happen between songs, but it does take a little focus, coordination, and rehearsal. You'll be glad you did and it will send a very strong message to the audience and judges: you're focused on taking them on a journey and they're in good hands.

Blocking and Stage Placement

Your group doesn't need to be the Temptations, but it does help if you've given some thought to how you place yourselves on the stage. We don't mean choreography (at all), but rather the stage picture you're creating and making sure your singers are near the people they need to be able to hear in the group. The stage will likely be larger than your rehearsal space and you'll likely be dealing with some mic issues. All of this needs to be considered.

Choreography is not necessary, but that doesn't mean that you don't need movement on stage. Use movement to your advantage. Even the smallest movements can help you relax and get in rhythm with the other singers. A simple step-touch or sway is preferable to standing perfectly still, unless the music calls for it. If you're the soloist, allow your face and body to flow with the music. Don't stand perfectly still unless you have a very good, very intended reason to do so. Otherwise, it will look like you're scared or bored.

Variety

If you haven't yet decided what to sing, choose your strongest songs. If they're all strong, then go for variety. Different soloists, different tempos, different styles. If you have a great arranger, sing his or her arrangements. Wonderful vocal percussion? Use it. Your group is funny? Has perfect tuning? Moves very well? Make sure that the audience and judges see the very best of what you can do.

Audiences and judges (especially judges) like to see a range of talent and technique from a group. Play to your strengths, no doubt, but show off as many different strengths as you can.

Breathe

It may sound stupid, but this is the single most important thing you can do before you get on stage and while you're on stage. Your nerves will be up, which will cause your muscles to tense, and you'll likely be only getting a fraction of the air you've been used to getting during rehearsal.

To counter this, take a few long, slow breaths. Breathe in deeply and exhale fully. The effect of this is significant, as you'll slow your heart rate, relax your muscles (especially your diaphragm), and literally reset your overall system, reducing stress.

Have Fun

Wasn't that first on the list? Yes, but it is so important that it bears repeating. People forget the importance of this and tend to focus their rehearsals on things they can fix. Then, on stage, they get carried away with their technical duties. Once you hit the spotlight, it's time to let go, relax, and trust your director, your experience, your rehearsals, your memory. You might want to use a couple of words at the beginning of each song to trigger the mood, but that's it. Let go, ride the wave, and focus on performing.

Don't sweat the details, don't get caught up in technique, and don't drift into autopilot—all of those things take you away from the crowd. Look at your fellow singers, smile, connect, then turn and share that energy with the audience. And that's it. That's the whole thing. That's performing.

There's an added bonus for your group if you're in the mindset of having fun: once you walk off the stage, you're not done! The best part of the night is still ahead of you: Who wins? Who cares! Let the judges do what they will. Focus on the experience: a great performance on stage, a great time meeting the other singers, listening to and learning from other groups, greeting the audience, making new fans, and enjoying the afterglow.

Advice for ICCA

Given all that we have said to this point, we know that groups want to do well when they compete. Amanda Newman, Executive Director of Varsity Vocals, offers this additional advice when competing in the ICCA: "Number one point: it's a game, so play the game! The best groups look up the judging criteria and then rehearse to those criteria. The "best" group is subjective based on our system, but if you're in the ICCA seeking to be named the best group in the ICCA, then follow the criteria!"

In other words, the ICCAs fully admit and embrace the fact that there are categories and know that each year's winners are actively looking to successfully tick each box. Go to their website to ensure you have the most up-to-date information.

Amanda Newman also offers some very specific advice about using professionals to assist your group. "Don't arrange your own music unless you are very, very good at it. Don't choreograph your set unless you are very, very good at it. The best directors know their limits and know when to seek outside help. It's amazing to me that groups come to the ICCA with no one having seen their performance but their own friends. Get real feedback. There's a huge community of real professionals out there. Hire them to help you!"

Collegiate a cappella is, in most cases, a student organized and student directed endeavor. Amanda's suggestion is clear: the best groups will look beyond their own abilities to find outside help and guidance so that every aspect of their performance is excellent. Lest this sound like cheating, remember that every single sound, movement and emotion on stage comes entirely from amateur collegiate singers. There is no shame in contacting experts to make sure that you're maximizing your potential and learning from the best. This pays dividends down the road as every future arrangement, rehearsal and performance benefits from what you've learned.

Advice for ICHSA

Andrea Poole is the Director of ICHSA. Andrea started working for Varsity Vocals in 2007 as the ICHSA Midwest Producer. At the time, she was a senior at Michigan State University and still singing in Capital Green.

For those who are considering participating in ICHSA, Andrea's advice is to take the leap and apply. Don't worry about the competition aspect, but focus on the opportunity to learn from other groups and meet other singers who love a cappella. At a typical ICHSA event, students from multiple groups mingle before and after the show, sing together backstage, and even teach each other vocal percussion. Groups are encouraged to sit in the audience when they're not on stage to get a chance to see the other competing groups. The high school a cappella community is encouraging and supportive and they are often the biggest cheerleaders for each other.

Andrea's tips:

> "Directors, approach the competition as an opportunity for your students to learn something new, and challenge them to be at their personal best. Network with the other directors. Encourage your students to support each other and the other competing groups."

> "Students, have fun. Work hard to prepare a set that you're really proud of. Watch the other groups and take mental notes (or actual notes) of awesome things that they're doing on stage. Cheer loudly for everyone—you know how it feels to be up there, too! Introduce yourself to students in the other groups. Sing with them. Teach them something new. Last, but definitely not least, thank your director for their support that allows you to have an a cappella group at your school. It's not the norm, and it's an experience you'll remember forever."

One additional note from Amanda Newman: "Emphasize quality over quantity. Groups are getting bigger and bigger. Ten years ago groups were 8-12 members. Fifteen was a huge group. Now our smallest groups have fifteen singers, and some groups have 24 or more members, and it's never a good thing."

It is important for high school directors to motivate as many singers as possible to sing, but when it comes to a national competition, more is rarely better.

Advice for The Harmony Sweepstakes

Perhaps the single best thing about The Harmony Sweepstakes is its judging metric, which has remained the same since day one:

50% musicality

50% performance

What does that mean? It is left up to the judges to decide and there is no training or orientation for the judges whatsoever. Judges are respected professionals chosen from the fields of music, performing, and the media. They decide who wins based on what they prefer.

This is perhaps maddening to an educator or barbershopper who is used to very specific targets (5% vowel matching, 10% diction, etc.), but the upside is that this competition does not influence creative decisions. Groups competing at the ICCA, for example, often feel a need to create elaborate choreography because they want a high score in the movement category. Without a movement category, an a cappella group will not add choreography unless they're already so inclined.

So, what should your strategy be? There is none. That's the beauty of these criteria. There is no way to game the system, no way to overthink what the judges will expect, which means that the Harmony Sweepstakes has effectively no impact on the contemporary a cappella style. No specific emphasis on tuning, or soloists, or choreography. Do what you think works, and then the judges will decide if they liked it.

Refreshingly simple, powerfully effective.

Advice for *The Sing-Off* (or any reality show)

The Sing-Off is not a competition in which most groups will have an opportunity to participate, but there are still lessons to be learned. Perhaps greater than actual winning *The Sing-Off* is "winning" an invitation to be a part of the show.

Although the advice given here is specific to this televised competition, there are great general pointers included.

Be Yourselves

This is first because it's central to your success. Unless you're all brilliant actors, it's not going to work for you to re-imagine your group and your personalities based on some assumption of what the judges want. They want talent and they want variety. It's that simple. If you're young, be young. If you're old, be old. If you're overweight and one of your members is 7 feet tall and you usually yodel, then embrace being the big & tall men's yodelers. You have to be comfortable in your skin or else you'll never translate well on camera.

Know and Show Your Style

The show is a popular music show and every group will be singing popular music from the past 40 years, but they'll be singing it from their own stylistic perspective. Maxx Factor sang with a Sweet Adelines-sensibility and Voices of Lee kept their choral jazz sound. Make sure one of your songs is your very best song and it shows off the core of your style.

Choose Your Set Wisely

You will be asked to bring three songs and two of them need to be well known pop/rock covers. One of the most important things you can do to prepare is pick the right songs. Think carefully and choose songs that show off your group's strengths and style. Got a killer rock tenor? Pick a rock song. Don't have a single fantastic soloist? Choose group anthem pieces. Terrible at dancing? Pick simple, effective motions to keep your set visually interesting. Got zany personalities? Choose at least one song that shows off your hilarity. If you ring a lot of chords, pick a song that will allow you to do that: perhaps a ballad instead of a fast rock tune. The show will be presenting all of the groups with various challenges and the judges and producers need to know that you understand your sound and can make it work with current repertoire.

Feature Your Absolute Best Soloist(s)

There are very few absolutes when it comes to competition advice, or musical advice in general, but this one is pretty universal. Assuming you want to win the competition (which should only be one goal among many), your soloist HAS. TO. BE. GOOD. Or maybe more accurately, your soloist's abilities have to fit the needs of the song. A cappella is often about equality and equanimity, but television is about ratings and stars. Do not be shy about picking your very best soloist to sing your audition songs, as a soloist is the focal point of your group. There's no way you'll be chosen for the show without at least one stellar lead singer. We are firm believers that groups should spread the love and the solos during their shows . . . but when you have 90 seconds in front of 7 million people; you absolutely have to put your best foot forward.

Why? Because the audience (and therefore the judges since they are part of the audience) will derive most of the song's energy, message, and emotional content from the soloist. Most of the time, we're looking at the soloist, the soloist's microphone will be the loudest, and the soloist has the lyrics. So don't pick a song just because you like it. Make sure it's one you—and especially your soloist—can sell very well, every time. The groups on *The Sing-Off* rarely used more than one or two soloists. Nothing wrong with that!

Voices of Lee is a great example of this. During The Sing-Off, they focused on one or two strong soloists and their great bass. Their arrangements played to their strengths: they showcased their best people and let the group sing a powerful backup, which is what they do well. It landed them in the final three. Follow that example.

Don't Underestimate the Importance of the Entire Group

Although your soloist can make or break you, don't think it's all about the soloist because the group is important too. Although you need great soloists to win the competition, if your group slacks in the background, you won't stand a chance. Why? Because it's a competition for your whole group and you're all up there. WE SEE YOU up there. There's no "back row" in a small a cappella group. There are no risers here. We're watching and hearing the whole lot of you and if the judges perceive any inconsistency in energy across the group, not only will it deflate the song, but you'll also lose your visual cohesiveness.

Have you ever seen a killer musical on Broadway or on another big stage? Of course, the leads were great, but it was probably the ensemble that really sold it. When a minor character at the back of the stage really gets into it, it shows the audience that there's no weak spot. It gives the audience license to relax and enjoy the show.

Pull Out All the Stops and Make a Lasting Impression

Be memorable. Assuming your pitch, rhythm, transitions, and dynamics are all there; you're going to make a lasting impression on the judges if your performance is memorable. Do you have flashy outfits? Wear them. Do you have great choreography? Bring da funk along with da noise. If you don't do choreography and wear street clothes, that's OK, too. Above all, be yourselves. But if you do have a song with some flashy moves, get it ready, as the visual aspect of performance on television is important. If you want to win, your job is to make your set so full of memorable moments that when the judges are deliberating, they'll see your group's name and have no doubt they should be their choice. What you don't want is: "Which group is that again?" "I think they had suspenders." "No wait, that was the other group." Instead, you want: "Oh my gosh! The group that did the classic rock medley!"

Weave in Your Specialties

Use your twelve minutes to your advantage. It's true that you can get up and sing three songs beginning to end and sit down and do well in the competition. But the groups that win tend to switch things up. Throw in a short, dazzling opener. Or put in a longer, highly creative medley. Or do something that's unusual. If you've got a great vocal harmonica sound or one of your members can do a standing backflip, by all means toss it in, provided it's not out of place. Fill in the time with greatness, from beginning to end and give it all you've got.

Arrangements

Tweak your arrangements. Once you've racked your brain devising the perfect set list, play with your songs a bit. Sure, you can just get up and perform Jay Sean's "Down" or Jason Mraz's "I'm Yours." But, if you add your group's personal flair, a la Nota, it will really shine.

Did you notice that every group on *The Sing-Off* had only about 90 seconds to sing their "song"? True, in some cases, it felt a little short. But not that much! As a general rule, a cappella songs, especially live, don't need to be as long as your favorite version on the radio. Cut out a verse; forget the third repeat of the chorus at the end. We get it.

Don't be too subtle. When it comes to arrangement tweaks and song choices and set programming, remember that your audience is kind of stupid. Quickly interpolating one short line from another song does not a fancy arrangement make. Stringing together four songs loosely based around one general theme is only half noticeable to many in the audience. If there's something you really want us to know about your group or your abilities or your set, make it clear. With that being said you want your arrangements to be clever, but no too clever. People like a good melody, they like harmony, and they like a clever quote or countermelody woven in. But they don't care about the carefully interwoven ♭9s and tritone substitutions as much as they care about a great performance and a great sound. Don't make things so technically challenging that you can't move and you can't smile and you can't emote. Not worth it.

But with that being said, arrangements are only kind of important. Don't think that your genius, fancy layering and totally original syllables are going to really impress every judge. Whether you sing jen or jin is really of little consequence. Nor do judges really know if your arrangement was hard to learn or if it looks amazing on the page. If you have to show the sheet music to someone to understand what you did, it's not effective. Nobody on *The Sing-Off* won with amazing arrangements. Difficulty is important, but it's not nearly as important as execution.

Have an Identity

Most performing artists today are carefully dressed, marketed, positioned and packaged. From Lady Gaga to Jack Johnson, audiences clearly understand who an artist is from a glance or cursory listen. This is important in today's media saturated world, as viewers quickly changing channels want to understand something quickly or they'll likely move on.

To this end, producers of the show are not only looking for talent (essential!) and presence (essential!), but also some kind of identity. Who are you? Southern boys who met at a church function? Music educators who didn't want to let their students have all the fun? It's not enough for you to just be a random assortment of people who happen to get together and sing because it makes the background story, wardrobe, repertoire selection difficult and confusing.

Know your story. Story? Well, yes, you have a story, or at least you will if you make it on the show. What makes you different, unique, interesting? What would people want to know about your group, your journey, your backgrounds? Reality television is about drama and there's very little time to give the audience a chance to get to know you so the "packages" for each group cut to the chase. Why should people root for your group? Think about it.

> Mind you, it's absolutely fine to have no identity as an a cappella group of people who like to sing together. I'm not suggesting that the a cappella community all immediately define themselves and one another within terms that the popular media can understand. I'm simply suggesting that you must do so if you're going to be on a network reality show.

Your identity could be formed by age, race, location, background or culture, but it also can be driven by focus, repertoire, common experiences, and so on. Give the producers something to hang their hat on, some simple way to describe you.

> *What you never want said about you: "It looks like someone just picked up a bunch of people at a bus stop. I don't know what we'd do with them."*

Say Something

Know the message of your songs and reflect that. If it's a happy, upbeat song, spread joy. If it's a heartfelt ballad, move us to tears. It's better to have an emotionally powerful yet imperfect group on the air than a group that's technically perfect but dull. The producers can work on tuning, but they can't manufacture sincerity and a powerful emotional delivery. Don't lose the heart in a quest for precision.

Cut from the Running? Here Is More Help

Why can't you "make it" onto insert-name-of show? The answer might just be that you're doing everything well and you're still not quite right. That's not very helpful so here are some key pointers that will increase your group's chances of making it onto shows like *The Sing-Off*.

Ask the Hard Questions

The fact is few people are going to go out of their way to tell you about your weaknesses and shortcomings. No one wants to and unless you're wildly popular, no one is either being paid to tell you or has a financial interest in telling you. Fans will either buy your album or not, stay to hear your set or walk away at intermission. However, if you're going to get better, you need to know.

> *What you never want said about you: "It's clear they have absolutely no clue that . . ."*

Start by videotaping yourselves and analyzing what you see. Don't critique the small picture—little hand gestures rarely matter—but think big: How do we look? How do we sound? What would someone who had never seen or heard a cappella think? And if you aren't getting very far, ask a good friend or two to be brutally honest.

You need to know if someone closes their eyes too often, looks bored, doesn't engage the audience, or dresses unflatteringly so that you can address all of these issues before you get in front of television producers, producers who see all and are paid to be extremely blunt because millions of dollars ride on every hour of television time. You know you sometimes get catty when flipping channels? . . . well, if the tables are going to be turned, you need to step up your game.

Engage with the Song and with the Audience

We have been beating the "presence" drum throughout this book and with good reason: the a cappella community appears to spend far more time focusing on tuning than they do on performing. The truth is, most people can't tell if a chord is in perfect tune, but they sure can tell if your group looks bored, disengaged, or distant.

What you never want said about you: "They don't care, I don't care."

If your group does not get frequent standing ovations, it's likely you're not really performing. We don't mean choreography or cruise ship banter or Vegas smooth. We are talking about focused, intense, emotionally engaged singing. If you're singing about sorrow, express sorrow. If you're singing about joy, smile! It should be obvious. However, because a cappella for many is an offshoot of choir, where the anonymity of the alto section, risers, and a distant audience give singers an apparent ability to get lost in the crowd, the emotional engagement is often missing.

There is no crowd in contemporary a cappella, even in the back row of a fifteen member group. You will be seen. You will be noticed. And your musings about where you'll have dinner while singing "I Can't Make You Love Me" will turn a poignant song into an unpalatable pabulum of amateur-hour Muzak. If you do not care about your music, no one else will.

If you're shy, work on it. Don't like to meet people's eyes? Work on it. Feel uncomfortable moving on stage? Singing a solo? Sharing your feelings? Work on it or decide that you're not really interested in prime time. It's okay—not every tennis player needs to aspire to the US Open. Those who do are the ones that practice and play with heart.

Vocaldente

Exit

Start Now

Sometimes a group has significant talent but they are too unpolished, too rough . . . because they are too new.

> *What you never want said about you: "Great soloists, great look, great talent . . . but just aren't working together."*

Have you ever watched an all-star or all-pro game where there are amazing players all lined up on both sides and the game is rather dull? That's because it doesn't matter how good you are in a team sport if you don't have chemistry as a group. You need to know where your teammates will be so you can anticipate their moves, finish their thoughts. Many teams with great players have fallen and many a Superbowl has been won on the backs of solid, yet unremarkable players who understand each other and make each other better.

Do not procrastinate. You pulled together some great singers for this year's auditions but didn't make a callback? Do not despair, do not disband. Keep singing every week, build a repertoire, perform, and relax into each other's company and friendship. It is essential to a great group sound and group energy. You will make each other better and "better" is what it takes to rise above so many great groups.

> *What you DO want said about you: "I love the look, the sound, the energy, and most of all how much they love singing together."*

ADDITIONAL INSIGHTS FROM DAVE BROWN

Enjoy the experience. Seriously. People say that a lot, and it's "Cheeseball USA," but it's true. Your group has been working very hard to prepare for the upcoming rounds of competition and it only gets more intense from here. But don't forget: you're in school! You're amateurs! You do this because you love it! Feel free to take it seriously and work hard, but don't let your intensity serve as an excuse for mistreating one another. The whole experience will be over in no time and all you'll be left with are relationships and memories so be sure to enjoy it along the way.

Imagine how much pressure the competitors on The Sing-Off felt in the weeks before the competition. Cameras in their hometowns and on their campuses. Interviews. The whole a cappella world looking in on them and judging them before they even set foot on stage. These groups were about to perform for millions of people. Talk about pressure! But every one of them has said that being on national television was such a tremendous experience, and, as they look back, they're just thrilled for the relationships they built and the fun they had along the way. Don't lose that!

Control your nerves. True, it's a new audience and a new venue, and it "really counts" this time. But nerves will hurt your pitch, your energy, and your precision, all of which are necessary if you're going to win. But a competition is a big deal, so what can you do?

Pretend you're not nervous. If you force your group to practice in front of tons of new audiences in lots of new circumstances, you'll get good at focusing on the show and not on your nerves. Even if you are nervous, do some self-affirmations to try to calm down, and at least put on a happy face. Sometimes an audience really can't tell the difference.

I'm not saying that you should be fake or disingenuous. But as a performer, you're really an actor up there. Get in the mood. And if you're not in the mood, or if you're nervous or distracted, force yourself to get in the mood! Or at least look like you're in the mood!

Music is the most important thing. Once you get up there, remember that it's a singing competition. If you have flaws in pitch or rhythm, it's hard for judges to give you the trophy. Sing well. Sing well. Sing well. The groups that succeeded in The Sing-Off all sang very well (after the first episode). Nota sang well from the very first performance and they went all the way.

Music isn't the only thing. Singing is crucial, but it's not everything. Don't forget, we're all sitting there in the audience. WE'RE WATCHING YOU. It's not a CD. If you are visually boring or your motions are stupid, judges can't give you the points for the visual aspect of your show. On The Sing-Off The Bubs were a prime example of putting on a great show and they made it to the final two. Frankly, just about every group on The Sing-Off gave a great visual performance. And guess what? You enjoyed it more because of it. The same goes for the ICCA and ICHSA audiences and judges.

Expect weird things. The sound on The Sing-Off was odd at times. The set was new. The competing groups even had to do a song they weren't prepared for. The monitors were reportedly not up to snuff, at least at first. Well, the same goes for the Varsity Vocals competitions: you never know what you're going to get! Maybe there will be an extra mic for your duet person, but probably not. Maybe you'll go last, maybe you'll go first. Maybe the stage will be smaller than you wanted. Maybe the stage will be huge! Maybe there will be monitors, maybe not. You have to be prepared for anything.

Do your best to find out as much information in advance as possible and then assume there's a decent chance that information will be incomplete or incorrect. You never know until you get to the venue what the real setup is. And at that point, you have to use your extra alone time as a group to make last-minute adjustments.

Is this a pain? Yes. But it goes with the territory! The most professional performers aren't the ones with demanding riders (though some of them do have demanding riders!), but rather those who can perform anywhere at any time under any conditions. Roll with the punches! The groups that win the ICCA and ICHSA every year are incredibly flexible. If you want to win, you should be flexible too.

Be likeable and award-worthy. Didn't it seem like all the groups on The Sing-Off were nice? I've spoken personally with several of the competitors from multiple groups and every one of them has had nothing but great things to say about every other group. By all reports, Nota is a total class act. Doesn't that make you want to really support them even more? And the Bubs were so nice when they lost, speaking very highly of Nota and congratulating them both publicly and privately. CLASS ACT!

Being nice isn't going to win you awards all by itself. But if you come across as arrogant or rude, it won't be easy for judges to give you awards. And, more importantly, when it's all over, what kinds of relationships will you have if you're jerks to everyone at the event? Be nice, reach out, and make friends. Stay humble.

The judges usually, sometimes, most of the time, almost always know what they're talking about. The Varsity Vocals producers work very hard to line up a panel of judges that understand not only contemporary a cappella, but also singing skills, performance skills, competitions, and everything related to what you are experiencing as a competitor. Judges do come with biases, preferences, and so forth, but none so terrible that it would affect any outcome.

So when you sit down to read the judges' comments, remember that they're not idiots, and they're legitimately trying their best to score the show accurately, as they see it from their chairs. They're trying to offer you useful feedback. Don't just throw it away; really read through it and consider it.

Obviously, a different set of judges may have scored the show slightly differently. You never know. Which is why, in the end, you can't define your value as a group based on your score in the show. This is only a moment in time. Although it's true that prizes can be awesome (if you win a prize or title, soak it up, issue a press release, put it on your website, enjoy it), but remember that your group will take away a lot more than prizes. Memories, friendships, future couches to sleep on when you tour, new fans, cash from sold CDs and merchandise. You name it. And perhaps more than anything, you should realize that the competition has made you rise to a level of quality you may not have otherwise ever had a reason to strive for. You're better than you would've been, and you've learned a lot along the way. Soak it up and be proud.

"My" Noteworthy ladies got booted off on the second episode on The Sing-Off. Were they upset? Sure, of course. But they walked away with their heads held high, proud of their performance, happy for what they learned, and with the memory of having been on national network television, something most a cappella groups will never have a chance to do. That made me more proud than anything they did or didn't do on the show.

Keep that positive attitude for yourself and your group. Work your butts off to make your set as amazing as possible, be flexible, don't be nervous, soak up the feedback, and have a blast. Once it's all over, learn what you can from it and use it to improve your next performance!

Fusion

CHAPTER 41

THE INTERNATIONAL CHAMPIONSHIPS OF A CAPPELLA AND AN INSIDE LOOK AT *PITCH PERFECT* AND THE REAL-LIFE BARDEN BELLAS

The 2012 musical comedy film *Pitch Perfect* was a huge success and showcased the world of a cappella to the masses. The movie grossed over $65 million domestically in the United States and $45 million internationally. It became the second highest grossing musical comedy film behind *School of Rock* and peaked at #3 at the box office. The plot follows an all-girl college a cappella group, The Barden Bellas, as they compete against another a cappella group from their college as well as other groups to make it to Nationals and ultimately win the coveted title. What fans of the movie *Pitch Perfect* may not realize is that the movie was inspired by actual events and is loosely adapted from Mickey Rapkin's non-fiction book *Pitch Perfect: The Quest for Collegiate A Cappella Glory*. The real-life Barden Bellas are a group known as Divisi and the competition the movie is based around is the International Championship of Collegiate A Cappella sponsored annually by an organization called Varsity Vocals.

Varsity Vocals is the organization that is self-defined as the "home of student a cappella." The organization gives college and high school singers the opportunity to interact, compete, learn from each other, get feedback from professionals, and perform in venues around the world. The Varsity Vocals International Championships of A Cappella is the only international tournament that showcases the art of student a cappella singing. The program includes both the International Championship of Collegiate A Cappella (ICCA) and the International Championship of High School A Cappella (ICHSA). Both competitions are dedicated to providing top-notch a cappella groups with valuable feedback from highly qualified judges. Participants have the opportunity to showcase their talent to an international audience and develop relationships with each other, cultivating the art of a cappella singing and a lifelong love of music.

The ICCA began in 1996 and the ICHSA began in 2005. Both began with five regions and have grown from there. Each year, the tournament takes place from January through April in regions across the United States and Europe. For the ICCA, each region holds several quarterfinal events and then the top two college groups at each quarterfinal advance to the college regional semifinals, and then the winner of each semifinal is invited to participate in the finals. For the ICHSA, the groups compete in regional semifinals only and the top high school group from each regional semifinal advances to the finals. There is also a wildcard round semi-final for both the ICCA and the ICHSA and the winners of those rounds are also then invited to participate in finals. The finals for both the ICCA and the ICHSA are held in New York City, where the groups compete for the coveted title of Grand Champion.

And now for an inside look at the ICCAs and ICHSAs and the real-life story behind the movie Pitch Perfect as told by Lisa Forkish. Forkish is an Oakland-based vocalist, composer, arranger, and music educator. She served four years as music director for the University of Oregon's acclaimed female a cappella group Divisi and then went on in 2006 to study at Berklee College of Music in Boston under a prestigious Vocal Performance scholarship. She has performed all over the country in various capacities and has released two full-length albums. Currently, she is on the Vocal Music faculty at Oakland School for the Arts where she teaches both middle and high school vocal music courses and is the founder/director of the high school's renowned a cappella group Vocal Rush. Here is her story:

The Real "Pitch Perfect" Story
by Lisa Forkish

Divisi: The Real "Barden Bellas"

April 30th, 2005: Twelve women in pin-striped pants, black button-down shirts, crimson red ties and heels had taken over a Chinese restaurant in the Upper West Side of Manhattan. It was the night of ICCA Finals and since we, the women of the University of Oregon's all-female a cappella group, had not been given the opportunity to deliver an encore performance at Lincoln Center for the 1000-person crowd, we performed instead for our own community of family and friends at this hole-in-the-wall restaurant. With up-dos coming undone and red lipstick nearly worn off, we sang the fan-favorite "Medley" as if we were still up on that stage at Alice Tully Hall. We kept our heads held high, despite the fact that we'd just lost the national a cappella championship title we'd worked so hard for; and that we'd delivered a performance that would go down in a cappella history, strengthening the notion of women's a cappella; and with an outcome that sparked Varsity Vocals to change their entire adjudication system; and inspired Mickey Rapkin to write a book that would later be made into a blockbuster hit film. This was Divisi, and this is our story.

Rewind to spring of 2004. It was only Divisi's second year competing in the ICCAs (just our third year in existence!) and we were determined to do well. The bar had been set high by our brother group at the University of Oregon, On the Rocks, who had made it to ICCA Finals in New York the prior year. We never saw ourselves as being less than as the only all-female group on campus, though we were all well aware of the stereotypes and prejudices surrounding all-female a cappella. Week after week we watched as folks showed up to see On the Rocks perform for our joint Friday a cappella showcase in the student union, only to see them get up and leave when it came time for Divisi's set. We heard repeated remarks about how sweet, soft, or even musical (like that's a bad thing!) we sounded, but how we weren't as entertaining and fun as our male counterparts; and everywhere we went, we were referred to as the "girls group" with the most subtle tone of condescension.

Divisi was also consistently surrounded by men each time we entered the a cappella scene, so it was no surprise when we found ourselves competing against mostly men at the 2004 ICCA Semi-Finals at Stanford University. The competition was made up of co-ed groups Extreme Measures from the University of Colorado and Reverse Osmosis from the University of Southern California; and three all-male groups: Fermata Nowhere from Mt. San Antonio College, Vocal Point from Brigham Young University and our very own On The Rocks—the latter two groups having placed at Finals in years past. We delivered a solid set, but didn't quite make the cut; we ended up placing third with Vocal Point and Fermata Nowhere in front of us. We wouldn't be going to the Finals that year. On the van ride home, we discussed ways in which we could strengthen our set for the following year's competition season, feeling like we had reached our highest point yet and struggling to envision where the next level would be for Divisi. This was the beauty of competing—it always pushed us to strive for more with what we were doing. We were disappointed with the fact that we would not advance to New York, but a fire was lit under us now, a newfound passion and drive to represent strong, confident and inspired women's a cappella at the ICCA Finals. We were determined to make 2005 *our* year.

In the fall of 2004, we said goodbye to only two members moving on from the group and admitted three new singers. Fortunately, since the second year of Divisi's existence when the group reached its capacity, we had had very little turnover; every woman who joined the group was excited about being a part of the foundation and setting the standards for future Divisi incarnations to come. Even though I was admitted about eight months after Divisi was founded in 2001, I considered myself a founding member, and I'm sure the other eight members who entered with me in the fall of 2002 felt the same. We collectively made the group what it was—a powerhouse of young determined women, a sisterhood. Joanne Caputo, Keeley McCowan and Mimi Kater came in fresh and ready to get down to work as newbies in September 2004. They joined Divisi co-founder Evynne Smith and founding members Erica Barkett, Anna Corbett, Suzie Day, Josi Henderson, Katie Hopkins, Sarah Klein, Megan McCornack and me.[1] We were mighty. Armed with a killer alto section; including Anna Corbett and me who won the "Testosterone Award" two years earlier at the 2003 ICCA Quarterfinals; confident, full-voiced sopranos; our new secret weapon, beatboxer Mimi Kater; multiple knock-out soloists; and our choreographer, Erica Barkett, who won "Outstanding Choreography" at every competition we had entered since she joined the group—we were ready to take on the ICCAs! These twelve women would take Divisi to New York in 2005. All we needed was a solid, stand-out set, something that would truly distinguish us.

Evynne Smith came to me one day that September and said, "Leese, I'm thinking of arranging 'Yeah' by Usher." Okay. This would be a daring song choice for us, but Evynne and I both agreed we could pull it off. She brought the arrangement to the group and we learned it in one night's rehearsal (it is only one repeated G minor chord, after all), knowing right away that this would have to be our competition set closer. We cast Erica on lead, and both Erica and Evynne interpreted the Ludacris rap, writing new Divisi-specific lyrics and making the feel of it relevant to our sound. It was really important to all of us that we make our rendition quintessentially Divisi and not just an imitation of the original. Some of the women in Divisi, me included, were concerned about our performance being misunderstood by the audience as cultural appropriation; and we had to be real and honest about the implications of a group of mostly white women performing a crunk/R&B hit. There was definitely a novelty factor in this song choice, one that most all-female groups would have steered away from; all-female a cappella had long been pegged as girl-ish with most groups at the time covering The Supremes, Indigo Girls, Sarah McLachlan or any number of other safe female artists/bands. It was pretty rare for us to see a women's group cover a male artist; and when we did, it was usually a ballad by John Mayer or Maroon 5.

Divisi

One of the most important components of our "Yeah" performance would have to be choreography, because this was NOT a ballad and we couldn't just stand in an arc. Enter Erica Barkett who put together some bold, original choreography that helped make our rendition wholly "Divisi" and pulled us further from the potential appearance of imitating or appropriating black music/dance, at least in my opinion. Erica was a stickler for uniformity, and we spent hours at her dance studio tightening up the moves so that every arm was at the same angle, every hip motion in unison, every step so polished that we were ready for Riverdance. (We also practiced making a formation that spelled the word "Yeah," an idea was vetoed by our choreographer, who must have been in the bathroom for the idea to have even been entertained in the first place. We were in good hands!) This standard of perfection, both in the realm of music and performance/choreography, is what would take us far. In rehearsal at the U of O School of Music, we added 7s and 9s to that G minor chord on repeat, and then we tuned that G minor 9 chord until it rang with overtones. Our beatboxer (Mimi) and bass (me) lined up the syncopation in the groove and locked in like a true rhythm section. We added some Lil' John shout-outs ("watch out!") and gave Katie Hopkins, our resident riff-master, free reign to contribute to the choruses with her own "yeah" runs. We wanted to give this song a full, womanly sound to catch people off guard—not only were we covering a male artist, but we were doing it in a mature, grown-woman kind of way. We recognized the irony in it being a club song about picking up a woman at a bar; and here we were, a group of self-proclaimed feminists, taking it on with conviction, and taking ourselves seriously as well. *That* was the power of our covering this song, at least for me. The content of American Top 40 is typically shallow and often sexist, but as a group of women covering a song that contained a message intended *for* us and instead having that message delivered *by* us (without changing pronouns, mind you), we turned the whole thing on its head. When I first saw the *Pitch Perfect* trailer, and it cut to a clip of the scene where the all-female group is singing "No Diggity" by Blackstreet while the others look on with shock and dismay, it confirmed for me that the film truly *was* inspired by Mickey Rapkin's book of the same name that told our story: Same concept, same affect on the audience. (Compare two lyric excerpts: "Baby you're a perfect ten, I wanna get in, can I get down so I can win" from "No Diggity" with Usher's "She's all up in my head now, got me thinking that it might be a good idea to take her with me, 'cuz she's ready to leave/I gotta keep it real now, 'cuz on a one to ten she's a certified twenty, but that just ain't me" from "Yeah.")

We knew how to end our set with a bang, but we still needed a strong beginning and middle. Sarah Klein, a talented arranger and soprano in Divisi, brought us her brand new arrangement of Joni Mitchell's "Woodstock." While there's a predictability to a female group covering Joni Mitchell, this song – and specifically Sarah's arrangement—was so ethereal, poignant, haunting, and contained a message that was important to us: Just a year and a half after the U.S. first invaded Iraq, we were still at war, and Joni's lyrics—"I dreamed I saw the bombers riding shotgun in the sky/they were turning into butterflies above our nation"—still held relevance 35 years after they were written during the Vietnam War. As a group, we would always talk about the meaning of the songs we sang together. There was never any one person leading these conversations; it would usually consist of all of us responding and relating to the lyrics, and in turn, responding and relating to *each other*. "We are stardust, we are golden and we've got to get ourselves back to the garden." These lyrics are both strong and feminine, a powerful combination unfamiliar to a lot of pop writing. They resonated with us as women who cared so deeply for each other and for the world in which we lived. Many of the Divisi ladies were religious and/or spiritual, many of us firm believers in the importance of staying connected to nature, and *all* of us were committed to our art. This song spoke to each one of us in different ways, but we were able to connect to the song as an ensemble and a unit. We shaped our dynamics to mirror the lyrical arc, and our arms and head movements were choreographed to compliment each line with grace and subtlety. Evynne was cast as the soloist, doing Joni justice with her soaring soprano and authentic delivery. The other 11 of us rehearsed the song with feet firmly planted and eyes directed outward at our imagined audience. Our spoken goal was to tell the audience a story, taking them with us on a journey to Woodstock. As young women in our late teens and early twenties, I don't think we fully understood the impact we would have singing this song, but we did truly access our inner old soul to call upon the year 1969 and to bring that same message to 2004.

In the realm of a cappella competitions, some say the closing song has to be the strongest because it's what you leave with your audience. Some say the opener is most important because first impressions matter. Others say the middle of your set has to be especially solid lest you lose your audience. All of these statements are equally true, and if you focus on each part of your performance (beginning, middle, end) being the strongest, you will end up with an exceptional set. Divisi's 2005 ICCA Set: "_____?" 'Woodstock.' 'Yeah.' How to fill in the blank? One of our group's strengths was delivering a song with authenticity and emotion as one connected ensemble. That characteristic then enhanced our musicality, phrasing, dynamics, stage presence, blend, intonation, cohesiveness . . . oh, am I naming categories on the ICCA adjudication sheet? So I am! For some it may be likened to the chicken/egg question, that one comes with the other and it doesn't matter which comes first. For us, for this group of Divisi women, the connectedness to each other and the song came first, and from there we had a solid foundation to build on all the musical and performance nuances (and ICCA adjudication categories, as it turned out).

All of that is to say that we chose our opening song based on the feeling of the song—the groove, the chords, the melody and melodic motifs that support it, the lyrics of the song, and the overall way it made us feel. This song was "Walking on Broken Glass" by Annie Lennox. It had been on the scene for over 10 years, so many a female a cappella group had already covered it; but we felt we had something new to bring to the table. For one, we had Anna Corbett's raw and impassioned voice to take on Annie's melody, spanning an octave and a sixth. We were a group of women who had all experienced the kind of heartbreak that Annie's lyrics address, and were close enough to speak openly with each other about those experiences and smart enough to put those emotions into our voices when we sang. And once again, we had a bad-ass choreographer who gave us fierce yet crisp movements that made us look like pillars of strength on stage, *contrary* to what the lyrics of the song might imply or dictate. For example, the lead singer (in our case, Anna) *appears* to feel hopeless, expressed through lines like "since you've abandoned me my whole life has crashed, won't you pick the pieces up 'cause it feels just like I'm walking on broken glass." In contrast though, the *feel* of the song is upbeat and peppy, almost clashing with the lyrics. The singer is in despair but wants to empower herself, and the uplifting feel of the song is helping her get there. It's the kind of song you put on a few weeks into a break-up when you're ready to get out of bed and get back out into the world. In discussing all of this as a group, we wanted to let Anna be vulnerable, so we decided she should bare her heart and soul to the audience, while the other eleven of us would stand behind her, simultaneously supporting her as she falls and sending her the strength to get back up. Months after we first discussed this idea, it came up again backstage at Lincoln Center as we prepared to go on. Before every performance, all of us knew exactly what we were about to put onstage; but that night in New York, there was a clarity to our set that came from preparation, commitment and once again, an emotional connection to what we were singing and to each other.

February 26, 2005: The ICCA Divisional event was held at South Eugene High School, which happened to be my alma mater, thus making it a stage I had sung on numerous times. We delivered our set with confidence: "Walking on Broken Glass," followed by "Woodstock," and closing with "Yeah." I remember hearing the audience's reaction when we broke into the catchy and immediately identifiable synth riff "ree ree, ree ree"—you could hear some folks gasp, but most responded with laughter. As the song continued, and especially when we got to the rap section, the audience reacted with cheers, laughter and shouting. We had made them feel something. And as an all-female group we definitely weren't used to being reacted to in this way, and especially not being perceived as funny. But because we took our performance of the song so seriously, the audience got it—the irony, the shock factor, the novelty. And because we executed that song so *well,* along with the other two songs in our set, we took 1st place that night.

March 5, 2005: Yes, these dates are correct. Our Semi-Final took place just one week after our Divisional. We made travel plans in a hurry, renting the usual 15-passenger van and heading down to the San Francisco Bay Area just days after our 1st place win in Oregon. The event was to take place at Dinkelspiel Auditorium on Stanford campus. We were familiar with this venue as we had been there one year earlier when we took 3rd place. *This* was the big night. *This* was the night that determined whether we would compete at the Finals on April 30th. The competition was stiff: UC Berkeley's California Golden Overtones, the all-female group who inspired Evynne to co-create Divisi back in 2001 and had placed 2nd at the Finals that same year;[2] Brigham Young University's Vocal Point who had a reputation that preceded them; and the group who beat us at Semis in 2004, Fermata Nowhere. But we were ready. Unstoppable. Unshakable. Unfaltering. Due in part to the depth of preparation leading up to this day, but also due to our love for each other, we were ready. As crazy as it may sound, I know that if you were to ask all twelve of the women who competed that year what our secret was or how we got so far, I'm certain that many would speak about how much we loved each other. And before we went onstage, we expressed that love. We sat in a circle in our holding room and each Divisi member turned to the woman next to her to tell her how much she meant to her. We went onstage with one unified goal, so deeply connected to each other and the music that we could genuinely share ourselves with an audience of hundreds.

Although I don't remember what happened after we went on to perform, I do know that we delivered a solid performance because of how confident I felt. After the judges finished deliberating, Julia Hoffman, our ICCA West producer, came onstage to give out the awards.

She announced the Outstanding Soloist award . . . "Evynne Smith!" We hugged and cheered! A well-deserved win, as she put her all into that performance. "The award for Outstanding Choreography goes to . . . Divisi!!!" Without intending to sound arrogant (and because I actually played such a small part in the winning of this award), I have to say I was not surprised, and I doubt the rest of the group was either—with Erica, we always cleaned up that award! The time had come to announce the 3rd, 2nd and 1st place groups. We stood onstage, eager to hear the results and ready to take on New York! Julia announced the 3rd place winner, BYU's Vocal Point! We cheered. We loved those guys and were happy for them. I closed my eyes. "Fermata Nowhere!!" At this point, I think we knew: When you feel confident that your performance was in the top three and your name hasn't been called yet, it usually means one thing. "And our ICCA West Semi-Final Champion, advancing to ICCA Finals at Lincoln Center is . . . DIVISI!!!!!" We jumped up and down. We cried. We screamed. Somewhere amidst all the excitement I remembered that as music director, I was supposed to go up and receive the award. As people often say about moments like these, it was surreal. We left that night feeling like champions. And as an all-female group, it felt like a win not just for us, but for women's a cappella around the country. We wanted to inspire other singers just as we had been inspired by the Overtones a few years earlier. All the negative stereotypes that surround women's a cappella came flooding to my mind. We had set out to defy those expectations and I felt confident that we had been successful. I felt so proud to be a part of this group. After a night of celebration with our a cappella community, we drove back in our van; but this time we didn't discuss how we could do better next year—instead we planned our trip to New York. We had already won. We had never before made it this far, and we felt honored just to be joining the other Regional Champions on stage at Lincoln Center.

Yes, we were honored and humbled to be in New York for the ICCA Finals; and we knew the other competing groups were going to be amazing. But I need to digress for a moment: Talk about a boys' club. We always had a sense of the staggering ratio of men to women in the a cappella world as we competed mostly against all-male and mixed groups. But here we were at Lincoln Center getting ready for sound check and we were the *only* women around, except for Amanda Newman, Executive Director of Varsity Vocals, and a few of her staff. Regardless, we were the only female competitors, that much was true, and we felt it. There *shouldn't* be a gender gap in collegiate a cappella because it's not something that is openly advertised or even implied to be for one specific group of participants. But when the best collegiate groups from around the country were picked, this is how it ended up—six groups, five of them all-male, and one all-female group. This reality hit hard, but Divisi wasn't the kind of group to let that intimidate us because we *knew* we weren't inferior. We knew that our sound was full and mature, just like what most people expect of an all-male group. We knew that our female basses were on it in spite of our higher vocal ranges. Our vocal percussionists were solid, our choreography tight and our music ready to move people. It shouldn't have meant anything that we were the only women's group. But it did mean something to us as women in the world, knowing more deeply how much the a cappella world really did resemble a "boys' club" in a lot of ways. We were more motivated than ever to change that.[3]

The University of Rochester's Midnight Ramblers, The Duke's Men of Yale, UNC Chapel Hill's Achordants, Indiana University's Straight No Chaser, and Boston University's Dear Abbeys. These were the five all-male groups that Divisi was up against. We interacted with them backstage, but I don't recall it being the warmest environment. Everyone was getting in their zone and no one seemed in the mood to make small talk with the strangers they were about to compete with.

The Divisi ladies always stuck together on competition day. We went to grab dinner as a group and ran a last-minute errand for hairspray and Ricolas. We walked around Lincoln Center together, commenting on how unreal it was that we were about to perform at this venue. Before sound check we walked through Alice Tully Hall, looking at the 1000+ empty seats and knowing that just a few hours later each one would be filled, many by family and friends (including our brother group, On The Rocks) who had traveled long distances to support us. After our sound check, we gathered in our dimly-lit dressing room together, applying the Divisi-red lipstick and helping each other tie our Divisi-red ties. We were very calm. In our pre-competition circle, we gave each other shout-outs and validation. We went over each song, reminding each other of all the small but important nuances: "Remember to come way down on the third verse of 'Woodstock;'" "Don't forget to breathe in between songs;" "Show you support for Anna while she sings;" "Let's perform 'Yeah' like we've never performed it before;" "Yes, totally!" "Oh, and remember to exaggerate the crescendo on the bridge in 'Broken Glass.'" The most important feeling to have after any performance is to know that you did your absolute best. We knew we were about to bare our souls on that stage. It was just a matter of letting it happen. Stage right, five minutes before we went on, the twelve women of Divisi held hands and whispered to each other: "I love you, Jojo!" "I love you, Suz!" "Love you, Katie!" "Love you too, Jos!" Here we go . . . "And our final competing group of the evening, from the University of Oregon, please give it up for DIVISI!"

> "I recall a sense of sisterhood as we sat in a circle preparing ourselves for the set mentally and emotionally. I don't remember much about actually being on stage, but based on the audience's impassioned response, I felt confident and exhilarated as we ran off stage." – Sarah Klein

> "My favorite memory of our 12-minute performance lasted only a moment. One of the traits that made our group unique was how close we were as girlfriends. We could be real, be our true selves, without worrying about snap judgments or intimidation. We weren't afraid to be silly and weren't afraid to bare our souls. In "Woodstock," we stood in an arc formation and at one moment in the song, we slowly raised our heads from looking down at the floor to making eye contact with the singer across from us. My spot was on the end and in this moment, I lifted my eyes to meet Josi's. Many times in

rehearsal, we would crack a smile or make a funny face to greet each other, letting our silly sides get the better of us. On that stage though, when I raised my head and my eyes met hers for that short moment, we were both living the story not only of the song but of our incredible connection with each other. It was an electric and powerful moment that I'll never forget." – Megan Perdue

"I guess it's been too many years now, but I can't really recall our performance on the Alice Tully stage. I know that we left all that we had on that stage, but for me, all that remains are several iconic Divisi photos from our performance— all showing the intensity on our faces, the tightness of our choreo & the unity of that group. That night truly felt like the end of an amazing journey, one that was better than we could have ever imagined." – Evynne Hollens

" I remember there was this buzz of nervous energy, but it was also underlined by this confidence that we were as prepared as we could possibly be. And we were so UNITED. I have never before or since been a part of a group that was so united in a singular goal and drive." – Keeley George

After the closing notes of "Yeah," we heard a roar of applause and the entire house took to their feet—we were the only ones to receive a standing ovation that evening. We exited stage right and walked briskly back to our dressing room. We had *never* performed like that before. The years leading up to this day with the goal of making it to ICCA Finals, the countless hours of rehearsal from September through April on these three songs, the time spent together outside of rehearsal learning to love each Divisi woman for *exactly* who she is, the cohesiveness we developed as a team working together toward a common goal, the significance of being the only women in the competition that night . . . we left *all* of that on the stage. And back in our dressing room, we relished our success, feeling proud of ourselves, grateful for each other and the music, and in awe of the moment itself, as if it came straight from a dream.

It was time for the International Champion to be announced and we waited with the other groups backstage. Barry Carl, the renowned bass singer from Rockapella and one of the night's esteemed judges, stood next to us. A few of the Divisi ladies turned to him and said thank you. He looked back at us and said, "Don't thank me yet." We didn't know what he meant, but our minds were preoccupied with the impending announcements and couldn't be shaken. In a close huddle at the front of the stage, we stood with our arms around each other so that everyone was connected. We probably smelled strongly of sweat and Aqua Net, but no one noticed or cared. At this point it was completely out of our hands, and we knew we had given it our all. Amanda announced all of the special awards. Divisi took the award for Outstanding Choreography again! "In 3rd place tonight . . . The Midnight Ramblers!!" We wanted 1st place and felt we were deserving. She wasn't going to call our name next. "Taking 2nd place tonight . . . Divisi!!" My heart sank. We looked at each other, then out at the audience and smiled graciously. I accepted the award on the group's behalf. I don't remember anything after that, but I know that Amanda crowned The Dear Abbeys as the 2005 National Champions.

Back in our dressing room, we gathered our belongings. The tone in the room was somber. Barry Carl popped his head in to say he was sorry and that he had really enjoyed our set—we were very moved that he went out of his way to do that. Amanda went to every group's room to give out the judges forms. We huddled up and I read aloud the scores and comments. Interesting. Two of the three judges placed us 1st in the subjective ranking category; but one judge didn't place us at all, and gave little constructive feedback on our adjudication form aside from the words "Thanks for bowing." How could one person (interestingly, the only female judge that night) think we deserved fourth place or worse, and two others rank us at the top? With 357 total points, we scored a whopping 85 points lower than our Semi-Finals score of 442. Right away I knew that was a huge discrepancy, as we had performed the same set (and, according to numerous people who attended both events, we performed much better at Finals). Of course the bar is higher at Finals, but this just didn't add up. Together we calculated that even if the judge who didn't place us at all had put is in 3rd place, we still would have won based on the adjudication system and our total number of points. I think Josi said it first, but I know we were all thinking it: "We were blackballed."

The lobby of Alice Tully Hall was abuzz as the singers greeted their family and friends. People approached me saying "you guys were robbed," and "I was so appalled that you didn't win" and "did you hear the audience gasp when they said your name in 2nd place!" One of the people who approached me expressing the same sentiment was a parent of one of the Dear Abbey guys. He apologized. It was so strange to hear so many people, many of them strangers, affirming what we already suspected from reading the adjudication forms. We made our way through the crowd of ICCA guests and competitors in the lobby, anxious for fresh air and the space to process what had just happened. The twelve women of Divisi gathered outside with our massive posse of family and friends, most of them sporting the "Divisi Groupie" T-shirts made by one of the parents. We stood on the sidewalk with our incredible community and just decided then and there—we *had* won. We put so much into our performance and had received such high marks from two of the judges and praise from our audience that we deserved to celebrate like we had won. In a giant clump of nearly 100 people, we found our way to a sweet little Chinese restaurant where we crowded around tiny tables and celebrated Divisi. I wish I could remember the name of this restaurant because they hosted one of the most memorable nights in my life. I would go back just to sit in that room and recall the way I felt that night—loved, grateful, humbled, and forever devoted to making music with others.

The Rushettes: Circle of Life

I finished my schooling at the University of Oregon in the spring of 2005, but opted to stick around Eugene and sing with Divisi for one more year before continuing my education at Berklee College of Music (I had been accepted three years earlier and kept deferring my admission in order to sing with Divisi). The last year of Divisi was amazing. We released our album *Undivided* to much acclaim and felt that we had finally established a reputation in the a cappella world. I knew this was going to be my last year, and I also knew that I would be leaving with most of the group's original members. It would be a sad spring with eight of us, including all but one of the founding members, moving onward. Years later, as a teacher of a scholastic group, I have a deeper understanding of how turnover affects a group, how each year is completely different from the last, but each group incarnation is special and important in its own way. I tell my students, "It's not going to be the same, but that's okay. It's going to be great in its own way" And that's the truth! At our final concert of the year in the spring of 2006, Divisi graduated Evynne, Suzie, Josi, Joanne, Anna, Erica, Megan and me. I moved to Boston a few months later with a heavy heart. Those had been the best four years of my life. And although I will always treasure that time, at the age of 21 I didn't yet know that I would have amazing years ahead of me.

Fast forward to spring of 2010. Since leaving Divisi I had spent three years at Berklee (taking one year off in between for professional development and growth) that were life-changing to say the least—that's a whole book in and of itself. I moved from Boston to the San Francisco Bay Area where most of my family resided and a thriving jazz scene awaited my husband and I. A cappella was something I did in college, but hadn't pursued since, aside from a brief stint with a female group in Boston that I founded and a couple of gigs with a Divisi-alum group called Luxe. In the Bay Area, I worked several music teaching/directing jobs and performed as a solo artist for about six months before I was hired to teach the premier high school choral ensemble at Oakland School for the Arts. It was a part-time job, about 10 hours a week, but it felt like full-time. After every rehearsal I felt emotionally and mentally drained. The 37 students in this choir were putting me through the ringer. I was a new, young teacher, encroaching on their turf midway through the year. Every day seemed like a test: "Will she quit if we do this? How about now?" I wanted so badly for this to work out. Teaching at a vibrant art school with a renowned vocal music program, an incredibly talented and diverse student body led by an esteemed faculty? Dream job! I was determined to gain the student's respect and prove myself to be at least competent – and hopefully much more. The School of Vocal Music was rich in diversity of genre and style, with resident faculty in opera and jazz, incorporation of world, spirituals and folk music, and an annual spring show that highlighted some of the best contemporary artists and styles including R&B, soul, pop, Motown, and rock. What did I have to offer that was unique? I knew that Contemporary A Cappella was in my wheelhouse from my years with Divisi and that if I could form a small, audition-only ensemble and teach them this art form, I could at least gain *those* kids' admiration and hope that it permeates the entire vocal department. I held auditions just two months into my time teaching at OSA. Sixteen students showed up to audition and ten of them were admitted – I will always cherish these ten kids for being willing to take a chance on a new teacher. I directed the group once a week after school through the spring and I was able to teach them about a cappella, watch them take on new leadership roles in the context of this small ensemble, and develop into a tight-knit ensemble. They called themselves Vocal Rush— and what ensued in the coming years was pretty incredible.

In the fall of 2011, I was brought on as full-time Vocal Music faculty at OSA and introduced Vocal Rush as an elective course in the program, no longer just an after-school ensemble. One student from the prior year had transferred schools and we admitted three new students for the 2011–2012 school year, bringing us up to twelve students in total. I had earned their respect, and I knew this because the students in my other classes who *weren't* in Vocal Rush treated me differently (I suspect many of them wanted to be in Vocal Rush at some point in the future and wanted to gain *my* respect). At the start of the school year, I told Vocal Rush about Varsity Vocals and the International Championship of High School A Cappella. "A competition?? Heck, yeah!" They were all in and more motivated than ever to excel. As there was no Semi-Final event in California, we planned to compete in Oregon at the Northwest Semi-Final. We chose and polished the set list ("Tightrope" by Janelle Monae, "Something's Missing" by Brandy and a Beyonce medley) and fundraised our behinds off to prepare for the trip. On January 28th, 2012, a group of teenagers who had been singing together for less than a year took the ICHSA stage at Rolling Hills Community Church in Wilsonville, Oregon. Vocal Rush delivered a strong set and was received with enthusiasm by the audience. We were all so proud—students, parents and teacher. When it came time to announce the results, Vocal Rush had come in 2nd place. There were tears (admittedly, the students weren't the only ones . . . it was emotional for me too) and I could see the disappointment in their faces as I approached them in the lobby. As we huddled together, talking through their performance and the evening as a whole, people kept approaching us saying things like "you guys were robbed," and "I thought you deserved to win." Deja vu. I was immediately taken back seven years to that fateful day in New York with Divisi. And it didn't stop there. I pulled out the adjudication sheets to read aloud to my kids. Flipping through, the first thing I saw was that two out of the three judges had placed Vocal Rush 1st but the third judge didn't place them at all, and they scored only nine points below the winning group. This was so crazy. It was a repeat of history, but with a different group, also directed by me. The irony was that Varsity Vocals had changed their adjudication system after what happened to Divisi at the 2005 ICCA Finals to require five judges, with the top and bottom scores thrown out; no judge could ever blackball a group again. The problem here was that it had become a challenge to find qualified individuals to judge the ICHSA/ICCAs, and Varsity Vocals' volume of events had increased drastically since 2005. The ICHSA Semis were more of a low-profile event, thus Vocal Rush had only three judges and . . . history had repeated itself. We piled into a van, the kids feeling defeated, while I was left feeling an interesting combination of confusion and nostalgia.

"It's not over," I told them. The ICHSA Wild Card round allowed groups who placed 2nd and 3rd at their Semi-Final event to submit a video performance of their set to have one last shot at getting to the Finals in New York. We made our audition tape, hopeful that this would pan out. Sure enough, Vocal Rush placed 2nd in the Wild Card round, and both 1st and 2nd place groups were invited to compete at the Finals. It was March 15th when we were notified, and the Finals were to take place on April 27th. All four of Vocal Rush's male singers and one female singer approached me saying that would not be able to go on the trip; these five singers had previously committed to other events that weekend and wanted to stay true to their word. We were in the middle of rehearsal for our department's big Spring Show, but flights needed to be booked within the next 24 hours if we were going to make it to the Big Apple. I pulled the remaining seven girls out into the hallway to deliver the news: "It's just you seven. I know you all can do it, but do you want to?" Without missing a beat, they all answered with an enthusiastic "yes." I explained that we would need to learn new repertoire because of the missing members, one of them would have to sing bass—essentially we would be starting from scratch, and we had only four weeks to make it happen. In what I now call true Vocal Rush form after directing various incarnations of this group for two and a half years, they insisted, "Let's do it."

Four weeks later, these seven extraordinary, hard-working and inspiring young women had put together a three-song set that included two brand new songs ("Gravity" and "Let Us Be Loving") and a revised-for-all-female third song from their previous set ("Tightrope"). On every song, it was one-on-a-part, with "Gravity" being the most challenging because there was no vocal percussion and the arrangement was in six-part harmony with loads of dissonant voicings. We rehearsed after school every day during the week of the competition, finalizing choreography for the new numbers, tuning the chords, working on balance, and practicing (only once) with individual miking. Then, the eight of us plus a few parent chaperones boarded a plane (the *first* time for two of these girls) and flew across the country to represent Oakland, OSA and Vocal Rush.

On April 27, 2012, I walked with these seven students from our hotel in Mid-Town to the Upper East Side where the competition was held. There is nothing like walking the streets of New York with a group of teenage girls, most of whom had never seen the city, to make you remember *why* it's such a magical place. We arrived for our sound check, where I was greeted with open arms by Amanda Newman. I hadn't seen her since I was there in 2005 with Divisi! All of this was a total trip for me. At our sound check, some of the Varsity Vocals staff were taking photos and videos, and there was a murmur in the hall. After we went back to our holding room, I stepped outside to let them change and do their hair and make-up. Several people approached me saying, "Your girls sound fantastic!" and "Where did you all come from?" I knew that Vocal Rush, or "The Rushettes" as they had decided to call themselves, was going to deliver an outstanding set. I knew that the other groups would be amazing (after all, these were the Finals) and had prepped the girls for the fact that they would be the smallest group by far and to not let the larger groups intimidate them. I also knew that while The Rushettes had something unique to bring to this competition, they were underdogs in a number of ways: 1) They weren't Regional Champions, but had come through the Wild Card round; 2) They were missing five of their members, including all of the boys; and 3) It was their first year competing and their first year in existence. We all talked about how much of an honor it was to have made it this far, especially given those circumstances, and to be grateful for the opportunity. I encouraged them to do what Divisi had done seven years earlier: "Leave it all on that stage. Give them your absolute best performance, and then it doesn't matter who wins because you all know you put your whole self into it." They were as ready as they could possibly be, given the four-week crunch. And I couldn't have been more proud.

After an incredible performance of their set, I ran backstage to greet them with love and encouragement. They were doubting themselves (as I've learned is more common with this age group than with college students) and wanting to critique their performance. I stopped them. I told them we could go through every detail of it later, but for now, savor the moment and feel proud of what you just did. We enjoyed watching the rest of the competitors, as well as a performance by Pitch Slapped (ironically, a group from Berklee College of Music), during the judges deliberations. The girls kept saying, "As long as Sarah wins best soloist, we can go home happy." Sarah Vela, a senior with an incredible voice who was a natural on stage, had been very well received by the audience—they cheered after she sang her very first line. The groups gathered on stage to hear the results. I stood in the back of the house, beaming with pride just to see those seven girls up there. It felt surreal to be back at it again, not onstage, but watching a group of young people that I worked with up there instead. No better feeling in the world, I will contend. The announcement for Outstanding Soloist was made . . . "Sarah Vela!!" I took a deep breath. So well-deserved, and I could see that my kids were above the clouds. It crossed my mind that they might take 3rd, but who knows? The competition was fierce. "In 3rd place, Limited Edition!!" The girls and I had enjoyed their set and were pleased. "Maybe," I thought, "just maybe 2nd place?" Emcee Dave Brown announced the 2nd place winner, "Forte!!" I exhaled and reminded myself how incredible it was that only seven of them were up on that stage, and that they had delivered an amazing performance. It literally did not occur to me that the next words I would hear out of Dave Brown's mouth were, "And our 2012 ICHSA Champions are . . . Vocal Rush!!!" The moments that followed are a blur. I know that I instinctively ran down the aisle toward them, not even realizing that I was running . . . and sobbing. I know that as I approached the stage, a group of about five Vocal Rush parents tackled me, wailing and shouting "Thank you, Lisa!" I know that I reached out to hug Dave Brown (who I knew from my years in Divisi when he was in Vocal Point) and accidentally pulled him over. I started to come to when my girls looked down from the stage and saw me, their faces smeared with make-up from their tears, all huddled up and jumping up and down. I reached up to hug them from the ground and shouted that they should just sing "Let Us Be Loving" again: We had never entertained the idea of needing an encore, and they knew only these three songs. I said to Vivian, "Just tell the audience what you're going to do and why." I sat down next to the parents, in awe of these amazing young people. Vivian got on the mic and said, "Our whole group wasn't able to be here, so we only know a few songs. We are going to do 'Let Us Be Loving' again. Hope you don't mind." The audience roared. Vivian thanked them and the song began.

Afterward in the lobby, Amanda Newman approached me and the first thing out of her mouth was, "Maybe this can make up for what happened with Divisi in 2005." I smiled and thought about how strange life is and how grateful I was for mine. As I wrote in an article for CASA last year, "In the end, this moment wasn't about me, it was about my kids, their hard work, perseverance and passion. But the moment was just too surreal *not* to recall my time on that New York stage. And that's when I fully realized just how important this a cappella—whether I'm onstage or watching students I've worked with onstage—scene is to me."

Life Lessons Learned

September 29th, 2006:

my dearest divisi,

it is just about 7:30 on friday over here in boston and i am thinking about that wonderful friday emu tradition that takes place as i write this. truthfully, this week has been the hardest for me since i left, and i think a lot of that has to do with the fact that divisi has begun it's next year and i am not a part of it. a whole piece of me is missing. right now, while listening to "broken glass" i am thinking about each and every one of you and how much i love you and miss you. a part of me just wants to hop on a plane and fly back to eugene so I can sing with you all again. but i know that would be silly. Anyway, what i'm trying to write through tears that block my sight of the computer screen, is how much i value the time i had singing with you beautiful, beautiful women. we were (and are) so fortunate to have shared in such amazing music, performance, laughter, love. i wish the best for all of you alum in this next year . . . remember i'm only a phone call away when you are having withdrawals. those of you that continue this year, please please don't take advantage of it. breathe it. be thankful. and kick some female a cappella ass. (as a side note, i feel like my experience with divisi puts me in a place well beyond the majority of my female vocalist peers at berklee . . . between the ear training we gain, arranging experience, performance, confidence, working in an ensemble with peers, developing range and emotion . . . the list goes on and on. and though i'm hoping it will change, i do feel like my experience as a singer/musician/performer, etc. with divisi won't even come close to comparing to my berklee experience. true story.)

all of my love,

lisa

This was an email I sent to my fellow Divisi ladies in the fall of my first semester at Berklee, just a few weeks into the very first school year in which I did not sing with an a cappella group. I discovered this email while doing research for the book (in other words, going down memory lane) and was so glad I found it. It's a gem. It's a reminder of what all I got out of Divisi and my experience in collegiate a cappella in general. Every year my memories grow dimmer, and although I know that I felt everything in that email at one point in time, I don't consistently feel it now. Why? I've grown up, and other things in life have become more important. But you know what? I would give anything to be 20 years old again and to re-live those years with my sisters in song. I still sing in an a cappella group, I still perform, I still travel, I still direct a group, and I'm still heavily involved in a cappella, but . . . this was something special. I know that many people reading this have also felt that special something and probably relate to most of the mushy sentiment from my 2006 email. I know my students do, as I have now graduated four classes of Vocal Rush members and watched them adjust to the world outside, cherishing the time they spent with their group and advising their younger peers not to take it for granted. And I will contend that much of the closeness, the feeling of one with a group of many, comes from competing with your ensemble.

Thus, I will leave you with a few pieces of advice or life lessons from someone who has spent a bit of time around the ICCA/ ICHSAs and has come to understand how my experiences shaped me as a person, in and outside the realm of a cappella:

Hard work will take you far, and may pay off in different ways than you might expect. For example, if it's doesn't reward with a win, it should reward through having done the work and being that much better at what you were working so hard on in the first place. As a kid (even during my years in Divisi) I would have scoffed at an elder who tried to tell me, "The reward for your hard work is being more knowledgeable, skilled or confident in the area you were working on." But as an adult, I know that doing the work is important and necessary, you may just not grasp or resonate with the pay-off right away or in the moment.

Know how to work effectively as a part of a team—it will prepare you for so much in life. Being able to listen to others' ideas, to work with people who aren't like you and love them unconditionally, to value the whole over the individual (i.e. learn to act selflessly and without your own agenda), to strive for something with others . . . these skills are absolutely invaluable – and harder to come by than one might think! There *is* no "I" in team, people! And teams show up all over the place: at your place of work; with your social groups; in your marriage; amongst your larger family; in addition to any a cappella or musical teams you may be involved in throughout your life.

It's okay to make yourself vulnerable and take risks. In fact, it's more than okay—it's encouraged! When you let yourself go and open your mind (to others, to your art, to your work), you free yourself of pretense and can get right to the heart of the matter. Specifically, through making music with a tight-knit group of people, you create a safe space to be yourself and let others be themselves. This is something that many people don't inherently know how to do, but is a skill that can be developed through working with people that you trust, and incidentally, learning to trust those same people is a skill in and of itself that will come from . . . wait for it . . . taking a risk and opening up! In the a cappella world, there is no such thing as competing and *not* taking a risk. Just by getting up there and doing it, you are acting courageously and learning how to do that affectively *with* others.

There is so much to be learned from others. Also, **humility goes a long way.** No one person has it all figured out, and if someone comes across in that way, they are fronting and most likely compensating for their own insecurities. If you go into a competition and hang out in your dressing room while the other groups perform, you are not only missing out on the opportunity to learn from your peers, you are also sending off a message that you have nothing left to learn.

As a musician *and* as a human being, I know that I will *never* stop learning and growing. And I know that this is true of any person—it's not just me that has more growing to do! Don't let your ego fool you into thinking any other way. Stay humble, stay grounded and have regard for where you came from *and* those who helped you get to where you are now.

Dream big and be fearless. What's the worst that can happen? You fail? Wouldn't it be more of a failure to have never set out with an inspired and lofty goal in the first place? I was a junior in high school when I auditioned for Divisi, a *collegiate* a cappella group, but I went for it anyway. It turned out they liked me, and could get around the high school thing if I just took one college course—it was just a technicality! I had very little teaching experience at the high school level when I applied for the job at OSA, but it was my dream job so I just went for it anyway, despite having doubts about my qualifications. The Vocal Music department chair, Cava Menzies, told me I was the first person to be interviewed and when I walked out, she already knew I was the one for the job. The morale of the story? You must dream big, because if you don't, you never even give yourself a fair shot at whatever life you would have dreamed for yourself if you'd allowed yourself to dream in the first place. Pretty straight-forward logic, right? Just go out and be you, do you, and never shy away or apologize for it.

Divisi

PREVIOUS WINNERS OF THE INTERNATIONAL CHAMPIONSHIP OF COLLEGIATE A CAPPELLA (ICCA)

YEAR	1ST	2ND	3RD
1996	Loreleis (UNC)	Duke's Men (Yale U.)	Other Guys (U. Illinois)
1997	Talisman (Stanford U.)	No Strings Attached (U. Illinois)	
2000	Men's Octet (U of Calif-Berkley)	Other Guys (U. Illinois)	Callbacks (Harvard U.)
2001	Golden Overtones (California U.)		
2003	Crosbys (Binghamton)	On the Rocks (U. Oregon)	Steiners (U. Maine)
2004	OneVoice (Milikin)	Fermata Nowhere (Mt. San Antonio College)	Chordials (Cornell U.)
2005	Dear Abbeys (Boston U.)	Divisi (U. Oregon)	Midnight Ramblers (U. Rochester)
2006	Vocal Point (Brigham Young U.)	Out of the Blue (Oxford U.)	Other Guys (U. Illinois)
2007	Noteworthy (Brigham Young U.)	Rocktavo (U. Nebraska)	Zumbyes (Amherst College)
2008	SoCal VoCals (U. Southern Calif.)	All-Night Yahtzee (Florida State U.)	N'Harmonics (New York U.)
2009	Fermata Nowhere (Mt. San Antonio College)	Out of the Blue (Oxford U.)	Beartones (Missouri State U.)
2010	SoCal VoCals (U. Southern Calif.)	Pitch Slapped (Berklee College of Music)	Accidentals (U. of Georgia)
2011	Pitch Slapped (Berklee College of Music)	Vocal Point (Brigham Young U.)	Melodores (Vanderbilt U.)
2012	SoCal VoCals (U. Southern Calif.)	ScatterTones (UCLA)	All The King's Men (King's College)
2013	Nor'easters (Northeastern U.)	ScatterTones (UCLA)	Chordials (Cornell U.)
2014	Pitch Slapped (Berklee College of Music)	ScatterTones (UCLA)	Vocal Point (U. of Delaware)
2015	SoCal VoCals (U. Southern Calif.)	Voices in Your Head (U. Chicago)	The G-Men (U. Michigan)

PREVIOUS WINNERS OF THE INTERNATIONAL CHAMPIONSHIP OF HIGH SCHOOL A CAPPELLA (ICHSA)

YEAR	1ST	2ND	3RD
2006	Men of Note (Cherry Hill High School West)	Baby Grands (School of Creative and Performing Arts)	5-Alone (Pioneer Valley Performing Arts School)
2007	Men of Note (Cherry Hill High School West)	Crimson (Cheyenne Mountain High School)	
2008	West Men of Note (Cherry Hill High School)	Mane Event (Leon High School)	
2009	Eight Notes (A&M Consolidated High School)	Soulfege (Pioneer High School)	
2010	Limited Edition (Port Washington High School)	Vocal Forte (Haddon Heights Baptist Regional School)	Town Criers (Weston High School)
2011	PFC (Douglas MacArthur High School)	Soul'd Out (Wilsonville High School)	Highland Voices (Northern Highlands High School)
2012	Vocal Rush (Oakland School for the Arts)	Forte (Centerville High School)	Limited Edition (Port Washington High School)
2013	Vocal Rush (Oakland School for the Arts)	Forte (Centerville High School)	Powder Room (Parkway North High School)
2014	Highland Voices (Northern Highlands High School)	Vega (Chaminade Julienne High School)	Crimson (Cheyenne Mountain High School)
2015	Vocal Rush (Oakland School for the Arts)	Forte (Centerville High School)	Falconize (Danvers High School)

PREVIOUS WINNERS OF THE HARMONY SWEEPSTAKES

YEAR	Winner
1985	Just Friends
1986	The Flips
1987	Pastiche
1988	Finesse
1989	Edlos
1990	The Knudsen Brothers
1991	Northshore A Cappella
1992	Acme Vocals
1993	17th Avenue All-Stars
1994	The Coats
1995	The Accidentals
1996	M-Pact
1997	So VoSo
1998	Metropolis
1999	Naturally 7
2000	Toxic Audio
2001	Sixth Wave
2002	Perfect Gentlemen
2003	Idea of North
2004	Chapter 6
2005	Groove For Thought
2006	Hi-Fidelity
2007	Moira Smiley and VOCO
2008	Vocaldente
2009	MAXX Factor
2010	Plumbers of Rome
2011	Da Capo
2012	Six Appeal
2013	Honey Whiskey Trio
2014	Women of the World
2015	Straighter Road

Kurt Zimmerman and Adam Chance, Street Corner Symphony

CHAPTER 42
THE SING-OFF SPEECH

By Deke Sharon

Imagine yourself just having arrived in Los Angeles, you've checked into the hotel, met many faces, had a long boring meeting with the legal department, and you're escorted into a large conference room where you see all of the other groups at once for the first time.

There might be a few familiar faces, and some eager smiles, but you're also a bit nervous as you eye the competition. What are your chances? Who is the group to beat?

Before you get a chance to muse for long, the doors close, and the only people in the room are singers and the music staff. And this is what I say:

> "Look around the room. These fine people are not the competition. These people will soon become your lifelong friends, and a decade from now, when NBC and Sony are distant memories, you'll still be in contact with many people in this room. In fact, you may find yourselves singing in a group with them.
>
> Your enemy is the remote control. The worst thing that could happen is for you to follow a group that has a bad performance, as no one will be watching you.
>
> Moreover, as you'll soon learn if you haven't already, the a cappella community is one of the most warm, inviting, supportive communities on the planet.
>
> Do not drink the Kool-Aid. Do not buy into the image and ethos of one group being better than the others. That's stupid. Art cannot be objectively judged.
>
> Think of this show as a two-hour infomercial for a cappella. A concert. A variety show, showcasing some of the nation's best a cappella.
>
> And each week we get to make another show, but alas we can't have as many groups on it. Who gets to stay? Three people will choose, and you won't always agree with them, but so what?

You already won.

Every single person in this room already won! You get to be on national television. You're getting paid to have an unforgettable vacation where you'll be working with some of the best singers and coaches and arrangers and choreographers you'll ever meet. You will work hard, but you'll love every moment of it, and it will be over far too soon.

Make these fleeting days about sharing your music with each other and the world. Do not compete against each other, but rather compete against your own potential. Be great, because the a cappella community at home is counting on you. You will inspire them to be their best, and inspire many young people to sing, giving them the gift of a lifetime of song."

And that's that. People drop their guards, and from then on the hot tub discussions and rooftop jams last into the wee hours of the morning.

Beelzebubs 50th Reunion

RockNacappella

No Sing Clef Behind

Eleventh Hour

CHAPTER 43
THE SING-OFF: LESSONS LEARNED

By Brody McDonald

One of the most transformative events in the history of our a cappella program was when Eleventh Hour (EH) was selected as the first high school group to compete on NBC's *The Sing-Off*. This is not because of the standard notions about TV exposure, but because the audition process fundamentally changed our culture for the better.

Learning from Failure

I first heard of *The Sing-Off* (hereafter listed as *TSO*) when I received an email from a casting agent. Someone involved in the show was doing research on possible groups and saw some YouTube videos of Eleventh Hour. While we were interested in the possibilities of the show, we pointed out that our group was comprised of high school students, and as such didn't meet the age requirement of 18. We were told to come to the audition anyway, and that if we were selected, they would get parental consent to deal with the age issue.

Because my daughter was only a few months old, I wasn't in a position to make the drive to Chicago for auditions. EH wanted to give it a shot, and so they made the trek with a parent chaperone.

When they returned the next day, I got a complete rundown of the audition. The kids sang well, but they had only been together about three weeks (it was the start of the school year) and they were stiff. They got overwhelmed and froze up in front of the producers. One of the casting agents started shouting, "Move around! Move around!" and jumped up and down among the singers for encouragement. EH made it through one-and-a-half of their three song audition and came back home.

The students and parents all said the same thing: "They wanted us to do well. We could see that they were hoping we'd do well, but we just didn't. We froze." I asked EH what they would do differently if they had the chance to do it all over again. The answer: "We'd bring it. No more holding back."

TSO aired over the holiday break and we all watched the eight groups who were selected for Season 1. We enjoyed the show, but couldn't shake the ghost of that failed audition. I decided to turn the energy around. During rehearsals when energy was low or when individual preparation waned, I simply said, "Do it like you wish you had done it in Chicago."

> **Lesson learned:**
> Sometimes you only get one shot to do something right. Give it your all, and if someone asks you to change for the better, do it. Don't let fear stop you from growing, or you'll live to regret it.

A Shot at Redemption

In the spring, *TSO* was renewed for a second season. Wonder of wonders, we got another casting email. I called EH into my office and asked them, "Do you want another shot at *The Sing-Off*?" They all said yes. After reading the casting announcement, I said, "If we do this, we can't play around. We aren't just prepping to get on the show; we're prepping to win."

The BHAG

What is a BHAG? Big Hairy Audacious Goal. Jim Collins and Jerry Porras coined it in their 1994 book, *Built to Last: Successful Habits of Visionary Companies*. They define a BHAG this way: "A true BHAG is clear and compelling, serves as unifying focal point of effort, and acts as a clear catalyst for team spirit. It has a clear finish line, so the organization can know when it has achieved the goal; people like to shoot for finish lines."

When we first auditioned for *TSO*, it was a lark. It didn't seem reasonable to think they would really want us on the show, so we didn't prepare adequately. The students just thought it would be a "neat experience."

Round two—well, that was a different story. Based on the overall interaction at Season 1 auditions, EH knew that they really had a shot at national television if they just dotted every "i" and crossed every "t." Getting on national television—that's a BHAG!

> **Lesson learned:**
> A BHAG is a galvanizing experience that is more motivating than "regular" rehearsals and concerts.

Training

In order to prepare for Season 2 auditions, we used the second habit from Steven Covey's *7 Habits of Highly Effective People*: begin with the end in mind. In order to prepare for success, we had to document what happened at the first audition, then break it into pieces, practice each piece, then reassemble them. We determined that our first audition came down to four components: singing, interview skills, group identity, and overall comportment. Then we had to consider all the general details, including such minutia as the size of each room and with whom we would interact.

The singing part was the easiest to handle. Naturally, we work on singing all year long. The biggest hurdle was to ensure we had energy to spare while performing and that we were never perceived as stiff. For the singing portion, we estimated the size of the performance space, and then recreated it in a special way. We put show choir platform risers together to make a mini-stage. That way, the singers knew exactly how much space they had to cover. We then created a visual plan for each song, changing positions regularly and creating opportunities to do coordinated, big moves. It wasn't a choreography plan; it was a visual energy plan.

The next part of the process was interviewing. We started by making a list of every question we could remember from the Season 1 interview. In addition, we added questions that *might* be asked. Each singer was given the list and an assignment to write out their answers. We read the answers aloud and decided which were the best. Everyone got a study sheet of the questions and the new "best" answers. We brought in a public relations specialist (my wife) to teach the singers interview techniques and run practice sessions. We found a room in the music wing that was roughly the same size as the audition site's interview room and practiced over and over.

From our Season 1 audition and from watching the show, we could tell that having a group identity was going to be important. Being high school students, we didn't have much life experience on which to draw. However, we did notice that each singer had a unique personality. Eleventh Hour did encompass many types of students. We decided to fill out our audition packets in a way that would highlight the students' personalities. Among the group, we had:

- The homecoming queen
- An Irish dancer
- An artist
- A computer "geek"
- A former athlete
- An honor student
- A songwriter

This led the producers to portray us as the "Breakfast Club," a group where many different types of students came together through their love of a cappella.

The last part of our preparation was on general comportment. We practiced how to enter rooms. We practiced what we would do when we were told to wait. We practiced how to speak to the producers in a casual setting (not the interview). At all times, we resolved to be upbeat, positive, engaging, and always smiling.

Lessons learned:
- Begin with the end in mind.
- There's more to your group than singing.
- Everything takes more preparation than you think in order to be outstanding.
- When working toward a goal, replicate the situation as much as you can— if competing on a large stage, practice on a large stage (and so on).
- Control everything you can control.

The Audition

We had done all we could to prepare for our audition, so we were excited when we arrived in Chicago. Unfortunately, there were more groups present than anticipated, and so our assigned "preferred audition time" was pushed back later and later. After hours of waiting, the kids were starting to lose energy. Finally, it was our turn.

I pulled EH together and said: "I am incredibly proud of you all. You've done an enormous amount of work this year and have really outdone yourself getting ready for this audition. I don't know if you're going to get on the show, but you have the ability to show the producers the group you really are. Just remember this—you will never get this chance again. Whatever you do in this room will be it, period. If you do all you can and don't get on this show, you can still be proud of yourselves. If you don't do all you can during this audition, that's fine, too, but I never want to hear about it. We will never again say 'coulda-woulda-shoulda.'"

The audition went great. The kids blew the producers away. From the back of the room, I could see EH lighting up the stage and the producers conversing with their heads nodding. When it was over, we were enthusiastically thanked, then led back to the holding tank to await our interview.

While waiting for the interview, we were approached by a producer who said, "Do NOT leave this building without seeing me." We took that as a good sign.

Another good sign came at the start of the interview. There was one lone woman in the room with her video camera. I was told that I would not be allowed to speak (*The Sing-Off* doesn't allow directors to assist groups in any way). The woman looked at our audition packet and said, "Wow . . . it says here 'These guys are soooooooo good! Seriously. So good.'" (She even counted the "o"s for emphasis.) After she asked many questions, she began talking to herself in a low voice: "If I put you in front of five million people, are you gonna clam up on me? Are you gonna clam up? What are you gonna do?" I couldn't take it any longer. I said, "I'm sorry. I know I'm not supposed to talk, but these kids are clutch players. They will deliver, I guarantee it." She changed her posture and said, "Okay, I have some more questions."

After the interview, we were escorted outside to make a test video for the producers at NBC. That meant we were on the "short list" but not yet on the show. Little did I know as we drove back home from Chicago (arriving in Kettering at 3:00 a.m. with 8:00 a.m. exams for the kids the next day) that our audition had only just begun.

> **Lessons learned:**
> - Preparation pays off.
> - If you prepare adequately and perform to the best of your ability, you can be proud of yourselves and avoid regrets. You can't control what others do, but you can control yourselves in order to maximize your chances of success in any situation.

The Post-Audition Audition

While we were now on the "short list," we had a period of about three weeks during which we continued to have some form of prolonged audition. Producers called various members of the group independently to ask them questions about their home lives, their school habits, and many other things to get a sense of whether our "home story" would be interesting to the viewers. We also had many discussions of the logistics that occur when minors appear on TV, legal issues that involved the school district and much more. Thankfully, we won out and were chosen to be one of ten groups on Season 2. The fun was just beginning.

Making the Show—The Prep Work, Performance, and Post Game

Prep Work

After being informed in late June that we were selected for the show, we were slated for a mid-July "home story" filming. We also had mountains of paperwork to complete, and the producers were constantly asking us for "demo" versions of songs to see if they were a good fit for the show. I would get a call on Monday asking for a demo of a song to be ready by Wednesday. This happened on many occasions. We decided to alleviate the problem of scheduling by agreeing to meet for rehearsal every day at 3:00. If there was nothing new to do, we'd split. If we had a demo to learn and record, we'd do that. We also had a song to learn for the home story ("Don't You Forget About Me" from the movie *The Breakfast Club*). During this period we learned the value of communication, the benefit of constant contact, and the challenge of learning a lot of new music quickly. Some of those benefits show up in other chapters in this handbook.

> **Lesson learned:**
> Do whatever the situation demands. The bigger the success, the bigger the investment.

Performance

In August we hopped a plane and headed for Los Angeles. Eleventh Hour left first, then I followed three days later. I knew in advance that I wouldn't be allowed to direct in any way, but I wanted to be around as a source of support. EH had to do everything themselves, just like the "big boys." They had costume fittings, rehearsals for the mass opening numbers, individual coachings, and many (many, many) adjustments to the arrangements they were to sing on the show. At one point, a staff arranger worked through the night to create the arrangement of "Just the Way You Are," which EH performed on the second episode. In order to make sure we didn't lose a minute of rehearsal, the arranger drove to a fast-food restaurant on a corner we would pass on our way from the hotel to the studio. When the traffic light turned red, he came running into the street to throw seven copies of the music through our van window. The light turned green, and we were off again with the new song in hand.

Throughout all of this, I learned the immense positive impact of student ownership. The group grew immensely due to the time they spent in charge of their own destiny. Of course, every group still needs a director, but I challenge you to create ways that your group can own pieces of their own development. These concepts also appear throughout this book. The success of Eleventh Hour as a self-contained group in this environment was the ultimate "final exam." Everything they had ever learned was put to the test for three weeks in California, across sixteen-hour days with almost zero down time.

Lessons learned:
- High school students are more capable than you ever dreamed, given the chance to prove it.
- Independence breeds growth, if monitored properly.

Post Game

Eleventh Hour was eliminated from *The Sing-Off* in the second episode. We returned home happy with our performance, and innocently thought that we would return to our everyday routine while we waited for the show to air in December. We couldn't have been more wrong.

The first thing that happened was the public announcement of the groups who made the show. We had newspapers and TV stations calling us for interviews and public interest segments. Our singers were regularly in front of the local media, so they had represent themselves well. We had to constantly remind ourselves of what we could say and could not say, and also communicate to the media what was "fair game." Certain aspects of the show were to be kept confidential. This process strengthened our internal communication and also taught the students the importance of *messaging*, the art of creating, and stating central themes that become "the party line."

The next curve ball came when we were asked to contribute a track to *The Sing-Off* Christmas album, *Harmonies for the Holidays.* Our lead singer, Kendall, had already moved to Nashville to attend Belmont University, so we had to coordinate her return to get "Santa Claus Is Comin' to

Town" in the can. It was an invaluable experience for the students to play "studio singer," learning the music on their own for a one-day recording session.

The show aired, and we were eliminated. We watched the rest of the season play itself out. As the end drew near, we received the phone call that we were being asked back to L.A. for the live finale. It was quite a fun and unexpected experience, but the ride didn't end there. Sony had approved a *Best of Season 2* CD, and we had to do a hurry-up session (again) to record a studio version of Justin Bieber's "Baby." This time it was Christmas break and the snow was falling. Kendall made it back from Nashville, but just barely. We had to record quickly to avoid being snow-bound in a studio.

> **Lesson learned:**
> If you commit to a large project, be ready for unforeseen side projects.

The Positive Side Effects of *The Sing-Off*

The Growth of the BHAG

We mentioned the Big Hairy Audacious Goal. *The Sing-Off* certainly was one. After such a process, we saw with great clarity the value of dreaming big and haven't stopped.

Instant Credibility

National TV is something that nearly every person on the planet perceives as special. After being part of *The Sing-Off*, everyone began to see us differently. We were always well received, but now we were sought-after. Our choir department, which was always respected, took a huge leap upwards in the eyes of the community and within the school district. When we performed at the state music conference and at the American Choral Directors Association National Convention, the rooms were packed.

Gigs, CDs, and $

Immediately after being on television, we were inundated with phone calls for performance opportunities that had previously been closed to us. Many were entertainment spots on national conventions, but some others included performances in other states for youth programs and the like. Everywhere we went we sold many more CDs, and our gig fee went up dramatically. We even sold more digital downloads on iTunes. In a year that was financially tough for our booster program, Eleventh Hour's new caché was keeping our heads above water.

Opening Doors

The biggest benefit of being on the show was how it opened doors for us—as a group and for individuals. Our singers made industry contacts that will pay off as they start their careers. Some were even offered jobs or internships when they finished high school. We were contacted by *America's Got Talent* (we didn't go) and *Extreme Makeover Home Edition* (we did go, portraying Christmas carolers on their holiday special). Kendall was selected to return in Season 3. All in all, this was a great experience for the students, many of whom plan to make music their livelihood.

The Negative Side Effects of *The Sing-Off*

Living in the Shadow (Or Is it the Shade?)

Unfortunately, one of the downsides to a large accomplishment is that the group immediately following can sometimes feel as if they are living in the shadow of their predecessors. Between the summer taping, the interviews, both CD projects, and the live finale, Eleventh Hour was living a split life. The "Sing-Off" Eleventh Hour was still reconvening and doing things while the "next generation" Eleventh Hour was trying to find their own identity. While the three new members were very gracious, it had to get old for them. Every time we sang a gig, well-intentioned people would ask, "What was it like to be on TV?" Sometimes it was like having a raspberry seed in your teeth that you just couldn't get out. Still, we reminded ourselves that whatever is good for any Eleventh Hour is good for all Eleventh Hours. After all, the "next-generation" singers are the ones who got to go sing many more gigs as a result of the notoriety. So, rather than "living in the shadow" of the "Sing-Off" Eleventh Hour, we liked to think of it as staying in the shade. Thanks to their accomplishment, our lives were just a bit better moving forward.

Oversaturation

Another consequence of garnering so much attention is oversaturation. Although everyone in the choir department was happy for Eleventh Hour, there comes a time when enough is enough. After a few months, we could almost hear the other students thinking, "If I hear about Eleventh Hour one more time, I'm gonna scream!" It is a natural tendency of young people to think that the elevation of one group's value leads to the devaluation of all others. While that simply isn't true, it is a feeling that crops up. When your group does something extremely special, be prepared for such reactions and be sensitive. Always be proactive in letting your department know that a win for one is a win for all.

Is it Over Yet?

This is like internal oversaturation. At some point, Eleventh Hour began to joke: "Is it over yet?" While being on TV is grand, at some point everyone wants to be valued for his or her next phase of development. Having so many "add-ons" after the show finished taping (roughly six more months of obligations) sometimes had a feeling of tying us to the past rather than the future.

Summary

Being selected for *The Sing-Off* was the ultimate learning experience. While there were a few negatives that could not be foreseen, the vast majority of the process was incredibly positive on multiple levels for all involved. While not every group will be able to have experiences that involve national television, every group can create BHAGs for themselves and create ways to foster the type of educational experiences that they bring.

One thing I cannot over-emphasize—in order to achieve maximum growth, it is important that your train your students to perform as if they are a professional group. If you try to be a good high school group, that's the best you'll ever be. You might also fall short of that goal, and end up being just another high school group. However, if you train to be a professional group and fall short, you can still far exceed the normal high school expectations. There are many professional singers, actors, and dancers who aren't yet 18-years old. Why not train your students to shoot for the stars?

The Melodores

Vocal Rush

CHAPTER 44

THE MOST IMPORTANT THING

By Deke Sharon

After spending months rehearsing, honing, polishing and perfecting, it is very difficult to keep perspective. And yet that is when you need it most of all. I offer these words for you not now, when you'll nod in approval, but the day of your performance, when tunnel vision will likely have you hyper-focused on the trophy:

Art is subjective. There is no absolute great art, like there is great science or great mathematics. One person's genius is another person's boredom. Beethoven's Ninth Symphony is a work of unparalleled genius . . . except by the people who think that Beethoven's introduction of a choir in the fourth movement is a failed experiment. Britney Spears is meaningless garbage . . . except that she isn't to the millions of people who love her music, her image, her story, her kitsch.

There are a few musical elements you can carefully measure, like tuning and rhythmic precision, but those alone are effectively meaningless. I'm sure you can think of some current popular music that's technically flawless but leaves you cold. Classic Motown, on the other hand, is out of tune by almost any standard . . . and incredibly fantastic by most people's measure.

As such, there is no single good way to determine the "best" group in a concert. All judges will have biases; all judging systems will put too much focus on some elements and not enough on others (not to mention how they can skew a group's choices from repertoire to choreography). Different audiences will affect a show's outcome, as will different judges, different halls, different nights. It's imperfect, it's messy, it's unfair, and any attempts to improve one area (like a more precise judging system) will have negative ramifications elsewhere (limiting a judges ability to reward risk taking and unconventional choices).

So, to summarize:

Art is subjective

Music can't be precisely measured for quality

Judging is messy and scoring systems are imperfect

389

No matter how hard you try to make every judge like you, you can't. No matter how hard you try to create perfect music, you can't. And no matter how hard you try to fit the precise mold of a perfect score based on judging criteria, you can't. It sounds very negative, because it is. It is important that you know you're swimming in muddy water.

Basically, you won't necessarily win by trying to win. Moving target, too many variables, imprecise, frustrating. You might as well not even bother, right?

Exactly!

The reason I'm saying all of this is because I want to make sure that when you're on stage, you're not thinking about winning, and you're not thinking about a perfect performance.

All of the training was necessary to create a unified sound and musical vision. But just as a great batter won't hit the ball as well if he's thinking about how he's shifting his weight and gripping his bat, your group will not connect with the audience if you're focusing on technical elements of music instead of sharing your love of music with the audience.

That's the most important thing.

Music is communication, and you have to remember to say something. The love of singing, the joy of music, the message of each song: these can deeply inspire an audience. Perfectly rung overtones and a flawless final pose are merely elements in the equation. They're not the point. Don't make them the point.

I've seen this happen time and time again at music performances. I remember an ICCA final at Carnegie Hall where a young director named John Stephens was at the helm of his collegiate group, the U Penn Counterparts, and they were about as tightly wound a group as you could find. Technically excellent, their songs had a jazzy cool . . . but it was clear they were all about winning. They walked past the other groups backstage, didn't intermingle, were 100% focused on winning.

Their sound check was a litany of orders and maneuvers, precision and perfection. And when they took the stage to perform, they were good, but people didn't feel a warmth behind their music, and although they were technically proficient, they didn't win. They didn't even place. They felt slighted, left after the show, and that was the last I saw of any of them.

Stanford Talisman, on the other hand, were relaxed and had absolutely no airs or attitude. Backstage they mingled with the other groups, and if they cared about winning, no one could tell. When they took the stage, they simply walked out, formed an arc, opened their mouths, and sang. No choreography, and in fact one of their soloists was blind. It was all about the music, the moment, the joy of singing. A pure expression. The audience was completely overwhelmed, and there was no question they had won the night. After the show they were gracious, wanted to get to know the other groups, wanted to meet the audience, and generally made it clear that that winning wasn't the point for them.

As it shouldn't be for you.

By the way, the director of the Penn Counterparts whose group didn't win or even place in Carnegie Hall? He changed his stage name to John Legend, and he's now doing just fine as a musician. That's another lesson to be learned: losing the ICCAs is hardly the end of one's musical career.

At this point, I feel like I should let you in on a little secret, which won't be much of a secret now that it's in print, but I feel it might help drive home my message.

The fact is, I hate musical competitions.

Yes, that's right: I'm one of the founders of the ICCAs, I was one of the producers of *The Sing-Off*, I started the Contemporary A Cappella Recording Awards, and so on. I'm probably responsible for more a cappella competitions and awards than anyone else in the world. And I hate them.

Why do I hate them? Because they taint one's musical experience. Because they warp singers' focus and relationship with the audience. Because people begin to think that winning a musical competition is the year's greatest potential accomplishment, and they measure their success in this way. As I said above, there's no way you can objectively measure art, so any decision is clearly imperfect, and usually leaves at least some of the audience and participants upset. I have a horrible, yucky feeling when I see a group single-mindedly driven to win an award, as it stands at odds with my greater goal: spreading harmony through harmony.

So then why did I do it? Why would I have been involved in so many competitive a cappella endeavors? Simple: audience.

Get some guys together in a college gym to play some basketball, no one watches. Make it the school's team, and you might get some of their friends to drop by. Have one school play another school, and you'll get some locals and some alums.

But if you create the definitive national tournament for college basketball, you have one of the world's most-watched sporting events.

The same goes for the arts, silly as it is (for the reasons above). Grammys, Oscars, Emmys, they're all a bunch of subjective popularity contests, given a veneer of legitimacy by a rarified, elite voting committee. And there are the Golden Globes, People's Choice Awards and the like, which tally the public's vote. Also flawed, in other ways (and yes, CASA created the A Cappella Community Awards, to tap into this zeitgeist as well).

Has your favorite movie of the year ever been the Oscar winner? Perhaps once, but it's unlikely to be the case very often. And yet the Oscars do award excellence, even if there's no ultimate excellence, so it's nice that someone gets a statue for cinematography, and the public spends a little time thinking about cinematography, even if the person chosen is merely one of the best as opposed to the ultimate supreme cinematographer. The Academy Award race inspires moviemakers, and gives movie studios a reason to make Great movies (with a capital G!), not just lowest-common-denominator blockbusters.

And most of all, an Oscar means more people will see your movie. It inspires people to go to the theater, or to stream the latest winners. It inspires discussion and consideration. That's the great value of an artistic award.

Now, I'll be honest: I don't care who wins the ICCAs. Or *The Sing-Off*, CARAs, ACAs, or any a cappella competition. The way I look at it, it doesn't matter, because the end result is that many more people will pay attention, and in that way we all win.

But my biggest problem with all of this is the fact that groups don't realize that awards are simply a large, flawed publicity machine. They drink the Kool-Aid, and care most of all about winning. It's too often that I'll speak with a group and their greatest goal for the year is to either win the ICCAs or get a track on BOCA. I do my best to give them the speech above, and some get it, but some don't care, as so much within our society is focused on winning and success and being number one that they can't see that it's flawed and ultimately doesn't matter.

So, if you're still reading this, and you're ready for the final "aha," here's the double-secret twist: an audience, and judges can tell if you're just in it to win.

It's perhaps subconscious, but there's something subtly different in a person's performance if their ultimate goal is to convince you they're the best as opposed to simply share their story with you. You can tell a sales job, a commercial, a self-promotion, or a legal argument from a gift, a message, a personal story. Genuine laughter and tears are more powerful than crocodile tears shed in hopes of getting something.

You can't fake it. You have to let go. You have to stop caring so much and trust in your training. You have to believe in what you've done and what you do, and just go out there and sing your heart out. That's all there is.

And once you realize that, once you can do that, there's a huge weight lifted off your shoulders. This isn't the Super Bowl, it's just a intercollegiate jam, where you get to meet the other singers, have fun, hear some great music, do some singing, then hang out after the show. Pretty much a perfect night. When you approach it this way, you've already won.

Imagine if someone asked you: "Hey, wanna come sing for a few thousand people in Lincoln Center with some other great college groups?" Your response would probably be "Yeah! Sounds great! Will there be a party afterwards?" not "What do we get if we're the best group on stage that night?" Sounds pretty self absorbed and petty when you think in those terms.

Music is a gift, not an entitlement. Singing is an act of generosity and communication, not posturing. How you approach your set mentally the day of the show could make all the difference, not only in terms of winning or losing, but in terms of what you and the rest of your group take away from the experience for the rest of your lives.'

That's what I want to say, if nothing else. The most important thing is that singing is communication, and you need to say something honest and real. And if you're simply saying "look and me! I'm great!" . . . it gets old.

Moreover, if you go into the competition with the specific goal of winning, then you'll either win or lose (and you're statistically much more likely to lose), whereas if your goal is to win over the audience, make friends and have a great time, you're guaranteed to win.

Guaranteed.

Sirens

APPENDIX A

Chapter 2: History of A Cappella as Popular Music

Gage Averill, *Four Parts, No Waiting: A Social History of American Barbershop Harmony* (New York: Oxford University Press, 2003).

Alan Clark Buechener, *Yankee Singing Schools and the Golden Age of Choral Music in New England, 1760–1800* (Boston: Boston University Scholarly Publications, 2003).

Joshua S. Duchan, Powerful Voices: The Musical and Social World of Collegiate A Cappella (Ann Arbor: University of Michigan Press, 2012).

John Michael Runowicz, *Forever Doo Wop: Race, Nostalgia, and Vocal Group Harmony* (Amherst: University of Massachusetts Press, 2010).

Chapter 24: Live Looping

1. http://voicecouncil.com/things-to-come/
2. http://www.livelooping.org/history_concepts/
3. http://equipboard.com/pros/ed-sheeran/chewie-monsta-looper
4. http://www.ted.com/talks/beardyman_the_polyphonic_me?language=en
5. http://voicecouncil.com/why-live-loop/
6. http://equipboard.com/pros/ed-sheeran
7. https://www.youtube.com/watch?v=HfBh3lZZi8Q
8. http://www.monolake.de/technology/ableton_live.html
9. http://www.highsnobiety.com/2014/10/14/ableton-ceo-gerhard-behles-interview/
10. http://www.beardyman.co.uk/category/beardytron-5000/
11. https://www.youtube.com/watch?v=Tkoj3tpcXpQ
12. https://www.youtube.com/watch?v=VQJbFFZiWVY
13. Beardyman, if you're reading this, email me plz
14. http://color-thought.com/downloads/a-squared

Chapter 29: Online Distribution

www.loudr.fm

www.patreon.com

www.tubularlabs.com

www.epoxy.tv

www.msclvr.com

www.cdbaby.com

www.distrokid.com

www.mondotunes.com

www.tunecore.com

www.aristake.com

Chapter 41: The International Championships of A Cappella

1. Married names in order of appearance: Joanne Herr, Keeley George, Mimi Matthew, Evynne Hollens, Erica Babjak, Suzie Metzger, Katie Purvis and Megan Perdue

2. Turns out that Divisi inspired a female a cappella group to form in the same way the Overtones had inspired us; at this same ICCA event, a woman named Esther Yoder from Brigham Young University approached Evynne and expressed that she had been so inspired watching Divisi at the previous years' event that she had founded her own all-female group at BYU called Noteworthy. Readers may know this group from their ICCA Finals win in 2007 or their appearance on The Sing-Off Season 1. They are regarded as one of the top collegiate female a cappella groups in the nation.

3. In January 2013, Evynne Hollens (formerly Smith) and I founded the Women's A Cappella Association (WACA), a non-profit organization dedicated to the growth and support of women in a cappella. Our first Women's A Cappella Festival SheSings took place in June of 2013 and will continue as an annual event. This organization was inspired by mine and Evynne's years in Divisi and was something we talked about constantly after graduating from the group in 2006. Divisi alumnae Megan Perduce (McCornack) and Rachelle Wofford also serve on our Board of Directors. www.womensacappella.org.

The authors would like to thank the a cappella community for the gracious use of the photos throughout the book. A special thank you to the following groups and photographers:

Front Cover:
Straight No Chaser
Home Free
Traces
The Swingles
Page v: Jiro Schneider
Page 20: Bobby Holland
Pages 25, 64, 352, 374, 378: Kristine Slipson

Page 132: Tory Stolper Photography
Page 176: Joseph Martinez
Page 224: Steve Austell
Page 239: Offer Gedanken
Page 305: Jeremy Daniel
Page 318: Joseph Martinez
Pages 356, 370: Ross Media

APPENDIX B

BIOGRAPHIES

Deke Sharon

Born in San Francisco, California, Deke Sharon has been performing professionally since the age of 8. As a child, he toured North America and shared the stage in operas with the likes of Pavarotti. Heralded as "the father of contemporary a cappella," he is responsible for the current sound of modern a cappella, having created the dense vocal-instrumental sound in college and subsequently spread it around the world.

As the founder, director and arranger for the House Jacks, the original "rock band without instruments," Deke has shared the stage with countless music legends, including Ray Charles, James Brown, Crosby Stills and Nash, Run DMC, The Temptations, LL Cool J, and the Four Tops, and performed for luminaries including President Bill Clinton. The House Jacks have eight albums and dozens of international tours to their name, including multiple appearances at Carnegie Hall. They performed the *Monday Night Football* theme with Hank Williams, Jr. in 2011. Deke produces *The Sing-Off* worldwide (USA, the Netherlands, and China), which had the highest ratings of any new, unscripted television show in the US in 2009, and was the third highest rated show on NBC in 2010. In addition, Deke served as arranger, on-site music director, and vocal producer for Universal's *Pitch Perfect* and *Pitch Perfect 2*, starring Anna Kendrick & Rebel Wilson.

Deke founded the Contemporary A Cappella Society while in college, and is responsible for many seminal a cappella programs, including the CARAs (Contemporary A Cappella Recording Awards), ICCAs (International Championship of College A Cappella), BOCA (Best of College A Cappella Compilation), the first contemporary a cappella conferences (the A Cappella Summit), the Contemporary A Cappella League, and the professional ensemble Voasis. He is also contemporary a cappella's most prolific arranger, having arranged over 2,000 songs, with many of them in print worldwide. His first book, *A Cappella Arranging*, was published in 2012.

He has produced dozens of award-winning a cappella albums for groups, including Straight No Chaser, Committed, Nota, Street Corner Symphony and the Tufts Beelzebubs. He has created a cappella groups for Disneyland and Disneyworld, and frequently tours the world teaching a variety of topics to students and professional singers. His voice can be heard in commercials and video games, most recently in *Just Dance Kids 2*.

Ben Spalding

Ben is the Choral Director at Centerville High School in Centerville, Ohio, where he directs all five of the choirs: Concert Choir, Women's Choir, Men's Choir, Symphonic Choir, and the a cappella group Forte. Forte has placed second overall at the International Championship of High School A Cappella three times. Forte has recorded 6 albums including 2 albums of all-original a cappella music that have won numerous Contemporary A cappella Recording Awards (CARAs) including the Best Overall High School CD in 2013. Forte has performed as part of *The Sing-Off* tour and has collaborated with artists like Kirstin Maldonado of Pentatonix. Symphonic Choir was a consortium member for Eric Whitacre's *Good Night Moon* and the choirs have also performed with Eliot Sloan of Blessid Union of Souls.

Ben holds a Bachelor of Music in Music Education from the University of Kentucky. Ben's a cappella roots go back to college, when he was a member of the University of Kentucky AcoUstiKats (as seen on NBC's *The Sing-Off*) and a semi-professional group called 5 by Tuesday. Ben is a founding member and has served as the Treasurer of the A Cappella Education Association. He has also served as the Program Manager for High School Outreach for the Contemporary A Cappella Society of America. He has served as a judge for both the Contemporary A Cappella Recording Awards and the International Championship of Collegiate A Cappella.

Ben would like to thank his wife Kylene and two daughters Hadley and Macy for their endless support through all of his musical endeavors. He feels truly blessed to have such a supportive family and is grateful for their many sacrifices at home. He would also like to thank his parents Ernie and Linda Spalding for all their love and support over the years as he would not be where he is today without them. Finally, he would like to say a special thanks to Ann Meyer for her dedication to the choral music program at Centerville High School and for always going above and beyond to help out in any way needed.

Brody McDonald

Brody McDonald is the director of choirs at Kettering Fairmont High School in Kettering, Ohio, and an adjunct music faculty member at Wright State University in Dayton, Ohio. His choirs have performed regularly at Ohio Music Education Association state conferences and at regional and national conferences of the American Choral Directors Association. They also have performed with internationally known artists including Kenny Rogers, LeAnn Rimes, The Beach Boys, Kenny Loggins and Pentatonix.

In 2010, his award-winning a cappella group Eleventh Hour was the first high school group to perform on NBC's *The Sing-Off*. The group also was featured on ABC's *Extreme Makeover Home*

Edition and won a gold medal in the Pop Choral Champions Division at the 2012 World Choir Games. Eleventh Hour's studio recordings have been included on multiple releases of *Best of High School A Cappella* and have won Contemporary A Cappella Recording Awards (CARAs) for Best High School Album and Best High School Song.

Brody is at the forefront of the educational a cappella movement, serving as a founder of the A Cappella Education Association and as a nominator and judge for the Contemporary A Cappella Society's CARA awards program. He has presented on pop a cappella in the classroom at numerous educational conferences and regularly lectures on the topic for ACDA chapters throughout the Midwest.

Brody is the author of *A Cappella Pop: A Complete Guide to Contemporary A Cappella Singing* and the co-founder of Camp A Cappella (www.campacappella.com), an immersive weeklong summer camp for students, educators and a cappella enthusiasts of all ages.

Brody is a graduate of Bowling Green State University, where he received a bachelor's degree in music education and a master's degree in choral conducting. He is an experienced barbershopper who sang in an international champion college quartet, a top-20 open class quartet and in a bronze-medal chorus. He has been named one of *Choral Director* magazine's Choral Directors of Note.

Josh Duchan

Josh is the author of *Powerful Voices: The Musical and Social World of Collegiate A Cappella* (University of Michigan Press, 2012), the first academic study of collegiate a cappella. He has presented on the history of a cappella at the National A Cappella Convention, Acappella Fest (Chicago), and at Camp A Cappella. Dr. Duchan serves regularly as an adjudicator for the ICCA and ICHSA competitions, and his arrangements have been featured on BOCA and nominated for CARA awards. He is Assistant Professor of Music at Wayne State University in Detroit.

Lisa Forkish

Lisa Forkish is an Oakland-based vocalist/composer/arranger/educator and a graduate of Berklee College of Music. She has been involved in a cappella since 2002 when she got her start as music director for the University of Oregon's award-winning female a cappella group Divisi, featured in the best-selling book "Pitch Perfect," later made into the blockbuster film.

Currently, Lisa is Assistant Chair of the Vocal Music Department at Oakland School for the Arts where she is also founder/director of the school's acclaimed group Vocal Rush, three-time ICHSA Champions and 3rd place winners on Season 4 of NBC's *The Sing-Off*. Lisa's arrangements have been nominated for CARAs as has her student group Vocal Rush and her ACA-dubbed "groundbreaking" women's quintet, The Riveters. She is also co-founder and Executive Director of the Women's A Cappella Association.

J.D. Frizzell

J.D. is a composer, conductor, and baritone. He currently serves as the Director of Fine Arts and Director of Vocal Music at Briarcrest Christian School in Memphis, TN. Winner of the 2007 Intégrales Composition Contest, he writes music for choir, orchestra, symphonic band, voice, handbells, chamber ensembles, and solo instruments. With music published by many major publishing houses, he has had best sellers throughout the world. Frizzell was chosen by the board of the Tennessee Music Educators Association as the 2011 Outstanding Young Music Educator. Additionally, he was awarded the Dr. Clair E. Cox Award for Teaching Excellence.

A leader in the contemporary a cappella movement, Frizzell is the co-founder and president of the A Cappella Education Association, a nonprofit dedicated to helping groups around the world. His high cappella group OneVoice is a SONY Recording Artist. They have produced numerous award-winning albums and have been hailed as "one of the most talented groups . . . on any level" and "one of the best [a cappella] groups, period".

Frizzell is active as a presenter, adjudicator, clinician, and guest conductor. As an active member of TNMEA, NATS, ACDA, and WTVMEA, he has served in multiple volunteer capacities. The board of the Cystic Fibrosis Foundation named him one of "Memphis' Finest" for his philanthropic efforts

Nick Girard

Nick had his first encounter with conemporary a cappella music as a freshman at the University of Vermont. Enticed by *The Top Cats* slogan, "Chicks Dig Guys Who Sing!," he auditioned and joined the group as a tenor. In 2006 Nick founded *Overboard*, a professional a cappella group in Boston. Eventually his talents as a director, performer, and arranger earned him a spot as a producer/engineer/arranger for *The Sing-Off*. In 2011, Nick joined the ranks of *The House Jacks* as a tenor and beatboxer. He produced the 2014 *House Jacks* album *Pollen,* featuring original music collaborations with 12 of the world's best professional a cappella groups. Nick is married to Clare Wheeler of *The Swingles* and resides in Guildford, Surrey while continuing to work in both the US and UK.

Joshua Habermann

Joshua Habermann was active in collegiate a cappella and is now in his seventh season with the Santa Fe Desert Chorale. Since joining the ensemble he has broadened its repertoire to include not only a cappella literature but also choral-orchestral masterworks, and unique concert experiences that combine music, poetry and the spoken word. In 2011, he was named director of the Dallas Symphony Chorus, the official vocal ensemble of the Dallas Symphony Orchestra, where he prepares the 185-voice chorus for classical and pops series concerts. A native of California, Habermann is a graduate of Georgetown University and the University of Texas at Austin, where he completed doctoral studies in conducting with Craig Hella Johnson.

Bill Hare

Bill Hare has been a full-time recording engineer/producer for over 30 years, and is recognized as a pioneer in bringing pop/rock production techniques to recorded contemporary a cappella. Over the decades, Bill has recorded and/or mixed acclaimed albums for some of the best-known Contemporary A Cappella groups around the globe—from The Swingle Singers to The King's Singers in the UK, Basix to Vocal Line in Denmark, Italy's Cluster, The Ghost Files, Alti & Bassi and Maybe6ix, German supergroups Wise Guys, Amarcord, and Maybebop as well as groups from dozens of other countries from Australia to Zambia. At the same time he also covered his home country from his base in California, working with top American acts including Pentatonix, Street Corner Symphony, NoTa, +4dB, Duwende, The Backbeats, The House Jacks, m-pact, and many more.

Bill is the world's most awarded individual Contemporary A Cappella producer, including more than 70 appearances on BOCA, over 100 CARA nominations, nearly 40 albums in the RARB "Picks of the Year" lists, and 11 "DeeBee" awards since 1987 in the Vocal Jazz category from Downbeat Magazine. In 2011, Bill received a Grammy Award* for his work on Christopher Tin's "Calling All Dawns," and in 2014 a Platinum Album for *Pentatonix*.

Christopher Given Harrison

Christopher Given Harrison has been playing with a cappella fire since UCLA's Awaken granted him group membership in the fall of 2000. Over the following three years, he cut his proverbial teeth with them as a music director and arranger. Nearly three years after that, he co-founded the group formerly known as Sonos and now called ARORA. Since then, he's operated as a stateside version of Nigel Godrich for ARORA, serving as principal arranger and "whisper-bass" performer as well as digging into sound and aesthetic design, album production, FX pedal shenanigans, and other miscellaneous mischief.

Peter Hollens

Peter Hollens is an American pop singer and producer best known for his work on YouTube as an a cappella cover artist. With over 1,100,000 subscribers, his videos have reached more than 150 million viewers since 2011. Hollens has collaborated with some amazing artists, including Jason Mraz, Hunter Hayes, Brian Wilson of the Beach Boys, Lindsey Stirling, George Watsky and many more. He has released over 100 digital singles and has been involved with a cappella music since 1999 when he co-founded the University of Oregon's male a cappella group On The Rocks. In 2010, he was featured on NBC's *The Sing-Off* Season 2 with On the Rocks. He advises many companies in the digital media space such as Youtube, Patreon, Loudr, and Tubular.

Jacob Reske

Jacob Reske is a music producer and composer. In undergraduate school he formed a.squared, a vocal group that remixes a cappella live. For the project, he created a system to incorporate multi-user looping and effects on one platform. He and a.squared were featured on NBC's *The Sing-Off* in December 2014. He is interested in soundscape studies, sound design, and the intersection between live performance and technology. Jacob produces all-vocal remixes under the alias colorthought.